Clive Oxenden
Christina Latham-Koenig

with **David Jay**
Beatriz Martín

New
ENGLISH FILE

Advanced
Teacher's Book

OXFORD
UNIVERSITY PRESS

OXFORD
UNIVERSITY PRESS

Great Clarendon Street, Oxford OX2 6DP

Oxford University Press is a department of the University of Oxford.
It furthers the University's objective of excellence in research, scholarship,
and education by publishing worldwide in

Oxford New York

Auckland Cape Town Dar es Salaam Hong Kong Karachi
Kuala Lumpur Madrid Melbourne Mexico City Nairobi
New Delhi Shanghai Taipei Toronto

With offices in

Argentina Austria Brazil Chile Czech Republic France Greece
Guatemala Hungary Italy Japan Poland Portugal Singapore
South Korea Switzerland Thailand Turkey Ukraine Vietnam

OXFORD and OXFORD ENGLISH are registered trade marks of
Oxford University Press in the UK and in certain other countries

ACKNOWLEDGEMENTS

*The authors would like to thank all the teachers and students round the world whose
feedback has helped us to shape New English File and also all those at Oxford University
Press (both in Oxford and around the world) who have contributed their skills and ideas
to producing this course.*

*Finally very special thanks from Clive to Maria Angeles, Lucia, and Eric, and from
Christina to Cristina, for all their help and encouragement. Christina would also like to
thank her children Joaquin, Marco, and Krysia for their constant inspiration.*

*The publisher and authors would like to thank Iain Saunders for his invaluable feedback
on the materials.*

*The authors and publisher are grateful to those who have given permission to reproduce
the following extracts and adaptations of copyright material:*

p.190 Extract from *Promise Me* by Harlan Coben. Copyright 2006 by Harlan
Coben. Reproduced by permission of The Aaron M Priest Agency and Orion
Books, an imprint of The Orion Publishing Group, London. Extract from *The
Palace of Strange Girls* by Sallie Day. © 2008 Sallie Day. Reproduced by permis-
sion of HarperCollins Publishers Ltd. Extract from *Beware of Pity* by Stefan
Zweig, ISBN 9781906548155. Reprinted by kind permission of Pushkin Press,
Ltd. Extract from *Spellbound* by Jane Green, published by Penguin Books Ltd.
Reproduced by permission of David Higham Associates Ltd. Extract from *Sex
and the City* by Candace Bushnell. Copyright © 1996 by Candace Bushnell.
Reproduced by permission of Abacus, an imprint of Little, Brown Book
Group, Grove/Atlantic, Inc., and Grand Central Publishing. Extract from
The Company of Cheerful Ladies by Alexander McCall Smith is reproduced by
permission of Polygon, an imprint of Birlinn Ltd. www.birlinn.co.uk. Extract
from *Bridget Jones's Diary* by Helen Fielding. Published by Penguin Group
USA. Reproduced by permission of Pan Macmillan and Aitken Alexander
Associates. Extract from *The Girl With the Dragon Tattoo* by Stieg Larsson.
Reproduced by kind permission of Quercus Books Plc.

p.232 *The Logical Song* by Rick Davies and Rodger Hodgson. Used by
permission International Copyright Secured. All Rights Reserved. p.235
Addicted to Love Composed by Robert Palmer © 1985 Bungalow Music
(ASCAP) All rights administered by WB Music Corp. By kind permission of
Warner Chappell Music Ltd. p.236 *Vincent* Words and Music by Don McLean
© Copyright 1971 Mayday Music, USA Universal/MCA Music Limited. Used
by permission of Music Sales Limited. All Rights Reserved. International
Copyright Secured. p.238 *Eye of the Tiger* Composed by Frank Sullivan and
James Peterik © 1982 Sony/ATV Melody, Rude Music Inc (BMI), Three Wise
Boys Music LLC (BMI), WB Music Corp. (ASCAP), Easy Action Music (ASCAP).
All Rights administered by Sony/ATV Music Publishing LLC and WB Music
Corp on behalf of itself and Easy Action Music. All Rights Reserved. Used by
kind permission of Sony/ATV Music Publishing and Warner Chappell Music
Ltd. p.233 *50 Ways To Leave Your Lover* Copyright © 1975 Paul Simon and Bruce
Woodley. Used by permission of the Publisher: Paul Simon Music. p.234 *A
Lady of a Certain Age* Words and music by Neil Hannon. © Copyright 2006
Universal Music Publishing MGB Limited. All Rights Reserved. International
Copyright Secured. Used by permission of Music Sales Limited.

Although every effort has been made to trace and contact copyright holders
before publication, this has not been possible in some cases. We apologize
for any apparent infringement of copyright and if notified, the publisher
will be pleased to rectify any errors or omissions at the earliest opportunity.

*The authors and publisher would like to thank the following for their permission to
reproduce photographs:*

Alamy pp.165 (Picture Partners), 191 (John Woodworth/money notes),
194 (Tom Prokop/Cast study 1), 232 (Agencja Free), *Allstar* p.237 (MGM),
Corbis p.236 (Michael Pole), *Getty Images* pp.157 (Bernhard Lang/40s male,
Barrry Austin Photography/student, B2M Productions/woman), 164 (Rob
Melnychuk), 191 (Superstock/money change), 192 (Hulton Archive/Elizabeth
Taylor, WireImage/S Granitz/Judi Dench, Kevin Winter/Kirsten Dunst,
WireImage/Gregg DeGuire/Cate Blanchett, Stephen Lovekin/Emily Blunt),
194 (Felbert+Eickenberg/Stock4B/Case Study 2, Elstermann/Case Study 3,
JoSon/Case study 4, Beowulf Sheehan/Case study 5, Aagamia/Case Study 7
Heather Weston/Case Study 8), 202 (Kent Horner/Martina Hingis), 219 (Bruno
Vincent/phone box, Tara Moore/mobile phones), 231 (Time and Life Pictures/
schoolboy), 233 (Colin Hawkins), 235 (Bridgeman Art Archive), *Fotosearch*
p.184 (1950's family), *Photolibrary.com* pp.184 (Dave J. Anthony/modern
family), 194 (Radius Images/Case Study 6), 219 (John Howard/operator),
Punchstock Association p.172 (AP/Ron Edmonds), *Reuters* p.202 (Hugo Sanchez),
Rex Features p.231 (Digital Vision/children playing), *Press* pp.202 (Nadia
Comaneci, Mark Spitz, Sergei Bubka), 234

Illustrations by: Jonathan Burton pp.166, 189, Cartoonstock/Ian Baker pp.162,
167, 171, 176, 187, 199, 221, 227, Phil Disley p.158, Joanna Kerr pp.197, 201,
Joe McLaren pp.188, 216, Meiklejohn Illustration/Peter Ellis pp.160, 168,
Gavin Reece pp.169, Linda Rogers Associates/Kay Dixey p.196, Kath Walker
Illustration pp.163, 186, 212, 223

Photocopiables designed by: Stewart Grieve

Picture research and illustrations commissioned by: Catherine Blackie

Syllabus checklist — 4

Introduction — 8

- **What do Advanced students need?**
- **Study Link**
- **Course components**
  Student's Book Files 1–7
  Back of the Student's Book
- **For students**
  Workbook
  MultiROM
  Student's website
- **For teachers**
  Teacher's Book
  DVD
  Class audio CDs
  Test and Assessment CD-ROM
  Teacher's website

Lesson plans — 12

Photocopiable activities — 154

Contents
Grammar activity answers
Grammar activity masters
Communicative activity instructions
Communicative activity masters
Vocabulary activity instructions
Vocabulary activity masters
Song activity instructions
Song activity masters
Dependent prepositions

Syllabus checklist

		Grammar	Vocabulary

1

4	**A** What motivates you?	discourse markers (1): linkers	work
8	**B** Who am I?	*have*	personality; family
12	**C** Whose language is it?	pronouns	language terminology

16	**WRITING**	A letter of application
18	**COLLOQUIAL ENGLISH**	Family secrets
19	**REVISE & CHECK**	Grammar and Vocabulary

2

20	**A** Once upon a time	the past: narrative tenses, *used to* and *would*	word building: abstract nouns
24	**B** Are there really 31 hours in a day?	distancing	*time*
28	**C** 50 ways to leave your lover	*get*	phrases with *get*

32	**WRITING**	An article
34	**COLLOQUIAL ENGLISH**	Time and technology
35	**REVISE & CHECK**	Grammar and Vocabulary

3

36	**A** Breaking the silence	speculation and deduction	sounds and the human voice
40	**B** Lost in translation	adding emphasis (1): inversion	describing books
44	**C** Are you suffering from *Affluenza*?	unreal uses of past tenses	money

48	**WRITING**	A review
50	**COLLOQUIAL ENGLISH**	Women and money
51	**REVISE & CHECK**	Grammar and Vocabulary

4

52	**A** History goes to the movies	discourse markers (2): adverbs and adverbial expressions	history and warfare
56	**B** Help yourself	verb + object + infinitive or gerund	compound adjectives
60	**C** Can't live without it	conditional sentences	phone language; adjectives + prepositions

64	**WRITING**	Discursive essay (1): a balanced argument
66	**COLLOQUIAL ENGLISH**	Fact or fiction?
67	**REVISE & CHECK**	Grammar and Vocabulary

Pronunciation	Speaking	Listening	Reading
word stress and rhythm	talking about jobs you would hate / love to do	radio programme about happiness at work; interview with *innocent drinks* employee	Successful people talk about their inspiration and motivation
rhythm and intonation	talking about your personality; having debates about family	an audio guide describing the painting *The Family of Carlos IV*; song: *The Logical Song*	What's your personality type?
sound–spelling relationships	talking about learning and using English	two people talk about being non-native speakers of English	Whose language?
word stress with suffixes	talking about childhood and early memories	five people talk about their earliest memory; a radio interview about memories	When we were young
linking	talking about time	a radio phone-in about how to deal with wasting time	Multitasking = 31/7 and The great myth of multitasking
words and phrases of French origin	talking about revenge	author talking about research she did for her book *Love by Numbers*; song: *50 Ways to Leave Your Lover*	Getting your own back
consonant clusters	talking about sounds and music	BBC radio interview about noise pollution	Breaking the silence
words with 'silent' syllables	describing books and talking about reading tastes	an interview with a professional translator	First and last lines quiz; Lost in translation
ea and *ear*	talking about 'affluenza'	a lecture on the relationship between money and happiness; song: *A Lady of a Certain Age*	*Affluenza*; I wish I had married for money, not love
stress in word families	describing a historical film	a film critic talks about how historically accurate *Titanic* and *Braveheart* are	History goes to the movies
intonation in polite requests	talking about self-help	a radio programme where people discuss four self-help books	The persuaders
sounds and spelling /ʃ/, /tʃ/, /ʒ/, /dʒ/	talking about obsessions	a journalist talks about her week without her mobile; five people talk about obsessions; song: *Addicted to Love*	Are we hooked on addiction?

		Grammar	Vocabulary
5			
68	**A** Who's in control?	permission, obligation, and necessity	word formation: prefixes
72	**B** Just any old bed?	verbs of the senses	place and movement
76	**C** Trick or treatment?	gerunds and infinitives	health and medicine; similes
80	**WRITING**	A report	
82	**COLLOQUIAL ENGLISH**	Art and artists	
83	**REVISE & CHECK**	Grammar and Vocabulary	
6			
84	**A** A moving experience	expressing future plans and arrangements	travel and tourism
88	**B** Pets and pests	ellipsis and substitution	the natural world
92	**C** The promised land?	adding emphasis (2): cleft sentences	words that are often confused
96	**WRITING**	Discursive essay (2): taking sides	
98	**COLLOQUIAL ENGLISH**	Encounters with animals	
99	**REVISE & CHECK**	Grammar and Vocabulary	
7			
100	**A** A recipe for disaster	nouns: compound and possessive forms	preparing food
104	**B** Sport on trial	*so* and *such*	word building: adjectives, nouns, and verbs
108	**C** The funniest joke in the world?	comparison	humour
112	**WRITING**	A complaint	
114	**COLLOQUIAL ENGLISH**	Cooking round the world	
115	**REVISE & CHECK**	Grammar and Vocabulary	
116	**Communication**		
121	**Listening**		
136	**Grammar Bank**		
157	**Vocabulary Bank**		
168	**Sound Bank**		

Pronunciation	Speaking	Listening	Reading
intonation in exclamations	talking about proposed laws	a talk about *QI*, the TV show and books	Welcome to Nannyfornia
extra stress on important words	talking about art	an art expert talks about two works of art; song: *Vincent*	In a season of calm weather
word stress	talking about alternative and mainstream medicine	a doctor talks about some commonly-held medical beliefs; four people talk about their experience of alternative medicine	Trick or treatment? Alternative medicine on trial
homophones	talking about what kind of traveller you are	radio programme about a memorable travel experience; song: *I Wish I Could Go Travelling Again*	My 25,000 Wonders of the World
weak and strong pronunciation of auxiliary verbs and *to*	debates about animals	two news broadcasts, one about wolves and the other about foxes	Pets and owners 'become more alike over time'
intonation in cleft sentences	various conversations about emigration, your town, the school, etc.	two people talk about emigrating to another country	an extract from *The Joy Luck Club*
-ed adjective endings and linking	talking about food and cooking	four people describe cooking disasters	My Last Supper
homographs	talking about sport and the influence it has on athletes and spectators	a psychoanalyst talks about sport and whether it has a positive influence; song: *Eye of the Tiger*	Battle of the workouts
augh and *ough*	talking about humour	a journalist talks about jokes and humour around the world	Famous put-downs, *Yes, Minister*, and *First date*

What do Advanced students need?

When students reach an advanced level of English they are, by definition, highly proficient users of the language. As a result, learners typically feel very positive about the language and their classes, but it can be hard to make them feel they are actually improving their English. We believe that advanced learners are best motivated by a strong focus on *lexis*, both in terms of expanding their knowledge of phrases, idioms, and collocation and in developing an awareness of levels of formality and informality (register). Equally important is the need to engage and stimulate students through meaningful, and motivating contexts and topics – 'advanced' should not mean 'dull and over-serious' – and through setting clear aims and challenging tasks.

Grammar, Vocabulary, and Pronunciation

At any level, the basic tools students need to speak English with confidence are Grammar, Vocabulary, and Pronunciation (G, V, P). In *New English File Advanced* all three elements are given equal importance.

Grammar

Advanced students need
- to be able to use a wide range of structures to express different concepts.
- to be able to use more sophisticated grammar structures with fluency.
- to develop awareness of the register of different grammatical structures in order to use them appropriately.

At this level students will have already studied most of the common grammatical structures. However, the more complex structures such as past modals need revising and several new advanced structures, such as inversion and ellipsis, will be introduced. Grammar is often presented functionally, e.g. the structures to use for distancing, or for adding emphasis, which allows students to revise and extend certain structures without feeling that they are retracing their steps. There is always a focus in the **Grammar Banks** on the register of structures to make students aware of the different levels of formality and informality.

The photocopiable Grammar activities in the Teacher's Book can be used for practice in class or for self-study. These now include both consolidation and activation of the grammar.

Vocabulary

Advanced students need
- systematic expansion of their vocabulary in a wide range of lexical areas.
- to enrich their vocabulary by focusing on idioms, synonyms, and collocation.
- to focus on the register of lexis to enable them to use the appropriate word or phrase according to the context or situation.
- to further develop their ability to 'build' new words by adding affixes.

At this level, expanding students' vocabulary is the most visible and motivating measure of their progress. Every lesson in *New English File Advanced* has a clear lexical aim. Many lessons are linked to the **Vocabulary Banks** which help present and practise high-frequency, topic-based vocabulary in class and provide a clear reference bank designed to aid memorization.

All reading activities and many listening exercises include a new feature, **Lexis in Context**, which focuses on useful words and expressions that come up in the text or listening script. Students can practise using the vocabulary from all the **Vocabulary Banks** with the **MultiROM** and the *New English File* Student's website, which also includes further practice of items from **Lexis in Context**. There is also a photocopiable activity to revise the vocabulary from each lesson.

Pronunciation

Advanced students need
- 'fine-tuning' of pronunciation of difficult sounds.
- to continue to develop their instinct for spelling – pronunciation rules and patterns.
- to be able to use natural rhythm and intonation in conversation.
- to develop awareness of how sentence stress can convey meaning, e.g. contrastive stress.
- to be able to use phonetic symbols in their dictionary to check pronunciation.

Every lesson has a pronunciation focus, which often prepares students for a speaking activity, or by analysing features of authentic speech helps them both to understand and pronounce better.

The pronunciation focus is linked to the **Sound Bank**, the *New English File* system of learning the phonetic symbols through 'sound pictures' which illustrate an example word for each sound. There are also two pages of common spelling rules for each sound, which students can print, on the *New English File* Student's website.

Speaking

Advanced students need
- up-to-date, stimulating topics to get them talking and exchanging opinions.
- practice in more extended speaking, e.g. roleplays and debates.
- the key words, phrases, and idioms necessary to discuss a topic.
- practice in recognizing and using discourse markers in speech.
- to improve <u>accuracy</u> as well as further developing their fluency.

Every lesson in *New English File Advanced* gives students many opportunities to speak and put into practice grammar, vocabulary, and pronunciation that have been worked on earlier in the lesson.

Photocopiable Communicative activities can be found in the Teacher's Book. These include pairwork activities, roleplays, debates, discussions, and quizzes.

Listening

Advanced students need

- motivating, integrated listening material.
- achievable tasks with the right level of challenge.
- exposure to longer listenings and to a wide variety of accents.
- regular exposure to authentic and colloquial spoken language.

For many students listening is still the hardest skill. *New English File Advanced* has motivating listening texts, and tasks which are challenging but hopefully always achievable and which expose students to a wide variety of accents, both native and non-native.

Most of the listenings in *New English File Advanced* are unscripted, and there is often a focus on features of natural speech such as hesitation, or saying the same thing in different ways. The Colloquial English lessons give students further practice in listening to unscripted authentic speech.

Reading

Advanced students need

- exposure to a wide variety of totally authentic texts.
- challenging tasks which help them read better.
- to develop an awareness of register.
- practice in guessing the meaning of unknown lexis.

Many students need to read in English for their work or academic studies, or may want to read about their personal interests on English websites. Reading also plays an important part in helping to extend students' vocabulary and to consolidate grammar. In *New English File Advanced* reading texts are taken from a variety of real sources (newspapers, magazines, the Internet) and have been chosen for their intrinsic interest, which we hope will stimulate students to want to read them and will help spark classroom discussion.

Writing

Advanced students need

- clear models of common text types, including ones required in international exams.
- regular practice in planning, organizing, writing, and checking.
- to develop an ability to vary register according to the context and text type.
- a focus on 'micro' writing skills, e.g. writing a good introduction, topic sentences.

The ever growing amount of email communication and Internet-based writing (e.g. blogs, etc.) continues to raise the importance of writing skills. Students at this level may also be thinking about taking public exams where writing quickly and accurately is a vital skill. *New English File Advanced* has one Writing lesson per File, now two pages as opposed to one page in the lower levels. These have two parts, a first stage where students analyse a model, focusing on useful language for each text type as well as micro skills such as writing introductions or topic sentences, and then a second stage where students plan the content before starting to write.

Colloquial English

Advanced students need

- regular exposure to authentic colloquial speech.
- to be able to deal with different speeds and accents.
- to expand their knowledge of high frequency colloquial phrases and idioms.

In the seven *Colloquial English* lessons students listen to unscripted and authentic English. The lessons consist firstly of an interview with a person who is an expert in his / her field (one of the File topics). In the second part of the lesson students hear street interviews where people answer questions related to the lesson topic. There is also a focus on 'Common phrases' where students listen again and complete high-frequency expressions used in spoken English.

The Colloquial English lessons are also on the *New English File Advanced* DVD which teachers can use instead of the class audio. Using the DVD will make the lessons more enjoyable and will help students to understand faster speech with the help of paralinguistic features. On the MultiROM students have the opportunity to watch and listen to more street interviews.

Revision

Advanced students need

- regular revision.
- motivating reference and practice material.
- a sense of progress.

The higher the level, the harder it is to see your progress. Advanced students need to feel that they are increasing their knowledge, improving their skills, and using English more fluently and effectively. At the end of each File there is a Revise & Check section, which revises the grammar and vocabulary of each File. These pages are designed to be used flexibly according to the needs of your students.

The photocopiable Grammar, Communicative, and Vocabulary activities also provide many opportunities for recycling.

StudyLink

The Study Link feature in *New English File Advanced* is designed to help you and your students use the course more effectively. It shows **what** resources are available, **where** they can be found, and **when** to use them.

The Student's Book has these Study Link references:

- from the Colloquial English lessons ○ MultiROM.
- from the Grammar Bank ○ MultiROM and Student's website.
- from the Vocabulary Bank ○ MultiROM and Student's website.
- from the Sound Bank ○ MultiROM and Student's website.

These references lead students to extra activities and exercises that link with what they have just studied.

The Workbook has these Study Link references:

- the Student's Book Grammar and Vocabulary Banks.
- the MultiROM.

The Teacher's Book has Study Link references to remind you where there is extra material available to your students.

Student's Book organization

The Student's Book has seven Files. Each File is organized like this:

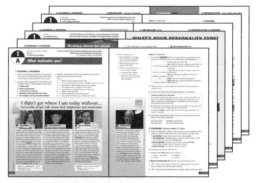

A, B, and C lessons Three four-page lessons which form the core material of the book. Each lesson presents and practises **Grammar** and **Vocabulary**, and has a **Pronunciation** focus. There is a balance of reading and listening activities, and lots of opportunities for spoken practice. These lessons have clear references ⬤ to the Grammar Bank, Vocabulary Bank, and Sound Bank at the back of the book.

Writing A two-page section which focuses on different text types and writing skills, looking at layout, register, spelling, and pronunciation.

Colloquial English One-page lessons where students develop their ability to listen to authentic English and learn common collocations, idioms, and colloquial vocabulary. The lessons link with the *New English File Advanced* DVD.

Revise & Check A one-page section revising the **Grammar** and **Vocabulary** of each File.

The back of the book

In the back of the Student's Book you'll find these three Banks of material:

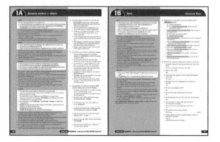

Grammar Bank (*pp.136–156*)
One page for each File. Part of the page has the grammar rules and the other part has practice exercises. Students are referred ⬤ to the Grammar Bank when they do the grammar in each main A, B, and C lesson.

Vocabulary Bank (*pp.157–167*)
An active vocabulary resource to help students learn, practise, and revise key words. Students are referred ⬤ to the Vocabulary Bank from the main lessons.

Sound Bank (*p.168*) A one-page section with the *English File* sounds chart for all sounds. Students are referred ⬤ to the Sound Bank from the main lessons.

You'll also find:

- **Communication activities** (*pp.116–120*)
  Information gap activities and roleplays.
- **Listening scripts** (*pp.121–135*)
  Scripts of key listenings.

More for students

Workbook Each A–C lesson in the Student's Book has a three-page section in the Workbook with revision and practice of Grammar, Vocabulary, Pronunciation, and Lexis in context, as well as more Reading practice and vocabulary development. Each section ends with:

- **Listening**, which gives students extra listening practice based on the theme of the lesson. The material is on the audio section of the MultiROM.

- **Exam practice** with an exercise which recycles key language from the File and from earlier in the course.

Each Colloquial English lesson has a one-page section in the Workbook with practice of the Common phrases and a reading activity.

It is available with or without key.

MultiROM

The MultiROM has two functions:

- It's a CD-ROM, containing revision of **Grammar**, **Vocabulary**, **Pronunciation**, **Colloquial English** (with extracts from the DVD), **Dictation** activities, and **Exam Practice**.

- It's an audio CD for students to use in a CD player. It has the audio material for the Workbook listening activities.

Student's website

www.oup.com/elt/englishfile/advanced

Extra learning resources including

- grammar activities
- vocabulary puzzles
- pronunciation practice as well as Sounds and spelling rules
- Colloquial English activities
- Lexis in context
- learning records
- weblinks
- idioms and collocation
- text builder

More for teachers

Teacher's Book The Teacher's Book has detailed lesson plans for all the lessons. These include:

- an optional lead-in for every lesson.
- **Extra idea** suggestions for optional extra activities.
- **Digital extra idea** suggestions for optional extra whiteboard or Internet activities.
- **Extra challenge** suggestions for ways of exploiting the Student's Book material in a more challenging way if you have a stronger class.
- **Extra support** suggestions for ways of adapting activities or exercises to make them more accessible for weaker students.

All lesson plans include keys and complete listening scripts. Extra activities are colour coded in blue so you can see where you are at a glance when you're planning and teaching your classes.

You'll also find over 85 pages of photocopiable materials in the Teacher's Book:

Photocopiable Grammar activities *see pp.157–177*

There is a photocopiable Grammar activity for each A, B, and C lesson.

Photocopiable Communicative activities *see pp.183–203*

There is a photocopiable Communicative activity for each A, B, and C lesson.

Photocopiable Vocabulary activities *see pp.208–228*

There is a photocopiable Vocabulary activity for each File.

Photocopiable Song activities *see pp.232–238*

A photocopiable Dependent prepositions list *see pp.239–240*

All the photocopiable material is accompanied by clear instructions and keys.

DVD The DVD episodes link with the Colloquial English lessons in the Student's Book. There is an episode in each File and each episode is divided into two parts: the first is an extended interview with a person who has first-hand experience of one of the topics from the File, e.g. File 5 an American painter talking about art; the second part contains shorter interviews with members of the public answering some general questions about the topic. All the interviews are unscripted and provide an opportunity for students to practise listening to English spoken at a natural speed and to learn some high-frequency vocabulary. Each episode can be used with the tasks in the Student's Book Colloquial English lessons as an alternative to the Class CD.

The *New English File Advanced* package also includes:

- **Four class / audio CDs**
  These contain all the listening materials for the Student's Book.

- **Test and Assessment CD-ROM**
  Tests as PDFs and customizable Word documents.

- **Teacher's website**
  www.oup.com/elt/teacher/englishfile
  This gives you extra teaching resources, including
  – a guide to *New English File* and the Common European Framework of Reference
  – wordlists
  – mini web-projects
  – customizable cloze tests
  – customizable crossword maker
  – student learning records
  – listening scripts

G discourse markers (1): linkers
V work
P word stress and rhythm

1A What motivates you?

File 1 overview

In the first File (**1A–1C**) the grammar has a strong revision element, but groups and presents key structures again in a challenging way. Each lesson has a substantial input of new vocabulary, which reflects the importance of lexis at this level. In lesson **1A** the grammar focus is on discourse markers (linking expressions of reason, result, purpose, and contrast), and the lexical area is words and phrases related to the world of work. The grammar focus of **1B** is on the main meanings and uses of the verb *have*, and the lexis is phrases and idioms related to family, while in **1C** the grammar focuses on an overview of pronouns and the lexical area is language terminology.

Lesson plan

The dominant theme of this first lesson is personal motivation. In the first half of the lesson famous people write about what inspired them or drove them to succeed in life. The context provides an opportunity for SS to discuss their own motivation to succeed in work, study, or in becoming fluent English speakers. The four reading texts have been selected from the regular feature in *The Times* newspaper. Examples from the text provide a lead-in to the grammar focus, which is on linkers expressing reason, result, purpose, and contrast. In the second half of the lesson the focus moves to what motivates people to feel happy at work and SS hear about a survey which established the top ten factors. They then listen to an interview with a woman who works for *innocent drinks*, a UK company whose employees are among the happiest workers in the country according to a recent survey.

SS then expand their lexis with advanced expressions related to work and job satisfaction. Pronunciation focuses on word stress and rhythm, and the lesson ends with a speaking activity where SS describe jobs they would love or hate to do.

Optional lead-in – the quote

- Write the quote at the top of *p.4* on the board (books closed) and the name of the author or get SS to open their books and read it.
- Point out that G.K. Chesterton (1874–1936) was an English journalist, novelist, poet, and philosopher, most remembered today for his Father Brown detective stories.
- Ask SS whether they identify with Chesterton's opinion or disagree, and try to get a short discussion going about the usefulness of advice from parents, teachers, and friends. Try to elicit some anecdotes of where people have followed or ignored advice (particularly regarding studies and work) and what happened. Contribute your own experiences if you have any.

1 READING & SPEAKING

a
- Focus on the task and point out that SS can either talk about someone they know personally or a famous person they admire. You could demonstrate the activity by talking about someone yourself first.
- Get SS to talk about their person with a partner first and then get feedback from individual SS. Try to establish, and write on the board, some common reasons for success, e.g. *having great determination, being very ambitious, having financial backing*, etc.

b
- Focus on the article and point out that this was a regular feature in *The Times* newspaper (a well-known UK daily paper).
- Focus on the four photos and find out if SS know any of the people. Set SS a time limit to read the article once and match the headings to the paragraphs. Then give SS time to compare and discuss their answers with a partner before checking answers.

1 D	**2** B	**3** E	**4** A

c
- Focus on the task and give SS time to read the article again and write the initials of the person next to each question. Again, give time for SS to compare answers before eliciting them from the class.

1 MW	**3** PC	**5** PC	**7** JM
2 AP	**4** JM	**6** MW	**8** AP

d
- Put SS in small groups of three or four. Focus on the questions and get SS to discuss them. You could appoint a secretary in each group to organize the answering of the questions. Monitor while the groups are discussing the questions, helping with vocabulary and noting down any general problems.
- Find out from some SS what impression they got of the four people's personalities and who of the four people in the article they identified with most and why. Also get brief feedback from the class about what / who motivates SS in the different areas of their lives.

LEXIS IN CONTEXT

e
- This is the first of a regular exercise-type focusing on useful lexical items that occur in reading and listening texts. Point out to SS that in this type of exercise, they should get into the habit of making sure the form of the word matches the definition, e.g. verb in the infinitive, noun in the singular, etc.
- Focus on the first part of the task, emphasizing the importance of trying to guess the meaning of words and phrases from the context. Get SS, in pairs, to look at each highlighted phrase in turn and try to guess its meaning. Set a time limit for this.
- When the time limit is up, focus on the second part of the exercise where SS now check their guesses by matching the highlighted phrases to definitions 1–7.

Check SS understand the abbreviations IDM (= idiom) and PHR V (= phrasal verb). Focus also on *sb* in 6 and elicit that it stands for *somebody*, and that when phrasal verbs are separable, this is how they are given in a dictionary, e.g. *pay sb back*.

⚠ Remind SS that they should write the verbs in the infinitive, and that if there is a pronoun, e.g. *my*, they should change it to *your* (which is what a dictionary gives).

● Give SS time to complete the exercise and compare in pairs before checking answers.

1	know your own mind	5	grit your teeth
2	stick to your guns	6	fill sb in
3	in a sense	7	catch up
4	your comfort zone		

● You may want to point out / elicit that:
 – *stick to your guns* has its origins in warfare where the expression meant not to abandon your artillery (= heavy weapons, e.g. cannons) when under enemy attack. Highlight that the idiomatic meaning of sticking to your beliefs despite opposition is considered a <u>positive</u> quality.
 – *grit your teeth* also has a literal meaning of pressing your teeth together which you could demonstrate to the class.
 – *catch up* (with someone) also has a literal meaning of running or walking faster to reach someone who is in front of you (e.g. *Don't wait for me, I'll catch you up.*).

f ● This exercise encourages SS to use reading texts to help extend their vocabulary. Give SS a few minutes to choose five more words and phrases, which they think would be useful to learn. Get them to compare their choices with a partner before getting some feedback from the class. Emphasize the importance of writing down new lexis in context, e.g. *I was a <u>determined</u> and <u>rebellious</u> kid* with the meaning of the word alongside it.
● You may want to systematically ask SS to choose more words or phrases to learn after each reading or listening text, even if this is not one of the lesson stages.

Extra support

At this point you could go through the text pointing out useful words and expressions, and eliciting meaning and pronunciation. For text 3 you may need to explain the idiom *work like a trouper* (= work very hard; a trouper is a member of a theatrical company) and the use of *no... whatsoever* (= none at all).

g ● Focus on the **Looking up idioms** box and go through it with the class. The rule of thumb regarding looking up idioms in the dictionary is to look under the first 'full' word (e.g. noun or adjective, etc.) and if it isn't there, then try under the other word(s).
● Highlight that if it is an idiom involving a very common verb, e.g. *get*, then you will need to look under the next 'full' word, e.g. *get into trouble* would be under *trouble*. However, a phrasal verb like *get on with sb* would be under *get*.
● Highlight also that when SS look up an idiom, it is a good idea to copy down, as well as the definition, a clear example if one is given.

● This would be a good moment to make sure that your SS have a good monolingual Advanced dictionary such as the *Oxford Advanced Learner's Dictionary*, as well as a good bilingual dictionary.

h ● This exercise gives SS practice in looking up idioms. If SS haven't got dictionaries with them in class, you could set this for homework or choose SS to look up each word within a time limit.
● Before they begin, ask SS where in the dictionary they would expect to find the idioms: *speak your mind* and *cross your mind* should be under the respective verbs, **speak** and **cross**; *mind your own business* and *be in two minds* should be under **mind**.
● Check answers.

> **speak your mind** = to say exactly what you think in a very direct way
> **mind your own business** (*informal*) = to think about your own affairs and not to ask questions about, or try to get involved in, other people's lives and problems, etc. *I was minding my own business* and *Mind your own business!* are both informal, but the second one when said to sb else is rude.
> **cross your mind** = to come into your mind, occur to you, e.g. *It never crossed my mind to ask him how his father was.*
> **be in two minds about something** = to be unable to decide what you think about sb or sth, or whether to do sth or not

Extra challenge

Ask SS to use their dictionaries to find more idioms with *mind*, which they think are useful.

2 GRAMMAR discourse markers (1): linkers

a ● Focus on the task. Remind SS not to look at the text and give them a few moments to try and remember more or less how the sentences continue.

> **Suggested answers**
> 1 the nuns thought I was stupid.
> 2 my clothes / the way I dressed.
> 3 it was hard for me.
> 4 tell him (the good and bad things) about my day.

Extra support

You could do this as a whole class activity, eliciting the sentences from the class.

b ● Get SS to look back at the text to see if they were right. Check answers, and tell them what the exact words were.

c ● Draw SS' attention to the bold linking expressions in sentences 1–4 and get them to complete the task.

> | | | |
> |---|---|---|
> | 2 Because of | 3 to | 4 even though |

d ● Tell SS to go to **Grammar Bank 1A** on *p.136*. If your SS have not used the *New English File* series before, explain that all the grammar rules and exercises are in this part of the book.

- Focus on the term *discourse markers*. Explain to SS that discourse markers are words and expressions, often adverbs or adverbial expressions, which help you to understand:
  – the connection between what a speaker is saying and what has already been said.
  – the connection between what a speaker has said and what he / she is now going to say.
  – what the speaker thinks about what he / she is saying.
- Tell SS that here they are focusing on discourse markers which express connections (those which give information about a speaker's attitude are focused on in **4A**).
- Go through each example and its corresponding rule with the class, or give SS time to read the examples and rules on their own, and answer any queries.

Grammar notes

In this lesson SS revise discourse markers in these four areas (reason, result, purpose, and contrast), and learn some more sophisticated expressions, e.g. *due to / owing to*, *yet*, etc. There is also a strong focus on register to enable SS to use these markers appropriately. Highlight that using a variety of discourse markers will make their English sound more advanced.

- Focus on the exercises for **1A**. SS do the exercises individually or in pairs. If SS do them individually, get them to compare with a partner. Check answers after each exercise. When checking answers to **b**, ask SS which sentences are formal.

a	1	as	b	1	because of
	2	so that		2	so
	3	in spite of		3	Nevertheless (formal)
	4	Nevertheless		4	to
	5	though		5	though
				6	due to (formal)

c 1 In spite of our seats being a long way from the stage, … / In spite of the fact that our seats were a long way from the stage, we enjoyed the play. We enjoyed the play in spite of our seats being a long way from the stage. / …in spite of the fact that our seats were a long way from the stage.

2 We took ages to get there because of the heavy traffic.

3 I took the price off the bag so that she didn't know / so that she wouldn't know how much it had cost.

4 Keep the receipt for the sweater in case your dad doesn't like it.

5 Even though Susanna is an only child, she isn't at all spoilt.

6 Prices have risen due to increased production costs.

- Tell SS to go back to the main lesson on *p.5*.

e ● **1.1** This exercise highlights the way discourse markers help a listener predict how a sentence will continue. Focus on the task and demonstrate the activity by playing the first sentence (or the first two), then pausing the CD player to elicit possible continuations from the class. Accept any that make sense and write them on the board. Point out that later SS will hear how the original sentences finish.

- Play the CD, pausing after each sentence for SS to write down how they think it might continue. Highlight that the idea is to guess logical continuations rather than the exact words of the original sentence.

> **1.1**   CD1 Track 2
>
> 1 Demand for new cars is falling and as a result…
> 2 Even though we'd only just met, …
> 3 The picnic was cancelled at the last minute because of…
> 4 She didn't tell him what she really thought of his new suit so as not to…
> 5 Despite not getting very good reviews, the film…
> 6 The accused is only 12 years old and therefore he…
> 7 The flight is delayed until 14.25 due to…
> 8 I want to find a job nearer home so that I don't…

f ● **1.2** Check answers by eliciting possible endings for each sentence 1–8 and writing them on the board. Then play the CD, pausing after each sentence for SS to compare the original with the guesses on the board.

> 1 many workers have lost their jobs.
> 2 we felt as if we'd known each other for ages.
> 3 the terrible storm.
> 4 hurt his feelings.
> 5 was a huge commercial success.
> 6 cannot be named.
> 7 technical problems.
> 8 don't have to spend so much time commuting.

> **1.2**   CD1 Track 3
>
> 1 Demand for new cars is falling and as a result many workers have lost their jobs.
> 2 Even though we'd only just met, we felt as if we'd known each other for ages.
> 3 The picnic was cancelled at the last minute because of the terrible storm.
> 4 She didn't tell him what she really thought of his new suit so as not to hurt his feelings.
> 5 Despite not getting very good reviews, the film was a huge commercial success.
> 6 The accused is only 12 years old and therefore he cannot be named.
> 7 The flight is delayed until 14.25 due to technical problems.
> 8 I want to find a job nearer home so that I don't have to spend so much time commuting.

3 SPEAKING & LISTENING

a ● Focus on the task and go through the ten factors making sure SS understand everything, especially *human resources* (= department in a company that deals with employing and training people), *rewarding* (= makes you happy and satisfied because you think it is a job which is worth doing), and *supportive* (= who support you, i.e. give help, encouragement, or sympathy).

● Set a time limit for SS in pairs to discuss the factors and to try to agree on the two most and least important. Point out that they will later find out what the order was in the original survey.

● Then get some feedback from pairs of SS and see if there is any kind of consensus. <u>Do not tell them the answers at this stage.</u>

Extra idea

If you have a class where some SS work (or have worked) and others are studying, you could divide the class into these two groups before sub-dividing into pairs or small groups. Then you could later contrast the possibly different perspectives of the two groups.

b ● Focus on the task and go through the statements before giving SS a few minutes to discuss them and mark them probably true or probably false. You could get some quick feedback from the class to see what the general view is on each factor.

c ● **1.3** Play the CD for SS to check their answers to **a** and **b**. Play the recording again as necessary. You could pause the CD after **John** says *Apparently not* (see the space in the script) and check answers to **a** before playing the rest of the recording and checking the answers to **b**.

● Check answers and find out whether SS were surprised by any of the results of the survey and why.

---

a The two most important factors are:
1 Having friendly, supportive colleagues.
2 Doing enjoyable work.
The two least important factors are:
1 Having your achievements recognized.
2 Earning a competitive salary.
b 1 T 2 F 3 F 4 F 5 T 6 F 7 T

1.3 CD1 Track 4

(script in Student's Book on *p.121*)
P = presenter, J = John
P Welcome to *Workplace* and in today's programme we're looking at the results of two recently published surveys, which both deal with the same topic – happiness at work. John, tell us about the first survey.
J Well, this was done by a human resources consultancy, who interviewed more than 1,000 workers, and established a top ten of the factors which make people happy at work. The most important factor for the majority of the people interviewed was having friendly, supportive colleagues. In fact, 73% of people interviewed put their relationship with colleagues as being the key factor contributing to happiness at work, which is a very high percentage. The second most important factor was having work that is enjoyable per se, that is people actually liking what they do. The two least important factors were having your achievements recognized, and, rather surprisingly, earning a competitive salary.
P So we're not mainly motivated by money?
J Apparently not.

P Any other interesting information in the survey?
J Yes, for example 25% of the working people interviewed described themselves as 'very happy' at work. However 20% of employees described themselves as being 'unhappy'.
P That's quite a lot of unhappy people at work every day.
J It is, isn't it? And there were several more interesting conclusions revealed by the survey. First of all, small is beautiful: people definitely prefer working for smaller organizations or companies with less than 100 staff. We also find out that, generally speaking, women were happier in their work than men.
P Yes, we're a miserable bunch, aren't we?
J And workers on part-time contracts, who only work four or five hours a day, are happier than those who work full-time. The researchers concluded that this is probably due to a better work–life balance.
P Are bosses happier than their employees?
J Yes, perhaps not surprisingly, the higher people go in a company, the happier they are. So senior managers enjoy their jobs more than people working under them.
P Does the period of time you spend with the same company affect how happy you are?
J Well, according to the survey, happiness declines the longer people stay with the same company or organization. The most contented people were those who'd been with a company for less than two years, and the least contented were those who'd been in the same place of work for more than ten years.
P So you can stay too long in the same place.
J So it seems. And lastly, according to the survey, apparently the happiest workers of all are those who are 55 years old or older, probably because they feel they're working at the peak of their powers.
P Presumably, though they haven't spent more than ten years in the same job.
J Exactly. So how long have you been here then, Michael?
P Eight years! Maybe I should start thinking about looking for a new job…

Extra support

If there's time, get SS to listen again with the script on *p.121*, focusing on any new vocabulary, and getting feedback on phrases SS didn't understand, e.g. because the words were run together.

● Finally, focus on the **Listening to English in the media** box and go through it with the class. This would be a good moment to find out what SS are listening to outside class in terms of news websites, language learning websites, films on DVD, etc. and for SS to 'exchange notes' on what they find useful or what problems they might be having.

d ● Focus SS' attention on the photos and ask them to read the text *Working where the grass is always greener* and find out whether they would like to work for *innocent drinks* or not and why.

e ● **1.4** Tell SS that they are going to hear the second part of the radio programme they listened to earlier, in which an employee of *innocent drinks*, Becka Walton, is interviewed.

● Focus on the two questions and tell SS that the first time they listen to the interview they just have to try and answer these questions. Warn them that Becka speaks quite quickly.

● Play the recording once, playing it again only if most SS seem to be struggling, and elicit answers to the questions. Check answers.

1 Yes, she does.

2 People work long hours (because they are passionate about their jobs).

1.4 CD1 Track 5

(script in Student's Book on *p.121*)

P = presenter, B = Becka Walton

P The second survey we're looking at in today's programme is a *Sunday Times* survey which was all about the best UK companies to work for. Apparently, one of the best small companies to work for is *innocent drinks*. Well, I have with me in the studio Becka Walton, who works for *innocent drinks*. Becka, tell us what made you apply for the job at *innocent*.

B Well, I've always really liked them as a company, I'd always followed their website and their weekly newsletter, I'd always thought that they would be people that I would like to work for, so it was a case of just keeping my eyes on the job page and waiting for something that I thought I could do to come along.

P In a recent survey about what makes people happy at work, *innocent* was listed as one of the top companies to work for. You obviously think it is a happy company. Now why do you think that?

B Well, I can see how we would have scored quite highly on that scale, I think there's quite a big emphasis on a team environment at work, we're all mixed up so nobody sits according to the group of people that they work with, which means that you get to make friends in different areas of the business. Everybody's aware of the projects that people are working on, the pressures that they're under so it makes for a really good team environment. I think that's important.

P And how does that compare with other companies that you've worked for?

B I've not really worked for any big corporations before – *innocent* is the biggest company that I've worked for. I know friends of mine complain about really dry working environments, we're really quite informal in our outlook, things are quite relaxed and a lot of my friends are quite surprised that we don't have to dress up to come to work, you know often people don't even wear shoes, we have a grassy floor in our office, and it's just kind of, it's a relaxed place to work.

P What would you change about the company if there was something that you could change?

B Oh, I, I'm not really sure how to answer that question, I think that a thing that does come up when we survey people is perhaps the work–life balance, I think people are quite passionate about their jobs, and that's a good thing, but it can lead to people working very long hours.

P So you are overworked?

B I wouldn't have gone quite that far but it would be easy to be overworked, yes.

P You're obviously very happy in your work, but is there a high staff turnover? Do people generally stay for a long time?

B I know that Daisy, my line manager, was the first girl employed by the company and we're coming up for our tenth birthday. She's only leaving now, so I think that she's quite happy. Obviously we have people on short-term contracts, but as a general rule I would say that people, people are happy and people do tend to stay at *innocent* for quite long lengths of time.

P OK, in the other survey, the one about the ten things that make people happy at work, the issue of a competitive salary was the last in the list. What's your view on that?

B Well, I've thought about this and I hope it doesn't make me sound terribly shallow, but I struggled to think of ten things that might be more important, of course, it's important to, you know, for a good work–life balance and to, I suppose, have fun at work and to enjoy the people you work with, but I think it probably is quite important to feel like you're adequately financially rewarded for what you do.

P OK. And finally, I should ask you, do you drink smoothies yourself and if you do, are they always *innocent*?

B I really love, I really love smoothies and if I didn't, it would be the wrong place for me to work, and, and of course they're always *innocent* smoothies. I think that the working environment reflects in the passion that we all have and I think that's because we know we've got a really good product.

P Thank you very much, Becka Walton.

---

f • Play the recording again, this time pausing after each question and answer (see spaces in the script) to give SS time to write their answers to each question. You could get SS to compare their answers in pairs. Play the recording again if necessary.

1 She had always liked them as a company (and followed their website and weekly newsletter).

2 They mix people up from different departments so you make friends with people in different areas of the business (and are therefore aware of the projects others are working on and the pressures they are under).

3 Employees don't have to dress up to go to work / people often don't wear shoes / there is a grassy floor in the office.

4 People tend to stay at the company for a long time.

5 No, she thinks it's important to 'feel like you are adequately financially rewarded for what you do.'

6 She loves smoothies and always drinks *innocent* smoothies. (She thinks that she and her colleagues feel passionate about their work because they know they have a good product.)

g • Get SS to go to *p.121* and play the recording a final time with SS reading the script. Get feedback about any words and phrases that SS found difficult to hear when they previously listened, and deal with any vocabulary problems.

h • Ask the question to the whole class and try to elicit some different opinions.

Digital extra idea

You could show the class the *innocent drinks* website at http://www.innocentdrinks.co.uk/ .

4 VOCABULARY work

a ● Focus on the task and give SS time to complete it. <u>Don't</u> check answers yet.

b ● 1.5 Explain to SS that they will hear the answers in some brief extracts from the Becka interview so they need to listen carefully. Play the CD for SS to check their answers. Check, and elicit the meaning of the phrases from the class.

> 1 **D** short-term contracts (= work contracts which are for a short space of time, usually just a few months. Opposite *long-term contracts*)
> 2 **A** work–life balance (= the relative amount of time people spend at work and the time they spend on other aspects of their lives, e.g. family and hobbies. People try to achieve a *good work–life balance.*)
> 3 **E** working environment (= the physical conditions existing where you work, e.g. behaviour of colleagues and superiors, level of comfort, noise, etc.)
> 4 **F** line manager (= the person who is your day-to-day boss, and who is usually one position above you in the company)
> 5 **C** staff turnover (= the rate at which employees leave a company and are replaced by other people. We talk about *high / low staff turnover.*)
> 6 **B** competitive salary (= a salary which is good compared to those offered by similar companies)

1.5   CD1 Track 6

1 …obviously we have people on short-term contracts, but as a general rule I'd say that people, people are happy and people do tend to stay at *innocent* for quite long lengths of time.
2 …a thing that does come up when we survey people is perhaps the work–life balance, I think people are quite passionate about their jobs and that's a good thing, but it can lead to people working very long hours.
3 I think the working environment reflects in the passion that we all have.
4 I know that Daisy, my line manager, was the first girl employed by the company.
5 You're obviously very happy in your work, but is there a high staff turnover? Do people generally stay for a long time?
6 OK, in the other survey, the one about the ten things that make people happy at work, the issue of a competitive salary was the last in the list.

---

c ● Tell SS to go to **Vocabulary Bank *Work*** on *p.157*. Focus on section **1 Adjectives describing a job** and get SS to do it individually or in pairs. Check answers and elicit / model the pronunciation of tricky words as necessary.

> **1 D   2 B   3 C   4 F   5 E   6 A**

● Highlight:
– the difference between a *challenging* job, which tests your abilities and energies in a positive way, and a *demanding* job, which tests the same things but has negative connotations. *Rewarding* is a synonym of *satisfying* but with an even more positive meaning. It suggests the work is hard but worth it. Point out that the adjective comes from the noun *reward* (= sth you are given for doing sth good, working hard, etc.)
– that *monotonous* and *repetitive* are very similar in meaning, but *monotonous* stresses that a job is both repetitive and boring.

● Now focus on section **2 Nouns that are often confused** and get SS to do it individually or in pairs. Check answers and elicit / model the pronunciation of tricky words as necessary.

> | | | | |
> |---|---|---|---|
> | 1 | post | 9 | employer |
> | 2 | profession | 10 | staff |
> | 3 | career | 11 | training |
> | 4 | salary | 12 | qualifications |
> | 5 | wages | 13 | skills |
> | 6 | bonus | 14 | hours |
> | 7 | perks | 15 | timetable |
> | 8 | staff, employees | | |

● Highlight that:
– *career* refers to the series of jobs that a person has in a particular area of work, usually involving more responsibility as time passes, e.g. *a career in journalism.* It can also refer to the period of your life that you spend working, e.g. *He had a long career as a tennis player.*
– *post* (synonym *position*) is normally used when talking about having or applying for a specific job in a large organization.
– *profession* usually refers in a general sense to jobs that require special training or qualifications, e.g. *the medical profession.*
– *wages* = the money paid weekly to do a job, whereas *salary* = the money that you are paid monthly or annually to do a job, especially professional employees
– *bonus* = an extra amount of money that is added to your wages / salary as a reward, e.g. *a productivity bonus*
– *perks* = an advantage you get from a company or employer in addition to the money you earn, e.g. a company car. In formal English, e.g. in a job description, you can also use *benefits* as a synonym.
– *staff* = all the workers employed in an organization considered as a group, e.g. *Only company staff can use the canteen.* It normally takes a plural verb. *employees* = the workers seen as individuals. You may want to point out that *employee* can also be stressed *employee*.
– *skills* = particular abilities required in a job, whereas *qualifications* usually refers to exams passed
– *training* = the process of learning the skills you need for a particular job
– *hours* = a fixed period of time during which people work, an office is open, etc., e.g. *I work very long hours.*
– *timetable* = a plan of when things are supposed to happen (e.g. school timetable) or a bus / train is supposed to leave or arrive, e.g. *There's a bus timetable on the wall.*

● Now focus on section **3 Collocations** and get SS to do it individually or in pairs. Check answers and elicit / model the pronunciation of tricky words as necessary.

> 1 charge, deal, responsible, off
> 2 team, opportunity, prospects, promoted
> 3 rise, temporary, short-term, security
> 4 sacked, run, part-time
> 5 redundant, out, voluntary, unpaid, experience

- Highlight especially:
  - dependent prepositions in phrases like *in charge of*, *deal with*, etc.
  - the meaning of *maternity leave* (= period of time when a woman temporarily leaves her job to have a baby (*paternity leave* for a father)).
  - the difference between *good prospects* in a job (= good possibilities of future promotion) and the *opportunity* / *chance* to travel, to use your English (= have the possibility now to do these things). In this phrase *prospects* is always plural.
  - the difference between *get a promotion* (= be given a higher post in the company) and *get a rise* (= be paid more than before).
  - the difference between *off work* (= temporary absence because of illness or if you are having a baby) and *out of work* (= you don't have a job or have lost the one you had).
  - the difference between *a temporary job* (= a job you may do only for a few months; opposite *a permanent job*) and *a part-time job* (= a job where you only work some hours a day; opposite *a full-time job*).
  - the difference between being *sacked / fired* (= made to leave your job because you did it badly / did something wrong, etc.) and being *made redundant* (= losing your job because a company / employer no longer has work available for you).
- Finally, focus on the instruction 'Can you remember the words on this page? Test yourself or a partner.'

Testing yourself

You can suggest that for **Adjectives describing a job** SS cover sentences 1–6 and look at sentences A–F and try to remember the adjectives. For **Nouns that are often confused** they can cover the **Noun** column while looking at the sentences and saying the missing words. For **Collocations** SS can look at the bold words and phrases and remember their meaning.

Testing a partner

Alternatively, SS can take it in turns to test each other. **B** closes the book and **A** defines or explains a word for **B** to try and remember, e.g. *a verb which means you lose your job because the company no longer has work for you to do* (be made redundant). After a few minutes, SS can change roles.

In a monolingual class, SS could also test each other by saying the word in their L1 for their partner to say in English.

Study Link SS can find more practice of these words and phrases on the MultiROM and on the *New English File Advanced* website.

- Tell SS to go back to the main lesson on *p.7*.
- d • This is a quick revision exercise on the lexis SS have just studied in the Vocabulary Bank. Give SS time to explain the differences between the pairs to each other, before feeding back answers.

For answers see key for exercise **c**

5 PRONUNCIATION word stress and rhythm

Pronunciation notes

Encouraging SS to improve their control of word stress is still important at this level as misplaced stress on an individual word can cause a breakdown in communication. Stressing the right words in a sentence will help SS speak English with a good rhythm and make them sound more fluent. Remind SS that we stress the *content* words in a sentence and do not usually stress the *structure* words (personal pronouns, articles, conjunctions, etc.). This gives English its characteristic beat or rhythm, sometimes referred to as the 'music of English'.

a • Focus on the task and give SS time to underline the stressed syllables in the bolded words.

b • **1.6** Play the CD sentence by sentence, pausing after each one for SS to check their answers. Elicit answers from the class.

> 1 I managed to get a **challenging** and **motivating** job.
> 2 I don't have any **qualifications** or **experience**.
> 3 There's no **job security** and I might be made **redundant**.
> 4 I've had a very **rewarding career** in publishing.
> 5 The job has a **competitive salary** and excellent **benefits**.
> 6 It's a **stimulating working environment** with good **opportunities** and **prospects**.
> 7 The **employees** don't enjoy their work as it's very **monotonous**.
> 8 After she **retired**, she did **voluntary** work at her local hospital.

1.6   CD1 Track 7

1 I managed to get a challenging and motivating job.
2 I don't have any qualifications or experience.
3 There's no job security and I might be made redundant.
4 I've had a very rewarding career in publishing.
5 The job has a competitive salary and excellent benefits.
6 It's a stimulating working environment with good opportunities and prospects.
7 The employees don't enjoy the work as it's very monotonous.
8 After she retired, she did voluntary work at her local hospital.

---

c • Play the CD again. Elicit that SS shouldn't stress the non-content words (they should say them say as lightly as possible). They should stress content words as well as stressing the stressed syllable within some of these words.

• Put SS in pairs and tell them to practise saying the sentences.

Extra support

Play the recording sentence by sentence and get SS to copy the rhythm by saying each sentence.

6 SPEAKING

a ● Focus on the task and go through the questions. You could demonstrate the activity yourself by talking about two jobs you would love / hate to do and why. Give SS a few minutes to prepare their answers to the questions.

b ● **1.7** Focus on the task and play the CD once. Check answers to the first question. Elicit the reasons why the man would love to be an archaeologist and the woman would hate to be a hairdresser.

> (archaeologist) Pros: travelling around the world, visiting exotic places
> (hairdresser) Cons: having to stand up all day and touch people's hair, dealing with complaints

● Now tell SS to listen again and listen out for the noises the two speakers use when they are thinking what they are going to say next. Check answers.

> The two noises are 'Er' and 'Um'.

● Encourage SS to use these noises to give themselves time to think rather than a noise they may use in their own language for the same purpose.

1.7   CD1 Track 8

1 Ever since I was a child I wanted to be an archaeologist. I love history, I have, I love reading historical books, I love going to museums, and looking at artefacts and reading where they came from and, you know, when they date back to, and it's just something that I've always wanted to do, the idea of travelling around the world, going to visit, you know, visiting far away places and doing excavating and stuff has always fascinated me. A friend of my father-in-law's in fact is an archaeologist and the tales she tells are quite extraordinary. I think she's in, well, she's somewhere very exotic right now, and I'm always very envious when I speak to her.

2 The thing I'd hate to do is to be a hairdresser. I can think of absolutely nothing worse than having to stand up all day touching people's hair. And dealing with complaints, and I think that would be my idea of absolute hell. I do know two people who are hairdressers, actually, and each one of them have had horror stories where they've completely destroyed somebody's hair. A friend of mine left a perm in someone's hair too long once and all the hair burnt off and it went orange, what can you do? I mean that's just horrendous. And the other person just completely messed up a haircut, and the woman had complete hysterics in the shop and was really tearful. So I just think it would be terrifying.

---

c ● Put SS into groups of three. SS take turns to describe the jobs they would love to do and explain why, etc. Monitor and help with any vocabulary SS need.

d ● SS now do the same for the jobs they would hate to do.

e ● Get feedback from each group to find out which of the jobs that were described sounded the most attractive to the other group members.

● If there's time, you could also find out which of the jobs that were described sounded the least attractive to the other group members.

Extra photocopiable activities

Grammar
discourse markers (1) *p.157*
Communicative
Have I got the job? *p.183* (instructions *p.178*)
Vocabulary
Work *p.208* (instructions *p.204*)

HOMEWORK

Study Link **Workbook** *pp.4–6*

1
B
G *have*
V personality; family
P rhythm and intonation

Who am I?

Lesson plan

This lesson has two main contexts. The first half of the lesson focuses on assessing personality using a quiz based on similar ones devised by psychologists. SS revise previously learnt words and phrases to describe personality and learn some new ones. The grammar focus is on different uses of *have* (e.g. *have* as a main and auxiliary verb and its special use in phrases such as *have your photo taken*), and the first half of the lesson ends with a song which revises adjectives of personality. In the second half of the lesson the focus changes from self to family. The context is the story behind a famous Goya painting of the Spanish royal family. This leads to SS expanding their vocabulary related to family before discussing family related issues in general and talking about aspects of their own family. SS are encouraged to use more sophisticated expressions for agreeing and disagreeing, and the pronunciation focus is the rhythm and intonation of these expressions.

Optional lead-in – the quote

- Write the quote at the top of *p.8* on the board (books closed) and the name of the author or get SS to open their books and read it.
- Point out that Maya Angelou (1928–) is a black American writer, famous in particular for her autobiography, *I Know Why the Caged Bird Sings*.
- Ask SS if they agree whether the three situations the writer gives are a good way to assess someone's personality. Ask SS if they can think of any other situations which are a good guide to someone's personality.

1 READING & SPEAKING

a - Put SS into pairs and focus on the task. First, tell them to decide if they think the adjectives describe positive or negative qualities and to give reasons. Set a time limit for this.

- Check answers by eliciting the meaning (and pronunciation) of the adjectives one by one, and whether the class think they are usually positive or negative qualities.

> **cautious** /'kɔːʃəs/ = not taking any risks. Can be positive or negative according to the situation.
> **conscientious** /ˌkɒnʃiˈenʃəs/ = taking care to do things carefully and correctly. Usually positive if not taken to extremes, though can imply a lack of imagination.
> **curious** /'kjʊəriəs/ = having a strong desire to know about things and people, interested in things. Usually positive. Compare with *nosy* = being too interested in other people's affairs.
> **easy-going** = relaxed and happy to accept things without getting angry or worried. Usually positive.
> **independent** = confident, without needing help from other people. Usually positive.
> **logical** = thinking and acting in a sensible and reasoned way. Usually positive.

> **loyal** = remaining faithful to sb or to a company or cause and supporting them / it. Usually considered positive.
> **mature** /məˈtʃʊə/ = behaving in an adult and sensible way. Positive.
> **quiet** = tending not to talk very much. Often considered a negative quality.
> **rebellious** = unwilling to obey rules or accept normal standards of behaviour, dress, etc. Usually negative, but can be positive, e.g. *many people think teenagers ought to be a bit rebellious.*
> **self-sufficient** /ˌself səˈfɪʃənt/ = not needing other people's help or company. Positive.
> **sensitive** = aware of and able to understand other people's feelings or easily offended or hurt. The first meaning is positive, but the second is negative.

- Now get SS to tell each other if they would use any of the adjectives to describe themselves.

b - Focus on the questionnaire and point out that this is based on similar questionnaires used by psychologists. Give SS time, in pairs, to circle their own answers to the questions 1–3. Then tell them to turn to **Communication** *What can you see?* on *p.116* and follow the instructions. Try to get them to do this without giving them time to read the options in question 4. When time is up, tell them to answer question 4. Then give them time to answer the rest of the questions. Monitor and help with any words or expressions SS can't guess from the context.

c - Tell SS to go to **Communication** *Who am I?* on *p.116*. Here they follow the instructions to identify their personality type (*Big Thinker, Counsellor*, etc.). Finally, they read the description of their personality type.

- Get SS to ask their partner for his / her personality type and read their description too. SS then tell each other how accurate they think the description is.

Extra idea

As a final light-hearted activity, tell SS they are going to do a psychological test. Tell them to close their books. Then tell them to write down the first three adjectives of personality that come to their minds.

Then tell them that the first adjective they have written is how they see themselves, the second is how others see them, and the third is how they really are.

LEXIS IN CONTEXT

d - Focus on the **Collocation** box and go through it with the class, and highlight the importance of recording common combinations of words, e.g. *a rough itinerary* (= an approximate list of the places you will go to on a journey). Point out that *rough* also collocates with *idea, sketch, guess*, etc. with the same meaning.

- Now focus on the task and give SS time to complete the exercise and compare their answers with their partner. Check answers.

1	book	5	go with
2	get	6	face
3	make	7	tell, hurt
4	catches	8	keep

e ● Now get SS to ask each other questions 1–8 to recycle the collocations.

f ● Give SS a few minutes to look back at the questionnaire and choose five more words or phrases they think will be useful for them to learn. Get SS to compare the words / phrases they have chosen with their partner and then get some feedback from the class.

2 GRAMMAR *have*

a ● Focus on the task and highlight that sentences A–H all contain an example of the different uses of the verb *have*. When SS have completed the task, check answers.

1	F	2	G	3	E	4	H	5	A	6	C	7	D	8	B

b ● Focus on the questions and give SS a few minutes to answer them. Check answers.

> 1 a) *have* is a main verb in B, D, G, and H.
> b) *have* is an auxiliary verb in A, C, E, and F.
> 2 When *have* is a main verb, you use an auxiliary verb (*be, do / will / would*, etc.) to make questions and negatives, e.g. *Do you have any money? I didn't have my car serviced yesterday because I didn't have enough time.*
> When *have* is an auxiliary verb (with *got*, and for perfect tenses), you reverse *have* and the personal pronoun to make questions and add *not* to *have* to make negatives, e.g. *Have you got time to help me with my homework? I haven't got Internet access at home.*

c ● Tell SS to go to **Grammar Bank 1B** on *p.137*. Go through each example and its corresponding rule with the class, or give SS time to read the examples and rules on their own, and answer any queries.

Grammar notes

The verbs *have* and *have got*, because of their different meanings and uses, are verbs that even advanced SS sometimes have doubts about. Here the uses and meanings are pulled together and revised.

● When explaining that *have* in its meaning of *possess* is a stative verb, you may want to go into the concept of stative verbs in more detail, explaining that they are verbs which refer to states or conditions which continue over a period of time, not actions, and are not normally used in continuous tenses (e.g. *we have a new car* NOT *we are having a new car*).

● Common stative verbs include mental and emotional states, e.g. *believe, know, like* and *love*, sense verbs, e.g. *see, hear, smell*, and other verbs that describe a state, e.g. *belong, agree, seem, include, possess*, etc. You may want to refer SS to a grammar book for a more complete list.

● Focus on the exercises for **1B** and get SS to do them individually or in pairs. If SS do them individually, get them to compare with a partner. Check answers after each exercise.

a 1 ✓
  2 ✓
  3 Does your husband have to work tomorrow…
  4 ✓
  5 How long have you had…
  6 ✓
  7 …had many problems…
  8 I haven't had…
  9 ✓

b 1 hasn't got / doesn't have any brothers or sisters.
  2 to have a family photograph taken every year.
  3 visitors to this site have to wear a hard hat.
  4 hasn't seen his father since 2009.
  5 hasn't got / doesn't have the right qualifications for this job.
  6 don't have to do it now. / haven't got to do it now.
  7 …we had a swim every morning.
  8 …have you got on…
  9 …to have the central heating fixed…

● Tell SS to go back to the main lesson on *p.8*.

d ● This is a grammar activation exercise. Demonstrate the activity by telling SS if the first sentence is true for you and why (not). Then get SS to go through each statement one by one and take turns to say if they are true for them or not and why. Monitor and help.

● Get some feedback from the class by asking some SS whether a sentence was true for them or not.

3 1.8 SONG ♫ *The Logical Song*

● This song was originally made famous by Supertramp in 1979. For copyright reasons this is a cover version. If you want to do this song in class, use the photocopiable activity on *p.232*.

> **1.8**   CD1 Track 9
>
> *The Logical Song*
>
> When I was young, it seemed that life was so wonderful,
> A miracle, oh it was beautiful, magical
> And all the birds in the trees, well they'd be singing so happily,
> Oh joyfully, oh playfully watching me
> But then they sent me away to teach me how to be sensible,
> Logical, oh responsible, practical.
> And then they showed me a world where I could be so dependable, clinical, oh intellectual, cynical.
>
> **Chorus**
> There are times when all the world's asleep,
> The questions run too deep
> For such a simple man.
> Won't you please, please tell me what we've learned
> I know it sounds absurd
> But please tell me who I am.
>
> I say now watch what you say or they'll be calling you a radical,
> A liberal, oh fanatical, criminal
> Won't you sign up your name, we'd like to feel you're
> Acceptable, respectable, oh presentable, a vegetable
>
> **Chorus**

4 LISTENING & SPEAKING

a • *The Family of Carlos IV* was painted by the Spanish painter Francisco de Goya between 1800 and 1801. Goya was employed as the royal painter at the time that he painted this portrait of the Spanish royal family. However, rather than paint the traditional flattering portrait it is believed that Goya's intention was to paint the Spanish royal family 'as they really were'. The painting can be seen in the Prado Museum in Madrid.

• Focus on the painting and the task. Give SS, in pairs, time to discuss and answer the questions. Make sure SS understand *heir to the throne* in 1, and elicit that *heir* is pronounced /eə/, and is another word in the small group of words beginning with a silent *h*.

Digital extra idea

You could show SS the painting and zoom in on the people as you focus on them. Google *wikimedia commons* and in the search box type *Goya* or *La familia de Carlos IV*.

b • **1.9** Tell SS that they should imagine that they are in the Prado Museum looking at the painting and listening on headphones to the audio guide, in English, giving information about Goya's famous painting.

• Play the CD once all the way through for SS to answer the questions. Get them to check their answers in pairs and play the recording again as necessary. Check answers.

Extra support

You could pause the CD after each person is mentioned to give SS a little more time to assimilate the information they are hearing (see spaces in the script).

> 1 The man who is second from the left in the group (Prince Fernando is number 3)
>
> 2 The king's sister (number 4) is the old woman behind Prince Fernando.
> The king's brother (number 10) is the old man behind the king.
>
> 3 There are two theories:
> a) She may be Princess Maria Amalia, one of the King's daughters, who had died in childbirth three years before the picture was painted. She's looking away because she is dead.
> b) The other (more popular) theory is that she represents the woman that Crown Prince Fernando would marry in the future. In this case she is looking away because she didn't actually exist at that time.
>
> 4 The queen's brother is second from the right (number 12).
>
> 5 Goya made the Queen, Maria Luisa, (number 7) the central figure in the painting because she had a very strong personality and she completely dominated her husband the King.
>
> 6 He is the painter, Goya.

1.9   CD1 Track 10

(script in Student's Book on *p.121*)
In the spring of 1800, the court painter, Francisco de Goya was commissioned by the Spanish King Carlos IV, direct ancestor of King Juan Carlos, to paint a portrait of the royal family. At the time, the royal family were all staying at the summer palace of Aranjuez, near Madrid.

First on the left is Prince Carlos, the King's second son, and next to him is his older brother Prince Fernando, who was the heir to the throne. Fernando grew up hating his parents, especially his mother, but in fact, he took after his mother in that he was very vain and authoritarian, and when he eventually became king he was extremely unpopular.

The old woman just behind Prince Fernando is Maria Josefa, the King's sister. Single and childless, she died shortly after the painting was finished.

Next to Maria Josefa is a young woman whose face we cannot see because she is looking away, and she is the 'mystery person' in this painting. There are two theories about her identity. One theory is that she is Princess Maria Amalia, one of the King's daughters, who'd died in childbirth three years before the picture was painted. The fact that she's looking away would be to show that she was, in fact, dead. However, the other more popular theory is that she represents the woman that Crown prince Fernando would one day marry. It would have been important to put her in the picture to show that the prince would marry one day, and have a son to carry on the dynasty. If this theory is true, the woman would be looking away because she didn't actually exist at that time. In fact, Fernando did marry, not once but four times.

The young girl next to the mystery woman is Princess Maria Isabel, the King's youngest daughter. She went on to marry her cousin, and had twelve children.

Next to her is the Queen, Maria Luisa. Goya made her the central figure in the painting because she had a very strong personality, and she completely dominated her husband the King. As a young woman she had been very beautiful and was rumoured to have had numerous lovers. In middle age, as she is here, she was still very vain. She tried to compensate for the fact that her beauty was fading by wearing exquisite dresses and jewellery, as we can see in the picture.

The little boy with the Queen is her youngest son, Prince Francisco. He was a very sensitive boy and he suffered all his life due to the fact that he looked incredibly like one of his mother's lovers. As a result, people assumed that he was not in fact the King's son.

The King, who is standing next to him, was a weak man. Although he came to the throne full of ideas and dreams, his wife and his advisors made sure that he never managed to achieve any of them and he died frustrated and disappointed.

The King's brother is standing behind him, and on his right, although you can only actually see part of her head, is the King's eldest daughter Carlota. Her parents arranged a marriage for her when she was only ten years old. She was an ambitious girl and eventually became Queen of Portugal.

The final group of three figures shows the Queen's brother, Don Luis de Parma, his wife, Maria Luisa and their first child, a baby boy. In fact, Maria Luisa was not only Don Luis's wife, she was also his niece, as she was the King's second daughter. In fact, Don Luis was supposed to have married the King's eldest daughter, Carlota, but he fell in love with Princess Maria Luisa, who was lively and intelligent, and he insisted on marrying her.

The royal family didn't all pose together for the painting – it would have taken too long. Instead Goya made individual studies of each family member and later used them to create this work. The painting took him two years to complete, and it was the last royal portrait he ever painted. Incidentally, he included himself in the painting – he is standing in the background on the left, behind the two princes.
Carlos IV called this painting 'the family all together picture', and it was originally hung in the Royal Palace in Madrid.

c ● Focus on the task and point out that a letter can be used more than once. Play the CD again as necessary. Check answers and then elicit any other pieces of information about the painting that SS can remember.

1 B, E	2 A, D	3 A	4 C	5 A

Extra support

If there's time, get SS to listen again with the script on *p.121*, focusing on any new vocabulary, and getting feedback on phrases SS didn't understand, e.g. because the words were run together.

d ● Focus on the task and give SS time to do a quick diagram of their 'family portrait'. Suggest they do the people as outline silhouettes which they could number and on a separate piece of paper list who the people are. You could demonstrate the activity by doing a diagram of your own family portrait on the board and telling SS about the people.

e ● SS take it in turns to show the diagram to their partner and talk about who each person is, saying a little bit about them. Encourage SS to talk about each person's personality to recycle adjectives and expressions describing personality.

5 VOCABULARY family

a ● Focus on the task and give SS a couple of minutes to complete it in pairs or you could just elicit the answers from the whole class.

6 and 12	niece and uncle (SS may also say *sister-in-law* and *brother-in-law*, as her uncle married one of her sisters.)
8 and 4	nephew and aunt
13 and 9	grandson and grandfather

b ● Tell SS to go to **Vocabulary Bank** *Family* on *p.158*. Focus on section **1 21st century families in the UK** and go through the four paragraphs with the class eliciting the meaning and pronunciation of the bold expressions.
  ● Highlight:
    – the difference between a *stepbrother / -sister* and a *half-brother / sister*. A *stepbrother* is the son of your *stepmother / stepfather*, i.e. the woman married to your father or man married to your mother but who is not your biological parent. A *half-brother / -sister* is a boy or girl who has either the same mother or same father as you. Elicit also *stepson / -daughter*.
    – a *single parent* = a man or woman who is bringing up a child alone
    – a *father figure* – could either be your real father or another male who acts as an emotional substitute and role model for a child who has no father

– *great-grandparents* are the parents of your grandparents; *great-great-grandparents* are the parents of your great-grandparents. Elicit also *great-grandson / -daughter*.
● Focus on section **2 Describing families** which tests common collocations related to family. Give SS time to choose the correct option and then check answers. Remind SS not to write the correct word in the sentences as later they can test their memory by covering the circled option and looking at the sentence.

1 takes after	5 close	9 grown
2 distant	6 ✓	10 relationship
3 an only	7 brought up	11 ✓
4 alike	8 grew up	12 ancestors

● Highlight:
  – the pronunciation of *close* /kləʊs/ as an adjective and compare with the pronunciation of *to close* /kləʊz/ as a verb. A *close family / friend* suggests intimacy and trust as well as enjoyment in each other's company.
  – the difference between *take after* and *look like* (*take after your father* means to look or behave like your father or other older member of your family; *look like your father* means to have a similar appearance to your father, but it cannot be used to express similarities in behaviour).
  – the meaning of *bring up* (= to care for a child and teach him / her how to behave). Compare with *educate* (= teach sb at school, university, etc.). Teach the noun *upbringing* and also the verb *raise*, which is common in AmE as a synonym for *bring up*.
  – the difference between *grow* (= increase in size) and *grow up* (= develop into an adult), e.g. *My children are all grown up now.*
  – the meaning of *relationship* = the way in which friends, partners, countries, etc. behave towards one another
  – the difference between *ancestors* (= a person in your family who lived a long time ago) and *descendants* (= children, their children's children, and all the people who live after them who are related to them)
● Now focus on section **3 Family idioms** and give SS time to match idioms 1–8 to meanings A–H. Check answers and make sure SS are clear about the meaning of the idioms.

1 F	2 A	3 C	4 H	5 B	6 G	7 D	8 E

● Finally, focus on the instruction 'Can you remember the words on this page? Test yourself or a partner.'

Testing yourself

For **21st century families in the UK** SS can look at the bold expressions again and try to remember their meaning. For **Describing families** they can cover the pairs of words and look at the gapped sentences again and try to remember the missing word or expression. For **Family idioms** they can cover sentences 1–8 and try to remember the idioms by reading meanings A–H.

Testing a partner
See **Testing a partner** *p.18*.

Study Link SS can find more practice of these words and phrases on the MultiROM and on the *New English File Advanced* website.

• Tell SS to go back to the main lesson on *p.11*.

c • Focus on the quiz, which recycles vocabulary SS have just learnt. Set a time limit for SS to do it in pairs and check answers.

1 great-grandmother
2 extended family
3 single-parent family
4 *A stepbrother* is the son of your stepmother / stepfather, i.e. not your biological parent.
   A half-brother is a boy who has either the same mother or same father as you.
5 A *nuclear family* is a family which consists of a mother, father, and children.
   An *extended family* is a family group which includes not only parents and children but also uncles, aunts, grandparents, etc.
6 *take after your father* means to look or behave like your father; *look like your father* means to have a similar appearance to your father.
7 My sister and my cousin aren't on speaking terms.
8 My brother and I don't see eye to eye about politics.
9 Who wears the trousers in their marriage?
10 I'm sure they have a few skeletons in their cupboard.

d • This is a vocabulary activation exercise. Give SS time, in pairs or small groups, to answer the questions. Encourage SS to give as much information as they can. Monitor the pairs / groups and keep the activity going until most groups seem to have answered all the questions.

6 PRONUNCIATION & SPEAKING rhythm and intonation

a • Put SS into small groups of three or four and focus on the task. Give SS time to choose what they want to debate and make brief notes. Make sure that they choose different topics within the group. Monitor and help with any words or phrases SS need.

Pronunciation notes

SS at this level can normally express an opinion with some fluency, but can still often sound rather flat or abrupt when they agree or disagree with someone else's opinion. Exercise **c** focuses on using a lively and polite intonation, and the right stress, when SS use the kind of high frequency phrases given in exercise **b**.

b • **1.10** Focus on the phrases and make sure SS know what they mean. Play the CD and get SS to underline the stressed syllables. Check answers.

See script 1.10

• Point out that *quite* in *I quite agree* = I completely agree. Highlight that you can't say *I quite disagree*.

• Play again as necessary. Then get SS to repeat the phrases, copying the rhythm and intonation. Play the recording again pausing after each phrase and getting individual SS to say the phrase.

1.10	CD1 Track 11

1 I quite agree.
2 I totally agree.
3 That's what I think too.
4 Absolutely.
5 I take your point, but…
6 I see what you mean, but…
7 I agree up to a point, but…
8 I completely disagree
9 I don't agree at all.

c • Set a time limit for each debate, e.g. 5–8 minutes. SS take turns to open the debate on the subject they made notes on. The student opening the debate should give their opinion on the topic and try to give a clear reason(s) to justify their point of view. Then the rest of the group give their opinion and the debate ensues. When the time limit is up, say *Next debate!* and another student opens the next debate in their group, etc. Remind SS before they start to try to use the **agreeing / disagreeing** expressions in exercise **b** during the debates.

Extra photocopiable activities

Grammar
have p.158
Communicative
The family *p.184* (instructions *p.178*)
Vocabulary
Family *p.209* (instructions *p.204*)
Song
The Logical Song p.232 (instructions *p.229*)

HOMEWORK

Study Link Workbook *pp.7–9*

1 C

G pronouns
V language terminology
P sound–spelling relationships

Whose language is it?

Lesson plan

The main topic of the lesson is introduced by an extract from a thought-provoking article that originally appeared in the *Financial Times*. The article questions whether, in the future, English will 'belong' more to non-native speakers than to native speakers, and leads to a discussion about how important (or not) grammatical correctness is as most conversations in English nowadays are between non-native speakers of the language. The grammar focus is on pronouns, revising what SS should already know and introducing advanced points such as the use of *they* to refer to a singular subject when the gender of the person is not specified or known. SS then discuss comments from around the world referring to learning and using English. In the second half of the lesson SS listen to interviews with two non-native speakers of English, who have lived for many years in the UK, talking about their sometimes amusing experiences as language learners. There is then a lexical focus on terminology used to describe aspects of language, e.g. *metaphor, slang, idioms*, and *register* – terms which will be used throughout the course – and this is consolidated through a language quiz. The pronunciation focus is on common sound–spelling relationships in English and gives TT the opportunity to refer SS to the Sound Bank at the back of the book as a reference, also to be used throughout the course.

Optional lead-in – the quote

- Write the quote at the top of *p.12* on the board (books closed) or get SS to open their books and read it.
- Elicit / explain that *lingua franca* means a shared language of communication used by people whose main languages are different, and originally referred to a common language (Frank) consisting of Italian mixed with French, Spanish, Greek, and Arabic that was formerly spoken in Mediterranean ports. You might also want to check that SS known that *anon.* is short for *anonymous*.
- Ask SS if they think the quote is serious or ironic (it's ironic). Find out if SS use the expression *lingua franca* in their L1.

1 READING & SPEAKING

a • Focus on the task and tell SS to cover the article *Whose language?* Focus on the statements and get SS, in pairs, to quickly discuss them and then mark them probably true or probably false.

b • Give SS a time limit to read the <u>first</u> half of the article to check their answers to **a**. Check answers, getting SS to tell you why the statements are true or false.

> 1 False (Around one-quarter of the world's population can communicate reasonably well in English.)
> 2 True
> 3 True

c • Focus on the task and give SS, in pairs, a couple of minutes to correct the mistakes. Check answers and find out if SS think they make these kinds of mistakes and how important they think they are.

> 1 starts
> 2 a restaurant
> 3 ~~the~~ women … ~~the~~ men
> 4 advice
> 5 I phoned ~~to~~ my brother…
> 6 We discussed ~~about~~ global warming…

d • Focus on the two questions and then set SS a time limit to read the second part of the article. Check answers.

> 1 All of them.
> 2 a The writer thinks grammatical accuracy is important in written English, for example, if you want to get an article published in an academic journal.
> b The writer thinks it does not matter in spoken English, where simply being understood is the main aim especially as in most cases both speakers are non-natives.

LEXIS IN CONTEXT

e • This would be a good moment to highlight that at this level of English it is important for SS to develop an awareness of '**register**', i.e. the level of formality or informality in a piece of writing or speech, and to be able to recognize whether it is appropriate for the situation. The article they have just read, for example, is fairly academic and is written in quite a formal style, which is appropriate for the subject matter and the target reader. It would also be appropriate language for a lecture on the same subject. However, the same language might sound rather odd in an informal conversation between friends, where phrases like *conduct business* would sound too formal for the occasion.

- Now focus on the **Being aware of register** box and go through it with the class. Then focus on the task and get SS to match the highlighted words in the article to their less formal equivalents. Get SS to compare their answers in pairs before checking answers.

> | 1 | remain | 5 | notion | 9 | thus |
> | --- | --- | --- | --- | --- | --- |
> | 2 | poor | 6 | omit | 10 | transcribe |
> | 3 | conduct | 7 | require | | |
> | 4 | adhere to | 8 | view | | |

Extra support

Ask SS to choose five other words or phrases they would like to learn from the article and get them to compare their choices. Get some feedback from the class as to the words or phrases they have chosen and deal with any vocabulary problems that arise.

f ● In this exercise SS give their response to some of the issues raised in the article. Put SS into small groups of three or four and ask them to discuss the questions. Then get some feedback from the whole class.
   ● Alternatively, you could do this as an open-class activity.

2 GRAMMAR pronouns

a ● Focus on the task and give SS time to mark the sentences right or wrong, and correct the wrong ones. Get them to compare their answers in pairs. Check answers. Some SS may correct sentence 1 to *his or her phone*, which would be correct too but *their phone* is a neater and more concise way of including both genders.

1 ✓	5 talking to each other
2 There used to be, ✓	6 ✓
3 ✓	7 one another
4 shave ~~myself~~	8 ✓

The mistake in sentence 5 would probably cause a communication problem as *talking to themselves* has a completely different meaning to the intended meaning of *talking to each other*.

b ● Tell SS to go to **Grammar Bank 1C** on *p.138*. Go through each example and its corresponding rule with the class, or give SS time to read the examples and rules on their own, and answer any queries.

Grammar notes

Advanced SS should be familiar with most of these uses of pronouns; however, the majority have never been overtly focused on, e.g. *one*, *one another*, the use of *they / their* to mean *he* and *she*, and the emphatic use of reflexive pronouns.

● Focus on the exercises for **1C**. SS do the exercises individually or in pairs. If SS do them individually, get them to compare with a partner. Check answers after each exercise.

a	1 ✓
	2 you
	3 ✓
	4 herself
	5 their
	6 ✓ *him* (or *her*) might be used, but would imply that you were only talking about a man (or a woman)
	7 They
b	1 their, they
	2 herself
	3 They
	4 each other / one another
	5 –
	6 yourself / yourselves
	7 you / one
c	1 it, There
	2 There, It
	3 it
	4 It, It
	5 There
	6 It, There

● Tell SS to go back to the main lesson on *p.13*.

3 SPEAKING

a ● **1.11** Focus on the task and give SS time to underline the word(s) which they think have extra stress when you wish to emphasize that something is your own opinion. Then play the CD for them to check their answers. Give SS practice in saying the phrases by playing the recording sentence by sentence and getting them to copy the stress and intonation.

> See script 1.11

1.11	CD1 Track 12
1 I'd say that…	
2 If you ask me, …	
3 Personally, I think that…	
4 Personally speaking…	
5 In my opinion, …	
6 In my view…	
7 I feel that…	
8 My feeling is that…	
9 As far as I'm concerned…	

b ● Focus on the task, and get SS to read the comments about English and learning English. Then set a time limit for SS to discuss them in pairs saying whether the situation is the same or different in their country and how they feel about it. Encourage SS to use the emphasizing expressions in **a**.
   ● When SS have discussed the five comments, get feedback on each topic from the whole class.
   ● Alternatively, you could get SS to discuss a topic for a set time, then get feedback from the class before moving on to discuss the next topic.

4 LISTENING & SPEAKING

a ● Focus on the instructions and go through the glossary with the class.

b ● Focus on the two questions and give SS time to answer them in pairs. Do not ask for feedback at this stage as SS will do it in **c**.

c ● **1.12** Now play Cristina and Zoltán's answers to the first question, and pause. Play the CD once more. Then elicit their answers from SS, and ask them who they identify with and why.

Cristina finds non-native speakers who speak standard English easiest to understand. She has problems with some regional accents, e.g. a friend from Glasgow, and with non-native speakers where she is not used to their accent from certain places, e.g. some Asian speakers of English.
Zoltán says as regards pronunciation, he finds it easier to understand native speakers who speak with these standard accents, e.g. BBC English. He sometimes has problems with some regional accents, e.g. Scots, Geordie, or New Zealand.
As regards content, he finds it easier to understand non-native speakers because they don't use idiomatic expressions, obscure cultural references, phrasal verbs, or regional slang, and they are more direct (they don't use allusions and metaphors).

- Now play Cristina and Zoltán's answers to the second question, and pause. Play the CD once more. Then elicit their answers from SS, and ask them who they identify with and why.

> **Cristina** doesn't mind. Her children, who are bilingual, often correct her.
> **Zoltán** doesn't mind but doesn't like being corrected by non-native speakers whose English he thinks is not as good as his. He also thinks that non-native speakers often spell better than native speakers – a native speaker recently corrected his spelling of *accommodation* (he thought it was spelled with one *m*) but Zoltán was right (it has a double *m*).

1.12 CD1 Track 13

(script in Student's Book on *p.121*)
I = interviewer, C = Cristina, Z = Zoltán
I Do you find it easier to understand native or non-native speakers of English?
C Well, it all depends where they come from. I suppose it's more or less the same. Some non-natives are more difficult than others if you're not used to the accent. For instance, I used to find some Japanese and Chinese speakers difficult to understand, but then because of work I went to the Far East lots of times, and then it became OK. Natives, again it all depends. I was taught RP, and one assumes that everybody speaks that. And of course I had friends from lots of parts of Britain who did not speak RP, in fact, it is pretty rare thing these days. So we have a good friend from Glasgow and it was always embarrassing for me because I could not understand most of what he was saying – I still don't.
I How do you feel about having your English corrected?
C I don't mind. My children used to love correcting me – they still say I speak very funny English. But usually adults in this country do not correct you. I would like to be corrected.

I Do you find it easier to understand native or non-native speakers of English?
Z It depends what you mean. As far as pronunciation goes, it's a lot easier to understand native speakers with a 'standard' accent like BBC English or General American and for me some of the regional dialects are quite easy to understand as well. Other dialects are a lot harder to decipher like Scots, or Geordie, or New Zealand, are really hard to understand.
As far as content is concerned, it's a lot easier to understand non-native speakers, because they don't use idiomatic expressions or obscure cultural references, they don't use regional slang. They also use the Latin verb instead of a phrasal verb, for example like *continue* rather than *carry on*, which is less easy to confuse. And the other thing about non-native speakers is that they are a lot more direct, when they speak in English, they say what they mean, there are no allusions and metaphors, and references to other things.
I How do you feel about having your English corrected?
Z I don't mind. I'm sometimes annoyed with myself for making a recurring mistake again like mixing up *he* and *she*. And I find it a bit weird when a non-native speaker who's less fluent than me corrects my English. I also think that non-native speakers, good non-native speakers, are often better at spelling than native speakers because we learn words with their spelling, whereas native speakers learn the word first and learn the spelling years later. Just recently an English friend of mine corrected my spelling of *accommodation*, which I'd spelled with double *c* and double *m*, and he insisted that it was spelled with a single *m*. In fact, *I* was right!

---

d ● Focus on the task, and get SS to answer the questions with a partner. Elicit anecdotes and opinions.

e ● **1.13** Now play the second part of the interview, pausing after they answer the question *Do you have any funny or embarrassing stories…?* Play the two anecdotes again, and then elicit what they were about.

> **Cristina** had a misunderstanding when her phonetics professor at university (whom she liked) said 'See you later' she wondered where she was going to see him later. She didn't realize he was just saying goodbye.
> **Zoltán** had a misunderstanding about kites. When an English friend said he had seen a kite near his house, Zoltán thought he was talking about the kites children fly. In fact, he was talking about a kind of bird.

Digital extra idea

Go to Google images and type the word *kite* to show images of both meanings of *kite*.

● Repeat for the last question, and elicit answers.

> **Cristina** says her problem is cultural things she doesn't know about. She mentions *The Simpsons* as an example of the kind of cultural knowledge that a non-native speaker may not have, however fluent their English is.
> **Zoltán** says he prefers to use his own language when he is counting.

1.13 CD1 Track 14

(script in Student's Book on *p.122*)
I Do you have any funny or embarrassing stories related to misunderstanding someone?
C Yes, misunderstanding and being misunderstood, several. Some I don't think I would like to tell you about. But I'll tell you one. I was a student at the University of Michigan, in the United States, and my phonetics professor was *very* handsome, and therefore I did extremely well, not in all subjects, but it was worth studying that one. But I remember my first tutorial when he said, 'See you later.' And I thought, 'Mmm, interesting. Where?' And in class he'd said, I'd asked a question and he'd said 'Interesting question', so I thought 'Great! He thinks I'm clever, and maybe he thinks I'm interesting to meet somewhere else.' But I couldn't understand how I was going to find out where or when. I luckily didn't ask. It would have been very embarrassing.
I Is there anything you still find difficult about English?
C Yes, I think that there are things that have especially to do with cultural aspects. I used to find when my children were little that I didn't know the same nursery rhymes that you know here, I didn't know the actions. And I still don't know lots of things. It's, I don't know, to give you an example, say I had learned American English but I still didn't know who the Simpsons were.
I Do you have any funny or embarrassing stories related to misunderstanding someone?
Z Hungarians aren't generally interested in birdwatching – and most Hungarians I know can't tell one bird from another. And recently a friend of mine told me about seeing some kites over the fields near their house the previous weekend, and I said that flying kites is really popular in Budapest too, meaning that people go into the hills at the weekend to fly their home-made paper kites. It never occurred to me for a second that she may be talking about a bird. I don't think a Hungarian would ever tell someone else about seeing some birds several days before.
I Is there anything you still find difficult about English?
Z Not really. I've been learning English for 26 years. If I had to say anything, I would say counting, numbers. If I have to count anything, I have to switch back to Hungarian, even if the person I'm speaking to will need the English sum.

- Finally, ask the class which of the two speakers they found easier to understand and elicit reasons.
- Following on from what Zoltán says, you may want to tell SS that according to some research there are three things people always tend to do in their first language but not in a foreign language, however well they speak it: count, pray, and swear.

5 VOCABULARY language terminology

a • Focus on the task and tell SS to read the eight definitions first before they try to match them to the words in the list. Get SS to check their answers in pairs before eliciting the answers from the class. Make sure SS can pronounce all the words and phrases correctly and get them to mark the stress on the multi-syllabic words.

1	an idiom	5	slang
2	collocation	6	colloquial
3	register	7	a synonym
4	a phrasal verb	8	a metaphor

b • This quiz recycles language terminology and also lexis from the three lessons in the File. Set a time limit and get SS, in pairs, to do the quiz. Check answers.

1 Idioms
1 refuse to change your mind about something even when other people are trying to convince you that you are wrong
2 say exactly what you think in a very direct way
3 were determined to continue despite the difficult circumstances
4 don't agree with each other
5 is the dominant partner

2 Phrasal verbs
1	catch up	4	bring up
2	put off	5	grow up
3	take after		

3 Synonyms and register
a (and b)
1	E (*one* is more formal)	5	H (omit)
2	D (consequently)	6	C (however)
3	F (owing to)	7	A (adhere to)
4	B (benefits)	8	G (require)

4 Collocation
1	completely	4	distant
2	hurt	5	security
3	close		

6 PRONUNCIATION sound–spelling relationships

Pronunciation notes

- At this level SS usually have a well-developed ability to predict the pronunciation of new words from their spelling and it is important to encourage them to do this every time they learn a new word. However, it is also important for SS to be able to use a dictionary to check pronunciation in the case of words which have a very irregular sound–spelling relationship.
- SS who have previously used *New English File* will be familiar with the 'sound pictures' used throughout the course to provide SS with a clear model of all the sounds of English and to familiarize them with the phonetic symbol for that sound. If your SS have not used *New English File* before, this would be a good moment to introduce them to the Sound Bank on *p.168*. There are also two pages of common sound–spelling rules on the *New English File* Student's website, which SS can print. Tell them to go to www.oup.com/elt/englishfile/advanced. Highlight that these resources will help them to check the pronunciation of new words in the dictionary by using the phonetic transcription and will also help them to predict pronunciation from spelling. It will also help them to 'fine tune' their own pronunciation.
- The exercise below is to help remind SS of common sound–spelling 'rules' in English and, in some cases, exceptions to those rules.

a • Focus on the information box and go through it with the class, highlighting that English pronunciation is a lot less irregular than many people may think.
- Focus on the task and give SS, in pairs, time to mark the sentences **S** if all the pink letters make the same sound or **D** if one word is different, in which case they should circle the different sound.

b • **1.14** Play the CD pausing after each sentence for SS to check their answers, playing the recording again as necessary. Then check answers eliciting the rule in each case and any more exceptions that SS can think of.

1 heir /eə/
Rule: the letter *h* is nearly always pronounced /h/. Common exceptions: *heir, honest, honour, hour, exhausted, rhythm*
2 power /ˈpaʊə/
Rule: the letters *ow* are often pronounced /əʊ/ as in *blow, window, below*, but are also often pronounced /aʊ/ as in *frown, towel, now*. ⚠ Occasionally, the same letters have different pronunciations according to the meaning, e.g. *row* /raʊ/ (= argument) but *row* /rəʊ/ (= a line of seats).
3 river /ˈrɪvə/
Rule: the letter *i* + consonant + *e* is usually /aɪ/ Common exceptions: *river, give, live* (the verb), *since, liver*, etc.
4 whose /huːz/
Rule: the letters *wh* are nearly always /w/, but occasionally /h/, e.g. *whose, who, whole*.
5 All the same pronunciation
Rule: the letter *j* is always pronounced /dʒ/.

6 machine /məˈʃiːn/

Rule: the letters *ch* are occasionally/ʃ/, e.g. *machine, chef, cliché,* or /k/, e.g. *chemist, architect,* but nearly always /tʃ/.

7 sure /ʃɔː/

Rule: the letter *s* at the beginning of a word is nearly always /s/.

Common exceptions: *sugar* and *sure* where the *s* is pronounced /ʃ/.

8 All the same pronunciation

Rule: the letters *aw* are always /ɔː/.

9 work /wɜːk/

Rule: the letters *or* are usually /ɔː/, but occasionally /ɜː/ e.g. *work, word, world.*

10 require /rɪˈkwaɪə/

Rule: the letters *ir* are nearly always /ɜː/, but are pronounced /aɪə/ when followed by an *e*.

1.14		CD1 Track 15
1	/h/	hurt heir adhere hardly himself
2	/əʊ/	throw elbow lower power grow
3	/aɪ/	alike despite river transcribe quite
4	/w/	whenever why whose where which
5	/dʒ/	jealous journalist reject job enjoy
6	/tʃ/	change achieve machine catch charge
7	/s/	salary satisfying spontaneous synonym sure
8	/ɔː/	awful saw flaw drawback law
9	/ɔː/	short corner work ignore reporter
10	/ɜː/	firm dirty third T-shirt require

c • This exercise shows how SS can use their instinct to predict pronunciation from spelling and can also use the phonetic script in a dictionary to check their guess.

• Focus on the task and get SS to cover the phonetics and definitions. Tell SS to guess the pronunciation from the spelling of the words and elicit what they think. Then tell SS to uncover and check the pronunciation by looking at the phonetic transcription.

Extra photocopiable activities

Grammar
pronouns *p.159*
Communicative
Language quotes *p.185* (instructions *p.178*)
Vocabulary
Language terminology *p.210* (instructions *p.204*)

HOMEWORK

Study Link Workbook *pp.10–12*

Lesson plan

This is the first of seven Writing lessons; there is one at the end of each File. In today's world of email communication, being able to write in English is an important skill for many SS, and at this level many SS are also preparing to take formal exams, which include a writing paper. We suggest that you go through the analysing and planning stages in class, but set the actual writing (the last stage) for homework.

In this lesson the focus is on writing a letter of application. The writing skills focus is on error correction and using appropriate register.

ANALYSING A MODEL TEXT

a • Focus on the text type (a letter of application) and tell SS that in this lesson they will be writing an application for a job. If you apply for a job in the UK, you normally send a CV (Curriculum Vitae) and a covering letter or email, which explains briefly what post you are applying for, who you are, and why you think you are suitable for the job. The same is true if you are applying for a grant or scholarship, or for a place on a course of study.

• Focus on the **Key success factors** and go through them with SS.

• Now focus on the job advert, and give SS time to read it. Then ask SS if they would be interested in applying and elicit opinions.

b • Focus on the instructions and the email. You might want to point out to SS that the email has mistakes in it, but they shouldn't worry about it at this stage. Tell SS to read it quickly, and elicit the contents of the three main paragraphs.

> 1 Information about qualifications and skills (his studies and his level of English)
> 2 Information about his work experience
> 3 Why he thinks he would be suitable for the job

c • Focus on the **Improving your first draft** box and go through it with SS.

• Focus on **1** and then on the first sentence which has been crossed out (My name is...). Elicit that it is inappropriate (and not done in a letter), as you give your name at the end of the letter. To include it here as well is unnecessary and repetitive. Then tell SS to find the other three inappropriate (this refers to register here) or irrelevant sentences. Get them to compare with a partner, and then check answers and elicit whether they are irrelevant or inappropriate.

> I had an American girlfriend during this period... (irrelevant)
> He is, in fact, distantly related to my mother. (irrelevant)
> I would definitely know how to look after myself if I got into a fight! (inappropriate, too informal)

• Now focus on **2** and on the crossed out mistake *Miss*. Elicit that as we do not know whether Emma Richards is married or not, the appropriate way to address her is *Ms Richards*. (Nowadays most women prefer to use this title.)

• Set a time limit for SS to find 12 more mistakes. Get SS to compare with a partner and check answers.

> **on** the festival UK website (line 3)
> **P**hysical **E**ducation (line 5)
> **for** six months (line 6)
> programm**e** (line 7)
> **h**igh school (line 7)
> **handling** money (line 14)
> on occasion (line 14)
> **keen** on world music (line 17)
> apart **from** my experience (line 19)
> calm and patient (line 21)
> send me **some** information (line 26)
> a**cc**ommodation (line 26)

d • Ask the question to the class and elicit opinions. (In fact he probably would be given an interview as, despite some mistakes, the letter is well organized and gives all the necessary information.)

USEFUL LANGUAGE

e • Focus on the task and on the example. Elicit that although they both mean the same thing, the slightly more formal / professional sounding style in *I am writing to apply...* is more appropriate. Take this opportunity also to remind SS that in this kind of letter they should not use contractions.

• Then get SS to continue individually or in pairs. Check answers.

Extra support

If you think your SS will have problems remembering the expressions, get them to quickly re-read the text first.

> 2 I am a final year student at the University of Berlin and I am doing a degree in Physical Education.
> 3 I have a high level of spoken English.
> 4 I have some relevant experience.
> 5 I was in charge of selling tickets.
> 6 I would welcome the chance to be part of this event.
> 7 I believe I would be suitable for the job advertised.
> 8 If you require any further information, I would be happy to provide it.
> 9 I would be grateful if you could send me some information about accommodation.
> 10 I look forward to hearing from you.

• Highlight that these phrases would be appropriate, with the relevant adjustments, in most letters of application (e.g. for a grant or course of study).

Extra idea

Test SS on the phrases by saying the informal phrase and getting them to say the more formal one.

PLANNING WHAT TO WRITE

a ● Focus on the task. Set a time limit for SS to read the advertisement and make notes.

b ● Now get SS to compare with a partner. Then get feedback from individual SS.

● Finally, go through the tips with SS.

Extra support

If you think your SS may have forgotten how to begin and end letters, elicit the rules from them and write them on the board.

1 If you know the name of the person you're writing to, begin *Dear* + title + surname. If not, begin *Dear Sir* or *Dear Madam*.

2 Finish your letter with *Yours sincerely* if you know the person's name, and *Yours faithfully* if you don't.

3 If you are writing a letter rather than an email, print your name underneath your signature.

WRITING

Go through the instructions and set the writing for homework.

Test and Assessment CD-ROM

CEFR Assessment materials
File 1 Writing task assessment guidelines

COLLOQUIAL ENGLISH FAMILY SECRETS

Lesson plan

This is the first in a series of seven Colloquial English lessons, where SS practise listening to authentic unscripted speech. Each of these lessons picks up on one of the topics of the preceding File, and consists of a studio interview with a person who has some expertise or experience related to the topic, and then some shorter street interviews where members of the public give their opinions about the same topic. In both parts of the lesson there is a focus on colloquial expressions used by the speakers.

We suggest that TT let SS listen a final time while reading the scripts. This will let them see what they did / didn't understand, and help them to further develop their awareness of features of spoken English such as elision, false starts, discourse markers, hesitation devices, etc.

In the first part of this lesson the person interviewed is David Shepherd, an amateur genealogist who, with his wife, has spent many years researching their family tree. He first outlines how to go about this kind of research and then talks about his own research and the discovery he made about his father's side of the family and how he felt about it. In the second part of the lesson, people in the street are asked how much they know about their own family tree, whether they have ever done any research into their ancestors, and if there is anyone in their family they would like to know more about.

Study Link These lessons are on the *New English File Advanced* DVD which can be used instead of the class CD (See Introduction *p.9*). SS can get more practice on the MultiROM, which contains more of the short street interviews with a listening task and scripts.

Optional lead-in (books closed)

● Write the following definitions on the board (or read them out) and get SS to write the words individually and then check with a partner. All the words occur in the listening and 1–3 are recycled from the Vocabulary Bank.

1 a person in your family who lived a long time ago (*ancestor*)

2 your grandparents' parents (*great-grandparents*)

3 sth shocking, embarrassing, etc. that has happened to you or your family in the past and that you want to keep secret (*skeleton in the cupboard*)

4 a woman on her wedding day (*bride*)

5 a man on his wedding day (*bridegroom*)

6 a diagram that shows the relationship between members of a family over a long period of time (*family tree*)

7 the study of family history (*genealogy*)

● Check answers making sure SS can pronounce *genealogy* (/dʒiːniˈælədʒi/) and elicit the person who does research into family history (*a genealogist*).

THE INTERVIEW

a ● Books open. Focus on the task and on the glossary. Go through it with the class eliciting from them how to pronounce the words and names.

Extra support

You may want to pre-teach some other words and phrases before SS listen to the interview (see script 1.15).

b ● **1.15** Focus on the questions and give SS time to read them. Encourage SS not to write anything down when they listen the first time. Tell them that they should listen and try to get the gist of what he is saying, and then discuss the questions with their partner.

Play the CD once (**Part 1**). Give SS time to discuss the questions and tell each other what they understood. Then play the CD again, pausing after each of David's answers to give SS time to make notes and compare with their partner again. Play the recording again as necessary. Elicit and check answers.

1 He and his wife were given a family tree computer program.
2 By asking living people what they know. However, this can be dangerous because of 'family myths' and the information you are given may not be accurate.
3 Because they give you the name of the bride's and bridegroom's parents.
4 Because to start your research you had to go to two different places in London (Births, marriages, and deaths and also the building where census records were kept). Then further research involved travelling around the country to visit churches to read parish registers.
5 It's easy to get back to 1837 using just birth, marriage, and death records. With more work involving parish registers you can get back to the late 1700s.
   It's easier if you have an unusual name and your family come from a small village and not London.
6 He has researched one branch of the family back to 1490. This is thanks to the research done by another researcher and because this branch of the family were richer than the others so there are more documents (wills, etc.).

1.15   CD1 Track 16

(script in Student's Book on *p.122*)
I = interviewer, D = David Shepherd
I   Why did you start researching your family history?
D   Well, it was mainly, I think, because in 1995 we were given a present by a friend of ours of a computer program, that was a family tree program and we'd been talking about it from time to time, but this was the incentive, if you will, to start typing in what we knew and then we realized how much we didn't know, so that's where we started.

I   When you start researching, what's the first step, the first thing you do?
D   Well, the first thing you do is to ask living people about what they know, but that can be very dangerous because family myths grow up and you can often find that what you're told isn't accurate, so then you start with birth certificates and marriage certificates and you keep going back because the marriage certificate will give you the name of the parent of the bride, the parent of the bridegroom, and then you go back to birth certificates, so you work back using those two.
I   In practical terms, what difference has the Internet made to researching family history?
D   Oh, it's made an absolutely massive difference. There is no comparison. In the days before the Internet, it involved going to London, initially, to two different places, one to look at births, marriages, and deaths and the other a completely different building to look at census records, and then, of course, once you've got back as far as you could, then it involved travelling perhaps over, around the country to visit a church, to get parish records. It was fun, but also vastly time-consuming. It's so much simpler now.
I   How far could most people expect to be able to trace back their families?
D   It's fairly easy to get back to 1837 when the birth, marriage, and death registers were compiled and started, most people can get back there. With a little bit more work involving parish registers, you can usually get back to the late 1700s and it gets progressively more difficult after that. It's easier if you have an unusual name and it's easier if they come from a small village, as opposed to London.
I   How far back have you managed to trace your family?
D   Well, one particular branch, thanks to the very helpful material from a lady in Oxfordshire, I've got back to 1490, but this is only because that particular branch were somewhat better off than the others, so there were wills left and records of business deals and things like that, but that's an awful lot of hard work, and this lady must have spent years and years researching it and very generously shares it with me and other people.

c ● **1.16** Focus on the task. Play the CD once (**Part 2**) and tell SS just to listen. Then give SS time to discuss the questions and tell each other what they understood. Now play the CD again, pausing to give SS time to make notes and compare with their partner again. Play the recording again as necessary. Elicit and check answers.

1 He thought he only had two aunts (on his father's side) but in fact there were seven other children (including triplets) about whom he had never known.
2 He felt angry as his father had never mentioned them and frustrated because now there is no way of finding out what happened to them.
3 There is no record of their birth or death. They might have been given away (to orphanages or for adoption) in which case their surname would have changed. There is no living relative to ask. The only hope is the next census in ten years' time.
4 Some births that were very near the marriage date.
5 His secret hope was that he would find that the highwayman Dick Shepherd was an ancestor of his, but he hasn't been able to find this out.

1.16 CD1 Track 17

(script in Student's Book on *p.122*)

I Was there anything in particular that you hoped to find out when you began researching?

D Yes, I really didn't know anything about beyond my grandparents because it wasn't something that was ever discussed in the family, so I was curious to find out where they came from, things like that.

I Have you found out anything surprising, any skeleton in the cupboard?

D Yes indeed, in fact it was this year when the 1911 census was released, it was released two years early, I discovered that instead of just having two aunts and my father there were another seven children, which I had no knowledge of at all, including triplets who were one month old, so, and they were never spoken about and there's no way of finding out what happened to them or where they went.

I And how did you feel when you found this out?

D I think it made me angry, to be honest, because my father had never ever mentioned anything like that, and they were a lot of kids, there were triplets, there were two more brothers and it may just have been as though they hadn't lived at all, because there was no mention ever in the family about it. And frustratingly, of course, there's no, absolutely no way I can find out, so that's a shame.

I Why is there no way you can find this out?

D Well, there's no record of their birth, there's no record of their death, if they were given away, which I don't think is impossible, because they were a poor family, then the surname would have changed and there would have been no record of that, so, and there's no living relatives that I can talk to.

I So have you just given up?

D You hate to give up on it and you rack your brains and think, 'Is there any way I could find out?' and of course, the only possibility with the Shepherd family I mentioned in the 1911 census is when the next one comes out in another ten years, there might be some possibility of seeing if they were around somewhere then, but that's a long way away.

I Did you find out anything else surprising?

D I did in fact find some births that were quite close to the marriage dates, and that was a little unexpected, but my secret wish, I suppose, was to hope that Dick Shepherd, the highwayman, might have been somewhere in the family tree, but if he is, I haven't got that far back, but I wouldn't mind at all. It would be quite exciting to have that sort of ancestor, I think.

I Do you think that research into family histories is addictive?

D Oh yes, yes I think any hobby can become so, but this is a fascinating hobby. Perhaps fortunately both my wife and I work and we're still working, so time available is dictated by work schedules, but yes it can be, it's a fascinating, fascinating hobby.

d ● **1.17** This exercise gives SS intensive listening practice in deciphering phrases where words are often run together, and introduces them to some common expressions and idioms used in spoken English. Focus on phrases 1–6 and give SS time to read them. Play the CD, pausing after the first phrase and replaying it as necessary. Elicit the missing words, and then the meaning of the whole phrase. Repeat for the other five phrases.

1 **time-consuming** (= taking up a lot of time)
2 the **late 1700s** (= the end of the eighteenth century, i.e. the last decade)
3 **that's a shame** (= idiomatic way of saying sth is sad or disappointing)

4 **rack your brains** (= idiom meaning *think very hard or for a long time about sth*)
5 a **long way away** (= very far in the future)
6 **that far back** (= I haven't been able to research into the past *as far as that point in time yet*)

1.17 CD1 Track 18

1 It was fun but also vastly time-consuming. It's so much simpler now.
2 … you can usually get back to the late 1700s…
3 …there's no, absolutely no way I can find out, so that's a shame.
4 You hate to give up on it and you rack your brains and think, 'Is there any way I can find out?'…
5 …there might be some possibility of seeing if they were around somewhere then, but that's a long way away.
6 …but if he is, I haven't got that far back…

Extra support

If there's time, get SS to listen again with the scripts on *p.122*, focusing on any new vocabulary, and getting feedback on phrases SS didn't understand, e.g. because the words were run together.

e ● Focus on the questions and get SS to answer in pairs and then get feedback from the whole class, or do this as an open-class discussion.

IN THE STREET

a ● **1.18** Focus on the task and play the CD once for SS to answer the questions. Get them to compare their answers with a partner and then write the answers on the board. Leave the three questions the interviewer asked on the board as SS will use these later.

Questions
1 How much do you know about your family tree?
2 Have you ever researched it?
3 Is there anyone in your family you'd like to know more about?

Jeremy has personally done some research. Tim seems to know the least.

1.18 CD1 Track 19

(script in Student's Book on *p.122*)
I = interviewer, S = Sheila, N = Naomi, T = Tim, J = Jeremy

Sheila

I How much do you know about your family tree?

S Not a great deal actually.

I Have you ever researched it?

S I haven't, but my cousin has and she's looked into the family history of my mother's side of the family. And it would be really interesting to find out what she's learned really.

I Is there someone in your family that you'd like to know more about?

S Both my grandfathers. So my grandfather on my mother's side, he was a musician, professional musician, and travelled a lot during the war and I think he made quite a lot of money because I've got lots of photographs of him with racing cars and motorbikes. I think he was a bit of a boy racer, so it would be quite interesting to find out more about him. And my other grandfather on my father's side, he, I think he was a code breaker in the war, so he's got a bit of a secretive side that it would be interesting to research.

Naomi

I   How much do you know about your family tree?

N   I have to admit that I personally don't know all that much about my own family tree, really. A little bit, I probably can go back a couple of generations, maybe.

I   Have you ever researched it?

N   I haven't researched it personally but my dad has. He's done some research on it, and I think my grandmother on my mother's side also did some research a while back.

I   Is there someone in your family that you'd like to know more about?

N   Yeah, probably my dad's mother. She was a single mum basically and she raised my dad on her own and I think if she were alive now, I'd probably like to ask her a few more questions about what that was like and how she felt and what it was like growing up as well, because I think it would have been different for her.

Tim

I   How much do you know about your family tree?

T   I wouldn't say I know too much extensively about my family tree. I know I'm Polish and French-Indian. But I only know up to my grandparents. I've never really researched into the history of my family or my family tree that much.

I   Is there someone in your family that you'd like to know more about?

T   Probably my grandfather on my father's side – he died when I was pretty young. And I know he had a lot of hobbies that I'd be interested in. But I didn't really get a chance to spend a lot of time with him.

Jeremy

I   How much do you know about your family tree?

J   I know a little bit about my family tree. We've done some research on my mother's side, less on my father's side, which is a bit of a mystery. My grandfather, in fact, he wrote his sort of memoirs of his childhood and his parents and grandparents, which I've kind of helped my mum type up. So I know about them. He was a chauffeur, his father worked as, I think, a footman in some country house and his grandfather was, I think, something, I don't know what he did, but something like that.

I   Are there any other people in your family you'd like to know more about?

J   I'd like to know more about my father's side, because I take after my dad, everyone says I look like him and I don't really know much about his parents or his grandparents, so that would be interesting to find out about them.

b ● Focus on the task and give SS time to read questions 1–7. Play the recording again all the way through and then give SS time to try and answer the questions. Then play it again pausing after each speaker this time for SS to check their answers. Play again as necessary. Elicit and check answers.

> 1 Sheila (speaker 1) and Jeremy (speaker 4)
> 2 Naomi (speaker 2)
> 3 Tim (speaker 3)
> 4 Naomi (speaker 2)
> 5 Sheila (speaker 1)
> 6 Tim (speaker 3)
> 7 Jeremy (speaker 4)

c ● **1.19** Focus on the phrases and give SS time to read them. Play the CD, pausing after the first phrase and replaying it as necessary. Elicit the missing words, and then the meaning of the whole phrase. Repeat for the other three phrases.

> 1 **a great deal** (= informal way of saying *a large amount*)
> 2 **pretty young** (= informal way of saying *quite young*)
> 3 **a while back** (= informal way of saying *quite a long time ago*)
> 4 **a bit of** a mystery (= informal way of saying *quite mysterious*)

> **1.19**   CD1 Track 20
> 1 Not a great deal actually.
> 2 Probably my grandfather on my father's side – he died when I was pretty young.
> 3 I think my grandmother on my mother's side also did some research a while back.
> 4 We've done some research on my mother's side, less on my father's side, which is a bit of a mystery.

Extra support

If there's time, get SS to listen again with the script on *p.122*, focusing on any new vocabulary, and getting feedback on phrases SS didn't understand, e.g. because the words were run together.

d ● Finally, get SS to ask each other the three questions that the interviewer asked the interviewees. Then get some feedback from the whole class.

HOMEWORK

Study Link **Workbook** *p.13*

The File finishes with a page of revision, which focuses on the grammar and the vocabulary (including Lexis in Context) from the File. These exercises can be done individually or in pairs, in class or at home, depending on the needs of your SS and the class time available. If SS do them in class, check which SS are still having problems, or any areas which need further revision.

GRAMMAR

a 1 though
2 their
3 got
4 there
5 one
6 as
7 herself
8 so
9 have / get
10 because

b 1 to have them mended
2 If one learns a few phrases,
3 despite the heavy traffic / despite the traffic being heavy / despite the fact that the traffic was heavy
4 was cancelled due to the fog
5 see each other
6 by themselves
7 haven't seen him since
8 so as not to be recognized
9 we won't have to do the washing up
10 hasn't got any pictures yet

VOCABULARY

a 1 teeth   4 trousers
2 mind   5 guns
3 run   6 terms

b 1 career   4 half-sisters
2 part-time   5 take after
3 alike   6 synonym

c 1 of   4 off
2 off, up   5 in
3 up   6 with, on

d 1 challenging   4 rebellious
2 competitive   5 enjoyable
3 unsuccessful   6 repetitive

Test and Assessment CD-ROM

File 1 Quicktest
File 1 Test

2A

G the past: narrative tenses, *used to* and *would*
V word building: abstract nouns
P word stress with suffixes

Once upon a time

File 2 overview

The second File (**2A–2C**) again combines consolidation and extension of previously taught language with new structures. Lesson **2A** contrasts narrative tenses with *used to* and *would* + infinitive for describing past habits; the lexical area is the formation of abstract nouns; **2B** focuses on the use of 'distancing' phrases to make language more impersonal and SS learn expressions and phrases related to time; **2C** looks at grammatical and lexical uses of *get*.

Lesson plan

The main context of the lesson is childhood memories. The theme is explored first through extracts from an anthology, *When we were young*, in which famous people write about their childhood. The grammar focus here is on past forms. SS revise narrative tenses (past simple and continuous, and past perfect simple and continuous) for describing specific incidents in the past. They also revise *used to* to describe repeated past actions and learn an alternative form, *would* + infinitive. The first half of the lesson ends with oral and written practice talking about childhood, where SS put into practice what they have just learnt.

In the second half of the lesson SS listen to an interview about a new book which talks about research that has been done into our earliest memories (what age we have them and what they usually consist of) and SS talk about their own first memories. Finally, there is a lexical and pronunciation focus on abstract nouns, e.g. *childhood*, *boredom*, *fear*, etc.

Optional lead-in – the quote

- Write the quote at the top of *p.20* on the board (books closed) and the name of the author or get SS to open their books and read it.
- Point out that Sam Ewing (1921–) is an American writer and broadcaster.
- Ask SS what they think the writer was trying to say in the quotation. Find out if any SS have left their own hometown and if so what they miss and why.

1 READING

a • Focus on the task and the texts and point out that they are extracts from a book called *When we were young*, where different people, including several well-known writers, describe aspects of their childhood. Set a time limit for SS to read the extracts and match the correct heading to each one.
- Before they start, go through the glossary. Highlight that *tea* in English can be either a hot drink or a light meal usually eaten around five or six in the evening. SS tend to think that the tradition in the past of 'tea at five' referred to having a cup of tea, whereas in fact it refers to the light meal.
- You may also want to give some more background information about some or all of the contributors to the article:

CS Lewis (1898–1963) was a close friend of J.R.R. Tolkien. His best-selling children's book, *The Chronicles of Narnia: The Lion, the Witch and the Wardrobe*, was made into a film in 2005.

Kofi Annan (1938–) was the very active and popular head of the United Nations from 1997–2006.

Jung Chang (1952–) is a Chinese-born writer now living in London, famous for her autobiography *Wild Swans*, in which she was highly critical of the Chinese communist regime of Mao Tse-tung causing the book to be banned in China.

Agatha Christie (1890–1976) will be familiar to SS as one of the world's best-selling authors of hundreds of detective novels. A play based on one of her books, *The Mousetrap*, is the longest running play in history.

Arthur Ransome (1884–1967) was an author and journalist. His best-selling series of books, *Swallows and Amazons*, tell of school holiday adventures in the Lake District of the UK.

Anaïs Nin (1903–1977) A French writer who is most famous for her journals which span nearly 60 years of her life. For a time she was the partner of the American writer Henry Miller.

Kathleen Cassidy (1927–) is a minor celebrity having been the tea lady at Newcastle United Football club for more than 40 years, serving tea to journalists.

- Give SS time to compare their answers in pairs before checking answers. You might want to explain that in British English *professor* usually means *a university teacher* but here Kofi Annan uses it to refer to a secondary school teacher. In case of any confusion, point out that number 3 is mainly about <u>food</u>, although also about school while number 5 is mainly about <u>school holidays</u> (arriving home from boarding school at the end of the term), but also mentions food.

1 Nightmares	5 School holidays
2 School	6 First love
3 Food	7 Illness
4 Toys and games	

LEXIS IN CONTEXT

b • Focus on the information box and remind SS about 'register', i.e. the style and level of formality (formal, informal, or neutral) of a piece of writing, and how a good dictionary will give important information about the level of formality of words and phrases. Highlight the importance of recording this information and remind them, in the case of very formal / literary words to also note down the neutral synonym, e.g. in the case of *spectre* (formal), they should also note down the neutral or normal word, *ghost*. They should also do the same if, for example, the word in the text had been *spook*, a very informal word for *ghost*.

- Focus on the task and give SS time to read the texts again and find the synonyms (numbers 1–7 refer to the extract where they will find the word.). Check answers, highlighting that *spectre* would rarely be used in modern, non-literary language, and that *skinny* has connotations of being unhealthily thin.

1	spectre	4	splendid	5	a rite
2	outlook on		liable to	6	scold
3	misery		No wonder skinny	7	germs

- Highlight the prepositions after *outlook* (*on*) and *liable* (*to*).

c • Focus on the questions and set SS a time limit to answer them. Some of the questions require some interpretation rather than straight comprehension. Get them to compare their answers with a partner before checking answers. Deal with any vocabulary doubts SS may have.

1 Insects, e.g. spiders
2 Perhaps it made him think that you should always try to see 'the bigger picture' rather than get distracted by small details.
3 From the Hans Christian Andersen story 'Little Match Girl' and from her teacher
4 Because of its action – it moved in all directions which made riding it very exciting.
5 Putting his hand into the waters of the lake as a way of saying 'hello' and to convince himself that he really was at home again.
6 They pretended to let her go without saying anything because they thought it was amusing.
7 As a reward for taking the unpleasant medicine or to take away the bitterness of the cod liver oil.

d • Focus on the task and get SS to do it in pairs. You could either get SS to cover the texts and remember together or get **student A** to cover the text and try to remember while **student B** (text uncovered) checks and prompts.
- Now open the discussion to the whole class, by asking *Which paragraph reminds you most of your childhood?* and eliciting responses and reasons.

Extra support

Ask SS to choose five other words or phrases they would like to learn from the text and get them to compare their choices. Get some feedback from the class as to the words or phrases they have chosen and deal with any vocabulary problems that arise.

2 GRAMMAR the past: narrative tenses, *used to* and *would*

a • Focus on the task and give SS a couple of minutes to answer the questions with a partner. Check answers.

1 Paragraphs 2 and 6
2 Paragraphs 1, 3, 4, 5, and 7

b • Focus on the task and again give SS a few moments to answer it with a partner before eliciting suggestions.

Paragraph 6: past simple (*was, arranged, watched,* etc.), past perfect (*had been scolded*), past continuous (*was waiting*)
Paragraph 7: past simple + *always* (*was always frightened*), *used to* (*used to give us, used to hold*), *would* + infinitive (*would refuse*)

c • Tell SS to go to **Grammar Bank 2A** on *p.139*. Go through each example and its corresponding rule with the class, or give SS time to read the examples and rules on their own, and answer any queries.

Grammar notes

SS should be totally familiar with narrative tenses, though they may still have problems differentiating between past perfect simple and continuous. They should also be very familiar with *used to* for past habitual or repeated actions. The structure which may be new to them is the use of *would* + infinitive. It is important to stress to SS that past simple, *used to*, and *would* are alternative structures to use when describing repeated past actions, and that varying structures will make their language sound more fluent and advanced.

- Focus on the exercises for **2A**. SS do the exercises individually or in pairs. If SS do them individually, get them to compare with a partner. Check answers after each exercise.

a 1 was sitting, had been crying
  2 ✓
  3 ✓, had died
  4 didn't use to look
  5 ✓, ✓
  6 had crashed, was pouring
b 1 spent / would spend / used to spend
  2 had died
  3 cooked / would cook / used to cook
  4 took / would take / used to take
  5 was invited / had been invited
  6 told
  7 was going
  8 tried
  9 got
  10 decided
  11 was sleeping
  12 wanted
  13 had been told
  14 climbed
  15 saw
  16 had been asking
  17 refused / had refused
  18 heard
  19 realized
  20 had got up
  21 was coming
  22 opened
  23 had caught
  24 had forbidden

- Tell SS to go back to the main lesson on *p.21*.

3 SPEAKING & WRITING

a ● **2.1** Focus on the task and play the first extract and elicit the phrase the speaker uses to refer to her age (*From the age of about seven till I was 16...*). Then play the rest of the CD for SS to write down the rest of the phrases, playing the recording again as necessary. Check answers and highlight that:

– you can say *When I was small...* instead of *When I was little...*

– *kid* is more informal than *child*.

– you can also say *As a child...* instead of *When I was a child*.

---

2 When I was little...

3 When I was a young child...

4 When I was at primary school...

5 When I was a kid...

2.1	CD1 Track 21

1 From the age of about seven till I was 16 I went to an all girls school in North London...

2 When I was little, and actually still now, I was absolutely terrified of spiders...

3 When I was a young child, I used to have a lot of nightmares...

4 When I was at primary school, I used to hate school dinners...

5 When I was a kid, we always used to go on holiday down to Cardigan in West Wales...

Extra challenge

Get SS to write down the whole sentence for each person. Then focus on the phrase used to refer to the speakers' ages.

b ● Focus on the task and make it clear to SS that they have to talk about <u>habitual actions</u>. Demonstrate the activity by talking about some of the headings yourself. Then get SS in pairs to take turns to talk about each heading. Highlight that they should be using past forms / *used to* and *would* + infinitive to describe their experiences.

c ● Focus on the instructions and highlight that this time they should use narrative tenses to describe a specific incident they can remember from their childhood.

● Give them some thinking time to choose a heading and an incident.

● Monitor and support, helping SS with vocabulary and correcting any wrong use of tenses. Fast finishers could choose another heading and describe another incident from their childhood.

d ● Focus on the task, which you could either do in class or set for homework. These could be displayed in the classroom or on the class website if you have one.

4 LISTENING & SPEAKING

a ● **2.2** Focus on the task and play the recording once the whole way through for SS to number the emotions. Play the recording again as necessary. Check answers.

---

surprise 3	sadness 5	fear 2
disappointment 4	happiness 1	

2.2	CD1 Track 22

(script in Student's Book on *p.123*)

I = interviewer, Sp = speaker

I What is your earliest memory?

Sp 1 Um, I was born on the Atlantic coast of New England and my earliest memory is swimming between my mother and my father in the Atlantic Ocean.

I Oh, wow.

Sp 1 Because I swam before I could walk and it was wonderful.

I How amazing! How old were you then?

Sp 1 I think I was like, actually, I must have been really really young, maybe, maybe I'd already walked by that point, I must have been one and a half when I had that memory. Really young, it was really, it was a beautiful experience then, I'm sure and remembering it makes me very happy.

Sp 2 My earliest memory is of being completely by myself, lost in what seemed to be a great big forest, it probably wasn't. I was about 18 months old and we were living in Cornwall, which is where I was born, and I was on a sort of path in the middle of a really really dark forest and I remember looking behind me and it was just darkness and, and big dark trees and the same ahead of me, and just having this feeling of being completely on my own, and calling out for my sister, Lynn, who was seven years older than me, who was supposed to be minding me and not being able to find her.

Sp 3 I guess I was about three or maybe four, and I remember sitting on my father's shoulders and we were going to the zoo and there was an elephant, and the elephant took my ice cream...

Sp 4 I remember it was 1966 and I was sitting on a bus with my grandmother, and I'd been given a brand new one penny coin, it was brand new, it was sparkling, and it was beautiful, and I remembered deciding then and there that this was going to be my earliest memory, I was going to remember this day in 1966 when I was sitting there with this brand new penny. And then I remember the bus conductor came along and wanted the fares, and my granny was a penny short, so that was the end of my penny.

Sp 5 One of my very earliest memories is pulling away in a car looking out of the window seeing our dog Sam, sort of pining for us through a window, and we were basically having to say goodbye to Sam because we were moving to a flat where they didn't allow dogs. So we were having to say goodbye to him, and it was very sad, he was sort of pining in his new home and we were pulling away. It was horrible.

---

b ● Focus on the questions. Point out that not all the speakers say exactly how old they were. Play the CD again for SS to answer the questions. You could pause between each extract to give SS more time. Get SS to compare in pairs before checking answers.

---

1 **Age:** 1½ **Memory:** swimming in the Atlantic Ocean with her mother and father

2 **Age:** About 18 months old **Memory:** being lost in a forest and not able to find her older sister

3 **Age:** 3 or 4 **Memory:** visiting the zoo with her father and an elephant took her ice cream

4 **Age:** doesn't say **Memory:** being given a brand new penny by his grandmother but then having to give it to the bus conductor as his grandmother didn't have enough money to pay for the fare

5 **Age:** doesn't say **Memory:** saying goodbye to the family dog who they were leaving behind in his new home

---

Extra support

If there's time, get SS to listen again with the script on *p.123*, focusing on any new vocabulary, and getting feedback on phrases SS didn't understand, e.g. because the words were run together.

c ● Tell SS that they are going to hear an interview in which someone will talk about a book about memory called *How Memory Shapes our Past* by Professor Douwe Draaisma, a Dutch professor and expert on memory.

● Get SS, in pairs, to discuss questions 1–5, all of which will be answered in the interview. Get some feedback from the class but <u>don't check answers</u> at this stage.

d ● **2.3** Play the CD for SS to check their answers to the questions. Play the recording again as necessary. Check answers. Find out if SS were surprised by anything they heard in the interview. You could also ask if, as a result of what they have heard, they think that any of the memories in **a** may not be true memories.

Extra support

Pause the CD where indicated in the script (see spaces) to give SS time to note their answers.

---

1 b (2–4 years)
2 Because we don't have a clear sense of ourselves as individuals and because we usually can't use the past tense yet.
3 a) strong emotions, e.g. happiness, unhappiness, pain, surprise, fear
   b) the birth of a baby brother or sister, a death, or a family visit. Festive celebrations.
4 Mostly visual
5 Because they might not be real memories but something someone has told us or we have seen in a photo.

2.3   CD1 Track 23

(script in Student's Book on *p.123*)
P = presenter, J = John Fisher
P Are our first memories reliable, or are they always based on something people have told us? What age do most people's first memories come from? John Fisher has been reading a fascinating new book about memory by Professor Draaisma called *How Memory Shapes our Past*, and he's going to answer these questions for us and more. Hello John.
J Hello.
P Let's start at the beginning then. At what age do first memories generally occur?
J Well, according to both past and present research, 80% of our first memories are of things which happened to us between the ages of two and four. It's very unusual to remember anything that happened before that age.

P Why is that?
J There seem to be two main reasons, according to Professor Draaisma. The first reason is that before the age of two, children don't have a clear sense of themselves as individuals – they can't usually identify themselves in a photo. And you know how a very small child enjoys seeing himself in a mirror, but he doesn't actually realize that the person he can see is him. Children of this age also have problems with the pronouns *I* and *you*. And a memory without *I* is impossible. That's to say, we can't begin to have memories until we have an awareness of self.

P And the second reason?
J The second reason is related to language. According to the research, first memories coincide with the development of linguistic skills, with a child learning to talk. And as far as autobiographical memory is concerned, it's essential for a child to be able to use the past tense, so that he or she can talk about something that happened in the past, and then remember it.

P I see. What are first memories normally about? I mean, is it possible to generalize at all?
J Early memories seem to be related to strong emotions, such as happiness, unhappiness, pain, and surprise. Recent research suggests that three quarters of first memories are related to fear, to frightening experiences like being left alone, or a large dog, or having an accident – things like falling off a swing in a park. And of course this makes sense, and bears out the evolutionary theory that the human memory is linked to self-preservation. You remember these things in order to be prepared if they happen again, so that you can protect yourself.

P Are first memories only related to emotions or are there any specific events that tend to become first memories?
J The events that are most often remembered, and these are always related to one of the emotions I mentioned before, are the birth of a baby brother or sister, a death, or a family visit. Festive celebrations with bright lights were also mentioned quite frequently, much more frequently than events we might have expected to be significant, like a child's first day at school. Another interesting aspect is that first memories tend to be very visual. They're almost invariably described as pictures, not smells or sounds.

P First memories are often considered unreliable, in that perhaps sometimes they're not real memories, just things other people have told us about ourselves or that we have seen in photos. Is that true, according to Professor Draaisma?
J Absolutely! He cites the famous case of the Swiss psychologist, Jean Piaget…

---

e ● **2.4** This exercise gives SS practice in understanding a short narrative by focusing on the key 'content' words in the story (i.e. the words that the speaker will tend to stress more strongly). Listening for 'key' words is an important aspect of understanding native speakers and especially understanding rapid speech.

● Tell SS that they are going to hear a short anecdote about the first memory of the famous Swiss psychologist, Jean Piaget. The first time they listen they should just write down any words they hear. Play the CD once.

● Now play the CD again for SS to try and fill in the rest of the story. Get them to compare with their partner and see if they can retell the story together.

● Finally, elicit the story from the class and write it on the board.

Suggested key words in bold
He was **sitting** in his **pram** as a one-year-old **baby**. A **man tried** to **kidnap** him. He remembered his **nanny fighting** to **save** him. His **parents gave** her a **reward** (a watch). **Years later** when he was **15** the **nanny** wrote his parents a **letter** and **returned** the **watch**. She **confessed** that she had **made up** the whole story.

2.4   CD1 Track 24

P First memories are often considered unreliable, in that perhaps sometimes they're not real memories, just things other people have told us about ourselves or that we have seen in photos. Is that true, according to Professor Draaisma?

J Absolutely! He cites the famous case of the Swiss psychologist, Jean Piaget. Piaget had always thought that his first memory was of sitting in his pram as a one-year-old baby when a man tried to kidnap him. He remembered his nanny fighting the kidnapper to save him. The nanny was then given a watch as a reward by Jean's parents. But many years later, I think when Jean was 15, the parents received a letter from the nanny in which she returned the watch to them. The nanny, who was by now an old woman, confessed in the letter that she'd made up the whole story, and that was why she was returning the watch. Of course Jean had heard the story told so many times that he was convinced that he'd remembered the whole incident.

f • Focus on the task and go through the talking points. If you have a good early memory story to tell, contribute it at this point.

    • Put SS in pairs or small groups of three or four. Tell SS to take turns to talk about any of the topics where they have a clear memory and are happy to recount it. If you have time, you could find out whether anyone has a funny / surprising / dramatic memory to retell to the whole class.

5 VOCABULARY & PRONUNCIATION
word building: abstract nouns; word stress

a • Focus on the information in the box about abstract nouns and elicit some examples from the class, e.g. *love, jealousy, hunger, attraction*, etc.

    • Focus on the task making it clear that to form some of the nouns SS will have to add a suffix and for others (the final column) SS have to form a new word instead of adding a suffix. Do the first two words *adult* and *afraid* with the whole class as examples.

    • In pairs, give SS time to complete the task. Check answers.

+ hood
adulthood, childhood, neighbourhood
+ ship
friendship, membership, partnership, relationship
+ dom
boredom, freedom, wisdom
+ ness
happiness, illness, kindness, sadness
+ tion
celebration, competition, imagination
word changes
afraid – fear, ashamed – shame, believe – belief, dead – death, hate – hatred, lose – loss, poor – poverty

b • **2.5** Focus on the task and tell SS to use their instinct to underline the stressed syllables in the words. Then play the CD for them to check their answers. Elicit which suffix ending(s) can cause the stress to change.

1 <u>a</u>dult – <u>a</u>dulthood
2 <u>ce</u>lebrate – cele<u>bra</u>tion
3 com<u>pete</u> – compe<u>ti</u>tion
4 free – <u>free</u>dom
5 <u>hap</u>py – <u>hap</u>piness
6 re<u>la</u>tion – re<u>la</u>tionship

The endings *-hood*, *-ship*, *-dom* and *-ness* <u>never</u> affect the stress of the word they are added to.
Multi-syllable nouns ending in *-ion* are always stressed on the syllable <u>before</u> the ending. This sometimes causes the stress to shift, e.g. <u>ce</u>lebrate – cele<u>bra</u>tion, in<u>form</u> – infor<u>ma</u>tion, but not always, e.g. ex<u>press</u> – ex<u>pres</u>sion.
You may want to point out that the same rule applies to words ending in *-ian*, e.g. *electrician, magician*, etc.

2.5   CD1 Track 25

1	adult	adulthood
2	celebrate	celebration
3	compete	competition
4	free	freedom
5	happy	happiness
6	relation	relationship

    • Now get SS to go back to the chart in **a** and practise saying the words correctly. Make sure they know where to stress the words which don't have a suffix, e.g. bel<u>ief</u>, <u>po</u>verty, etc.

c • Focus on the task and set pairs a time limit to complete the quotations. Sometimes more than one abstract noun will make sense in a quotation but the idea is for SS to try and guess the original words. Check answers.

1	hatred	5	poverty
2	Fear	6	boredom
3	happiness	7	illness
4	Imagination	8	freedom

Digital extra idea

You could show the class photos of the people as they look at each quote.

d • You could do this exercise in pairs or as a whole class activity.

Extra photocopiable activities

Grammar
past: narrative tenses, *used to* and *would* p.160
Communicative
Childhood questionnaire *p.186* (instructions *p.178*)
Vocabulary
Abstract nouns *p.211* (instructions *p.204*)

HOMEWORK

Study Link Workbook *pp.14–16*

Are there really 31 hours in a day?

Lesson plan

The topic of this lesson is time, how we try to save time through multitasking and how other people waste our time. In the first half of the lesson SS read two articles about multitasking. One of the articles is about how multitasking is enabling us to cram even more hours into the day whilst the other questions whether it is a myth that we actually save time by multitasking. The grammar focus of the lesson is on distancing, i.e. using certain language (e.g. *apparently, it seems*, etc.) to 'distance' ourselves from information we are giving to others.

In the second half of the lesson SS listen to a radio phone-in about 'Time Bandits', i.e. people or situations which waste our precious time. Here there is a pronunciation focus on linking words together in rapid speech. The vocabulary focus is on expressions related to time and the lesson finishes with SS answering questions in a time questionnaire, which recycles this lexis.

Optional lead-in – the quote

- Write the quote at the top of *p.24* on the board (books closed) and the name of the author or get SS to open their books and read it.
- Point out that Will Rogers (1879–1935) was an American cinema actor, comedian, and journalist, who in his day was a world famous figure.
- Ask SS whether they identify with Will Rogers's opinion or disagree, and try to get a short discussion going about how people try to save time these days and whether they think this is a useful thing to do.

1 READING & SPEAKING

a ● Focus on the task and quickly go through questions 1–4. Then set a time limit for SS to discuss the questions.
  ● Get some feedback from the class.
b ● Put SS into pairs, **A** and **B**. Focus on the task, and the information that SS **A** and **B** will have to tell their partner after they have read their respective articles (**A** looks at the first four points and **B** looks at the next five points). Set a time limit and monitor while SS are reading and help with any words or phrases they cannot guess from the context.
c ● When the time limit is up, SS take it in turns to tell their partner the main points of their article using the information in **b** to help them.
  ● Finally, give SS time to read the article they have not read in preparation for the next exercise.

Extra challenge

You could skip this final stage, and get SS in **d** to find the words from the text they read and then teach them to each other.

LEXIS IN CONTEXT

d ● Focus on the task and get SS to work together to find the words in the two articles that match the definitions. When SS have completed the task, check answers.

1	gadget	**6**	juggle
2	frenzy	**7**	engrossed
3	blizzard	**8**	cope
4	catch up with	**9**	clog
5	peak	**10**	overcome

  ● Focus on the **Metaphors** box and elicit / remind SS of the meaning of *a metaphor* (= a word or expression that is used in a non-literal sense to make your writing or speech more interesting or powerful).
  ● Finally, ask SS what other two words in exercise **d** are also used metaphorically in the respective articles (*peak* and *juggle*).
e ● Focus on the questions and elicit opinions and experiences from the class.

Extra support

Ask SS to choose five other words or phrases they would like to learn from the articles and get them to compare their choices. Get some feedback from the class as to the words or phrases they have chosen and deal with any vocabulary problems that arise.

2 GRAMMAR distancing

a ● Do this as a whole class activity and elicit that the phrases all distance the writer from the information, i.e. they imply that it might not be a definite fact.
b ● Tell SS to go to **Grammar Bank 2B** on *p.140*. Go through each example and its corresponding rule with the class, or give SS time to read the examples and rules on their own, and answer any queries.

Grammar notes

- Distancing expressions are often used, particularly in journalism where a speaker or writer wants to stress that the information is second-hand and comes from a specific source or sources, rather than being their own knowledge or opinion. Expressions like *It is said that…* are also often used where a writer is not sure of the sources, and by using these expressions they can avoid the possibility of libel.

- SS should have come across most of these expressions before, but will probably never have focused on their exact function, and may well not be familiar with the two possible ways of using *seem* and *appear*. You may want to point out that *appear* is slightly more formal than *seem*.

- Focus on the exercises for **2B**. SS do the exercises individually or in pairs. If SS do them individually, get them to compare with a partner. Check answers after each exercise.

a 1 seems / appears
    2 would
    3 seems / appears
    4 said / supposed
    5 According
    6 seems to / appears to
    7 There
    8 to
    9 that

b 1 appear / seem that people who work night shifts die younger.
    2 have escaped to France.
    3 expected to make a statement this afternoon.
    4 has been announced (by the company) that the new drug will go on sale shortly.
    5 are believed to be responsible for the rise in life-expectancy.
    6 to the manual, you have to charge the phone for at least 12 hours.
    7 appears to be intending to lower interest rates.
    8 has been suggested that the painting is fake.
    9 seem / appear to be more cyclists than there used to be.

- Tell SS to go back to the main lesson on *p.25*.

c ● Focus on the task. Tell SS that they should choose a headline and invent the details; they should distance themselves from the information they give. Monitor and help while SS are doing this.

Extra support

You could do this in pairs or small groups.

- Finally, get SS to read each other's paragraphs before collecting them in to check for accuracy.
- Alternatively, you may wish to set the writing of the paragraph for homework.

3 PRONUNCIATION & LISTENING linking

a ● Focus on the programme information and elicit an answer to the question (*They are people and situations that steal our time*).

b ● **2.6** Tell SS that the focus here is on deciphering phrases when the speaker runs two or more words together. This is called 'linking' and of course is one of the reasons why understanding fast speech can be so difficult.

Pronunciation notes

- The focus here is on three specific areas where words are commonly linked, i.e. when a word ends with a consonant sound and the next word begins with a vowel sound (e.g. *She went out at eleven o'clock.*), the inserted /r/ sound when a word ends in *r* or *re* and the next word begins with a vowel sound (e.g. *They're easy to please.*), and when one words ends and the next word begins with the same consonant sound (e.g. *We should get together.*). Other aspects on linking are dealt with in later lessons, e.g. the added /w/ sound when a word ending in a vowel + *w* is followed by a word beginning with a vowel sound.

- Focusing on linking and getting SS to practise doing it themselves, apart from making SS' speech sound more natural, will help them to decipher linked speech when they are listening.

- Play the CD once for SS to complete the sentences, pausing after each sentence for SS to write. Play again as necessary. Check answers getting feedback from SS as to which phrases they found most difficult to understand and why.

  1 …for all
  2 First of all…,
  3 For example,…
  4 And I will always arrive…
  5 …such a waste of…
  6 …great talking…

> **2.6**   CD1 Track 26
> 1 I think that's quite a common problem for all of us.
> 2 First of all don't complain out loud…
> 3 For example, I've got this friend of mine and…
> 4 And I will always arrive on time…
> 5 It's just such a waste of time…
> 6 It's been great talking to you…

c ● Focus on the instructions. Get SS to read the **Linking** box and then look at the phrases they have written in **b**. Check answers.

1 rule 2	4 rule 1
2 rule 1	5 rule 1
3 rule 2	6 rule 3

⚠ There are some other words linked according to rule 1 in these phrases, e.g. *quite a* in 1, *complain out* in 2, *friend of* in 3, and *and I* in 4. You may want to point these out to SS.

- Ask SS to practise saying the sentences, linking the words. They can do this quietly by themselves or with their partner. Then ask some individual SS to say the sentences.

Extra support

You could use the recording (2.6) to model the sentences with SS repeating after each sentence.

d ● **2.7** Focus on the task and play the CD, pausing after each caller to give SS time to write a summarizing sentence. Check answers, writing the summaries on the board.

Caller 2	He often wastes time waiting for people who are late.
Caller 3	She wastes time helping her husband look for things he can't find.
Caller 4	She wastes time trying to decide what to wear in the morning.
Caller 5	She wastes time in the supermarket when the person in front of her in the queue chats to the cashier.

2.7
CD1 Track 27

Caller 1 Right, I have this friend who's always phoning me and, well, she just won't let me get off the phone – I waste so much time just listening to her telling me every single thing she's been doing and every little problem that she has.

Caller 2 I am a very punctual person, you know, it's something I pride myself on, and I do spend a lot of my time, wasting my time really waiting for people. Like, for example, I've got this friend of mine, and we'll often have like an informal lunch together or something and I will always arrive on time, I'll arrive at the restaurant on time, but I have to wait for him, well, it's at least ten minutes, sometimes more, for him to arrive.

Caller 3 Well, it's my husband. He always expects <u>me</u> to help him find whatever he can't find, you know, usually his car keys or a particular shirt he wants to wear. Even when I'm busy and I spend too much time helping him and not getting on with doing what I'm supposed to be doing.

Caller 4 Every morning when I get up, I spend ages just standing in front of the wardrobe, and try and decide what to wear. It's just such a waste of time! Especially as I end up then wearing the same thing again and again.

Caller 5 I have kids and I work full-time, so as you can imagine I don't have much spare time, and I'm often in a hurry when I go to the supermarket. And somehow I always manage to have someone in front of me in the queue who seems to have all the time in the world, you know, who's really slow and, even more annoying, gets into a conversation with the cashier. Do you have any tips?

e ● Give SS time to discuss each problem and come up with some good advice.

f ● **2.8** Focus on the task and then play the CD for SS to match a piece of advice (A–E) to each caller. <u>Don't check answers at this stage.</u>

2.8
CD1 Track 28

Advice A
I got this advice from a friend of mine who works in fashion. She recommends you completely re-organize your wardrobe. Set aside ten minutes one day, make a list of your five favourite outfits, and hang them all together. Then stick the list inside the door of the wardrobe and when you can't think of what to wear, just look at the list and wear one of the outfits. Well, I tell you, my friend swears it saves her a lot of time.

Advice B
Rule number one, Judy. Look, never, ever, drop what you're doing to go and help. Now, if he shouts at you from another room, just tell him you can't hear him properly, let him come to you. Pretend you're really busy even if you aren't.

Advice C
Say you'd love to chat, but you can't right now and you'll ring back another time. How about that? Or say you've only got five minutes and mean it, I mean say goodbye when the five minutes are up. Use a finishing-up expression like, 'Oh, it's been great talking to you, but I really must go now.'

Advice D
I do know what you mean because I've got friends like that too. I think the best thing to do, and speaking from experience, is send your friend a text or email on the morning of your get-together, and tell them you're a bit short of time today so you don't want to hang around too much. And ask him or her to let you know if they're going to be late! That should make them get the message.

Advice E
Well, first of all, don't complain out loud, because that might easily annoy the other person and make them take even longer. No, the thing to do is just politely interrupt and ask the cashier a question. Now this should bring the person ahead of you back to reality. And that will remind the cashier that there are other people waiting to be served.

g ● **2.9** SS now listen to the whole programme and check their answers to **f**. Check answers and find out from the class how similar / different their advice was to the expert's. If the SS' advice was different, you could ask them *Whose advice do you think is best and why?*

Caller 1	Advice C
Caller 2	Advice D
Caller 3	Advice B
Caller 4	Advice A
Caller 5	Advice E

2.9
CD1 Track 29

(script in Student's Book on *p.123*)
H = host, C = caller, R = Richard

H And now it's time for our weekly dose of *Time Bandits*, the section of the show where we try to deal with your time issues. And we're going to be talking to our time management guru, Richard. And now we're going to line 1, which is Jade from North London. Hi Jade.

C 1 Hello, hi, right I have this friend who's always phoning me and, well, she just won't let me get off the phone – I waste so much time just listening to her telling me every single thing she's been doing and every little problem that she has.

H Yeah, I think that's quite a common problem for all of us – so Richard, what advice have you got?

R Well, look, say you'd love to chat, but you can't right now and you'll ring back another time. How about that? Or say you've only got five minutes and mean it, I mean say goodbye when the five minutes are up. Use a finishing-up expression like, 'Oh, it's been great talking to you, but I really must go now.'

C 1 Yeah, OK, thank you.

R Not at all.

H That's great advice Richard. Must remember to use that with the mother-in-law. Right, we're going to line 2 now. We're talking to Nigel from Bury. Hi Nigel.

C 2 Hiya, it's Bury, actually. What I wanted to say was I am a very punctual person, you know, it's something I pride myself on, and I do spend a lot of my time, wasting my time really waiting for people. Like, for example I've got this friend of mine, and we'll often have like an informal lunch together or something, and I will always arrive on time, I'll arrive at the restaurant on time, but I have to wait for him, well, it's at least ten minutes, sometimes more, for him to arrive.

H OK Nigel, so, over to you, Richard.

R Well, look Nigel I do know what you mean, because I've got friends like that too! I think the best thing to do, and I'm speaking from experience, is send your friend a text or email on the morning of your get-together, and tell them you're a bit short of time today so you don't want to hang around too much. And ask him or her to let you know if they're going to be late! That should make them get the message.

H That's great advice, Richard. Right moving punctually on to line 3 which is Judy from Horndean. Hello Judy.

C 3 Oh hello. Oh dear. Well, it's my husband. He always expects me to help him find whatever he can't find, you know, usually his car keys or a particular shirt he wants to wear. Even when I'm busy, and I spend too much time helping him, and not getting on with doing what I'm supposed to be doing.

H Right I see. OK, Richard, what do you make of that?

R Rule number one, Judy. Look, never, ever, drop what you're doing to go and help. Now, if he shouts at you from another room, just tell him you can't hear him properly. Let him come to you. Pretend you're really busy even if you aren't.

C 3 Oh, I'll try.

H That's fantastic, Richard. Thank you. Now, moving on to caller 4, who's Wendy from Leeds. Wendy, what's your problem?

C 4 Hi. Every morning when I get up, I spend ages just standing in front of the wardrobe and try and decide what to wear. It's just such a waste of time, especially as I end up then wearing the same thing again and again.

H I know how you feel, Wendy. Richard, what's your advice?

R OK. Straight up, Wendy. I got this advice from a friend of mine who works in fashion. She recommends you completely reorganize your wardrobe. Set aside ten minutes one day, make a list of your five favourite outfits, and hang them all together.

C 4 Right.

R Then stick the list inside the door of the wardrobe. And when you can't think of what to wear, just look at the list and wear one of the outfits. Well, I tell you, my friend swears it saves her a lot of time.

C 4 Wow! Thank you.

H That's great advice, Richard. I should remember that myself. Now, time's ticking swiftly on so we need to take our last caller and that is Sue from Staines. Hello Sue.

C 5 Oh, hi. Am I on?

H Yes, you are. What's your problem?

C 5 I have kids and I work full-time, so as you can imagine, I don't have much spare time, and I'm often in a hurry when I go to the supermarket. And somehow I always manage to have someone in front of me in the queue who seems to have all the time in the world, you know, who's really slow and, even more annoying, gets into a conversation with the cashier. Do you have any tips?

H Any tips, any tips for Sue, there Richard?

R Of course, of course, well, first of all, don't complain out loud, because that might easily annoy the other person and make them take even longer. No, the thing to do is just politely interrupt and ask the cashier a question. Now this should bring the person ahead of you back to reality, and that will remind the cashier that there are other people waiting to be served.

C 5 All right.

R All right?

H That's great advice, Richard. I think a lot of people could use that. Right, I'm afraid time's up for now, but thank you all for your calls…

Extra support

If there's time, get SS to listen to the phone-in again with the script on *p.123*, focusing on any new vocabulary, and getting feedback on phrases SS didn't understand, e.g. because the words were run together.

h ● Open the discussion to the whole class and elicit from the class things which waste their time, and the best way to deal with them.

4 VOCABULARY expressions with *time*

a ● Focus on the task and point out that all the sentences are from the radio phone-in. Give SS a few moments to complete the missing words. <u>Don't</u> check answers at this stage.

b ● **2.10** Play the CD for SS to listen, check their answers, and elicit what the phrases mean.

1 **wasting** my time = using time badly
2 **spare** time = more time than you need (that you could use to do something else)
3 **saves**…time = allows you do something quicker (and perhaps avoid wasting time)
4 **short** of time = you don't have enough time
5 time's **up** = the time allowed for something has come to an end

1 …wasting my time really waiting for people.
2 I have kids and I work full-time, so as you can imagine, I don't have much spare time.
3 …my friend swears it saves her a lot of time.
4 …tell them you're a bit short of time today…
5 Right, I'm afraid time's up for now, but thank you all for your calls.

c ● Tell SS to go to **Vocabulary Bank** *time* on *p.159*. Focus on section **1 Verbs with *time*** and get SS to do it individually or in pairs. Check answers and elicit / model the pronunciation of tricky words as necessary.

1	waste	7	give
2	save	8	spare
3	kill	9	take up
4	take	10	have
5	make up for	11	run out of
6	take		

● You may want to highlight that:
  - *waste time* = use time badly. Contrast with *lose time* (= take longer), e.g. *We lost a lot of time because we took the wrong exit off the motorway.*
  - *save time* suggests that you do sth to reduce the amount of time sth would normally take, e.g. *I would have been late, but I saved time by getting a taxi to work.*
  - *kill time* suggests that you want to make time pass quickly because you are bored
  - *make up for lost time* = try to compensate for time or opportunities missed in the past
  - *take up* (*time*) = fill your time
  - *can't spare the time* = you don't have enough time to devote any of it to another activity
  - *run out of time* = not have any time left to do sth

● Now focus on section **2 Prepositional phrases with *time*** and get SS to do it individually or in pairs. Remind SS to write their answers in the **Prepositions** column and <u>not</u> in the sentences. Check answers and elicit / model the pronunciation of tricky words as necessary.

1	on	4	in	7	in, for
2	before	5	at	8	from, to
3	By	6	off	9	at

● You may need to elicit / explain:
  - the difference between *on time* (= punctually, at the agreed time) and *in time* (= arriving early enough to do sth, e.g. catch a train)
  - *before my time* = before I was old enough to be aware of / remember this
  - *by the time* = all the time up to a certain point, e.g. *By the time we got to the top of the mountain we were exhausted* = we had been getting progressively more exhausted during the climb.
  - *in four days' time* (or *in four days*) = in four days from now
  - *at the time* = at that moment
  - *time off* = time at home, not working
  - *from time to time* = occasionally
  - *at times* = sometimes

- Now focus on section **3 Expressions with *time*** and get SS to do it individually or in pairs. Check answers and elicit / model the pronunciation of tricky words as necessary.

1 I	**3** J	**5** F	**7** E	**9** A
2 B	**4** D	**6** G	**8** C	**10** H

- You may need to elicit / explain:
  – *time left* = time remaining
  – *time to spare* = with more than enough time
  – *short of* = synonym of *pushed for time* but *pushed for time* is less formal
  – *time on my hands* = more free time than I actually want
  – *for the time being* = for the moment
  – *it's a question of time* = it's inevitable that something will happen
  – *time's up* = the allotted time for something has expired
- Finally, focus on the instruction 'Can you remember the expressions on this page? Test yourself or a partner.'

Testing yourself

For **Verbs with *time*** SS can cover the sentences and look at the verbs in the list and try to remember the sentences. For **Prepositional phrases with *time*** they can look at the prepositions only and try to remember the context. For **Expressions with *time*** SS can look at sentences 1–10 and try to remember sentences A–J.

Testing a partner

See **Testing a partner** *p.18.*

Study Link   SS can find more practice of these words and phrases on the MultiROM and on the *New English File Advanced* website.

- Tell SS to go back to the main lesson on *p.27.*

5 SPEAKING

- Focus on the time questionnaire and give SS time to read through the questions.
- Tell SS to give examples when they answer the questions, and remind them of *For example... / For instance...*
- Then get SS in pairs to work through it answering the questions together.
- Monitor while SS are doing this, correcting any slips in the time phrases, and noting down any other problems to deal with later.
- Finally, get feedback from the whole class.

Extra photocopiable activities

Grammar
distancing *p.161*
Communicative
Time: Proverbs and sayings *p.187* (instructions *p.178*)
Vocabulary
'Time' race *p.212* (instructions *p.204*)

HOMEWORK

Study Link Workbook *pp.17–19*

2C

G *get*
V phrases with *get*
P words and phrases of French origin

50 ways to leave your lover

Lesson plan

This lesson deals with the topic of relationships – first SS discuss a light-hearted list of 'best break-up lines' before reading the true stories of how three women got their own back on a boyfriend / husband, who left them or was unfaithful to them. Then in pronunciation they look at French words and expressions (e.g. *rendezvous*), which are commonly used in English but pronounced in a way that is close to their French pronunciation. There is then a lexical focus on verbs and idioms related to the verb *get*, probably the most versatile verb in English.

In the second half of the lesson SS discuss certain often-asked questions about relationships such as 'Do opposites attract?', 'Should you try to get back in touch with an ex?'. Then they listen to a journalist talking about academic research that has been done into these topics and the statistical evidence available. The grammar focus is also on different meanings of *get* and the lesson ends with a questionnaire which recycles both lexical and grammatical examples of this verb.

Optional lead-in – the quote

- Write the quote at the top of *p.28* on the board (books closed) and the name of the author or get SS to open their books and read it.
- Point out that Ivana Trump (1949–) was a Czech born Olympic skier, who emigrated to the USA where she met and married Donald Trump, the American property millionaire. When they divorced, Ivana is reported to have won a settlement of more than 20 million dollars.
- Point out that *mad* in American English means *angry* and ask SS what they think Ivana meant in this quote (don't get angry, get as much money, property, etc. as you can) and whether they think it is good advice. You could also ask SS whether they think it is right that spouses of wealthy people often receive huge divorce payments from their ex-partner even when they weren't married for very long.

1 READING & SPEAKING

a • Focus on the title of the lesson and elicit from SS that it is the title of a song by Paul Simon (a version of which SS will listen to later in the lesson).
- Focus on the task and get SS to decide in pairs which they think are the best / worst. Get feedback from the class.

Extra challenge

Alternatively, you could start the lesson with books closed and ask SS for their own ideas of the best break-up lines. Write these up on the board before opening books and comparing SS' ideas with the ones in **1a**.

b • Focus on the three stories and the title *Getting your own back*, and elicit the meaning (taking / getting revenge on sb for sth). Read aloud the quote 'Hell hath no fury...' and elicit its meaning (*There is no one more dangerous than a woman who has been rejected by a man.*). Establish that all three stories involve a woman taking revenge on her ex-partner / husband. You may want to tell SS that the composer mentioned is Michael Nyman.
- Focus on the gist reading task and the five questions. Set a time limit for SS to read the three stories. Tell SS not to worry about the meaning of every word or try to guess the missing words, but just to find out exactly how the woman took revenge in each case and why.
- Get feedback from SS about which act of revenge was the most ingenious / satisfying, etc.

> Students' own answers

LEXIS IN CONTEXT

c • Focus on the task and give SS time to complete it. Get SS to compare their answers with a partner before checking answers. Where useful, elicit the meanings of some of the wrong options. Check answers.

1 b dumped (informal)	7 b created
2 a turning	8 c crowning
3 c ridiculed	9 a get over
4 a replaced	10 c took
5 a unwillingly	11 b set about
6 c posted	12 b stamped on

d • Focus on the task and elicit from the class what the first number (50) refers to (*50 Ways to leave your lover*, a song by Paul Simon). Then get SS to continue in pairs, telling them to look back at the stories if they can't remember. Check answers.

> **107** – the number of women to whom Sophie Calle sent her ex-boyfriend's email
> **30** – the number of emails the famous composer used to send Jane Slavin before he suddenly broke off contact with her
> **more than 100** – the number of emails the famous composer sent 'Lucia'
> **42** – the age of Sarah Graham-Moon's husband's lover
> **32** – the number of her husband's suits, jackets, and coats which Sarah Graham-Moon damaged by cutting off part of a sleeve
> **1,000** – the value in pounds of some of the suits, jackets, and coats which Sarah Graham-Moon damaged
> **25** – the number of Havana cigars in a box that Sarah Graham-Moon stamped on
> **24** – the number of her husband's bottles of alcohol that Sarah Graham-Moon gave away

Digital extra idea

Go to YouTube and type *Sophie Calle* in the search box. The clip called *52nd Venice Biennale 2007* shows people going around the exhibition. Or Google *Sophie Calle paramnesic pleasures* and watch an interview where Sophie Calle explains what she did and why; you can also see her work. Only the first half of the interview is relevant. You might want to warn SS that Sophie has a strong French accent.

e ● Focus on the sayings, and elicit their meanings.

> *Revenge is sweet* = people enjoy taking revenge
> *Revenge is a dish best served cold* = it is better not to take revenge in the heat of the moment, but later
> *In revenge, woman is more barbarous than man* = women are more cruel in their revenge than men
> *An eye for an eye makes the whole world blind* = taking revenge harms you as much as the other person

● Then elicit from the class which saying they think best suits each story and why. You could also ask SS if there are any sayings about revenge in their country.

Extra support

Ask SS to choose five other words or phrases they would like to learn from the stories and get them to compare their choices. Get some feedback from the class as to the words or phrases they have chosen and deal with any vocabulary problems that arise.

2 PRONUNCIATION words and phrases of French origin

Pronunciation notes

Throughout the centuries a feature of English has been that it has always borrowed words from other languages (called 'loan words'), typically where there is not an English word available to describe, e.g. a custom, type of food, a technology, which has been imported from another country. Common examples of loan words are *sauna* (from Finnish), *pasta* (from Italian), and *robot* (from Czech). The pronunciation of these words is usually anglicized. However, there is quite a large group of French loan words and phrases most of which are pronounced in a similar way to the way a French person would say them, e.g. *nouveau riche* /ˌnuːvəʊ ˈriːʃ/ (an expression to describe a person who has recently become rich and likes to show it off in a very obvious way). An advanced dictionary will give these words and phrases and their pronunciation.

a ● Focus on the information box and go through it with the class. Then give SS time to complete the task and elicit the meaning of the words and phrases. At this stage do <u>not</u> worry about pronunciation.

> 1 *faux pas* /ˌfəʊ ˈpɑː/ = an action or remark that causes embarrassment because it is not socially correct.
> 2 *déjà vu* /ˌdeɪʒɑː ˈvuː/ = the feeling that you have previously experienced sth that is happening to you now
> 3 *avant-garde* /ˌævɒ̃ ˈɡɑːd/ = new and very modern, sometimes surprising or shocking

> 4 *entrepreneur* /ˌɒntrəprəˈnɜː/ = a person who makes money by starting and running businesses, especially if this involves taking financial risks
> 5 *cliché* /ˈkliːʃeɪ/ = a phrase which has been used so often it loses its meaning and interest
> 6 *bouquet* /buˈkeɪ/ = a bunch of flowers arranged in an attractive way
> 7 *fiancé* /fiˈɒnseɪ/ = the man that a woman is engaged to (*fiancée* for a woman)

b ● **2.11** Play the CD once all the way through, then sentence by sentence for SS to repeat the French word or phrase. Then get individual SS to say the sentences.

Extra challenge

You could write on the board all or some of the following French words / phrases used in English and ask SS to tell you what they mean and how they are pronounced: *apéritif, art nouveau, au pair, bourgeois, café, chauffeur, connoisseur, croissant, cuisine, décor, denouement, genre, Grand Prix, piste, raconteur, sabotage*, etc.

2.11	CD1 Track 31

1 I made a real faux pas when I mentioned his ex-wife.
2 When we were introduced I had a sense of déjà vu, though I knew we'd never met before.
3 For our first date, he took me to a concert of avant-garde music – there was no second date.
4 She's engaged to a well-known local entrepreneur.
5 I know it's a cliché, but it really was love at first sight.
6 On our anniversary, he always buys a huge bouquet of flowers – he's so predictable!
7 I met Jane's fiancé last night. They told me they're getting married next year.

3 VOCABULARY phrases with *get*

a ● Give SS a few moments to complete the task and check answers.

a get your own back	b get over

b ● Tell SS to go to **Vocabulary Bank** *get* on *p.160*. Focus on section **1 Expressions with *get*** and get SS to do it individually or in pairs. Check answers and elicit / model the pronunciation of tricky phrases as necessary.

⚠ Remind SS that, as *get* is a very common verb, idioms with *get* are likely to be found in the dictionary under the next full word, e.g. *get on sb's nerves* will be under *nerves*; *Get a life* under *life*, etc.

> 1 get the impression = think, have an idea or opinion
> 2 get a shock = be very surprised, especially by sth unpleasant
> 3 get the chance = have the opportunity
> 4 get the joke = understand a joke
> 5 get to know = discover what sb or sth is really like
> 6 get hold of = make contact with
> 7 get rid of = throw away, make yourself free of sb / sth
> 8 get my own back on = take revenge on sb
> 9 get into trouble = find yourself in a situation in which you can be criticized or punished
> 10 get out of the way = move to one side to allow sb or sth to pass

- Now focus on section **2 Idioms with** *get* and get SS to do it individually or in pairs. Check answers and elicit what the phrases mean.

1 I	3 A	5 D	7 E	9 H
2 J	4 F	6 C	8 B	10 G

- Highlight especially that:
  - *Get real* = see things as they really are, don't act in a stupid / unreasonable way
  - *Get a life* = used to talk about your own life or to tell sb to do sth more exciting with their life
  - *get on sb's nerves* = to annoy sb
  - *get your act together* = to organize yourself more effectively in order to be able to achieve sth
  - *get on like a house on fire* = to get on very well with sb
  - *get the wrong end of the stick* = to misunderstand sb when they explain a situation to you or plans / arrangements
  - *to be getting on* (always in the continuous form) = to be getting old
  - *get the message* = understand what sb is trying to tell you
  - *get your own way* = get or do what you want, especially when sb has tried to stop you
- Finally, highlight that all these idioms are informal and that some are rather rude, e.g. *Get a life!*
- Now focus on section **3 Phrasal verbs with** *get* and get SS to do it individually or in pairs. Check answers.

1 J	3 K	5 B	7 L	9 F	11 I
2 A	4 D	6 C	8 E	10 G	12 H

- Highlight that:
  - you *get over* a broken relationship, death, illness, or other trauma
  - *get by* can also be used to mean manage in the context of speaking languages, e.g. *I know enough French to get by when I go on holiday there.*
- ⚠ Remind SS that phrasal verbs with *get* will be found in the dictionary under *get*.
- Finally, focus on the instruction 'Can you remember the expressions on this page? Test yourself or a partner.'

Testing yourself

For **Expressions with** *get* SS can look at the expressions in the list and see if they can remember what they mean. For **Idioms with** *get* they can look at sentences A–J and see if they can remember the idioms. For **Phrasal verbs with** *get* they can look at definitions A–L and see if they can remember the phrasal verbs.

Testing a partner

See **Testing a partner** *p.18*.

Study Link SS can find more practice of these words and phrases on the MultiROM and on the *New English File Advanced* website.

- Tell SS that the expressions taught in this Vocabulary Bank will be recycled in the *get* questionnaire at the end of the lesson, which pulls together lexis and grammar.
- Tell SS to go back to the main lesson on *p.29*.

4 🔊 2.12 **SONG** 🎵 *50 Ways to Leave Your Lover*

- This song was written and recorded by Paul Simon in 1975. For copyright reasons this is a cover version. If you want to do the song in class, use the photocopiable activity on *p.233*.

2.12	CD1 Track 32

50 Ways to Leave Your Lover

(See photocopiable *p.233*)

5 SPEAKING & LISTENING

a ● Focus on the back cover of the book and establish that this is a real book. Get SS to read the 'blurb' (i.e. the information on the back cover telling you about the book) and ask why the book is called *Love by Numbers* (Because it contains a lot of academic research using statistics to try to answer common questions about relationships).

- Tell SS, in pairs, to discuss the six questions in the 'blurb'. Get some feedback from the class regarding their opinions on the topics.

b ● 2.13 Now tell SS that they are going to listen to the author of *Love by Numbers* talking about some research that has been done. SS have to listen for the answers to the questions in **a** according to the research.

- Play the CD once for SS to listen to the answers to the questions and then get them to compare answers with their partner. Check answers.

1 Yes. Researchers found that both men and women felt happier and were more committed to each other when their friends approved of their relationship.

2 A car. It is a small and confined space so ideal for an argument.

3 No. Research proves that 'like attracts like', i.e. we are generally attracted to people who are similar to us.

4 As good as any other method. According to research, the success rates of relationships that started online are very similar to offline methods of meeting people, such as meeting people at work or socially.

5 Only if you are single. Research showed that single people often got back together successfully with their 'lost loves'.

6 No. Most people felt anxious and sorry afterwards, not happier. Most of all they still felt angry.

2.13	CD1 Track 33

(script in Student's Book on *p.124*)

1 No relationship is an island; it's surrounded by friends and family, all of whom have something to say about it. In a study undertaken by Illinois University, researchers found that both men and women felt happier and were more committed to each other when their friends approved of their relationship. When friends tell a couple that they are a good match, and how much they enjoy going out with them, that couple start believing that they really are a couple. Also when a couple stays together for a while, their two groups of friends start to make friends with each other, and as a result the couple's relationship gets stronger.

2 Cars are small confined spaces, which makes them ideal to fight in. A survey conducted for a driving magazine found that one driver in ten will be arguing with a partner within 15 minutes of starting the journey. About 40% of the arguments are caused by men criticizing their partner's driving, and another 10% by the man taking control of the car stereo. At least disputes about map reading can now be solved by satellite navigation!

3 Relationship research would say that it's conclusively proven that like attracts like, in other words that we are generally attracted to people who are similar to us. This research shows that couples usually share religious and political beliefs and are about the same age. They are fairly similar in education, intelligence, and what they think matters in life. Most people also go for someone as good-looking or as plain are they are. You may, however, be familiar with the phrase 'love is blind', suggesting that you can fall for anyone, should you get the chance to meet them. But psychologists argue that such 'blindness' is temporary: after three months you can 'see' again, and then you usually go off the person.

4 Today the Internet is one of the most popular ways for people to get dates. On the one hand, the opportunity to remain anonymous for a while is an advantage. People feel that they can express their emotions more readily online and get to know each other more quickly. On the other hand, people can lie more easily, the most common lies being about weight, age, and of course about already being married. But if you have reasonable expectations, online dating is a good way to start looking for dates. Increase your success by posting a photo and a truthful profile. Online agencies advise getting a photo taken where you look friendly, rather than seductive. Best of all, use a dictionary when composing your profile. The biggest turn-off, apparently, is profiles with poor spelling. But once you've found a date, will the relationship last? A study in the US of over 3,000 adults found that 15% knew someone in a long-term relationship that had started online and according to research the success rates of these relationships are very similar to offline methods of meeting people, such as meeting people at work or in a bar.

5 Early loves are incredibly powerful and, with the Internet, increasingly accessible. A survey in *Time* magazine found out that nearly 60% of people interviewed still thought about their first loves. In another study by Dr Nancy Kalish, California State University got randomly selected American adults to agree to be interviewed about their first loves. One third said they would reunite with their first loves if they could. Then, by advertising in the media, Dr Kalish got data on 2,500 first love couples who got back in contact with each other. With the ones who were single when they found their lost loves, things moved quickly with 40% of them together again within three weeks, and most of them then getting married (and still together several years later). But there was a different story with the couples who were already in committed, usually happy relationships. Most of these people had casually Googled their old love in a speculative fashion with no plan for what to do if they found that person. 80% of these people finished up getting involved with their lost love again, and generally they became unhappy as a result. Dr Kalish strongly warns people who aren't single not to Google lost loves because of the destruction it can cause families and relationships.

6 You've just been dumped by your partner and you want revenge. But will it make you feel better? In a Canadian study, the most popular methods of revenge were flirting with friends or enemies of their ex, damaging their car, or breaking something they own, and writing nasty letters or emails. The question is, what will the revenge achieve? Another study by Stephen Hoshimura at the University of Montana asked people what act of revenge they had carried out, and what they had wanted to achieve, and how they felt afterwards. The research showed that most people felt anxious and sorry afterwards rather than feeling any happier. But most of all, they still felt angry. It seems that unfortunately, for most people, revenge is *not* sweet.

c • Focus on the questions and give SS time to read them. Play the CD, pausing after each section and giving SS time to discuss the answers in pairs. Play again as necessary. Check answers.

> 1 When friends tell a couple that they are a good match, they help them to believe this is true. Secondly, if both partners' friends begin to make friends with each other, this makes the relationship stronger.
> 2 Men criticizing their partner's driving, men taking control of the car stereo, and map reading. The last one is becoming less common thanks to satellite navigation.
> 3 It is only a temporary condition. After about three months the person can 'see' again and they see what they don't like in their new partner and stop finding them attractive.
> 4 Advantages: Being able to remain anonymous, feeling able to express your emotions more easily online, and getting to know the other person more quickly.
>   Disadvantages: People often lie about their weight, age, or marital status.
>   Advice regarding profiles you post on a website: Increase your success by posting a friendly rather than seductive photo and a truthful profile. Use a dictionary when composing your profile as poor spelling is the biggest turn-off.
> 5 A survey in *Time Magazine* found out that nearly 60% of people interviewed still thought about their first loves.
>   80% of people already in a relationship who got back in touch with a first love ended up getting involved with them again.
> 6 Flirting with friends or enemies of their ex, damaging their car or breaking something they owned, and writing nasty letters or emails.

Extra support

If there's time, get SS to listen again with the script on *p.124*, focusing on any new vocabulary, and getting feedback on phrases SS didn't understand, e.g. because the words were run together.

d • Open out the discussion to the whole class and elicit different opinions.

LEXIS IN CONTEXT

e • 2.14 This exercise focuses on some useful expressions in the listening text and gives SS some practice in listening for a particular phrase.

• Play the CD for SS to complete the missing phrases playing again as necessary. Check answers and elicit the meaning of the phrases.

1 **good match** = being very compatible with 'matching' personalities
2 **fall for** (sb) = (informal) to be strongly attracted to sb; to fall in love
3 **go for** = be attracted by and try to attract
4 **go off** = stop liking
5 **long-term** = that is long lasting and appears to be permanent
6 **turn-off** = sth which stops you being attracted to sth
7 **getting involved** = starting to have a relationship
8 **carried out** = done

2.14 CD1 Track 34

1 When friends tell a couple that they are a good match and how much they enjoy going out with them…
2 …suggesting that you can fall for anyone, should you get the chance to meet them.
3 Most people also go for someone as good-looking or as plain are they are.
4 After three months you can 'see' again, and then you usually go off the person.
5 A study in the US of over 3,000 adults found that 15% knew someone in a long-term relationship that had started online.
6 The biggest turn-off, apparently, is profiles with poor spelling.
7 80% of these people finished up getting involved with their lost love again.
8 Another study by Stephen Hoshimura at the University of Montana asked people what act of revenge they had carried out…

6 GRAMMAR *get*

a • Focus on the task and give SS, in pairs, time to answer the questions. Check answers.

1 C	2 B	3 A

b • Tell SS to go to **Grammar Bank 2C** on *p.141*. Go through each example and its corresponding rule with the class, or give SS time to read the examples and rules on their own, and answer any queries.

Grammar notes

Apart from the many phrases and idioms involving *get*, *get* is also frequently used as a main verb, often as a more informal alternative to another verb, e.g. *get / receive*. In spoken English, *get* is also often used in certain grammatical structures, e.g. as an alternative to *be* in the passive, or instead of *have* in the structure *get sth done*. Here all these different uses are pulled together.

• Focus on the exercises for **2C**. SS do the exercises individually or in pairs. If SS do them individually, get them to compare with a partner. Check answers after each exercise.

a 1 becoming
2 buy
3 persuade / convince
4 have
5 received
6 catch / take
7 arrive / be
8 fetch / bring
9 be
10 persuade / convince

b 1 got my work permit renewed
2 get used to driving
3 nearly got killed
4 get my sister to babysit
5 get all the locks changed
6 got stopped
7 get my eyes tested
8 got bitten

• Tell SS to go back to the main lesson on *p.31*.
c • This exercise activates both the lexical and grammatical uses of *get* in the lesson.
• Put the class into pairs. Then get SS to read the questionnaire and tick ten questions they would like to ask a partner. SS take turns to ask each other their questions.
• Finally, tell SS to cover the questionnaire and get them to ask you some of the questions from memory.

Extra photocopiable activities

Grammar
get p.162
Communicative
Reconciliation? *p.188* (instructions *p.179*)
Vocabulary
get phrases *p.213* (instructions *p.205*)
Song
50 Ways to Leave Your Lover p.233 (instructions *p.229*)

HOMEWORK

Study Link Workbook *pp.20–22*

2 WRITING AN ARTICLE

Lesson plan

In this lesson the focus is on writing an article. The writing skills focus is on choosing a good title, paragraphing and discourse markers, and on making your writing more interesting by using synonyms and a richer range of vocabulary. This lesson does not have a **Useful Language** section; since the content of an article will vary depending on the title, it is difficult to pinpoint any often recurring language.

ANALYSING A MODEL TEXT

a ● Focus on the text type (an article) and tell SS that they may want to write an article for an English language magazine or website or they may be required to do this for an exam (such as Cambridge Advanced). There are certain tips and strategies that SS will learn in this lesson which will help them to write good articles.

● Focus on the **Key success factors** and go through them with SS.

● Focus on the task, and get SS in pairs to discuss what factors they might include if they were writing about their country, e.g. the way schools have changed. Get feedback and write their ideas on the board.

b ● Set a time limit for SS to read the article and see what ideas were included, and also to choose a title. Get feedback about which title they prefer and why.

> The best title is probably *Changing childhood*, which sounds more interesting and engaging than *How childhood has changed*. *My childhood* is not appropriate, as the article is about childhood in general.

c ● Now get SS to read the article again and answer the questions with a partner. Check answers. When checking answers to 4, elicit that the discourse markers used are either to introduce the main ideas (*Firstly*, etc.) or to express cause and result (*As a result, due to*, etc.).

> 1 The direct question engages the reader and tells him / her exactly what the article will be about. The question is answered in the conclusion.
>
> 2 The first paragraph focuses on the writer's memories of his childhood, and gives examples of how he spent his free time, e.g. playing in the street, playing board games with his brothers and sisters, etc.
>
> 3 Families are smaller and there are more only children, because parents both work nowadays, or can't afford more than one child. As a result, children spend a lot of time alone. Children don't play outside any more, because parents think playing outside is dangerous. Children play more on their own, because the popular toys today are computer and video games, which you can play without another person.
>
> 4 SS should have underlined *Firstly, As a result, Another major change, this is due to the fact, so, Finally.*

d ● Focus on the task and give SS time to find the synonyms. Get them to compare with a partner and then check answers.

> 1 these days, today, nowadays
> 2 boys and girls, youngsters, young people
> 3 by themselves, on your own
> 4 pastimes

● Now go through the **Using synonyms** box. Stress that it isn't that you can't repeat a word or phrase (*children* is used six times), but that also using *youngsters, boys and girls*, etc. makes the vocabulary more varied.

● You may want to suggest that SS could use a thesaurus, e.g. *The Oxford Thesaurus of English.*

e ● Focus on the task and get SS to try to do it without looking back at the article. Then check answers.

> 1 enormously
> 2 neighbourhood children
> 3 racing
> 4 hazardous
> 5 scarcely
> 6 could possibly afford
> 7 idyllic

Extra challenge

You could elicit other synonyms that the writer could have used, e.g. 1 hugely, 2 local children, 3 dashing / rushing, 5 hardly (ever), etc.

● Finally, go through the **Using richer vocabulary** box with SS.

PLANNING WHAT TO WRITE

a ● Focus on the task and article titles, and give SS time to choose a topic to brainstorm in pairs.

● Get brief feedback from different pairs for the three different topics.

● Then tell them to individually choose the two or three changes that they would focus on in their article.

● Get feedback asking SS why they have chosen these changes.

b ● Finally, get SS to individually think of titles for their article, and compare / discuss them with a partner.

● Get feedback and help SS to improve their titles where appropriate.

● Finally, go through the tips with SS.

WRITING

Go through the instructions and set the writing for homework.

Test and Assessment CD-ROM

CEFR Assessment materials
File 2 Writing task assessment guidelines

Lesson plan

In the first part of this lesson the person interviewed is Tony Hawks, a multitasker *par excellence*, well known in the UK as a comedian, author, composer, and charity worker. He talks about how he manages to juggle his different jobs and organize his time, as well as giving his opinion about the effects on us of modern technology.

In the second part of the lesson, people in the street are asked to say what piece of technology has most improved their life, what piece of technology they would disinvent if they could, and what gadget or piece of technology they waste most time with.

Study Link These lessons are on the *New English File Advanced* DVD which can be used instead of the class CD (See Introduction *p.9*). SS can get more practice on the MultiROM, which contains more of the short street interviews with a listening task and scripts.

Optional lead-in (books closed)

- Ask SS if they know anybody who has more than one job, or is doing a full-time job and bringing up a family, or who is working and doing another time-consuming activity (e.g. doing voluntary work). Ask how successful these people are at managing their time.

THE INTERVIEW

a • Books open. Focus on the photo and information about Tony Hawks. Then focus on the glossary and go through it with the class, eliciting how to pronounce the words.

Extra support

You may want to pre-teach some other words and phrases before SS listen to the interview (see script 2.15).

b • **2.15** Focus on the questions and give SS time to read them. Encourage SS not to write anything down when they listen the first time. Tell them that they should listen and try to get the gist of what he is saying, and then discuss the questions with their partner.

- Play the CD once (**Part 1**). Give SS time to discuss the questions and tell each other what they understood. Then play the CD again pausing after each of Tony's answers to give SS time to make notes and compare with their partner again. Play the recording again as necessary. Elicit and check answers.

1 He delegated work to another person. It didn't work because he finished up having to chase the person he got to help him to see where they were with everything. His system doesn't work particularly well.

2 He works for a while on one thing and then on another. He uses the metaphor of wearing different hats to refer to his different jobs.

3 Because he loves sitting doing nothing (basking) in the sun. (There is a type of shark called a basking shark.)

4 **Pros:** It is very convenient and allows him to get a lot of work done. **Cons:** He is totally reliant on it so if his Internet connection fails, he feels 'like a baby without parents.'

5 He mentions it as another example of how people today rely too heavily on new technology. If it fails, they don't know what to do as many of them don't even carry maps in their cars.

2.15 CD1 Track 35

(script in Student's Book on *p.124*)
I = interviewer, T = Tony Hawks

I You're a comedian, a writer, a musician, a composer, you raise money for charity, how do you fit it all in?

T Well, some days I don't fit it in very well at all, I feel that it's all closing in on me. I sometimes open up my emails, sort of ten emails all on a different thing, and so you do have to try and get organized and I've tried in the past to delegate and it didn't go terribly well because I got somebody in to help, but then you end up, sort of, just having to chase them and find out where they are with everything, so I usually, what I usually do is try to say right for the next hour I'm working on this, I've got this hat on for the next hour I've got that on, that hat on, and some days you just realize that you've just neglected something hopelessly and someone phones you up and chases you, or tells you off, but, I wouldn't say I'm the best person in the world at doing it, I could be much better.

I How do you switch off?

T I play the piano, I actually go, I quite like a bit of physical exercise, I'll go for a run or a swim, I'll play tennis if I can arrange a game with someone like that. If the sun's out, I just love sitting in the sun and just bask, I'm a good basker, I'd be a good shark. I've picked a ridiculous country to live in obviously for basking in the sun, but things like that. I also have started to do five minutes or so of meditation if I can, so I try to concentrate on actually trying not to think of anything, so just spend five minutes trying to just follow my breath and, because it's amazing, it makes you realize how busy your mind is all the time. It's always thinking of stuff and that's quite, I'm not very good at it, but it's quite good to do.

I What is your attitude to modern gadgets? Would you say you were more of a technophile or technophobe?

T I think I'm probably more of a technophobe really. I mean I'm aware of the amazing advances that we've had and how they can improve our lives, possibly, but I almost feel, to some extent, we'd be better off without them because we would then not be reliant upon them. So my problem is I am now utterly reliant on email. I find it incredibly convenient, I can get so much done. It is actually fantastic. However, if the Internet goes down, or the connection goes down, I'm like a baby without parents, or food, you know, I'm 'errr', I have to go to, sort of, get on my bike, cycle to an Internet café try to, so, and I see the same with people who have, kind of, satellite navigation in their cars, which I haven't got for this reason alone, is because if that goes down, I know they don't even have maps in their cars half the time, they're completely lost and they just sit there and get weepy, and you think, 'How did you allow that to happen?'

---

c • **2.16** Focus on the task. Play the CD once (**Part 2**) and tell SS just to listen. Then give SS time to discuss the questions and tell each other what they understood. Now play the CD again pausing after each of Tony's answers to give SS time to make notes and compare with their partner again. Play the recording again as necessary. Elicit and check answers.

1 Remote controls, which enable us to 'flick round the channels', have been very bad for our attention spans and made us impatient as they encourage us to want everything (e.g. entertainment) immediately at the touch of a button.

2 They had five remote controls (all for different appliances) and he couldn't work out which one controlled the TV so he missed the match.

3 He feels nostalgic for the fact that there was no TV then in the daytime.

4 They had no TV on a Thursday. He thinks the idea of one day a week without TV should be reintroduced so everyone would go to the theatre, visit friends, or make their own entertainment.

5 He predicts that technology will grow and grow until it reaches 'meltdown' and we can no longer cope. The Internet might collapse from overuse, satellites collide, etc.

6 If there is a technological meltdown, the new heroes will be people with simple skills like how to grow things, how to build things.

2.16   CD1 Track 36

(script in Student's Book on *p.124*)

I Are there any gadgets you'd like to ban?

T Well, I don't know whether I'd ban it, but I'd certainly like to, you wouldn't expect me to say this probably, but I would like manufacturers to stop making things with remote controls. I don't know what was going on with that, I mean, the idea, just take a television. If you can't be bothered to get up and walk six feet to turn over the channel, you don't deserve a television, you know. OK, if you're disabled or something like that, then that's different, but for the general members of the public sitting there and just flicking round the channels, that I think has been disastrous for our attention spans, because, they're, people are so impatient, they want things immediately, they want entertainment, they want everything instantly and I think that remote control was the beginning of this. And the worst thing about remote controls is that because they have them for everything, you go into somebody's house, and they say, 'Oh, just watch television, we're going out now.' I went to someone's house once and they went out and there was a football match I really wanted to watch and they had a great big television and there were five remote controls sitting on this table, one was for the stereo, one was for the VCR, one was for the, all these things, and I didn't know which remote control worked what, and I missed the entire football match because I couldn't turn on the television, it was on BBC1, it was on our main terrestrial channel and I couldn't watch it. And from then on I've had it in for remote controls.

I Do you ever feel nostalgic for simpler times, when there was less technology?

T I do, well, I feel very nostalgic for, I think it's something that you have to be careful of because I think it's something to watch as we get older, we can become nostalgic just for the sake of it, we go, 'Oh I remember', because I remember when I was going to school, television, there was no television in the daytime, and in a way I am sort of nostalgic for the fact that there was so little television. I read a while ago that in Iceland in possibly the 70s or 80s they had no television at all on Thursdays, because there wasn't enough power or whatever to deal with it, and I thought that was a fantastic idea that we should introduce. We should just have a day of the week where there's no television, so everyone would have to go to the theatre, they'd have to go round to their friend's house, make their own entertainment, all of that sort of stuff.

I How do you imagine the future? Do you think we'll become more dependent on technology or do you think there will be a backlash against it?

T I don't think there'll be a backlash against technology, I think we'll, and we'll keep on growing and we'll keep wanting more and more, but I can foresee a time, maybe not in my lifetime where there's a kind of a meltdown, where we simply can't cope any more, the Internet kind of explodes or whatever, I don't even know how it works, but it, it gets full up and starts to overflow or satellites bash into each other, all the things that we rely on, all the things that we build our whole system around, just, they were predicting it a bit in 2000, weren't they, when in 1999 they thought things couldn't cope, they were wrong, but I do think there may well be a kind of meltdown and then we'll have to rely on people with simple skills and farmers and people that can grow things, build things, make things will be the new, new heroes.

d ● **2.17** This exercise gives SS intensive listening practice in deciphering phrases where words are often run together, and introduces them to some common expressions and idioms used in spoken English. Focus on phrases 1–7 and give SS time to read them. Play the CD, pausing after the first phrase and replaying it as necessary. Elicit the missing words, and then the meaning of the whole phrase. Repeat for the other six phrases.

1 **to some extent** (= partly, in some way, to some degree)

2 **goes down** (*computers* PV = stop working temporarily)

3 you **can't be bothered** (= idiomatic way of saying *you don't want to spend time or energy on sth*)

4 I've **had it in** for (= idiom meaning *feel very negative towards*)

5 for **the sake** of it (= for no real or particular reason)

6 a **backlash against** (= a strong negative reaction by a large number of people)

7 in **my lifetime** (= during the time that I will continue to live)

2.17   CD2 Track 2

1 …but I almost feel, to some extent, we'd be better off without them…

2 However, if the Internet goes down, or the connection goes down, I'm like a baby without parents…

3 If you can't be bothered to get up and walk six feet to turn over the channel…

4 And from then on, I've had it in for remote controls.

5 …we can become nostalgic just for sake of it…

6 I don't think there'll be a backlash against technology…

7 …but I can foresee a time, maybe not in my lifetime…

Extra support

If there's time, get SS to listen again with the scripts on *p.124*, focusing on any new vocabulary, and getting feedback on phrases SS didn't understand, e.g. because the words were run together.

e ● Finally, focus on the question. Get SS to answer in pairs and then get feedback from the whole class, or do this as an open-class discussion.

IN THE STREET

a ● **2.18** Focus on the task and play the CD once for SS to answer the questions. Get them to compare their answers with a partner and then elicit the answers onto the board. Leave the three questions the interviewer asked on the board as SS will use these later.

Questions

1 What piece of technology has most improved your life?
2 If you could, what piece of technology would you disinvent?
3 What gadget or piece of technology do you waste most time with?

Technology mentioned: computers, TV, BlackBerries, the Internet, warfare technology, security cameras, and mobile phones.

2.18   CD2 Track 3

(script in Student's Book on *p.124*)
I = interviewer, M = Matt, B = Brian, A = Amy, Ma = Mark

Matt
I What piece of technology has most improved your life?
M I'd have to say the computer for the ease of information and able to get as unbiased opinion as possible, as opposed to some of the older technologies.
I If you could, what piece of technology would you 'disinvent'?
M The television. I think it's completely harmful to our society. It causes people to stop thinking as a whole. It's easy just to shut off and, you know, be told what to do. Instead of actually thinking on your own and deciding what you want to do for your own life.
I What gadget or piece of technology do you waste most time with?
M Do I waste most time with? Definitely the BlackBerry™. It's for work and for my personal use, so it probably consumes about 18 hours a day.

Brian
I What piece of technology has most improved your life?
B I think the Internet and just being able to stay in touch with people who are far far away from me. So either talking to them or sending messages to them or sharing pictures and movies. I think it's really brought, my family is all over the place and so it's been nice to be able to keep in touch using the Internet.
I If you could, what piece of technology would you 'disinvent'?
B 'Disinvent'? Well, probably any warfare technology, I think we've gotten a little over our heads with regard to weapons and some of the privacy issues I think. There's cameras everywhere and I think you have to be careful with how pervasive your cameras are and who gets to see what turns up on cameras.
I What gadget or piece of technology do you waste most time with?
B Do I waste most time with? It's probably the television. It's great to learn new things, but it's on more than I would probably like to admit. So television I think. If I could just get rid of it, I would.

Amy
I What piece of technology has most improved your life?
A It's quite a typical answer, but it will have to be the mobile phone, because I feel a lot more in contact with friends and it's so much easier to communicate and as a girl you feel a lot safer being on your own. So having a mobile phone has definitely revolutionized life for me.
I If you could, what piece of technology would you 'disinvent'?
A It's really useful, but I think email has actually made people a lot more lax in the way they communicate with each other. So it stops people talking directly, so I would probably monitor the use of email rather than completely 'disinvent' it.
I What gadget or piece of technology do you waste most time with?
A The Internet, definitely. I go on lots of social networking sites and just browse in the web all the time in the evenings and it wastes a lot of time when you don't realize how long the time it takes up.

Mark
I What piece of technology has most improved your life?
Ma I would probably say bicycle, the bicycle, simply because it's my means of transport for getting to work, it's much faster than the car or the bus and, you know, it's a healthy option, it's environmentally friendly as well. So all in all, I'd say yeah, it's certainly improved my life.
I If you could, what piece of technology would you 'disinvent'?
Ma That's very tricky really. I think it's probably... I think it's more not about the technology, it's more about the way in which people use pieces of technology, to be honest. There are lots of, you know, people speaking on their phones in public, that sort of thing, it's quite irritating, but it's how people are using the phone, not about the actual phone itself. So if I really had to think of something to 'disinvent' then, I don't know, a weapon of war perhaps or something like that.
I What gadget or piece of technology do you waste most time with?
Ma The Internet, definitely, the amount of time I spend Googling pointless, pointless things...

b ● Focus on the task and give SS time to read questions 1–7. Play the recording again all the way through and then give SS time to answer the questions. Then play it again pausing after each speaker, this time for SS to check their answers. Play again as necessary. Elicit and check answers.

---

1 Amy (speaker 3)
2 Mark (speaker 4)
3 Brian (speaker 2) and Amy (speaker 3)
4 Mark (speaker 4)
5 Matt (speaker 1)
6 Brian (speaker 2)
7 Matt (speaker 1)

---

c ● **2.19** Focus on the phrases and give SS time to read them. Play the CD, pausing after the first phrase and replaying it as necessary. Elicit the missing words, and then the meaning of the whole phrase. Repeat for the other four phrases.

1 **to shut off** (= informal way of saying *stop thinking*)
2 **all over the place** (= informal way of saying *in many different places*)
3 **what turns up** (PV = what is found by chance, here on the recordings made by security cameras)
4 a **lot more lax** (= careless, not strict)
5 **very tricky** (= informal way of saying *difficult or complicated*)

2.19   CD2 Track 4

1 It's easy just to shut off, and you know, be told what to do.
2 …my family is all over the place…
3 …and who gets to see what turns up on cameras.
4 …I think email has actually made people a lot more lax in the way they communicate with each other.
5 That's very tricky really.

Extra support

If there's time, get SS to listen again with the script on *p.124*, focusing on any new vocabulary, and getting feedback on phrases SS didn't understand, e.g. because the words were run together.

d ● Finally, get SS to ask each other the three questions that the interviewer asked the interviewees. Then get some feedback from the whole class.

HOMEWORK

Study Link **Workbook** *p.23*

2 REVISE & CHECK

For instructions on how to use this page, see *p.35*.

GRAMMAR

a 1 I used to have / I had
2 The boss appears to have
3 Did you really use to wear
4 ✓
5 I need to get my passport renewed
6 ✓
7 ✓
8 ✓
9 Could you get your brother to have a look
10 she was wearing trousers

b 1 (that) I had made a big mistake
2 seems to have
3 you get the tap fixed
4 is expected to resign
5 According to the *Daily Mail*,
6 it will get broken
7 There are said to be
8 They don't usually get to the airport
9 the dog had been sleeping on my bed all night

VOCABULARY

a 1 friendship
2 Freedom
3 neighbourhood
4 fear
5 shame
6 poverty

b 1 take
2 spare
3 get
4 cope
5 left
6 know

c 1 lost
2 pushed
3 life
4 nerves
5 message
6 way
7 out

d 1 By
2 at
3 before
4 off
5 down
6 away
7 out
8 over

Test and Assessment CD-ROM

File 2 Quicktest
File 2 Test

3 A

G speculation and deduction
V sounds and the human voice
P consonant clusters

Breaking the silence

File 3 overview

As in the first two Files, **File 3** balances consolidation and extension of known language with a completely new advanced grammar point. Lesson **3A** pulls together grammatical structures, e.g. modals to speculate and make deductions. The lexical area is verbs and nouns to describe sounds and ways of speaking. Lesson **3B** introduces SS to using inversion to add emphasis to a sentence, and expands their knowledge of adjectives to describe books. Lesson **3C** provides an overview of special uses of the past, e.g. after *I wish...* and *I'd rather...*, and the vocabulary focus is on expressions and idioms related to money.

Lesson plan

This lesson has two main contexts which contrast noise and silence. The first half of the lesson focuses on noises which annoy us in our daily lives, both in the workplace and also in shops, bars, and restaurants. SS first expand their vocabulary of verbs and nouns to describe sounds and the human voice, and there is a pronunciation focus on consonant clusters which occur in many of these words, e.g. *screech*, *splash*, etc. SS then listen to an interview with an expert talking about how businesses are not paying enough attention to 'how they sound', e.g. the music they play while customers are shopping or eating, etc. They talk about their own tastes in background music. In the second half of the lesson the focus is on 'breaking the silence', i.e. the silence that exists between us and the people we see every day in the street or on the bus. This part begins with a grammar focus on speculation and deduction. SS then read about, and discuss, an experiment done by an Irish photographer who set out to speak to the strangers she passes daily on her way to work.

Optional lead-in – the quote

- Write the quote at the top of *p.36* on the board (books closed) and the name of the author or get SS to open their books and read it.
- Point out that Arthur Schopenhauer (1788–1860) was a German philosopher, most remembered today for his analysis of human will, which influenced many well-known thinkers such as Nietzsche and Freud.
- Ask SS what *impertinent* usually means (rude / disrespectful especially to sb older / more important) and what it means in this context (annoying). Ask whether they share Schopenhauer's opinion about noise and elicit some examples of where noise interrupts in an 'impertinent' way, e.g. a mobile phone ringing in a restaurant.

1 VOCABULARY & WRITING sounds and the human voice

a
- Focus on the questions and elicit what noises SS can hear in their classroom, e.g. traffic noise, noise from adjoining classrooms, etc. and find out which noises, if any, affect their concentration. If some of your SS work, ask them what noises annoy or distract in their workplace.
- You may want to elicit from SS the difference in meaning between a sound and a noise. Although they are similar in meaning, there is a clear difference (a *sound* is something you can hear and has a neutral or positive meaning, e.g. *I love the sound of the sea*. A *noise* is a sound which is often loud or unpleasant, e.g. *the noise of the traffic was deafening*).

Extra idea

You could start the class by telling SS to be completely silent, and to listen. Then elicit what sounds or noises they could hear.

b
- Focus on the cartoons and on the text, and get SS to read it. Then go through the list of the most annoying noises, and elicit the meaning of *slurp*, *tap*, *crunch*, and *hum*.
- Ask SS which noise they think was probably voted the most annoying and get feedback to see which noise(s) is the 'favourite' to win.

c ● **3.1** Play the CD for SS to check their answer to **b** and get them to number the phrases as they hear the noises. Check answers and find out which of the noises they find most annoying and which don't bother them.

Other people's mobile ring tones	[3]
People making personal phone calls	[6]
People slurping tea and coffee	[2]
People tapping the keyboard of their computer	[8]
The boss's voice	[4]
The crunch of people eating crisps	[1]
The 'hold' music on the telephone	[7]
The hum of the air conditioning	[5]

3.1   CD2 Track 5

[Sound effects]
8 People tapping the keyboard of their computer
7 The 'hold' music on the telephone
6 People making personal phone calls
5 The hum of the air conditioning
4 The boss's voice
3 Annoying mobile ring tones
2 People slurping tea and coffee
1 The crunch of people eating crisps

---

d ● Give SS, in pairs, a couple of minutes to think of other noises which annoy them and then feedback suggestions onto the board. Contribute your own ideas too. Then take a vote with a show of hands to find out which annoying noise is the 'winner'.

e • **3.2** Tell SS to go to **Vocabulary Bank** *Sounds and the human voice* on *p.161*.

• Focus on section **1 Sounds** exercise **a**, and play the CD for SS to hear the sounds, and point out how the words are often onomatopoeic.

3.2   CD2 Track 6

(See Student's Book)

[sound effect] a gun shot   [word] bang
(etc.)

• Now focus on **b** and get SS to do it individually or in pairs. Check answers and model and drill pronunciation as necessary.

b	1 tick	6 creak	11 hiss	16 slam
	2 sniff	7 buzz	12 drip	17 crunch
	3 click	8 hoot	13 roar	18 snore
	4 splash	9 tap	14 whistle	19 rattle
	5 bang	10 slurp	15 hum	20 screech, crash

Extra challenge

Play recording 3.2 again pausing after each sound and elicit the word from the class before they hear it.

• Now focus on section **2 The human voice** and get SS to do exercise **a** individually or in pairs. Check answers, making sure SS know what all the words mean.

a	1 scream	4 whisper	7 stammer
	2 yell	5 mumble	8 sob
	3 giggle	6 groan	9 sigh

• Focus on exercise **b** and get SS to answer it in pairs before checking answers.

b (suggested answers)
nervous – stammer
terrified – scream
lose their temper – yell
not supposed to be making a noise – whisper
not opening their mouth enough – mumble
relieved – sigh
misses a penalty – groan
very unhappy – sob

• Finally, focus on the instruction 'Can you remember the words on this page? Test yourself or a partner.'

Extra idea

Get SS to focus on the photos at the top of the page and elicit the seven words (*buzz, drip, click, splash, whisper, giggle*, and *scream*).

Testing yourself

In both sections SS can look at the words in the list and check they remember the sounds.

Testing a partner

See **Testing a partner** *p.18*.

Study Link SS can find more practice of these words and phrases on the MultiROM and on the *New English File Advanced* website.

• Tell SS to go back to the main lesson on *p.36*.

f • **3.3** Focus on the task and play the first sequence of sounds. Elicit them from the class and write them on the board. Then elicit a sequence of events from the class using the five sounds and write the paragraph on the board, e.g. *It was 12.30 at night and Mike had just fallen asleep. The clock was ticking quietly. Mike was snoring loudly. Suddenly he woke up. He could hear the buzz of a mosquito, which had just bitten him. He got up and killed it with his hand.*

• Now repeat the process for the second sequence of sounds, and then the third. You could get SS to write their paragraphs in pairs or do this as a whole-class activity eliciting sentences and writing the paragraphs on the board.

3.3   CD2 Track 7

[sound effects]

1 clock ticking
  man snoring
  mosquito buzzing
  man groans 'Oh no'
  bang (of man killing mosquito)

2 street noise
  woman yelling 'He's got my bag!'
  door slamming
  car driving off
  cars hooting
  screech of brakes
  car crash

3 wind whistling
  owl hooting
  man and woman whispering sth
  opening creaking door
  woman screams

---

2 PRONUNCIATION consonant clusters

Pronunciation notes

Consonant clusters are groups of consonants with no vowel in between, e.g. **spr**ing. Pronouncing them may be a problem for SS according to their first language. The typical error is to insert a vowel sound before, after, or in the middle of the cluster.

a • **3.4** Focus on the information box and go through it with SS. Then play the CD for SS first to listen to the words (line by line) and then to practise saying them.

Extra support

If these sounds are a problem for your SS, play the words one by one, and pause getting SS to repeat them.

3.4   CD2 Track 8

(See Student's Book)

---

b • **3.5** Play the CD for SS to repeat the sentences one by one. Get SS to practise saying them quietly to themselves. Then get individual SS to say the sentences out loud.

3.5   CD2 Track 9

(See Student's Book)

---

c ● Give SS time to invent their sentences while you monitor and help. Then SS exchange sentences and say them.

3 LISTENING & SPEAKING

a ● Ask the question to the whole class and get opinions.
b ● **3.6** Focus on the photo and the task and ask SS what they think an *acoustician* is (a scientist who studies sound).

● Focus on the task and the three summaries and play the CD all the way through. Check answers.

> The best summary is **a**.

3.6   CD2 Track 10

(script in Student's Book on *p.125*)
P1 = Presenter 1, P2 = Presenter 2,
J = Julian Treasure, Sp = speaker

P1 …time's 18 minutes to nine. Companies are losing millions of pounds by making the wrong noises. Greg Wood, who always makes the right ones, is here.

P2 Thank you so much, Ed. Some noises can be really annoying. I'm sure we all like or dislike inappropriate music in shops for example – most of them made by companies. A new book called *Sound Business* claims that businesses which spend enormous amounts on their images are doing nothing about the way they sound. We sent its author, Julian Treasure, out onto the streets to explain.

J This is a typical London street scene. So we've stepped into a well-known mobile phone retailer. There is quite a lot of street noise intruding into this store when the cars go past and they've got, over the top of a very nasty hum from the air-conditioning system, there's some music playing – I don't know who chose it. I don't know what it's got to do with this brand.

So we've stepped in for a quiet coffee which unfortunately is a contradiction in terms in most of London. And this coffee bar has got no absorbent surfaces at all, everything is hard and reflective so all the sound is crashing and bashing around inside. There's a lovely buzz in the background, you can hear, from a huge chiller cabinet, which is rattling and vibrating. On top of that when the barista makes a coffee, your nerves get shredded and your brain gets fried, so I'm afraid this is a long way from a relaxing coffee that really it should be.

P2 Espresso machines feature with chiller cabinets and diesel engines as the top three most annoying noises, but the important consideration for any business is that sound changes the way people think and act, the speed at which they shop or eat in restaurants for example. According to independent academic research, appropriate sound can boost sales in a shop by 30%. Bad music has the opposite effect on shoppers.

Sp 1 I hate most of the music they play in shops and it's a very good way of getting me out the store very very quickly.

Sp 2 I kind of switch off when I go into shops, and often I have headphones on.

Sp 3 Well, it depends on the kind of music. It's kind of relaxing.

Sp 4 I don't like it. I think it's too noisy. You can't think anything so you just go out again.

P2 And then, there's the office. It's claimed that the noise in open plan offices can cut the productivity of knowledge workers by two thirds.

J So we're walking now into what I think is a fairly typical BBC office and it's filled with the most distracting sound in the whole world, which is other people's conversation.

As a business, sound is an enormously powerful tool, and at the moment, it's just like firing a machine gun at random. There's noise and sound coming out of businesses in all directions, nobody is conscious of it, nobody's managing it, nobody is aware of the effect it's having on the people that they're trying to affect. Many organizations spend millions on how they look and nothing at all on how they sound.

P2 This is what the experts consider to be the right sort of noise: randomly generated from a computer-based selection, and used in this case to soothe the nerves of passengers at Glasgow airport. Sales at the airport shops rose by up to 10%, demonstrating that good sound can also be good business.

---

c ● Focus on the glossary and let SS read the definitions. The three words / phrases are used in the interview.

● Give SS time to read the questions and then play the interview again so they can answer them. Pause the recording where gaps have been inserted in the script to give SS time to answer the questions. Get them to compare with the person next to them. Play the recording again as necessary. Check answers.

> 1 The book claims that businesses spend enormous amounts of money on their images, but do nothing about the way they sound.
> 2 a) street noise, (hum of) air conditioning, music
>   b) the buzz of the chiller cabinet which is rattling and vibrating, the barista makes a lot of noise when he makes a coffee.
> 3 Espresso machines, chiller cabinets, and diesel engines
> 4 a) Appropriate sound can boost sales in a shop by 30%.
>   b) Bad music has the opposite effect on shoppers.
> 5 One person, who finds it relaxing
> 6 Other people's conversation
> 7 It's totally random, nobody is managing it or is aware of the effect it's having.
> 8 Randomly generated music from a computer-based selection
> 9 It was used at Glasgow airport to soothe the nerves of passengers. Sales at the airport shops rose by up to 10%.

d ● Do this as an open-class question and elicit opinions.
e ● Focus on the task and get SS to answer the questions in pairs before having some open-class feedback.

Extra support

You could discuss the first two or three places with the whole class, before letting SS continue with a partner.

Digital extra idea

SS could watch a five-minute talk given by Julian Treasure – Google Julian Treasure's name and then click on the *Julian Treasure Profile on TED.com* link. It is quite hard but good for a strong class or as homework.

4 GRAMMAR speculation and deduction

a ● Focus on the sentences and give SS time, in pairs, to circle the right answer. Try to elicit why the other form is wrong.

> **1** It can't be (*mustn't* is not used for speculation / deduction.)
>
> **2** He probably hasn't (*probably* goes <u>before</u> a negative auxiliary verb.)
>
> **3** It must have been (*must be* refers to the present, not the past.)
>
> **4** is likely to call (*likely* is an adjective, not an adverb, and is always used with the verb *be*. An alternative form would be: *It's likely that the woman will call the police.*)
>
> **5** must be working (*he must work* refers to a habitual action, e.g. *He must work in that office as I always see him going in there in the morning. He must be working* refers to what we think he is doing now.)

b ● Tell SS to go to **Grammar Bank 3A** on *p.142*. Go through each example and its corresponding rule with the class, or give SS time to read the examples and rules on their own, and answer any queries.

Grammar notes

SS should be familiar with the use of modal verbs *may* / *might*, *must*, and *can't* for speculation; however, it is a structure which most SS do not use with any fluency until advanced level. Here the structure is revised, and other expressions for speculation or deduction using adjectives or adverbs are also presented and practised.

● Focus on the exercises for **3A**. SS do the exercises individually or in pairs. If SS do them individually, get them to compare with a partner. Check answers after each exercise.

> **a 1** must have moved them
> **2** ✓
> **3** it must be
> **4** ✓
> **5** She definitely won't like it
> **6** bound to be late
> **7** ✓
> **8** she must still be studying
> **9** ✓
>
> **b 1** probably won't have time to call in and see us
> **2** may never get over
> **3** should have heard the news by
> **4** can't have left my credit card in the restaurant
> **5** is bound to like the scarf
> **6** is unlikely to resign
> **7** must have been in love with her
> **8** you definitely lock
> **9** likely that the couple will get divorced

● Tell SS to go back to the main lesson on *p.38*.

5 READING & SPEAKING

a ● Focus on the title of the article and get SS to read the introduction (the bold paragraph) and look at the photos. Ask them what they think the article is going to be about.

b ● Tell SS to read the rest of the article to answer the two questions. Elicit answers from the class and deal with any vocabulary problems.

> Susie Rea's project is to discover more about the strangers she passes every day. The paradox her project highlights is that thanks to the Internet and TV we know what is happening thousands of miles away day and night, but we often don't know anything about the people we see every day in the street.

c ● Tell SS, in pairs, to look at the photos and to speculate about their ages, jobs, etc. using the questions given.

d ● **3.7** Play the CD for SS to listen to Susie describing the people and get SS to check their answers to **c** and take notes about the people. You will probably need to pause between each person to give SS time to take notes. Play the recording again as necessary. Elicit what other information SS can remember about the people and find out if SS were surprised by anything.

3.7	CD2 Track 11

(script in Student's Book on *p.125*)

1 All I knew of the man with the beard and the Panama hat was that our paths crossed at about twenty past eight in the morning on the street I walked down daily. The rest of his story was my own invention, until I spoke to him last week. Eiran is a self-taught jeweller and artist. He passes me each day on his way back from the synagogue at the end of the street where he's training to be a rabbi.

2 I pass number 220 once or twice a day depending on my route and from time to time I see an older gentleman standing outside it leaning on the gatepost. I wonder when I pass him what he sees and what he has seen. When I talk to him he tells me his name is Clarence, and he's from Barbados. He arrived in Britain in 1957 and has been here ever since. He is in his 80s and has close family who live nearby.

3 As I leave for work each morning, the man who cleans my street is usually positioned with his cart at the corner of the first junction I pass and he never fails to smile and say 'Good morning.' When I introduced myself to him, he told me that his name was Gerard and he's from Ireland. He moved to London when he was a child.

4 Always together, the young man and the dog who work at the hardware store are regularly to be found in the doorway of the shop, side by side, observing the comings and goings on the street. Shyan is from Iran and his dog is German. Both have lived in London for many years. Shyan tells me that he's not sure if he is a Londoner, but says that he kisses the ground every time he returns to the city from a trip abroad.

5 My mother is a doctor and she does not approve of chips. On my way home from the bus stop, I watch as people of all ages enter George's Fish and Chip Shop to partake of the fried fare from the smiling men behind the counter and I wonder who they are.
Stauros is from Macedonia and Cebrail is from Kurdistan. They are George's Fish and Chip Shop Men. They sell a lot of fish and chips and sausages and pickled eggs to the hungry locals. Do they eat chips, I enquire? Twice a day is the reply.

6 The bun shop at the end of the road is an old fashioned bakery where you can get a no-nonsense cup of instant coffee and a doughnut covered in hundreds and thousands. When I pass it, the two ladies behind the counter are always busy feeding the local community. Tara is from St Lucia though her accent has faded. Her nickname at work is Cleopatra because she spends so long on her hair. Rita is from the Philippines and she does not like eating buns.

e ● Open the discussion to the whole class and try to get some differences of opinion.

f ● Focus on some responses that were sent to the BBC website in response to Susie Rea's experiment and on sentences A–I, which have been removed from the emails. Highlight that there are two extra sentences (which are not from any of the emails).

● Set a time limit for SS to read the emails and complete them with the missing phrases. Get SS to compare with a partner before checking answers.

1 H   2 E   3 B   4 I   5 A   6 C   7 D

LEXIS IN CONTEXT

g ● Focus on the task and tell SS to try and guess the meaning from context. If SS don't have dictionaries in class, elicit guesses and then check answers.

nickname = to give sb an invented name, often informal and humorous and related to their real name or to their appearance, etc.
day in day out = every day for a long period of time
childcare = the care of children, especially while their parents are at work
apply to = is also true about / relates to
come round = visit sb in their house for a short time
acknowledge = show you accept that sth is true
small talk = polite conversation about ordinary or unimportant subjects
overly = too, very
commute = travel regularly from your home to your place of work, usually to a city or large town
nod = move your head up and down to show you agree, understand or as an informal greeting

● Finally, ask SS which phrasal verbs are used in two of the extracts (5 and 7) to mean *approach* (*go up to* and *come up to*).

Extra support

Ask SS to choose five other words or phrases they would like to learn from the text and get them to compare their choices. Get some feedback from the class as to the words or phrases they have chosen and deal with any vocabulary problems that arise.

h ● Ask the question to the whole class and elicit SS' experiences.

6 WRITING

Focus on the task and establish that the style of the email should be informal or neutral rather than formal. You could do this in class or set it for homework. You could display SS' corrected work on the wall or the school website for other SS to read.

Extra photocopiable activities

Grammar
speculation and deduction *p.163*
Communicative
Sound or noise? *p.189* (instructions *p.179*)
Vocabulary
Sounds and the human voice *p.214* (instructions *p.205*)

HOMEWORK

Study Link Workbook *pp.24–26*

3 **B**

G adding emphasis (1): inversion
V describing books
P words with 'silent' syllables

Lost in translation

Lesson plan

The main context of this lesson is books and the lesson begins with a quiz in which SS have to match famous first and last lines from some classic or best-selling novels. This leads to SS learning some new adjectives commonly used to describe books or films, and talking about their reading habits past and present, which provides a good opportunity for TT to find out how much SS read in English and for SS themselves to exchange information and advice about suitable books / authors to read. The grammar focus is on inversion after adverbs or adverbial phrases for dramatic effect. The second half of the lesson begins with some pronunciation work where the focus is on words with silent syllables, e.g. *literature*. The topic now shifts to the role of the book translator and SS read an article from the British press about the impact a translator can have on the style of a translated novel and on the reader. SS then listen to an interview with a translator talking about the pros and cons and some of the trickier aspects of the job, and the lesson concludes with an optional activity where SS have a go at making their own translations of novel extracts.

Optional lead-in – the quote

- Write the quote at the top of *p.40* on the board (books closed) and the name of the author or get SS to open their books and read it.
- Point out that Marcus Tullius Cicero (106 BC to 43 BC) was a Roman philosopher, orator, and writer.
- Ask SS whether they share Cicero's opinion and find out how many SS in the class are regular readers of novels a) in their own language and b) in English.

1 READING

a
- Put SS into teams, trying to get a balance of ages, and focus on the task. Tell SS that first they have to decide if they think the lines are first or last lines from famous novels, and then try to match them to the novels themselves. Set a time limit and establish that the winning team is the one with the most correct answers in the time limit. Check answers from the class and deal with any vocabulary problems.

1	F, I	3	L, G	5	F, F	7	F, D	9	F, E
2	F, J	4	F, B	6	L, C	8	L, A	10	F, H

b
- Give SS time in their teams to answer these questions before getting feedback from the class.

Extra support

You could discuss these questions with the whole class.

2 VOCABULARY & SPEAKING describing books

a
- Focus on the task and highlight that the comments about the books explain the meaning of the adjective.
- Give SS time in pairs to complete the sentences, telling them to try to guess the meaning of words / phrases they haven't seen before. Check answers and check SS know which syllable is stressed.

1	moving	6	intriguing
2	thought-provoking	7	implausible
3	heavy-going	8	fast-moving
4	gripping	9	depressing
5	entertaining	10	haunting

- You might want to highlight:
  – the literal meaning of *grip* = to hold sth strongly
  – *haunt* = literally what a ghost does, staying in a house after a person has died. Figuratively it means to keep coming into your mind.
  – *implausible* = not seeming likely to be true
  – *heavy-going* = difficult to follow or understand and so becomes tiring / boring
  – *intriguing* = interesting because unusual and with an element of mystery

b
- SS work in pairs. Highlight that the same book or film can be used for more than one adjective. Get some feedback from the class.

c
- **3.8** Focus on the short listening task and play the recording twice for SS to write down the four adjectives. Point out that the adjectives are not necessarily from **a**. Check answers.

great, fast-moving, exciting, incredible

- You may want to point out that Wilbur Smith is a white African-born author. In fact, *The Burning Shore* is set in Africa, not Australia. The speaker made a mistake.
- Highlight that when we talk about books / films in an informal context, we often use a variety of common adjectives, e.g. *great / amazing / incredible* as well as more sophisticated ones like *fast-moving, intriguing*, etc. However, in a more formal written review we would tend to use more the kind of adjectives in exercise **2a**.

3.8 CD2 Track 12

A There's an author called Wilbur Smith…
B Oh yeah, yeah…
A And I usually really don't like his work actually, but I read, the first one I read of his was *The Burning Shore*…
B Right.
A …, which was the first of about a five-part series I think, and it was just great, I had never read anything like this, it was so fast-moving, so exciting, great characters, set in Australia, and it was just incredible, it was just, I read it all the way through, straight away…

---

d • Focus on the task and the talking points. You could demonstrate the activity by talking about your own books, before getting SS to continue in pairs. When they have finished, get some feedback from the class.

Extra idea

This would be a good moment, if you have not done so already, to find out what your SS are reading in English and to suggest authors they might read. SS can share their own experiences with the class and make recommendations.

3 GRAMMAR adding emphasis (1): inversion

a • Focus on the task and highlight that the five sentences are all taken from real novels. Give SS time to complete the task and compare with a partner before checking answers.

> 1 B 2 A 3 D 4 C 5 E

b • Focus on the questions and elicit answers.

> The normal order of subject verb has been inverted. It makes the sentence more dramatic.

• Highlight that this is quite a formal device not usually used in informal conversation although it might be appropriate in a speech or lecture.
• Finally, ask the class to tell you the normal form for each phrase:

> 1 I didn't understand until later what he meant…
> 2 He had never been so unnatural…
> 3 Venus Maria was an adored and controversial superstar and she was also…
> 4 I haven't been ready to confess until now…
> 5 As soon as one campaign had come to an end.

c • Tell SS to go to **Grammar Bank 3B** on *p.143*. Go through each example and its corresponding rule with the class, or give SS time to read the examples and rules on their own, and answer any queries.

Grammar notes

Inverting the subject and verb after some (mainly negative) adverbial expressions is commonly used for dramatic effect in English. SS should be encouraged to use inversions where appropriate, but not to overuse them as this would make their English sound unnatural.

• Focus on the exercise for **3B**. SS do the exercise individually or in pairs. If SS do it individually, get them to compare with a partner. Check answers.

> 1 years later did I realize my mistake
> 2 had we seen such magnificent scenery
> 3 did they dislike her, but they also hated her family
> 4 we had read his autobiography did we understand what he had really suffered
> 5 had we started to eat when we heard someone knocking at the door
> 6 have I read such a badly written novel
> 7 the sun set did we put down our tools and rest
> 8 was the hotel room depressing, but it was cold as well

> 9 it was unusually cold did they light the fire
> 10 had he gone to sleep than there was a knock on the door
> 11 did I realize the full scale of the disaster
> 12 had I destroyed the evidence when the police arrived
> 13 has he regretted the decision he took on that day
> 14 I had spoken to the manager was the problem sorted out

• Tell SS to go back to the main lesson on *p.41*.

d • Focus on the task and give SS time to think of sentences. They could do this in pairs or individually and then compare with a partner. Go round monitoring and correcting. Elicit sentences from the class, writing some good ones on the board.

4 PRONUNCIATION words with 'silent' syllables

Pronunciation notes

As well as words having silent consonants there are also words in English which have silent vowels, which result in the words having a silent syllable such as *literature* /ˈlɪtrətʃə/, *interesting* /ˈɪntrəstɪŋ/, and *comfortable* /ˈkʌmftəbl/. SS will sound a little strange if they pronounce these silent syllables, and should be advised to cross them out if they occur in new vocabulary. SS should be encouraged to fine-tune their pronunciation of common words with silent syllables (like the ones in the exercise), which some SS may have been mispronouncing for years.

a • **3.9** Focus on the task and emphasize that SS don't have to write down the whole sentence, just the last word. Play the CD and SS write down the words. Play the recording again as necessary. Check answers, writing the words on the board, and eliciting the sentences.

> | 1 | literature | 6 | frightening |
> |---|---|---|---|
> | 2 | restaurant | 7 | medicine |
> | 3 | interesting | 8 | comfortable |
> | 4 | different | 9 | temperature |
> | 5 | history | 10 | dictionary |

> **3.9**   CD2 Track 13
> 1 He's a professor of English literature.
> 2 I loved the scene in the restaurant.
> 3 I thought the main character was really interesting.
> 4 The novel and the film were very different.
> 5 My worst subject at school was history.
> 6 I found the last part of the film really frightening.
> 7 I've just read a new book about alternative medicine.
> 8 The seats in the new cinema complex are incredibly comfortable.
> 9 It's important to drink wine at the right temperature.
> 10 If you don't know what *gripping* means, look it up in the dictionary.

b • Focus on the information box and go through it with the class. Then give SS time to cross out the vowels which they think are not pronounced in the words they wrote down in **a**. Get them to compare with a partner.

c ● **3.10** This time SS hear just the words not the whole sentence and check their answers to **b**. Elicit the answers from the class.

● Then get SS to practise saying the words to themselves quietly. Finally, elicit them from individual SS.

3.10		CD2 Track 14
1 lit[e]rature	6 fright[e]ning	
2 rest[au]rant	7 med[i]cine	
3 int[e]resting	8 comf[or]table	
4 diff[e]rent	9 temp[e]rature	
5 hist[o]ry	10 diction[a]ry	

5 READING

a ● Ask the question to the whole class and elicit responses.

b ● Focus on the task and give SS time to read the two translations and answer the questions with a partner. Then elicit answers from the class.

1 In the first translation (but not in the second) you find out the name of the piece of music in English. The piece is referred to as 'the overture'.

In the second translation (but not in the first) you find out that the caller was a woman, and the name of the piece of music in Italian. The piece is referred to as 'the prelude' (in fact it is normally referred to as 'the overture').

2 a) In translation 1 past forms are used to set the scene. The cooking of the spaghetti is described in detail (boiling, potful).

In translation 2 the 'dramatic present' is used. There is a quirky invented adjective 'spaghetti-cooking' to describe the music.

b) In translation 1 there is only one (long) sentence. In translation 2 there are four shorter sentences.

3 Students' own answers.

c ● Focus on the task and set a time limit for SS to read the article and answer the questions. Check answers.

1 The author thinks that translators are undervalued and underappreciated as their translation can make a huge difference to the style and tone of a book.

2 Birnbaum's translation, perhaps because his style is more unusual and original.

3 Because some critics think that her translations weren't faithful to the original novels – she made them too 'English'. She was also accused of translating major novelists like Tolstoy and Dostoyevsky in such a similar way that they were indistinguishable.

4 'a smooth lawn mowed in the English manner' meaning correct, neat, tidy, and dull, i.e. not wild or exotic

5 in order to make it more readable, much shorter, have a happy ending, and be 'more peace less war'

LEXIS IN CONTEXT

d ● Focus on the task, emphasizing that SS should look at each adjective / adverb in context and have a go at guessing the meaning of ones they don't know. Then, they should look at definitions 1–12 and match them to the adjectives / adverbs. Check answers and deal with any other vocabulary queries or problems SS might have.

1 barely	7 quirky
2 profoundly	8 lowly
3 arguably	9 staccato (Italian, musical term)
4 vast	10 neatly
5 bland	11 smooth
6 awkward	12 faithful

Extra support

Ask SS to choose five other words or phrases they would like to learn from the article and get them to compare their choices. Get some feedback from the class as to the words or phrases they have chosen and deal with any vocabulary problems that arise.

e ● Ask the question to the whole class and elicit opinions.

6 LISTENING

a ● Focus on the task and give SS time to think of questions they might like to ask the translator. Get them to compare their questions with a partner and then elicit them onto the board.

b ● **3.11** Play the recording once all the way through for SS to see which of their questions (if any) the translator was asked and answered.

3.11   CD2 Track 15

(script in Student's Book on *p.125*)
I = interviewer, T = translator
I What made you want to be a translator?
T It was something that I'd done when I was at university and when I moved to Spain it was difficult to get a job that wasn't teaching English, so I went back to England and I did a postgraduate course in translation. After doing the course I swore that I would never be a translator, I thought it would be too boring, but I kept doing the odd translation, and eventually I came round to the idea because I liked the idea of working for myself, and it didn't require too much investment to get started. And actually, I enjoy working with words, and it's very satisfying when you feel that you've produced a reasonable translation of the original text.
I What do you think is the most difficult kind of text to translate?
T Literary texts, like novels, poetry, or drama because you've got to give a lot of consideration to the author, and to the way it's been written in the original language.
I In order to translate a novel well, do you think you need to be a novelist yourself?
T I think that's true ideally, yes.
I And is that the case? I mean are most of the well-known translators of novels, generally speaking, novelists in their own right?
T Yes, I think in English anyway. People who translate into English tend to be published authors, and they tend to specialize in a particular author in the other language. And of course if it's a living author, then it's so much easier because you can actually communicate with the author and say, you know, like, 'What did you really mean here?'

I Another thing I've heard that is very hard to translate is advertising, for example slogans.

T Well, with advertising, the problem is that it's got to be something punchy, and it's very difficult to translate that. For example, one of the Coca-Cola™ adverts, the slogan in English was 'the real thing', but you just couldn't translate that literally into Spanish, it just wouldn't have had the same power. In fact, it became *Sensación de vivir*, which is 'sensation of living', which sounds really good in Spanish but it would sound weird in English.

I What about film titles?

T They're horrific, too. People always complain that they've not been translated accurately, but of course it's impossible because sometimes a literal translation just doesn't work.

I For example?

T OK, well, think of, you know the Julie Andrews film, 'The Sound of Music'? Well, that works in English because it's a phrase, that you know, like 'I can hear the sound of music'. But it doesn't work at all in other languages, and in Spanish it was called *Sonrisas y lágrimas* which means 'Smiles and tears', in German it was called *Meine Lieder, Meine Träume*, which means 'My songs, my dreams', and in Italian it was *Tutti insieme Appassionatamente*, which means I think 'All together passionately' or I don't know something like that! In fact, I think it was translated differently all over the world.

I Do you think there are special problems translating film scripts, for the subtitles?

T Yes, a lot. There are special constraints, for example the translation has to fit on the screen as the actor is speaking, and so sometimes the translation is a paraphrase rather than a direct translation, and of course, going back to untranslatable things, really the big problems are cultural, and humour, because they're just not the same. You can get across the idea, but you might need pages to explain it, and you know, by that time the film's moved on.

I also sometimes think that the translators are given the film on DVD, I mean, you know, rather than a written script, and that sometimes they've simply misheard or they didn't understand what the people said. And that's the only explanation I can come up with for some of the mistranslations that I've seen. Although sometimes it might be that some things like humour and jokes, especially ones which depend on wordplay are just, you know they're simply untranslatable. And often it's very difficult to get the right register, for example with slang and swear words, because if you literally translate taboo words, swear words, even if they exist in the other language they may well be far more offensive.

I What are the pros and cons of being a translator?

T Well, it's a lonely job, I suppose, you know you're on your own most of the time, it's hard work, you're sitting there and, you know, you're working long hours, and you can't programme things because you don't know when more work is going to come in, and people have always got tight deadlines. You know, it's really rare that somebody'll ring you up and say, 'I want this translation in three months' time.' That just doesn't really happen.

I And the pros?

T Well, the pros are that it gives you freedom, because you can do it anywhere if you've got an Internet connection and electricity, and I suppose you can organize your time, because you're freelance, you know, you're your own boss, which is good. I like that.

I What advice would you give someone who's thinking of going into translation?

T I'd say that in addition to the language, get a speciality. Do another course in anything that interests you, like economics, law, history, art, because you really need to know about the subjects that you're translating into.

c • Focus on the task and go through the questions dealing with any vocabulary queries.
   • Play the CD for SS to answer the questions, pausing if necessary after each question is answered (see spaces in the script). Play the CD again as necessary. Get SS to compare with a partner and check answers.

| 1 c | 2 c | 3 b | 4 c | 5 b | 6 a | 7 c | 8 a |

Extra support

If there's time, get SS to listen again with the script on *p.125*, focusing on any new vocabulary, and getting feedback on phrases SS didn't understand, e.g. because the words were run together.

d • Ask this question to the whole class and elicit opinions.

7 WRITING

a • Focus on the task and ask SS to do it for homework and bring it in to the next class.

b • When SS have brought their translations in, get them to read each other's and see if they can identify the novels.
   ⚠ This activity will work best with a monolingual class who all know the same novels, and where you know the SS' L1.

Extra photocopiable activities

Grammar
adding emphasis (1) *p.164*
Communicative
Who wrote it? A man or a woman? *p.190* (instructions *p.179*)
Vocabulary
Adjectives and adverbs *p.125* (instructions *p.205*)

HOMEWORK

Study Link **Workbook** *pp.27–29*

3C

G unreal uses of past tenses
V money
P *ea* and *ear*

Are you suffering from *Affluenza*?

Lesson plan

The topic of this lesson is money and materialism. In the first half of the lesson SS read a review of a book by Oliver James in which he describes how many people in the developed world are being made depressed, anxious and unhappy by their obsession with money, consumer products, personal appearance, etc., a virus-like condition he has termed *Affluenza*. Then SS do a questionnaire to see if they themselves are suffering from the virus. The lexical focus is on words, phrases, and idioms related to money, and Pronunciation looks at the many different pronunciations of the letters *ea* and *ear* in English. In the second half of the lesson SS read an anonymous article which appeared in *The Times* newspaper in which a woman confessed that she wishes she had married for money rather than love. This leads into the grammar focus on special uses of the past tense after expressions like *I wish, I would rather*, etc. Finally, SS listen to a short lecture given by a Harvard professor about research into the correlation between money and happiness.

Optional lead-in – the quote

- Write the quote at the top of *p.44* on the board (books closed) and the name of the author or get SS to open their books and read it.
- Point out that Tennessee Williams (1911–1983) was an American playwright most remembered today for his play, *A Streetcar Named Desire*, which was later made into a film.
- Ask SS what they think Tennessee Williams meant by this quote (that it's easier to live off very little when you're young, e.g. when you are a student. When you are older, you don't want to have to economize on, e.g. food, heating, etc.) and whether SS agree with him and why (not).

1 READING & SPEAKING

a ● Focus on the lesson title and the task and elicit suggestions from the class as to the possible meaning of *Affluenza*.

b ● Set a time limit for SS to quickly read the product description and review of *Affluenza*. Highlight that they will have to interpret what they read to come up with a brief definition of *Affluenza* as it is not fully defined anywhere in the text. Elicit suggestions from the class.

Suggested answers to 1
According to Oliver James, 'affluenza' is a virus which is spreading through affluent countries. People with the virus define themselves by how much money they earn, the possessions they have, how attractive they look, how successful they are, etc. / An unhealthy obsession with money and material objects and values.

- Now focus on the second part of the task and elicit whether the review is positive or negative (positive). Ask SS which parts of the text they have underlined which show that the critic thinks *Affluenza* is a good book.

Suggested answers to 2
In this book he explores the idea further and it is terrific. (Highlight that *terrific* is a positive adjective. It often means *excellent*, e.g. *It was a terrific film – one of the best I've seen*, but can also mean *big*, e.g. *There was a terrific bang*. It <u>never</u> means *terrible*.)
A lot of readers…will want to cheer.
It's a wonderfully clear and cogent theory. *Affluenza…* is clearly recognizable as our way of life…

c ● Focus on the task and give SS time to read the texts again and answer the questions, comparing their answers with a partner. Check answers and deal with any vocabulary queries, e.g. *messed up* (= to be in a bad state), *show off* (= to try to impress others by talking about your abilities, possessions, etc.).

1 He travelled around the world interviewing people.
2 He wanted to find out why 'affluenza' is spreading and how we can strengthen our 'emotional immune system'.
3 'To fill up our emotional emptiness.' We buy things to make ourselves feel better.
4 Money, possessions, appearance, and fame.
5 When people buy things to make themselves feel better, it makes them feel worse, which then makes them want to buy more things.
6 Be a good person, worry about your interior self rather than your external appearance.

d ● Ask this question to the whole class and elicit opinions.

Extra support

Ask SS to choose five other words or phrases they would like to learn from the texts and get them to compare their choices. Get some feedback from the class as to the words or phrases they have chosen and deal with any vocabulary problems that arise.

e ● Focus on the questionnaire and set a time limit for SS to answer the questions.

f ● Tell SS to go to **Communication** *Have you got 'affluenza'?* on *p.117*. Here SS find that any 'yes' answer means that they have the virus. The more 'yes' answers they have, the worse they have the virus. Get feedback from the class as to how many people have the virus and whether they think the questionnaire is fair, e.g. by asking them which statements they think are negative qualities and which aren't.

g ● Give SS time to discuss the questions in pairs and then open it up as a class discussion.

2 VOCABULARY money

a ● Focus on the task and give SS time to complete the missing words. Check answers.

1 affluent, wealthy	**2** own	**3** luxury

b ● Tell SS to go to **Vocabulary Bank** *Money* on *p.162*. Focus on section **1 Nouns for money or payments** and get SS to do it individually or in pairs. Check answers and elicit / model the pronunciation of tricky words as necessary.

1 budget		**6** charge		**11** deposit
2 grant		**7** savings		**12** will
3 loan		**8** donation		**13** overdraft
4 fees		**9** fine		**14** lump sum
5 fare		**10** instalment		

● Now focus on section **2 Money in today's society**. Give SS time to read the sentences and discuss what the bold words and phrases mean. Check answers to **a** and do **b** as a whole-class activity.

a 1 **consumer society** = a society where buying and selling material goods is considered very important

  2 **standard of living** = the amount of money and level of comfort that a particular person or group has

  3 **income** = the money sb receives for their work
  inflation = the rise in the price of goods and services which results in a fall in the value of money
  cost of living = the amount of money you need to spend to cover the basic necessities, e.g. rent, food, transport, etc.

  4 **can't afford** = not having enough money

  5 **interest rates** = the percentage of extra money that you have to pay back when you borrow money from a bank

  6 **in debt** = owing money
  mortgage = money lent by a bank to buy a house

  7 **shares** = units of equal value into which a company is divided and sold to raise money
  stock market = the business of buying and selling shares and the place where this happens (also called the **stock exchange**)

  8 **currency** = the system of money that a country uses
  exchange rate = the amount of money you get when you change one currency into another

● Focus on section **3 Adjectives related to money**, and elicit that a thesaurus is a kind of dictionary which gives you synonyms for words. Get SS to do the exercise individually or in pairs. Check answers and elicit / model the pronunciation of tricky words as necessary

rich	**poor**
1 rich, wealthy	**1** poor
2 affluent	**2** penniless
3 well-off	**3** hard up
4 loaded	**4** broke

● Finally, focus on section **4 Idioms related to money** and get SS to do it individually or in pairs. Check answers and elicit the meaning of the idioms.

  1 D (cost a fortune = be very expensive)
  2 F (spend money like water = in large quantities)
  3 E (it's good value for money = its products / services are worth the price)
  4 H (can't make ends meet = can't live on the money you have)
  5 C (be in the red = have a negative bank balance)
  6 B (tight-fisted = mean)
  7 A (have more money than sense = have a lot of money but not know how to spend it)
  8 G (living beyond their means = living a lifestyle which they can't afford, i.e. spend more than you have)

● Finally, focus on the instruction 'Can you remember the words and expressions on this page? Test yourself or a partner.'

Testing yourself

For **Nouns for money or payments** SS can cover the definitions and look at the words in the list and try to remember their meanings. For **Money in today's society** they can look at the bold phrases and remember their meanings. In **Adjectives related to money** they look at the head words only and remember meanings. In **Idioms related to money** they look at sentences 1–8 and try to remember the idioms.

Testing a partner

See **Testing a partner** *p.18*.

Study Link SS can find more practice of these words and phrases on the MultiROM and on the *New English File Advanced* website.

● Tell SS to go back to the main lesson on *p.45*.

c ● Focus on the task and give SS time to choose the right word and to compare answers with a partner. Check answers.

1 broke (*penniless* too formal)
2 loan (*mortgage* is for a house / flat)
3 red (*in the black* = you do not owe the bank money)
4 in
5 loaded (*affluent* too formal)
6 exchange rate
7 standard
8 make

d ● Focus on the task and get SS to take turns to talk about people they know for as many categories as possible. Then have some open-class feedback.

Extra idea

Tell SS about some people you know first.

3 PRONUNCIATION *ea* and *ear*

Pronunciation notes

SS at this level should already know that new words that come up which have the combination of letters *ea* and *ear* need special care as there are many different ways they might be pronounced and no rules to fall back on. Instinct and a dictionary are SS' best tools.

a • Focus on the task and get SS to say the sentences individually or with a partner and to decide whether the pink sounds in each sentence are all the same or different.

⚠ If SS know the picture words from the Sound Bank, they can use these to identify the particular sounds.

b • **3.12** Play the CD for SS to check their answers, playing the recording again as necessary. Check answers.

> 1 Three different sounds: /eɪ/, /e/, and /iː/
> 2 Both the same sound: /ɪə/ (sometimes *really* is pronounced /ˈriːəli/)
> 3 Two different sounds: /ɜː/ and /ɪə/
> 4 Both the same sound: /ɜː/

3.12	CD2 Track 16
(See Student's Book)	

c • Elicit the seven sound words from the class (*chair, ear, bird, tree, egg, train, car*) and the sounds illustrated by each word: /eə/, /ɪə/, /ɜː/, /iː/, /e/, /eɪ/, /ɑː/.

   • Give SS time, in pairs, to put the words in the list in the right column. Get SS to compare their answers.

d • **3.13** Play the CD for SS to check their answers. Play again as necessary. Check answers.

3.13			CD2 Track 17
/eə/	bear pear wear		
/ɪə/	appear earring fear hear nuclear		
/ɜː/	earth learn		
/iː/	beat creak deal neatly please scream		
/e/	death jealous pleasure spread unhealthy		
/eɪ/	break steak		
/ɑː/	heart		

Extra support

You could play the CD word by word and get SS to say them. Then tell SS to cover the chart and look just at the words in the list and remember how they were pronounced.

Extra challenge

You could give SS some sentences with some *ea* / *ear* words you think they may not know, or be unsure of, and then get them to check the pronunciation in a dictionary. For example:

My brother has a **beard**.

I'm **dreading** going to the dentist tomorrow.

There was a cosy fire roaring in the **hearth**.

The hill was so steep I had to use first **gear**.

These water pipes are made of **lead**.

   • Finally, focus on the ⚠ box and remind SS to check new words with this spelling combination.

4 READING

a • Ask the class the questions and elicit ideas. SS can talk about people they know or celebrity couples.

b • Focus on the task and set a time limit for SS to read the article once. Then elicit reactions from the class for and against the woman who wrote the article.

c • Now set a time limit for SS to read the article again and then discuss the three points with a partner. Then elicit answers from the class.

> 1 At first she found it amusing that he had a relaxed attitude to money, but later when they had a family she began to get very envious of female friends whose husbands could provide them with a better standard of living than she had. She also gets frustrated that her husband is not ambitious.
> 2 Their husbands have better paid jobs, they live in bigger, more expensive houses, can afford private education, and can have several holidays a year.
> 3 She will try to convince them that they should look for a future husband with a very good income to provide them with a high standard of living.

LEXIS IN CONTEXT

d • Focus on the task and give SS time to work with a partner saying what they think the words and phrases mean. Encourage them to look at the phrase in context before deciding what it means. Check answers.

> 1 They can depend on their husbands to earn enough money to cover all their expenses.
> 2 made it difficult to live in the space they had in their flat and on the money they earned
> 3 not say what you really want to say because it might upset sb or cause an argument
> 4 try to get the job of deputy head at the school where he works
> 5 becoming thirteen, fourteen, etc. years old
> 6 wanting what other people have so much that it almost makes you feel ill
> 7 Even if he became head teacher, he wouldn't earn nearly as much money as her friends' husbands do.
> 8 complain about
> 9 do sth that corrects a bad situation
> 10 without her husband knowing
> 11 there are a lot of advantages to

Extra support

Ask SS to choose five other words or phrases they would like to learn from the article and get them to compare their choices. Get some feedback from the class as to the words or phrases they have chosen and deal with any vocabulary problems that arise.

e • Ask SS to choose which statement best sums up their opinion and then elicit opinions from the class. Try to find out if there is a consensus of opinion about the woman's attitude.

5 GRAMMAR unreal uses of past tenses

a ● Focus on the task and give SS time to complete it and check with a partner. Then check answers.

1 past
2 (a hypothetical) future
3 (a hypothetical) present
4 past
5 (a hypothetical) present
6 (a hypothetical) future
7 (a hypothetical) past
8 (a hypothetical) past

b ● Tell SS to go to **Grammar Bank 3C** on *p.144*. Go through each example and its corresponding rule with the class or give SS time to read the examples and rules on their own and answer any queries.

Grammar notes

SS at this level should be aware that past tenses are not only used to refer to past time, but also to hypothetical present / future time as in 2nd and 3rd conditionals. Here they focus on various structures which involve this use of past tenses, e.g. after *wish*, *if only*, *would rather*, and *it's time*.

● Focus on the exercises for **3C**. SS do the exercises individually or in pairs. If SS do them individually, get them to compare with a partner. Check answers after each exercise.

a 1	realized	6	had saved
2	lived	7	paid
3	were able	8	knew
4	didn't discuss	9	had gone / had been
5	stopped		

b 1 I'd rather you didn't smoke in here
2 I wish I could afford to
3 If only we hadn't painted the room blue
4 it's time you started to look / looking
5 If only he were less tight-fisted
6 Would you rather we came
7 I wish I had bought

● Tell SS to go back to the main lesson on *p.47*.

c ● Put SS in pairs, focus on the question prompts and highlight that SS have to ask *Would you rather...?* or *Do you ever wish...?* according to which they think makes best sense. Sometimes both are possible.

● Give SS time to decide which question stem is most appropriate.

● Demonstrate by asking SS to tell you what the first two or three questions are.

● Give SS time to ask and answer the questions and then elicit some answers from individual SS.

6 LISTENING

a ● Focus on the instructions, and tell SS they are going to listen to a university lecture given by a professor at Harvard University in the USA. Tell SS that this will give them practice in listening in an academic context, e.g. if they go on to study in an English-speaking environment.

● Focus on the three conclusions and get SS in pairs to choose one of them. Get feedback but don't tell them yet who is right.

b ● **3.14** Go through the glossary with the class and then play the first part of the lecture for SS to check their answers to **a**.

His conclusion is **b**.

3.14   CD2 Track 18

(script in Student's Book on *p.126*)
One of the most puzzling paradoxes in social science is that although people spend so much of their time trying to make more money, having more money doesn't seem to make them that much happier.

My colleagues Liz Dunn and Lara Aknin – both at the University of British Columbia – and I wondered if the issue was not that money *couldn't* buy happiness, but that people simply weren't spending it in the right way to make themselves happier. Liz had the great idea of exploring whether, if we encouraged people to spend money in different ways, we could uncover the domains in which money might lead to happiness.

We conducted a number of studies in which we showed that money *can* buy happiness, when people spend that money prosocially on others (for example, giving gifts to friends, donating to charities, etc.) rather than on themselves (say, buying flat-screen televisions).

---

c ● Now focus on the questions. Play the CD again, pausing after each question is answered (see spaces in the script) and giving SS time to discuss their answers. Play again as necessary and then check answers.

1 That although people spend a lot of their time trying to make more money, having more money doesn't make them happier.
2 Because they weren't spending their money in the right way.
3 The research showed that money can make people happier if they spend it on other people (prosocially), rather than on themselves.

d ● **3.15** Now focus on the multiple choice questions 1–5 for the second part of the lecture. Give SS time to read them, and check they are clear what all the options mean.

● Play the CD once the whole way through and tell SS just to listen and try to follow his arguments.

● Then play the CD again, pausing after each question is answered (see spaces in the script). Give SS time to discuss each question and choose an answer. Play again as necessary. Check answers.

1 b	2 a	3 c	4 b	5 a

3.15   CD2 Track 19

(script in Student's Book on *p.126*)

So what are the psychological factors involved when it comes to individuals and the feelings they encounter when they are giving away their money? Does it matter how wealthy you are? We found that it was the relative percentage of their money that people spend on others – rather than the absolute amount – that predicted their happiness. We did a study to look at the happiness of 16 employees of a Boston-based company before and after they received bonuses of between $3,000 and $8,000. This showed that the size of the bonus that people received had no impact on their long-term happiness. It was the percentage of that bonus they spent on others that increased their well-being.

In another study, we showed that spending as little as $5 over the course of a day, on another person, led to demonstrable increases in happiness. In other words, people needn't be wealthy and donate hundreds of thousands of dollars to charity to experience the benefits of prosocial spending; small changes – a few dollars reallocated from oneself to another – can make a difference.

Of course many of us equate having money with happiness, and a large body of research does show that people become happier as they move from being very poor to lower middle class, but after this point the impact of income on happiness is much weaker. Think of someone who makes $100,000 one year and $110,000 the next – do we really expect this additional income suddenly to make this person fulfilled, without a care in the world? Being informed about a raise certainly makes us happy, but the $10,000 doesn't make our siblings or in-laws any less difficult to deal with over the course of the following year. Although people believe that having money leads to happiness, our research suggests that this is only the case if at least some of that money is given to others.

We had one final question. We wanted to know whether *knowing* about the effect of prosocial spending might erase it, if people engaged in prosocial spending in a calculated manner in order to 'get happy'.

We conducted a research project in conjunction with the *New York Times* in which readers who had been told about our findings were invited to complete a brief survey in which they reported their happiness, as well as how much money they'd spent on others and on themselves so far that day. Consistent with our previous research, we found that spending more on others was associated with greater happiness among this sample of approximately 1,000 *New York Times* readers, even though the respondents had been exposed to our previous findings.

e ● Ask SS to what extent what Dr Norton says reflects their own experience, i.e. whether they agree that spending money on others makes them feel happier than if they had spent it on themselves.

7 **3.16** **SONG** ♫ *A Lady of a Certain Age*

● This song was a hit by The Divine Comedy in 2006. For copyright reasons this is a cover version. If you want to do this song in class, use the photocopiable activity on *p.234*.

3.16   CD2 Track 20

A Lady of a Certain Age

(See photocopiable *p.234*)

Extra photocopiable activities

Grammar
past simple and past perfect: unreal uses *p.165*
Communicative
Money questionnaire *p.191* (instructions *p.179*)
Vocabulary
Money *p.216* (instructions *p.205*)
Song
A Lady of a Certain Age p.234 (instructions *p.229*)

HOMEWORK

Study Link **Workbook** *pp.30–32*

Lesson plan

In this lesson the focus is on writing a review. The particular review chosen is a book review, but all the information could equally apply to writing a review of a film, play, or even a concert. The writing skills focus is using participle clauses and using a variety of adverbs of degree.

ANALYSING A MODEL TEXT

a • Focus on the text type (a review) and highlight that nowadays many people write reviews of books, films, hotels, etc., and post them on the Internet. They may also be asked to write a review in an international or final year school exam. The structure of reviews tends to be broadly similar, and you would normally include factual information, your opinion, and a recommendation.

• Focus on the **Key success factors** and go through them with SS.

• Focus on the task, and get SS in pairs to discuss what factors influence them to choose a book to read, or do this as an open-class discussion.

b • Focus on the task and the book review, and find out if any SS have read the book. Elicit that the author is Swedish so the English version is a translation. Set a time limit for SS to read the review and do the task individually. Get them to compare with a partner and then check answers.

> The strong points of the book   3
> The basic outline of the plot   2
> What happens in the end   DS
> Where and when the story is set   1
> The weaknesses of the book   3
> Whether the reviewer recommends the book or not   4
> How good the English translation is   DS
> Who the author is   1
> Who the main characters are   2
> How much the book costs   DS
> Who the book is suitable for   4

Extra idea

Ask SS what else would be included if this were a film review, e.g. who the actors were in paragraph 2, what their performances were like in paragraph 3, and maybe some mention of the soundtrack or the special effects.

• Elicit that a review would never mention what happens in the end (particularly of a detective or mystery novel or film) as this would put people off reading the book.

• Go through the information box with SS, and tell them that they are now going to look at a specific way of making the description of a plot more concise.

c • Focus on the task and the extract, and get SS to read the **Participle clauses** box. Check answers.

> *Because he is*, *he is*, and *who is* have been left out.

• Highlight that participle clauses are very common in written English, but very rarely used in spoken English.

d • Focus on the task and give SS time to rewrite the phrases. Check answers.

> 1 Believing him to be the murderer…
> 2 Armelle, forced to marry a man she does not love, …
> 3 Simon, realizing that…
> 4 First published in 1903, it has been…
> 5 Deeply ashamed of how he has behaved, …
> 6 Set during the First World War, it…
> 7 Hearing the shot, …

e • Focus on the task.

> *slightly* reduces the strength of the adjective and *absolutely* increases it.

f • Get SS to do the exercise in pairs. Elicit the meaning of *denouement* (= the end of a book, in which everything is explained or settled). Check answers.

> 1 ✓
> 2 *very* should be crossed out. It can't be used with strong adjectives like *fascinating*, *amazing*, etc. which already mean 'very interesting', 'very surprising', etc.
> 3 ✓
> 4 *rather* should crossed out. As it means 'quite', it is not usually used with a strong adjective such as *thrilling*.

g • Finally, get SS to discuss what differences in meaning / register there are between the adverbs in 1 and 3.

> 1 They all mean the same thing, but *a bit* is informal, whereas the others are neutral.
> 3 They all mean the same thing, but *pretty* is informal, whereas the others are neutral.

PLANNING WHAT TO WRITE

a • Focus on the task. Tell SS to choose either a book or film they have read recently, or one that they have read or seen several times and know well. Tell them not to worry if they can't remember, e.g. the names of actors or characters, as they can research this on the Internet when they come to write their full review.

• Set a time limit of about ten minutes for SS to write their paragraphs, using paragraph 2 in the review as a model. Monitor and help SS with vocabulary.

Extra support

Get SS in pairs to choose a book or film that they have both read or seen and do the task together.

b • Get SS to swap paragraphs with other SS and identify each other's books / films.

• Finally, go through the tips with SS.

WRITING

Go through the instructions and set the writing for homework.

Test and Assessment CD-ROM

CEFR Assessment materials
File 3 Writing task assessment guidelines

Lesson plan

In the first part of this lesson the person interviewed is Sarita Gupta, vice president of Women's World Banking (WWB), who explains the WWB's initiative to help women in developing countries escape from poverty by providing them with bank loans, which allows them to set up small businesses. In the second part of the lesson people in the street are asked whether they think they are good with money, whether women are better at managing money than men, and whether having more money would make them happier.

Study Link These lessons are on the *New English File Advanced* DVD which can be used instead of the class CD (See Introduction *p.9*). SS can get more practice on the MultiROM, which contains more of the short street interviews with a listening task and scripts.

Optional lead-in (books closed)

- Get SS to revise vocabulary related to money (Vocabulary Bank *Money p.162*). Put SS in pairs and tell SS **A** to test **B**'s memory (**B** has book closed or the page covered) by defining words, phrases, or idioms for **B** to guess. Set a time limit and when this is up SS change roles.

THE INTERVIEW

a
- Books open. Focus on the task and on the glossary. Go through it with the class eliciting from them how to pronounce the words and phrases.

Extra support

You may want to pre-teach some other words and phrases before SS listen to the interview (see script 3.17).

b
- **3.17** Focus on the questions and give SS time to read them. Encourage SS not to write anything down when they listen the first time. Tell them that they should listen and try to get the gist of what she is saying, and then discuss the questions with their partner.
- Play the CD once (**Part 1**). Give SS time to discuss the questions and tell each other what they understood. Then play the CD again pausing after each of Sarita's answers to give SS time to make notes and compare with their partner again. Play the recording again as necessary. Question 3 may require more attention than the others as SS have to extract the key points from quite a long explanation. Elicit and check answers from the class.

> 1 They discussed domestic violence, economic access, and education. They decided to focus on economic / financial independence for women.
> 2 They needed access to credit as they cannot borrow either from relatives (who are also poor) or from the bank (as they have no collateral).

> 3 The three innovations were: money is lent to a group of peers and they hold each other responsible for paying it back; the loan payments are broken into very small amounts that come out of people's daily income; an incentive system – the poor are first lent small amounts. If they pay these back successfully, they are then lent larger amounts.

3.17   CD2 Track 21

(script in Student's Book on *p.126*)
I = interviewer, S = Sarita Gupta
I Could you tell me who founded Women's World Banking and why?
S The idea behind Women's World Banking came out in a meeting that was held in Mexico in 1975. It was a United Nations first International Year of the Woman and really they were gathering women from around the world to discuss women and human rights and there was a small group that started to think if we could work on only one issue, because they were discussing domestic violence, you know, economic access, education, the whole plethora of human rights. So if we could only discuss one issue, sort of focus on one issue, put all our energies behind it, what would that be, what would be that catalyst? And they decided that it would be economic independence for women. So that if a woman has the access to financial independence, then she can choose, and she can have greater access to education, opportunity, well-being, and that's where the idea came about and Women's World Banking was really set up, the first mission was to give women all over the world a greater access to the economies in their own countries.
I Where did the idea of microfinance come from?
S The idea behind microfinance again goes back to the mid-70s. There had been, by that time, several decades of what we call 'the Western World' giving massive amounts of aid to the developing world and a realization that a lot of it was not working, there were still many people who were left poor. So, you know, Muhammad Yunus is credited as being the father of microfinance. He's an economist living in Bangladesh, a very poor country, and he looked around and he said, 'What is it that the poor lack? What is that they need?' And the answer is obvious: they need money. And all of us, in order to get started, have had access to credit. So, the poor can't get access to credit, they can't go to relatives to borrow because generally the relatives are as poor as they themselves are, and they certainly cannot go into a bank and borrow because they have no collateral.
I How did Dr Yunus solve these problems?
S There are really three innovations that he came up with that are brilliant in hindsight. One was, OK the poor have no collateral, but let's figure out a way to create collateral, which means collateral is basically if you're not going to pay back the loan that somebody's held responsible. So he came up with a lending methodology where there was a group of peers that were given the loan and they would be lending to each other and the group held each member accountable for paying back.
The second innovation that he came up with is that it is very difficult for the poor to gather a lump sum to pay back a loan, but if you can break up that payment into very small regular payments that are coming out of your daily income, then it's feasible to pay back the loan. So what microcredit did was break up the loan payment into these very sort of regular small payments.
And the third was really an incentive system, that the poor were not encouraged to borrow a large amount, they only borrowed what they could use in their business and then pay back, and if they paid back successfully, then they were eligible for a larger loan.

c ● **3.18** Focus on the task. Play the CD once (**Part 2**) and tell SS just to listen. Then give SS time to discuss the three case studies and tell each other what they understood. Now play the CD again, pausing after each of the case studies to give SS time to make notes and compare with their partner again. Play the recording again as necessary and check answers.

Case study 1
The Dominican Republic (DR)
She was making food in her kitchen and selling it to factory workers.
With the loan she was able to set up a 'cantina' in her living room and sell food and other things, e.g. beer. With a new loan she built an extra room on top of her house and rented it out. Eventually she was able to build a new house and rent out the old one, guaranteeing security in old age.

Case study 2
Jordan
She was young and looking after her much older husband who was sick. She could not earn money for herself or her children as it is not considered proper for a woman to go out and work.
With the loan she bought cosmetics and sold them from home to her neighbours (mainly women). This gave her extra money to use herself.

Case study 3
India
The woman and her husband were uneducated.
The husband and their son worked in the informal economy selling vegetables.
With the loan she bought materials and embroidered saris at home and sold them direct to a store. This way she was able to double her income without doubling her work as she did not, as in the past, have to go through a 'middle man', who took half the profit.

3.18   CD2 Track 22

(script in Student's Book on *p.126*)
I   Do you have any examples of individual success stories?
S   Oh, I love talking about individual success stories, because this is what sort of gets us up in the morning and, you know, gets us to come to work and stay late, and do this, this work. Since I've been at Women's World Banking I've been to the Dominican Republic, Jordan, and India, so I am happy to give you a story from each of the three countries.
The DR is a more established economy, if you will, and so the woman I met had already had successive loans she had taken from our partner in the DR and what she did was to start out, she was basically selling food from her kitchen, making excess food and selling it to the factory workers, took out a loan, sort of increased that business and then set up a little cantina out of her living room. So that along with food, she was selling cigarettes, beer, candy, etc. That business did well, took out another loan and built a room on top of her house and started to rent it out. And so over seven years what she's been able to do is to completely build a new home for herself and rent out the old one and this is going to ensure income in her old age, because at some point she's going to be too old to work in the kitchen, and to be, you know, standing on her feet behind the cantina counter and she's looking at these rental rooms that she has been able to put on as her, her old age security.

In Jordan, I'll tell you about a young woman that we met. You know, sort of the cultural norm in Jordan is that a fairly old husband can marry again and marry a fairly young woman, so the one that we met, her husband was now too old and sick so while he took care of having a roof over her head, she had absolutely no means of earning more money for herself or her kids, and at her socio-economic level it's not considered proper for a woman to go out and work. So the only thing that she was able to do, was she had taken a loan to buy cosmetics, and was selling them from her living room to her neighbours and this was considered to be an OK business for her because primarily she was dealing with other women, but it gave her that sort of extra money to use for herself. And then in India where I was recently in the city of Hyderabad, and Hyderabad is this up-and-coming city, you know, it's gleaming. Indians themselves are thinking of it as the next cyber city. But across town they have slums, where even now, both men and women have not gone to school, they're not educated, and their only recourse is to work in the informal economy. So the family that we met, the husband was a vegetable cart, a vegetable seller, so he took his cart and went out into the more affluent neighbourhoods. The son had dropped out of school to join his father to push a similar cart, and the mother had taken a loan to embroider saris. And she did this at home, sort of in her spare time and what she really wanted to do was to amass enough income so that she could cut out the middle man, because she basically got half of what the sari was worth, because she was handing it over to a middle man. So that if she could buy the materials herself, embroider it herself, and sell it herself to the store, she could in effect double her income without doubling her labour.

d ● **3.19** This exercise gives SS intensive listening practice in deciphering phrases where words are often run together, and introduces them to some common expressions and idioms used in spoken English. Focus on phrases 1–6 and give SS time to read them. Play the CD, pausing after the first phrase and replaying it as necessary. Elicit the missing words, and then the meaning of the whole phrase. Repeat for the other five phrases.

1   **focus on** (= give attention, effort, etc. to one particular subject)
2   **massive amounts** (= very large sums of money). *Massive* is also often used informally instead of *big*, e.g. *They have a massive house.*
3   in **hindsight** (= the understanding that you have of a situation only after it has happened)
4   **along with** (= in addition to, as well as)
5   **having a roof** over her head (IDM = to have somewhere to live)
6   **dropped out of** school (PV = to leave school early without completing your studies)

1 So if we could only discuss one issue, sort of focus on one issue…

2 There had been, by that time, several decades of what we call 'the Western World' giving massive amounts of aid to the developing world…

3 There are really three innovations that he came up with that are brilliant in hindsight.

4 So that along with food, she was selling cigarettes, beer, candy, etc.

5 …while he took care of having a roof over her head, she had absolutely no means of earning more money for herself or her kids…

6 The son had dropped out of school to join his father to push a similar cart…

Extra support

If there's time, get SS to listen again with the scripts on *p.126*, focusing on any new vocabulary, and getting feedback on phrases SS didn't understand, e.g. because the words were run together.

e ● Finally, focus on the question. Get SS to answer in pairs and then get feedback from the whole class, or do this as an open-class discussion.

IN THE STREET

a ● **3.20** Focus on the task and play the CD once for SS to answer the questions. Get them to compare their answers with a partner and then elicit the answers onto the board. Leave the three questions the interviewer asked on the board as SS will use these later.

Questions

1 Do you consider yourself good with money?

2 Do you think that women are better at managing money than men?

3 Do you think that having more money would make you happier?

Three people (Ian, Kate, and Jason) consider themselves bad at managing money. Two people (Sheila and Jerry) think they are good at it.

b ● Focus on the task and give SS time to read questions 1–5. Play the recording again all the way through and then give SS time to answer the questions. Then play it again, pausing after each speaker this time for SS to check their answers. Play again as necessary and check answers.

1 Kate (speaker 4)

2 Jerry (speaker 3)

3 Ian (speaker 1) and Jerry (speaker 3)

4 Sheila speaker 2)

5 Jason (speaker 5)

(script in Student's Book on *p.126*)
I = interviewer, Ia = Ian, S = Sheila, J = Jerry, K = Kate, Ja = Jason

Ian

I Do you consider yourself good with money?

Ia No, I think I'm pretty bad on the whole. It makes me anxious. It freaks me out. Yeah.

I Do you think women are better at managing money than men?

Ia On the whole, probably, yeah. I certainly think my wife's better. I think she and many women are better planners, I think. More sensible about these things. Yeah.

I Do you think having more money would make you happier?

Ia In a kind of banal way, I could get to do certain things more easily, yes, but maybe not in the bigger picture.

Sheila

I Do you consider yourself good with money?

S Yeah, I think so. I've never been in debt, so I think that's pretty good going seeing as I'm quite old now. And yeah, I spend a lot on shoes, that's my only weakness, I think.

I Do you think women are better at managing money than men?

S I don't really think it's a gender issue. I mean, I'm pretty good with my money, but my brother's rubbish, he's always in debt, but my husband's fine, so I'm not sure that there's a gender thing going on there.

I Do you think having more money would make you happier?

S Pretty happy as I am actually, so no.

Jerry

I Do you consider yourself good with money?

J I do actually, yeah. No, I do.

I Why?

J Because I never go overdrawn, I pay off my credit card, I try to make sure my savings get a reasonable rate of interest, I never run out of cash, I'm just a kind of an organized person money-wise.

I Do you think women are better at managing money than men?

J That's a tricky one. In some respects I think so. I wouldn't want to fall into stereotyping. I think men and women spend money on different things. I mean I do a lot of cycling, and if you see a man and woman out cycling together, the man always has a better bike. Always. It's quite amazing. So I think men like spending money on their things, whereas women might spend money more on family things, I don't know. So in that sense I think women have more of a perspective on money than men do.

I Do you think having more money would make you happier?

J I think having a bit more might. I think having a lot more it's difficult to say. I think a lot of people find large sums of money, if you won the lottery say, that would be quite hard to deal with, I think. But you know, an extra 10,000 a year I think would be just about right. Yeah.

Kate

I Do you consider yourself good with money?

K No, not at all. I spend it without thinking and just I'm very lazy looking for bargains and things, whereas I have friends who look really carefully for the cheapest option. I just can't be bothered to do that so I tend to spend money like water. It's awful.

I Do you think that women are better at managing money than men?

K Not necessarily, but now I think about it I think maybe women go, I know it's stereotypical to say, but maybe women go shopping more together as a sort of social activity, whereas men tend to, you know, I don't know, stay in their rooms or work or something. I don't know.

I Do you think that having more money would make you happier?

K I think it might, yes. I think I might be very happy with more money, I can, yeah, just not think about money at all, and spend all the money I want and go out, have nice meals, and go on holiday. That would be great.

Jason

I Do you consider yourself good with money?
Ja Not good enough, no.
I Why not?
Ja Why not? I'm not very good at making budgets and sticking to them.
I Do you think women are better at managing money than men?
Ja I think that depends. The ones I know probably are not.
I Do you think that having more money would make you happier?
Ja In New York, yes. In most places no.

c ● **3.21** Focus on the phrases and give SS time to read them. Play the CD, pausing after the first phrase and replaying it as necessary. Elicit the missing words, and then the meaning of the whole phrase. Repeat the process for the other four phrases.

---

1 It **freaks me out** (= informal way of saying you react strongly to something that makes you feel shocked, surprised, frightened, etc.)
2 pretty **good going** (= informal way of saying you are quite pleased with what you have achieved in a particular time period)
3 **money-wise** (PV = informal way of saying *regarding money*)
4 **bargains** (= things bought for less than the usual price)
5 **sticking to them** (= keep to a rule or limitation that has been imposed on you)

3.21   CD2 Track 25

1 It makes me anxious. It freaks me out.
2 …I think that's pretty good going seeing as I'm quite old now.
3 …I'm just a kind of an organized person money-wise.
4 …I'm very lazy looking for bargains…
5 I'm not very good at making budgets and sticking to them.

Extra support

If there's time, get SS to listen again with the scripts on *p.126*, focusing on any new vocabulary, and getting feedback on phrases SS didn't understand, e.g. because the words were run together.

d ● Finally, get SS to ask each other the three questions that the interviewer asked the interviewees. Then get some feedback from the whole class.

HOMEWORK

Study Link Workbook *p.33*

REVISE & CHECK

For instructions on how to use this page, see *p.35*.

GRAMMAR

a 1 Not only did we see the sights
   2 I think he might have got lost.
   3 ✓
   4 The waiter probably didn't notice
   5 it's time you went to bed
   6 ✓
   7 ✓
   8 must be baking
   9 ✓
  10 I'd rather you came

b 1 to arrive
   2 were we
   3 to have heard
   4 had they got / did they get
   5 hadn't bought
   6 be trying
   7 started
   8 had I seen
   9 work
  10 you didn't park

VOCABULARY

a 1 bite my tongue   4 cost a fortune
   2 beyond her means   5 spends money like water
   3 behind my back   6 can't make ends meet

b 1 slammed   4 sighed
   2 whispered   5 rattled
   3 whistled   6 screeched

c 1 buzz   6 fare
   2 drip   7 shares
   3 small talk   8 budget
   4 thought-provoking   9 fee
   5 bland   10 intriguing

d 1 wealthy   5 vast
   2 implausible   6 adhere to
   3 tight-fisted   7 profoundly
   4 penniless   8 vast

Test and Assessment CD-ROM

File 3 Quicktest
File 3 Test
Progress Test 1–3

4
A

G discourse markers (2): adverbs and adverbial expressions
V history and warfare
P stress in word families

History goes to the movies

File 4 overview

This File begins, in **4A**, with a second look at discourse markers, this time focusing on adverbs and adverbial expressions; the vocabulary focus is on history and warfare. In **4B** the grammar focus is on verb + object + gerund or infinitive, with a vocabulary focus on compound adjectives. Finally, in **4C** the grammar focus is conditional sentences, and the vocabulary covers two areas, phone language and adjectives with dependent prepositions.

Lesson plan

In this lesson the topic is history, as seen through the cinema, in historical films. The lesson begins by introducing the vocabulary of history and warfare through texts describing memorable scenes from historical films. The pronunciation focus is on shifting word stress in some of the word 'families' SS have just learnt, and they go on to describe film scenes of their own to each other. In the second part of the lesson the topic is historical accuracy in films. SS read the preface to an American book *History Goes to the Movies*, and then listen to a film critic discuss two films regarding their accuracy. Finally, the discourse markers, which SS have been exposed to throughout the lesson, are focused on and the lesson ends with the grammar put into practice though a communication activity *Guess the sentence*.

Optional lead-in – the quote

- Write the quote at the top of *p.52* on the board (books closed) and the name of the author or get SS to open their books and read it. Get SS to discuss what they think it means.
- Elicit that the film *Gone with the Wind,* which is set in the American Civil War (1861–1865), has a famous scene where the heroine, who no longer has any beautiful clothes, makes a dress out of a curtain. What the critic seems to be saying is that the film glamorized war and made it not seem as horrific as it really is.
- Ask SS if they think films tend to glamorize war or not, and elicit examples.

1 VOCABULARY history and warfare

a
- Focus on the instructions and get SS to discuss the films with a partner. Then open the discussion to the whole class. Finally, tell them that in general a film is considered historical when it is based on a real event, or is set in a historical period, so by these criteria all the films given are historical.

b
- Now focus on the three photos of film scenes and ask SS if they have seen any of the films and remember the scenes. If SS remember them, ask them to describe what happens in each scene.

- Focus on the instructions and the words in each list. Tell SS in pairs to work together to try to work out which word goes where, and to guess its meaning from the context. Encourage them to read the texts through once before they complete the gaps and to guess the meaning of any other new words, e.g. *shield.*

c ● **4.1** Play the CD, pausing after the first scene to check answers. Elicit from SS what they think the words mean and tell them that they will be going to the **Vocabulary Bank** to check. Repeat for the other two paragraphs.

Braveheart

2	overthrow	4	arrows	6	victorious
3	outnumbered	5	troops		

Gone with the Wind

1	Civil War	3	besieged
2	side	4	looted

Spartacus

1	weapons	3	rebellion	5	casualties
2	forces	4	defeat	6	capture

4.1 CD2 Track 26

1 The film is set in 13th-century Scotland. Mel Gibson plays the Scottish rebel William Wallace who tries to overthrow the English who ruled Scotland at that time. One of the most memorable scenes is the Battle of Stirling, when Wallace's army, hopelessly outnumbered, wait in an open field for the English to attack. The English fire thousands of arrows into the air but the Scots defend themselves with shields. Then the English knights on horseback charge at full speed, but at the last moment the Scottish troops raise their spears and the English knights are thrown from their horses and slaughtered. A fierce battle then takes place and Wallace's army are victorious. The scene is not a model of historical accuracy, but with its spectacular special effects and stunts, it's tremendous fun. 'They may take our lives, but they will never take our freedom!'

2 *Gone with the Wind* is based on the best-selling book by Margaret Mitchell. It tells the story of a manipulative woman, Scarlett O'Hara (played by Vivien Leigh), and an unscrupulous man, Rhett Butler (Clark Gable), who carry on a turbulent love affair in the American South during the Civil War. The Confederates, the side Scarlett's family supports, are losing, and Scarlett is living in Atlanta, which is besieged by the Union army. She escapes, and goes home, only to find her mother dead, her father disoriented, and her family home looted. She asks for food and is told the soldiers have taken everything. In this dramatic scene, Scarlett, starving and desperate, suddenly sees a turnip in the ground. She falls on it, pulls it from the ground and eats it. She is nearly sick, then rises from the ground, looks round the ruined land and vows, 'As God is my witness, I'll never be hungry again.'

3 This epic film tells the story of the rise and fall of a slave in the Roman Empire. Spartacus (Kirk Douglas) is trained as a gladiator, but he rebels against his Roman owner and escapes. He forms an army of slaves and becomes their leader. Although they have fewer weapons and are less well organized, they win several victories against the Roman forces which are sent to put down the rebellion. But a final climactic battle just outside Rome results in the total defeat of the rebel army, with heavy casualties on both sides, and the capture of many of the survivors, including Spartacus. Crassus (Laurence Olivier), the Roman general, promises the captives that they will not be punished if they will identify Spartacus. In this powerful scene, one by one, each surviving soldier stands and shouts out 'I'm Spartacus!' Crassus finally condemns them all to be executed in a mass crucifixion along the Appian Way.

d ● Tell SS to go to **Vocabulary Bank** *History and warfare* on *p.163*. Focus on section **1 Weapons** and get SS to do it individually or in pairs. Check answers and elicit / model the pronunciation of tricky words as necessary.

1	cannon	4	machine gun	7	bow
2	spear	5	arrow	8	sword
3	shield	6	bullet	9	missile

● Now focus on section **2 People and events** and get SS to do **a** and **b** individually or in pairs. Check answers and elicit / model the pronunciation of tricky words as necessary.

a	1	refugees	4	troops	7	the wounded
	2	casualties	5	snipers	8	survivors
	3	forces	6	civilians	9	ally
b	1	revolution	3	ceasefire	5	siege
	2	coup	4	civil war	6	treaty

● Highlight that *wounded* is also an adjective (*he was wounded in the war*) and that (*the*) *wounded* can only be used for deaths / injuries caused in wartime. For accidents in daily life use *injured* (adj.) or *the injured* (*The injured were taken to hospital.*).

● Highlight the collocations in the definitions, e.g. *heavy casualties, armed forces, a military coup,* etc., and the use of *the* in *the wounded* (*the* + adjective to refer to a group of people). You may also want to point out that the *p* is silent in *coup* /kuː/ because it is a French word.

● Now focus on section **3 Verbs describing warfare** and get SS to do it individually or in pairs. Check answers and elicit / model the pronunciation of tricky words as necessary.

1	overthrew	5	shelled	9	captured
2	broke out	6	withdrew	10	looted
3	blew up	7	surrendered	11	declared
4	retreated	8	defeated		

● Finally, focus on the instruction 'Can you remember the words on this page? Test yourself or a partner.'

Testing yourself

For **1 Weapons** SS can cover the words, look at the pictures and say the words. For **2 People and events** SS can cover the words, look at the definitions and say the words. For **3 Verbs describing warfare** SS can cover the **Verbs** column, look at the sentences, and say the sentences with the missing verbs.

Testing a partner

See **Testing a partner** *p.18*.

(Study Link) SS can find more practice of these words and phrases on the MultiROM and on the *New English File Advanced* website.

● Tell SS to go back to the main lesson on *p.53*.

e ● Focus on the task. You may want to elicit the first difference from the class before letting SS continue in pairs. Check answers.

> A **spear** is longer than an **arrow** and is thrown. An arrow is shot from a bow.
> **Survivors** are people who are not killed in a war or accident. **Refugees** are people who have to leave their homes because of a war or political situation.
> A **coup** is when a small group of people try to overthrow a government or change the political system. A **revolution** is when the mass of the population try to do so, as in the French Revolution, the Russian Revolution, etc.
> A **ceasefire** is when two sides agree to temporarily stop fighting. A **treaty** is when two or more sides sign an agreement.
> To **withdraw** means to move to another place for tactical reasons. To **retreat** means to move away from an enemy because you are in danger.
> To **defeat** sb means to beat them in a war or battle. To **overthrow** sb means to remove them from power using force.

f ● Focus on the instructions. Divide the class into groups of three and give each student a number (1, 2, or 3). Get them to re-read and memorize the information, and then to describe the scene in their own words.

Digital extra idea

You could show the class a clip of each film on YouTube.

2 PRONUNCIATION stress in word families

Pronunciation notes

SS sometimes make mistakes with shifting word stress in word 'families' (e.g. *history, historical*) because they tend to stress the same syllable as in the base word. It is important to point out that in many such 'families' the stress changes and SS need to check and underline the stress when they come across these words.

a ● Focus on the information box and go through it with SS. Then give them a few minutes to complete the chart individually or in pairs. Check answers.

See script 4.2

● Elicit /explain the difference between:
– *captive* (= person who has been captured) and *captor* (= person who captures sb)
– *civil* (= connected with the people who live in a country, or with the state) and *civilized* (= well organized socially, with a developed culture and way of life)
– *historical* (= connected with the past, e.g. historical documents) and *historic* (= important in history, e.g. a historic occasion)

● You may want to point out that *loot* can also be a noun when it refers to the object as opposed to the action.

b ● **4.2** Now give SS time to underline the stressed syllables. Then play the CD once or twice for them to check they have the right stress. Elicit that the 'families' where the stress changes are *civilization*, *execution*, *history*, and *rebellion*.

● Now ask SS, e.g. *What's the adjective of history?* and elicit *historical* or *historic*. Then get SS to test each other in the same way, taking care to stress the right syllable.

4.2   CD2 Track 27

capture captive / captor captive capture
civilization civilian civil / civilized civilize
execution executioner execute
history historian historical / historic
looting looter loot
rebellion rebel rebellious rebel
siege besiege
survival survivor surviving survive
withdrawal withdraw
victory victor victorious

---

3 SPEAKING & WRITING

a ● Focus on the information box and go through it with SS.

● Focus on the instructions. Remind SS that a historical film is one set in a historical period or based on a real event, so the term covers a wide range of films. Try to have the titles of a few well-known historical films to suggest for SS who are having problems thinking of one.

● Give SS time to make notes. Monitor and help with any vocabulary they may need.

b ● Put SS in groups of three or four and tell them to describe their scene, but without mentioning the title of the film, so that the others can guess it.

Extra challenge

Tell SS not to name the characters but to refer to them as, e.g. a man, a woman, a soldier, a slave, etc., in order to make it more challenging to guess the film.

c ● Set a time limit, e.g. ten minutes, for SS to write their paragraphs, or set this for homework. Tell them not to name the film, as you could then hand the descriptions out for SS from different groups to read and identify.

4 READING

a ● Do this as an open-class question and elicit opinions. You might want to point out to SS that this text is in American English.

b ● Focus on the question. Set a time limit for SS to read the text once. Get SS to compare with a partner and then check answers.

a

c ● Get SS to read the text again and choose the right answer. When they have finished, get them to compare with a partner before checking answers.

1 b   2 c   3 c   4 b   5 c

LEXIS IN CONTEXT

d ● Give SS time to go through the highlighted words with a partner and check they know what they mean. Explain the meaning yourself if SS don't have a dictionary handy.

---

female lead /liːd/ = the woman playing the main part
premiere = the first public performance of a film
the final credits roll = when the list of people involved is shown at the end of the film
plot = the series of events which form the story
dialogue sequences = a set of conversations
screen movies = show films (*screen* is a verb here)
the big screen = the cinema (you may like to point out that TV is sometimes referred to as *the small screen*)
period films = films that are set in a particular period of history
released = made available to the public
film review = a report in which sb gives their opinion of the film

---

e ● Get SS to complete the sentences with some of the highlighted words. Check answers.

1 released	4 plot
2 big screen	5 premiere
3 final credits	

Extra support

Ask SS to choose five other words or phrases they would like to learn from the text and get them to compare their choices. Get some feedback from the class as to the words or phrases they have chosen and deal with any vocabulary problems that arise.

5 LISTENING & SPEAKING

a ● Do this as an open-class question and elicit opinions from SS. If SS come up with a lot of things they think were inaccurate, you could write them on the board.

b ● **4.3** Focus on the instructions and the gist task. Remind SS that Joseph Roquemore is the author of *History Goes to the Movies*.

Extra idea

Get SS who have seen the films to predict how many stars he gave each one.

● Play the CD once and check answers.

Joseph Roquemore gave *Titanic* three stars and the critic agrees.
He gave *Braveheart* five stars and the critic disagrees – he wouldn't even have given it two stars.

4.3

CD2 Track 28

(script in Student's Book on *p.127*)

In the book *History Goes to the Movies*, the author Joseph Roquemore gives films stars according to their historical accuracy on a one-to-five scale – five stars means a film's very accurate and no stars means it's very inaccurate. I'm going to look at two of the best-known films that Roquemore features in his book.

The first film is the Oscar-winning movie *Titanic*, which was directed by James Cameron in 1997. The film *is* historically accurate as regards the events leading up to the collision with the iceberg – the Titanic was sailing too fast and the captain ignored warnings about ice. The collision and sinking are also very accurately portrayed with amazing special effects.

However, where the film falls down is in its characterization. I must say I entirely agree with Roquemore when he criticizes director James Cameron for what he calls 'class-conscious overkill'. What he means by that is Cameron depicts all the third-class passengers in the film as brave and good, and all the first-class passengers as selfish, stupid, cowardly, or downright evil. And this can't have been the case.

Then a large part of the film centres on the love story between Jack, a third-class passenger, played by Leo DiCaprio, and Rose, a first-class passenger, played by Kate Winslet. Obviously, these characters and their story are fictitious and were just added, presumably to sell the film to a younger audience. But many historians have pointed out that a romance between Jack and Rose is totally improbable, because at that time there was complete class segregation on board ship.

Roquemore also criticizes the film's portrayal of Captain Smith. He is made out to be indecisive and frankly useless throughout the disaster. But this contradicts everything which was said about him by survivors of the sinking.

And for me, though, even more indefensible was the film's portrayal of the ship's First Officer, William Murdoch. On the night of the sinking he behaved heroically. In his home town in Scotland there's even a memorial to him, but in the film he's shown taking a bribe from a passenger (in exchange for a place in a lifeboat), shooting passengers dead, and finally shooting himself in the head. In fact, the film company 20th Century Fox, who produced *Titanic*, were eventually forced to admit that there was no historical evidence that Murdoch did any of these things, and that they'd included these details purely and simply to make the story more interesting.

Roquemore gives *Titanic* three stars, describing it as 'Great pyrotechnics – mediocre history.' All in all, I think his assessment is about right. The main events are true but the characterization is definitely the weak point in the film.

Moving on to the second film, *Braveheart*, this is one of the films to which Roquemore gives five stars for historical accuracy. He gives the film five stars because despite what he calls some 'small fictions' he thinks *Braveheart* is, I quote, 'true to the spirit of William Wallace'. Well, that may be the case, but I'm afraid I have to take exception to the phrase 'small fictions'.

The historian Elizabeth Ewan described *Braveheart* as a film which 'almost totally sacrifices historical accuracy for epic adventure.' William Wallace is portrayed as a kind of poor primitive tribesman living in a village. In fact, he was the son of a rich landowner and he later became a knight.

You'll remember too that in the film Mel Gibson wears woad, a kind of blue face paint. Apparently, the Scots stopped wearing woad hundreds of years earlier.

And while we're on the subject of costume, in the film the Scottish soldiers wear kilts. No surprises there you might think, but in the 13th century, which is when the events of the film are set, the Scots did not wear kilts, and in fact, they didn't start wearing them until four centuries later.

Another of these 'fictions' is that in *Braveheart*, William Wallace has a romance with the beautiful French princess, Isabelle. However, the historical reality is that Wallace never met Isabelle and even if he had, she would only have been nine years old at the time!

Finally, anyone who's seen the film will remember the famous battle scene. The battle was the Battle of Stirling, so called because it was fought on Stirling Bridge in Scotland. Basically, the reason why the Scots won the battle is because the English soldiers got trapped on the narrow bridge. In *Braveheart* the bridge does not appear at all in the battle. In fact, Mel Gibson originally planned to film the scene on the actual bridge, but he found that the bridge kept 'getting in the way'. Apparently, when he mentioned this to one of the Scottish history advisors on the film, the man's reply was 'Aye, that's what the English found.'

Mel Gibson defended all the inaccuracies in the film saying that the film's version of history was more 'compelling cinematically'. Admittedly, it *is* a very entertaining film, and it does give you a strong feeling for William Wallace and how he must have inspired his countrymen, but I don't think you can give this film five stars or even two stars for historical accuracy.

c ● Focus on the task, and remind SS to take notes, not try to write full sentences. Play the CD until the end of his comments on *Titanic*. Then pause to give SS time to write. Let them compare notes with a partner and then play the CD again as necessary.

Titanic
All 3rd class passengers portrayed as brave and good, all first class passengers as selfish, stupid, cowardly, and evil.
Love story between Jack (3rd class) and Rose (1st class) totally improbable because of class segregation on board.
Capt. Smith portrayed as indecisive and useless, which contradicts everything said about him by survivors.
First Officer William Murdoch shown taking bribes, shooting a passenger, and shooting himself. No historical evidence for this (he is said to have behaved heroically).

● Repeat the process for *Braveheart*. Then check answers.

Braveheart
William Wallace portrayed as poor primitive tribesman – in fact son of rich landowner.
Scottish troops wear blue face paint – they had stopped doing this hundreds of years earlier.
Scottish soldiers wear kilts, which didn't happen until four centuries later.
William Wallace has romance with French princess, but he never met her – she would have been nine years old at the time.
The famous battle was fought on Stirling Bridge and this is why the Scottish won because the English got trapped. In the film it doesn't take place on a bridge.

Extra support

If you think your SS may struggle with the length of this recording, you could pause after each inaccuracy is mentioned to give SS more time to make notes and to lighten the memory load (see spaces in script 4.3).

● Finally, ask SS how important they think the inaccuracies are.

d ● Get SS to answer the questions in pairs or do as an open-class question.

Extra support

If there's time, get SS to listen again with the script on *p.127*, focusing on any new vocabulary, and getting feedback on phrases SS didn't understand, e.g. because the words were run together.

6 GRAMMAR discourse markers (2): adverbs and adverbial expressions

a ● **4.4** Focus on the instructions and sentences 1–5. Give SS time to read through them. Then play the CD, pausing after each sentence for SS to write the missing word(s).

● Check answers, and elicit for each discourse marker what its function is, i.e. what does it indicate the speaker is going to say next?

> **1 Obviously** = the speaker will say sth which is clearly true or easy to understand.
>
> **2 All in all** = the speaker is going to say sth having taken everything in consideration.
>
> **3 In fact** = the speaker is going to say sth which is surprising / unexpected or which contradicts in some way the previous information.
>
> **4 Apparently** = the speaker is going to give some information about sb / sth which they have heard / read.
>
> **5 Basically** = the speaker is going to give the most important reason (usually without going into details).

4.4   CD2 Track 29

1 **Obviously**, these characters and their story are fictitious…
2 **All in all**, I think his assessment is about right.
3 William Wallace is portrayed as a kind of poor primitive tribesman living in a village. **In fact**, he was the son of a rich landowner.
4 **Apparently**, the Scots stopped wearing woad hundreds of years earlier.
5 **Basically**, the reason why the Scots won the battle is because the English soldiers got trapped on the narrow bridge.

---

b ● Tell SS to go to **Grammar Bank 4A** on *p.145*. Go through each example and its corresponding rule with the class, or give SS time to read the examples and rules on their own, and answer any queries.

Grammar notes

● Recognizing discourse markers is an essential part of understanding both written and spoken English. Using them correctly is also an important aspect of communication that enables the reader or listener to follow your ideas.

● SS have already worked on discourse markers (commonly called linkers), which introduce a result, a purpose, a contrast, and a reason in **1A**. Here they focus on a more diverse group. SS should now be familiar with the term discourse marker, so when others come up refer to them that way for SS to add to their knowledge.

● Focus on the exercises for **4A**. SS do the exercises individually or in pairs. If SS do them individually, get them to compare with a partner. Check answers after each exercise.

a		b	
1	Basically	1	on the whole
2	In any case	2	anyway / in any case / besides
3	Obviously	3	After all / I mean
4	I mean	4	Talking of
5	at least	5	By the way / Incidentally
6	All in all	6	at least / on the other hand
7	By the way	7	Actually
8	Otherwise	8	in other words
9	In fact	9	As far as…is concerned
10	Talking of	10	Otherwise
		11	On the one hand, on the other hand

● Tell SS to go back to the main lesson on *p.55*.

c ● Tell SS to go to **Communication** *Guess the sentence* **A** on *p.117*, **B** on *p.119*.

● If your SS are not familiar with this type of activity, you may want to demonstrate it. Write the following sentence on a piece of paper: *I didn't win the race, but at least I didn't come last.*

● Don't show the sentence to SS. Then write on the board: *I didn't win the race, but at least I* _____. (–)

● Tell SS that you have this sentence completed on a piece of paper and they have to guess what you wrote. Elicit possible completions with a negative verb. If SS say something different from what's on your paper, e.g. *I wasn't the last one*, say 'Nearly. Try again' or give a clue until someone says the phrase *didn't come last*.

● Now go through the instructions. Emphasize that SS should write their ideas next to the sentence, but not in the gap, and only complete the gap when they have guessed the sentence correctly.

● SS continue in pairs. Monitor and help.

Extra photocopiable activities

Grammar
discourse markers (2) *p.166*
Communicative
Historical films quiz *p.192* (instructions *p.179*)
Vocabulary
History and warfare *p.217* (instructions *p.205*)

HOMEWORK

Study Link   **Workbook** *pp.34–36*

4
B

G verb + object + infinitive or gerund
V compound adjectives
P intonation in polite requests

Help yourself

Lesson plan

The topic of this lesson is self-help books. SS begin by reading a review of a recent self-help book about how to persuade people to do things for you, and then they read and re-tell extracts from it and assess the usefulness of the tips. This leads to the grammar focus, which is on the common pattern of verb + object + infinitive or gerund. The pronunciation focus is on intonation in polite requests.
In the second half of the lesson the focus widens and SS listen to a radio discussion about four more self-help books, and then go on to talk about self-help books or websites which they have used. The lesson ends with vocabulary, where SS extend their knowledge of compound adjectives.

Optional lead-in – the quote

- Focus on the lesson title and elicit two possible meanings (*serve yourself food* or *do something to improve yourself*).
- Get SS to read the quote at the top of *p.56*. Elicit / explain the meaning of *kleptomaniac* (= a person who cannot stop himself from stealing) and get SS to discuss what they think the quote means.
- Elicit / explain that it is a play on words, and that the first *helps himself* = serves himself (as when the host at a meal says *Help yourself*). The second (*he can't help himself*) is an idiom and means he can't do anything about it / stop himself doing it, as in *I can't help worrying*, etc.

1 READING & SPEAKING

a • If you didn't do the Optional lead-in, focus on the lesson title and elicit two possible meanings according to the context (*serve yourself food* or *do something to improve yourself*).
- Focus on the question and elicit answers from the whole class.

> The term self-help refers to guided self-improvement, e.g. economical, intellectual, or emotional, often with a substantial psychological basis. Self-help books are now a very popular genre, and aim to help people to help themselves in diverse areas of life, ranging from losing weight to finding a partner.

b • Focus on the book cover and the title of the review (**The persuaders**). Ask SS why they think there is a carrot on the cover, and elicit / explain that the 'carrot or stick approach' is a commonly used expression for the two different ways of getting someone to do something, and comes from the idea of either dangling a carrot in front of a horse to make it move, or beating it with a stick. Thus the 'carrot' means persuading somebody by use of a bribe or promise, the 'stick' by using force or aggression.
- Now focus on the task and set a time limit for SS to read the review and answer the questions in pairs. Check answers.

> **1** A man is selling *The Big Issue* outside a department store. He helped a woman to come out through the 'in' door, and she then bought a copy of *The Big Issue*.
> **2** Because it illustrated a principle (of reciprocity) identified by the author of the book.
> **3** Yes. He thinks it is a serious theory, not just 'popular psychology'.

c • Focus on the instructions and put SS in pairs, **A**s and **B**s. Set a time limit for SS to read their part, and encourage them to underline important phrases relating to the techniques and the research.

d • Check that **A**s and **B**s have both read their text carefully. Now get them to tell each other about the techniques and research. Encourage them to do this from memory and using their own words, only referring to the text itself when they can't remember a detail. Monitor and help.

e • Finally, get SS to discuss the two strategies together. Get feedback from the whole class and elicit situations where they think the strategies might work.

Extra support

Ask SS to choose five other words or phrases they would like to learn from the text and get them to compare their choices. Get some feedback from the class as to the words or phrases they have chosen and deal with any vocabulary problems that arise.

2 GRAMMAR   verb + object + infinitive or gerund

a • Focus on the sentences and give SS time in pairs to decide whether they are right or wrong, and to correct the mistakes. Encourage them to use their instinct, because although they may not have studied these structures before, they will have come across them frequently.

> **1** ✓
> **2** I was often made **to** do
> **3** I want **you to finish**
> **4** ✓
> **5** ✓
> **6** **you not finishing / if you don't finish**
> **7** suggest you **take** the 7.30 train
> **8** ✓
> **9** ✓
> **10** involves me **travelling** abroad

b • Tell SS to go to **Grammar Bank 4B** on *p.146*. Go through each example and its corresponding rule with the class, or give SS time to read the examples and rules on their own, and answer any queries.

Grammar notes

SS will be aware that when one verb follows another the second verb is in either the infinitive or the gerund. Here the focus is on the pattern verb + object + infinitive or gerund. SS will have been passively exposed to many of these structures, and have also studied verb + object + infinitive in reported requests, e.g. *I told him to be here at 7.00.* However, for many SS these structures may be problematic, especially where in their L1 they would tend to follow some verbs with a *that* clause where in English a gerund or infinitive is used.

- Focus on the exercise for **4B**. SS do the exercise individually or in pairs. If SS do it individually, get them to compare with a partner. Check answers.

1 answering their mobiles
2 me feel uncomfortable
3 for you to stay
4 Jane coming
5 you to think
6 you to pay for
7 you to stay
8 you travelling a lot
9 Hannah to do
10 you being
11 us to buy
12 us from crossing
13 me to call back / if I called back
14 the car breaking down

- Tell SS to go back to the main lesson on *p.57*.

3 PRONUNCIATION intonation in polite requests

Pronunciation notes

Native speakers of English tend to use a wide voice range when they make a polite request and even advanced students of English often fail to do this, which can tend to make them sound abrupt or unfriendly. The aim of the exercises here is to remind SS of the importance of intonation and give them some practice in using a variety of forms to make polite requests. It is important to highlight that using the right intonation is arguably more important than using a very polite phrase as far as getting the desired response from the listener. For example, *Would you mind opening the window, please?* said in a flat voice will not come across as polite as *Can you open the window, please?* said with a lively intonation.

a ● **4.5** Focus on the gapped phrases 1–6. Play the CD the whole way through for SS to listen. Then play it again, pausing after each sentence to give SS time to write. Check answers.

See **bold** sentences in script 4.5.

- Highlight that all the speakers have used polite language, but ask SS which forms are the most polite in terms of language used (Numbers 1, 4, 5, and 6).

4.5 (and **4.6**)   CD2 Track 30 and CD2 Track 31

1 **Would you mind opening the window?** It's a bit stuffy in here. (politely first)
2 To Victoria Station. **And can you hurry, please?** (politely second)
3 **Could you do me a favour?** I need someone to help me with this report. (politely first)
4 If you're going to the canteen, **do you think you could get me a sandwich?** (politely first)
5 **Would you mind asking your parents to come next weekend,** and not this one? (politely second)
6 **Could you possibly give me a lift to the station?** My car's being serviced. (politely second)

b ● **4.6** Focus on the instructions and play the CD once or twice if necessary. Pause after each pair and let SS discuss with a partner which they think is the most polite. Highlight that although all the speakers have used polite language in terms of the words used, it is the intonation which will most impact on the listener and affect their willingness to help.

- Explain that one of the sentences always sounds more polite because of the intonation (the fall-rise). The other one sounds either too abrupt or unfriendly. Check answers.

1 a 2 b 3 a 4 a 5 b 6 b

c ● **4.7** Play the CD pausing for SS to repeat, copying the polite intonation. Encourage SS to use a fall-rise intonation and wide voice range.

4.7   CD2 Track 32

The same requests as in 4.5 / 4.6 with polite intonation.

d ● Elicit the different ways of making a polite request in English as used in exercise **a**. Focus on the task and give SS time to think of something they would like someone to do for them.

- Then get SS to mingle, and try to convince at least three other SS to help them. Elicit the two tips SS learnt from the self-help book (always give a reason / only asking for a little).
- Tell SS they should only agree to do things for other people if they are really convinced by their powers of persuasion (and intonation).
- Get feedback from the class.

Extra idea

You could use the photocopiable 'Do you think you could possibly…?' on *p.193* to give SS ideas for favours to ask.

4 LISTENING & SPEAKING

a ● Focus on the instructions and get SS to answer the questions with a partner.
- Get some feedback and tell SS which ones, if any, you might be tempted to buy.

b ● Set a time limit for SS to read the extracts. Then ask the question to the whole class and elicit responses. Deal with any vocabulary problems.

Extra idea

You could also ask SS which one they think, from the extract, is the most light-hearted, serious, old-fashioned, new-age, etc.

c ● **4.8** Play the CD once for SS to do the gist task. Check answers.

> Two – *The Bluffer's Guide to Psychology* and *Idiot-Proof Diet.*

4.8　　　　　　　　　　　　　　　CD2 Track 33

(script in Student's Book on *p.127*)

P = presenter, M = Matt, A = Anita, K = Kate, D = Daniel

P Hello, good afternoon and welcome to today's edition of the *Book Programme*. Did you know that in every list of best-sellers, there's always one kind of book that's guaranteed to be there, and that's a self-help book? From how to make a fortune to how to bring up your children, there's a book that can give you advice on any problem you might possibly have. Today, our four contributors have each chosen a best-selling self-help book to talk about. First, Matt Crossley. What did you choose, Matt?

M Well, I have quite a few friends who are into psychology, and when I'm chatting to them I always wish I could make an intelligent comment, which would show that I know something about psychology too – which, in fact, I don't. So I chose *The Bluffer's Guide to Psychology*. The *Bluffer's guides* are a series of books which are supposed to help you to talk about a subject even if you don't really know anything about it. So there are *Bluffer's Guides* to economics, to opera, to wine, all sorts of things.

P And what did you think?

M Well, I have to say I was really impressed. It's a light-hearted introduction to psychology, which is both funny but at the same time extremely informative and scientifically-based. My feeling is that even people who really do know about psychology would find it a good read, and speaking personally, it actually made me want to find out some more about certain things like the gestalt theory…

P So you'd recommend it?

M Absolutely! I now understand some of the terminology of psychology and a little about the main theories, but above all I had a great time reading it. I actually laughed out loud at one point just reading one of the glossary entries.

P So, the *Bluffer's Guide to Psychology* recommended. Anita, how about you?

A Well, I chose a fairly recent diet book called *Neris and India's Idiot-Proof Diet*. I chose it firstly because India Knight is a journalist I like, and I often read her articles in *The Sunday Times*, which are usually very witty, and also because I see myself as a bit of an expert on diet books, I mean I've read them all and I've tried them all over the last ten years.

P And your verdict?

A Well, I'll just start by saying that I haven't actually done the diet yet…

P Obviously!

A Cheeky! I don't know if it really works, but I thought that the book was great. As Matt said about *The Bluffer's Guide*, this book was also, it was a good laugh, which is not something you can usually say about a diet book. But for me the two best points were that firstly, it's written by two women who were both extremely large, and they did the diet themselves.
Most diet books seem to be written either by men or by stick-thin women who've never had a weight problem in their lives. So the fact that the authors had done the diet themselves gave it credibility for me. And then the second reason is that really more than half the book is these two women talking about all the reasons that made them put on weight in the first place, and I'm sure that all these psychological reasons are at the heart of most people's weight problems.

P So, might you give the diet a try? Not that you need to, of course.

A Well, I don't know, I might actually. The diet obviously worked for them, because they're honest enough to include photos in the book of them at their fattest, and then how they ended up after doing the diet. So…

P Thank you Anita. So it's thumbs up for *The Idiot-proof Diet*. Kate, what was your choice?

K Well as you know, James and I recently got married, and when I saw the title of this book, it's called *The Rules of Marriage*: *Time-tested Secrets for Making Marriage Work*. I thought, 'That's the book for me'.

P And was it?

K Definitely not. To tell you the truth, I was actually horrified. The book is supposed to be a kind of manual of dos and don'ts for what to do from the engagement onwards, and if you ask me, it was something that could have been written 50 years ago, or more. The message is more or less that once you've *caught* your husband, you have to keep him satisfied in every possible way. And if you don't like it, then all they suggest is that you complain and moan to your girlfriends. According to this book, making a marriage work is entirely up to the wife, the husband doesn't have to do anything at all. The wife just has to try to be exactly what her husband wants her to be, and then everything will be just fine. I can't believe that in the 21st century such horrendous advice as this is being published and presumably, as it's a best-seller, being read by women in their thousands.

P So you wouldn't recommend *The Rules of Marriage*?

K Absolutely not! In fact, I think it should be banned.

P So to our last guest today, Daniel. And your book is…?

D My book is Paul McKenna's latest, which is called *I Can Make You Rich*. And I don't need to give any explanations about why I chose this book.

P So are we going to see you on the next list of the hundred richest people in Britain?

D No, I don't think so. In fact, I feel a bit like Kate did about her book. I couldn't take it seriously at all. The book promises to help you to see the world in a different way, which will make you 'think rich' and eventually 'live rich', all through doing mental exercises, which are supposed to help you find out what you want and focus on it. It has a sort of hypnosis-style CD with it, and I can't actually tell you much about it because I fell asleep after the first five minutes. Yeah, still I suppose that means it's relaxing. But after reading it, my suggestion would be, if you want to get rich, start by not wasting money on buying this book.

P So a big thumbs down for Paul McKenna too. Matt, Anita, Kate, and Daniel, thank you very much.

d ● Focus on the task and give SS a minute to read 1–8. Play the CD again. Get SS to compare answers with a partner, and then play the CD again if necessary. Check answers, eliciting for each statement what exactly the speaker said about the books.

Extra support

As this is a long listening, you could give SS more time and reduce the memory load by pausing the recording after each book has been discussed for SS to match two statements to each book (see spaces in the script).

1 D (It has a CD with it…)
2 B (Anita had read many other diet books.)
3 A (Matt has a lot of friends who are into psychology and this book will help him chat to them about the subject.)
4 B (Anita may try the diet.)
5 C (Kate recently got married.)
6 A (Matt intends to read more about psychology, e.g. the gestalt theory.)
7 C (It only gives the man's point of view.)
8 D (It promises to make you 'think rich'.)

Extra support

If there's time, get SS to listen again with the script on *p.127*, focusing on any new vocabulary, and getting feedback on phrases SS didn't understand, e.g. because the words were run together.

LEXIS IN CONTEXT

e ● **4.9** Focus on the gapped sentences and give SS a moment to read them, and see if they can remember any of the phrases.

● Play the CD once the whole way through. Then play it again pausing after each sentence for SS to write the missing words. Check answers.

See **bold** words in script 4.9

● Elicit / explain that:
– *quite a few* = more than a few
– *a bit of* (an expert) is quite informal
– *entirely* = totally, completely
– *at all* intensifies a negative phrase it comes after. It is very common after *nothing / anything* (*Did you understand anything? Nothing at all.*) and after a negative verb (*I didn't like it at all.*). Remind SS that we also often use the phrase *Not at all* to respond when sb says *Thank you*, as an alternative to *You're welcome*.
– *just* as a modifier here means *completely / absolutely*, but of course has many other meanings such as *only* (e.g. *just a minute*), *exactly* (e.g. *she looks just like her mother*), *at this moment* (e.g. *They're just leaving*).

4.9   CD2 Track 34
1 Well, I have **quite a few** friends who are into psychology.
2 I see myself as **a bit of an** expert on diet books.
3 According to this book, making a marriage work is **entirely up to** the wife.
4 …the husband doesn't have to **do anything at all**.
5 The wife just has to try to be exactly what her husband wants her to be, and then everything will be **just fine**.

f ● Do this as an open-class question to get SS to respond to the content of the listening.
g ● Focus on the task. Go through the topics and elicit the meaning of *DIY* (= do-it-yourself and refers to doing home repairs, assembling furniture, etc.). Then put SS in small groups and allow them time to discuss the topics, saying whether they have used any self-help books, DVDs, etc. and how helpful they found them.
● Get feedback and find out if SS have any recommendations.

5 VOCABULARY compound adjectives

a ● Focus on the information box and go through it with SS. They will already be familiar with compound nouns, but stress that, unlike compound nouns, compound adjectives are very often hyphenated (compound nouns sometimes are and sometimes aren't or are written as one word).
● Focus on question 1 and elicit the compound adjective formed by a word from each circle (e.g. *second-hand*). Then get SS to continue individually or in pairs. Check answers. Elicit / explain that in compound adjectives both words are stressed although there is slightly more stress on the <u>second</u> word, e.g. a <u>second-hand</u> car.

2 long-term	7 air-conditioned
3 last-minute	8 part-time
4 duty-free	9 narrow-minded
5 worn-out	10 well-behaved
6 home-made	

b ● Get SS to ask and answer the questions with a partner. Monitor and help where necessary.
c ● Focus on the task. You could set a time limit for SS to match the words. Check answers.

mass-produced	hands-free
short-sighted	first-class
high-heeled	easy-going
kind-hearted	left-handed
blue-eyed	absent-minded

● Now give SS a few minutes to write their questions. Get them to first ask you some of them and then ask each other.

Extra photocopiable activities

Grammar
verb + object + infinitive or gerund *p.167*
Communicative
Do you think you could possibly…? *p.193* (instructions *p.180*)
Vocabulary
Compound adjective race *p.218* (instructions *p.205*)

HOMEWORK

Study Link **Workbook** *pp.37–39*

4 C

G conditional sentences
V phone language; adjectives + prepositions
P sound and spelling: /ʃ/, /tʃ/, /ʒ/, /dʒ/

Can't live without it

Lesson plan

The topic of this lesson is behavioural addictions and obsessions, such as being addicted to shopping. Alcohol or substance addiction have not been included as these may be sensitive or even taboo subjects in some teaching situations. SS begin by revising typical phone language, and then read and listen to a journalist talking about an experiment in which she tried living without her mobile phone for a week. Then there is work on the pronunciation of four consonant sounds, which are often confused. The grammar focus revises conditional sentences, and introduces mixed conditionals and alternatives to *if* such as *supposing* and *provided that*, etc.

In the second half of the lesson SS read a newspaper article from the British press about people who are addicted to certain types of behaviour, for example tanning and using the Internet. They then do some work on dependent prepositions after adjectives, e.g. *addicted to, hooked on*, and finally they listen to some people talking about their obsessions, and then talk themselves about people they know who have similar behavioural problems. The lesson ends with the song *Addicted to Love*.

Optional lead-in – the quote

- Write the quote at the top of *p.60* on the board (books closed) and the name of the author or get SS to open their books and read it.
- Elicit / explain that Carl Jung (1875–1961) was a very influential thinker and the founder of analytical psychology.
- Get SS to discuss with a partner whether they agree with the quote or not and why.
- Open the discussion to the whole class and elicit ideas and opinions.

1 VOCABULARY & LISTENING

a
- Focus on the task and the quiz. Set a time limit for SS to do it in pairs. Check answers. You may want to highlight:
  Part 2 – you can also say 'to give sb a call' (*I'll give you a call tomorrow.*)
  Part 3 – *hang up* = end a phone conversation (old-fashioned phones often used to be fixed on walls). If someone (usually because they are angry) ends a phone conversation abruptly without saying goodbye, we say *He / She hung up (on me)*.

1	to call, to phone, and to ring				
2	**a** give		**b** make		
3	**a** up		**d** up		**g** speak
	b turn / switch		**e** out		**h** put
	c off		**f** through		
4	**a** charge		**d** missed		**g** pay phones
	b landline		**e** directory		
	c engaged		**f** voicemail		

Extra support

You could get SS to test each other's memory on the phone vocabulary by taking it in turns to give definitions for their partner to say the word, e.g. *What do you do if your mobile phone battery is low?* (charge it).

b
- Get SS to answer the question with a partner, and then get feedback from the whole class. Tell them your opinion too.
- Focus on the task. Set a time limit for SS to read the beginning of the article. Check answers.

> The experiment is to live for a week without a mobile phone.
> A 'nomophobe' is a person addicted to their mobile phone and who gets very stressed if they can't use it.

c
- **4.10** Focus on the task and give SS time to read the six sentences. Play the CD once and get SS to write the initials of the days of the week in the boxes. Get SS to compare their answers with a partner and play the recording again as necessary.

Extra support

As this is quite a long listening, pause after each day to give SS more time and to lighten the memory load.

1 W	**2** M	**3** F	**4** T	**5** Th	**6** M

4.10   **CD2 Track 35**

(script in Student's Book on *p.128*)
It's Monday.
Just five minutes after I'd agreed to abandon my phone, I got a text! But of course officially I didn't have a mobile any more, so I had to switch if off without reading the text and then I spent all afternoon wondering what crucial information there was in the message.
After work I missed my train, and I'd arranged to meet my flatmate for dinner. I knew I was going to be late – and I hate being late but there was just nothing I could do about it. I made it in time for dinner, but in the restaurant I kept feeling an urge to check my phone for messages or missed calls. It was weird and really stressful. And on top of it all, my flatmate had her phone sitting on the table in front of her.

It's Tuesday.
When I was on the way home, I suddenly thought that I *had* to ring my mother. If I'd had my phone, I'd have called her there and then, and it made me realize now that I always speak to my parents when I'm on the move. They're always complaining that we never have a conversation without traffic noise in the background. So for once, when I got home, I called her on the landline, and we had a whole half-hour of conversation without any interruptions. I have to say it was one of the most relaxing conversations we'd ever had in recent years. A real pleasure!

84

It's Wednesday.

The morning started badly because I needed to make a doctor's appointment before I went to work, but the surgery was engaged for half an hour. I eventually got through, but it meant I was late for work, and I felt under pressure all day. In the evening, I'd planned to go climbing with some friends at the climbing centre, so I rushed to get home early because one of my friends said he would need to call me to check the arrangements. I waited around for him to call, which he did, but late, so we both got to the climbing centre late and didn't enjoy it as much as we might have if we'd had more time.

It's Thursday.

After work I went to a friend's house, which was about an hour away. I actually had a good feeling about being without my mobile because it meant having a whole hour for me to relax and when no one could disturb me. The feeling lasted until I got off the bus and realized that I didn't know exactly where her street was and I got completely lost looking for it. So I was late for the fourth time.

It's Friday.

Well, this was the day when I ended up calling the bar trying to find my friends. First, I went to the theatre with my friend Alice. I got very panicky when I was waiting for her in the foyer, because we hadn't specified exactly where we were going to meet, and there were a lot of people, and she had the tickets. If I'd had my phone, I would have just sent her a text saying exactly where I was. Luckily, we did see each other. But then after the theatre the idea was to meet up with some friends and that's when I ended up spending nearly five pounds what with trying to get the number of the bar from directory enquiries, and then doing the whole thing again for a second bar. In the end we went to have a drink on our own. So that wasn't just being late, it was a social occasion that just didn't happen.

d ● Focus on the task and tell SS to make notes for each day. Play the CD again, pausing after each day. Then get SS to compare their notes and in pairs to retell her week.

e ● **4.11** Focus on the task and play the CD once or twice. Get SS to compare with a partner and check answers. Make sure SS know the meaning of the phrasal verbs *to stand sb up* (= to not turn up when you have arranged to meet sb on a date) and *to let sb down* (= to disappoint sb by not acting in the way they hoped or expected).

> The result of not having a mobile is that you end up waiting in the rain, or being stood up, or letting people down.
> Francesca decided she will keep her phone with her all the time and never switch it off.

4.11   CD2 Track 36

Saturday morning!
At exactly one minute past twelve I switched my phone on again. I was really excited to see what vital or hilarious messages I'd have, but in fact there weren't any. But I was absolutely clear by now that the supposed benefits of living without a mobile don't really exist. The reality is that you end up waiting in the rain, or being stood up, or letting people down. I admit it. My name is Francesca and I am a nomophobe. And as for all the anxiety and stress that we addicts are supposed to suffer when we are deprived of our drug, the answer is simple. In the future I will just keep my phone with me at all times. And I won't turn it off again ever.

---

f ● Do this as an open-class question.

2 PRONUNCIATION sounds and spelling: /ʃ/, /tʃ/, /ʒ/, /dʒ/

Pronunciation notes

This exercise gives SS the opportunity to fine-tune their pronunciation of four consonant sounds, which may still cause problems even at an advanced level.

/ʃ/	common spellings: *sh, ti, ci, x* (= /kʃ/) less common: *ss* (e.g. *pressure*), *ch* (e.g. *machine*), *s* as in *sugar*
/tʃ/	common spellings: *ch, tch, t* before *ure / ury* (e.g. *literature*)
/ʒ/	common spellings: *s* before *u* or *i* (e.g. *pleasure, decision*)
/dʒ/	common spellings: all *j* (e.g. *jury*), *g* before *e* (e.g. *wages*), *dge* and sometimes *g* before *i* (e.g. *imagine*)

a ● Focus on the instructions and the chart, and check SS know what the sounds are in each picture. Encourage SS to say the words in the list out loud before writing them in the columns.

b ● **4.12** Play the CD once for SS to check their answers. Then give them a few moments to practise saying the words themselves.

Extra support

Play the CD and get SS to repeat after each word.

4.12   CD3 Track 2

/ʃ/	/tʃ/	/ʒ/	/dʒ/
addiction	attachment	conclusion	arrangement
anxious	century	decision	engaged
condition	future	occasion	journalist
crucial	switched	pleasure	message
obsession			surgery
officially			
pressure			
technician			

---

c ● Get SS to practise saying the sentences with a partner. Encourage them to try to say them quite fast, linking words where appropriate.

3 GRAMMAR conditional sentences

a ● Focus on the task and give SS a few moments to match the sentence halves.

> **1** D   **2** F   **3** B   **4** E   **5** A   **6** C

b ● Focus on the questions and give SS time in pairs to answer them. Elicit that the sentences are all unreal conditionals, i.e. they are hypothesizing either about the present / future or about the past.

> **1** and **4** are third conditionals (*if* + past perfect, *would have* + past participle). They are used to talk about hypothetical situations in the past and their consequence.

3, 5, and 6 are second conditionals (*if* + past simple, *would* + infinitive). They are used to talk about hypothetical or improbable situations in the present / future, and their consequences.

2 is a mixed conditional (a combination of a second and a third conditional). It refers to a hypothetical situation in the present (*If I wasn't a journalist*) and the consequence it would have on the past (*I would never have done the experiment*). *If I wasn't* could also be *If I weren't* with no change of meaning.

- Elicit that in 2 the *if*-clause is like a second conditional (because it refers to the present) and the other clause is like a third conditional (because it refers to the past), but that mixed conditionals can also work the other way round, e.g. *If I hadn't passed all my exams* (3rd conditional, a hypothesis about the past), *I wouldn't be feeling so relaxed.* (the consequence in the present).

c ● Tell SS to go to **Grammar Bank 4C** on *p.147*. Go through each example and its corresponding rule with the class, or give SS time to read the examples and rules on their own, and answer any queries.

Grammar notes

- SS should be familiar by now with the two standard forms of unreal conditions, i.e. 2nd and 3rd conditionals, even though they may still make mistakes with the forms when speaking. It is worth reminding them that continuous forms (past continuous or past perfect continuous) can also be used in the *if*-clause, e.g. *If it were snowing now, I would leave work early.*
- Mixed conditionals are much less common than standard conditionals, but SS still need some practice in this area.
- One area not covered here is inversion in conditionals of the type, *Should you wish to..., Were I to...*

- Focus on the exercises for **4C**. SS do the exercises individually or in pairs. If SS do them individually, get them to compare with a partner. Check answers after each exercise.

a 1 ✓
   2 if the camp wasn't / weren't so crowded
   3 ✓
   4 ✓
   5 if she hadn't got injured last month
   6 ✓
   7 They would have got divorced ages ago
   8 If the storm hadn't been at night
   9 ✓

b 1 provided / providing   **7** even
   2 Even   **8** as / so
   3 long   **9** Supposing
   4 Had   **10** whether
   5 condition   **11** Had
   6 whether

- Tell SS to go back to the main lesson on *p.61*.

d ● Focus on the questions, and divide the class into groups of three or four. Give SS at least five minutes to discuss the questions. Monitor and correct any errors with conditional sentences.

4 READING

a ● Do this as an open-class question and elicit ideas. The photos will give SS some ideas (the Internet, tanning, and shopping) and they should be able to come up with some more.

b ● Focus on the task and the article. Set a time limit for SS to read it once and answer the gist questions with a partner. Check answers.

> Behavioural addictions are when people are addicted to a certain kind of behaviour, e.g. using their mobiles, having plastic surgery, etc.
> Most people think of addictions as being to substances like tobacco, alcohol, or drugs not to a kind of behaviour.
> They can be treated through a stay in a clinic or therapy.

c ● Focus on the task and set a time limit for SS to re-read the article and answer the questions. Get them to compare answers with a partner and try to justify their choices. Check answers.

> **1** c   **2** b   **3** a   **4** a   **5** c

LEXIS IN CONTEXT

d ● Focus on the first highlighted expression (*substance dependencies*) and elicit that it means being dependent on (i.e. addicted to) a substance, e.g. nicotine or alcohol. Then get SS to continue in pairs working out the meaning of the other highlighted expressions. Elicit the meaning from individual SS.

> **harmless** = not causing damage
> **behavioural addictions** = being addicted to certain types of behaviour, e.g. shopping
> **wrecking lives** = destroying lives
> **I feel edgy and tense** = I feel nervous, especially about what might happen (also *on edge*) and not at all relaxed
> **seeking treatment** = looking for treatment
> **she feels overwhelmingly anxious** = she feels completely dominated by her anxiety
> **gave me an enormous high** = made me feel extremely pleased and excited, as if I had taken a drug
> **overcome addictions to gambling and work** = was able to succeed in dealing with or controlling the problem
> **become hooked on anything** = (informal) become addicted to anything
> **compulsive behaviour** = behaviour that is difficult to stop or control

- Finally, deal with any other vocabulary queries SS have. You may want to explain that *breed* in the introduction normally means a kind of animal developed by people, but can also (as here) be used metaphorically to mean a kind of person.

Extra support

Ask SS to choose five other words or phrases they would like to learn from the text and get them to compare their choices. Get some feedback from the class as to the words or phrases they have chosen and deal with any vocabulary problems that arise.

e ● Either get SS to discuss the question in pairs and get feedback, or do as an open-class question. Try to keep the discussion general rather than eliciting cases of people SS know themselves as they will be talking about this later in the lesson.

5 VOCABULARY adjectives + prepositions

a ● Remind SS that certain adjectives have a dependent preposition, e.g. *tired of*, *opposed to*, and that it is important for them to learn the preposition with the adjective.

● Give SS time to complete the **prepositions** column. Check answers.

1	with	4	on	7	of	10	of
2	to	5	with	8	for	11	on
3	to	6	to	9	on		

b ● Get SS to test themselves by covering the **prepositions** column and saying the sentences with the prepositions.

c ● Focus on the first sentence and ask SS if they think it is true for their country, and elicit examples. Then get SS to continue in pairs with the other sentences.

Extra support

At this point you could give SS the photocopiable 'Dependent prepositions' on *pp.239–240*. This is intended mainly as self-study / reference material. You could get SS to learn the dependent prepositions at home and quickly revise them in class by getting everyone to cover the **Preposition** column and go through the sentences eliciting the preposition. To avoid overload you could give out one sheet one day and the other sheet on a later occasion.

6 LISTENING & SPEAKING

a ● **4.13** Focus on the instructions. Play the CD once, pausing after each person for SS to note down what they are obsessed with. Check answers. You may want to pre-teach / highlight that *Aussie* (in interview 2) is an informal way of saying *Australian*.

1	Arranging things in alphabetical order
2	Cleaning
3	Checking their hair in the mirror
4	Counting things
5	Healthy eating / ingredients

4.13   CD3 Track 3

(script in Student's Book on *p.128*)
I = **interviewer**, **Sp** = **speaker**
1
Sp What's the question? Do I have any obsessions? Well, I don't consider them obsessions, but I do have a habit of organizing myself in ways that other people might consider obsessive. I've walked into a friend's flat, where I was staying for a week or two, and instantly alphabetized their collection of CDs or DVDs of maybe a hundred or so because if I was going to be there, and I needed to find a piece of music, it just means…it was a lot easier to find it when it's alphabetized.
I Are all your book collections and record collections at home alphabetized?
Sp Absolutely. It just saves…I do it once and it saves a lot of time in finding things afterwards. I find it practical. I don't find it obsessive.

2
I Do you have any private obsessions, for example, you know, collecting things, exercise, tidiness, that stuff?
Sp Well, I do, I've got a complete obsession about cleaning and it's awful, it's the bane of my life, it's absolutely awful, I cannot relax unless everything is absolutely, you know, clean and tidy. I've had to let it go a bit because my husband's an Aussie and he's very laid-back and I just haven't been allowed to be as obsessed as I have been in the past, and of course having children stops the obsession a little bit because there's toys and stuff everywhere…
I Yeah, where did it come from?
Sp Well, I think it's just, it's a security thing, I feel when everything's clean and tidy I feel safe and comfortable, I think it's because when I was an early teenager my parents split up, they divorced, and that's when it started, I started cleaning. We had a smoked glass coffee table with chrome legs and I used to clean that because I couldn't stand the fingerprints on it and that's where it began, that then escalated and I started cleaning the kitchen and the bathroom…
I Oh my God, as a teenager?
Sp Yeah, I was absolutely, and then hoovering came into play, and I started hoovering, but ironically I've got a couple of friends, and their obsession with cleaning started as well with the same thing, their parents split up at around about the same age, early teenagers, and they have obsessions with cleaning as well. One who I work with, not very far from here today, and another girlfriend who, I went on a course, met on a course, and she has the same problems, so I don't know whether it's, there's anything in that.
I Do you clean when you're upset or do you…?
Sp Yes.
I Or do you just clean all the time… when you're upset?
Sp Particularly when I'm upset. Yeah, it occupies me and everything's all nice, but I have got a handle on it now, I'm a lot better than I used to be.
I Will you come over to my place and clean?
Sp Yes, that's what everybody says.

3
Sp Well, my mother is completely, pathologically addicted to checking her hair in the mirror all the time, she's got a real hang-up about her hair, completely obsessed by it, spends hours and hours checking out her hair and…
I 1 Does it interfere with her life?
Sp I think it's quite time-consuming and yes, I think it does, I mean she can get really upset, and if she goes to the hairdresser and sort of has anything done, she becomes really upset for days if it's slightly wrong, or she's really self-conscious about it.
I 1 Just about her hair?
Sp Yeah.
I 2 How long has it been going on for?
Sp Ever since she was a child. I discovered that her brother had curly hair when he was a child, beautiful curly hair, and big brown eyes, and I think he was the sort of favourite child, I think he was the favoured one…
I 1 And she has straight hair…
Sp And she has straight hair, and I think that's where it comes from. But she's absolutely, is really hung up about it.

4 There's a name for this condition but I can't remember what it is and I'm not sure what it's called but I do count things. If I come into a room, I will count the number of lights on the ceiling. The only thing is, I don't know how many there really are, because I count things so that they turn out to be in multiples of threes or nines, and I also count panes in windows, I will count panels in doors. But I like them always to get to up a 3 or a 30 or a 90 so it's a fairly useless thing, but it's just something I just do.

5 Yeah, my friend is obsessed with healthy eating, absolutely obsessed, and it makes going out for dinner with her really quite boring because you can't… anything on the menu she just goes on and on about how this is bad, that's bad, allergy to this, allergy to that, getting the waiter over to talk and, you know about certain things that are in each dish and it's just so, it really actually does interfere with like her social life, having fun with her because she's just completely obsessed by what she eats and it's just a bit, I don't know it's a bit boring.

Extra support

If there's time, get SS to listen again with the script on *p.128*, focusing on any new vocabulary, and getting feedback on phrases SS didn't understand, e.g. because the words were run together.

b ● Focus on the task and give SS time to read the questions. Play the CD the whole way through and get SS to compare answers. Play the recording again as necessary and then check answers.

> **A** 2 **B** 1 **C** 5 **D** 3 **E** 4

c ● Focus on the task. Point out that the questions (*How long has it been going on for?*, etc.) are things they should answer about the person they are describing.

   ● Demonstrate the activity by talking about a person you know, or about yourself if you have an obsession you don't mind talking about!

   ● Divide SS into groups, and give them time to think about people they know before they start.

   ● Monitor, looking out especially for any mistakes with prepositions.

   ● Get some feedback by asking the groups about any unusual obsessions that came up.

7 4.14 SONG 🎵 *Addicted to Love*

   ● This song was a hit by Robert Palmer in 1985. For copyright reasons this is a cover version. If you want to do this song in class, use the photocopiable activity on *p.235*.

4.14   CD3 Track 4

Addicted to Love

The lights are on, but you're not home
Your mind is not your own
Your heart sweats, your body shakes
Another kiss is what it takes
You can't sleep, you can't eat
There's no doubt, you're in deep
Your throat is tight, you can't breathe
Another kiss is all you need

Chorus
Whoa, you like to think that you're immune to the stuff, oh yeah
It's closer to the truth to say you can't get enough,
You know you're gonna have to face it
You're addicted to love

You see the signs, but you can't read
You're running at a different speed
Your heart beats in double time
Another kiss and you'll be mine, a one-track mind
You can't be saved
Oblivion is all you crave
If there's some left for you
You don't mind if you do

Chorus
Might as well face it, you're addicted to love (x5)

The lights are on, but you're not home
Your will is not your own
Your heart sweats your teeth grind
Another kiss and you'll be mine

Chorus
Might as well face it, you're addicted to love (x7)

Extra photocopiable activities

Grammar
conditional sentences *p.168*
Communicative
Case studies *p.194* (instructions *p.180*)
Vocabulary
Phone language *p.219* (instructions *p.205*)
Song
Addicted to Love p.235 (instructions *p.230*)
Dependent prepositions *pp.239–240*

HOMEWORK

Study Link **Workbook** *pp.40–42*

Lesson plan

In this lesson the focus is on writing a discursive essay. These are generally of two types, either a 'balanced argument' essay, where SS are expected to give both sides of an argument and draw a conclusion, or an 'opinion' essay, where SS decide whether they agree with a statement or not and give their reasons. The 'opinion' essay is focused on in Writing 6. The writing skills focus here is on the content of introductory and concluding paragraphs, and there is a **Useful language** focus on expressing the main points in an argument, adding supporting information, describing cause and effect, and weighing up arguments.

ANALYSING A MODEL TEXT

a • Focus on the text type (a discursive essay: a balanced argument). Tell SS that when they are asked to write an essay it is normally one of two types, either giving a balanced argument, i.e. showing the pros and cons of something , or giving their own opinion clearly in favour of or against a particular statement. Point out that the latter kind of discursive essay will be focused on in File 6.

• You should highlight to SS that although some essay titles make it clear which type of essay is required, some titles allow SS to decide for themselves which type they wish to write.

• Focus on the **Key success factors** and go through them with SS.

• Focus on the task, and get SS in pairs to discuss arguments for and against text messaging. Get feedback and write the arguments up on the board in two columns.

b • Focus on the task and main sections of the essay. Get SS to read it quickly and check the arguments against the ones on the board. Elicit that the main argument is given first in the 'in favour' section, and last in the 'against' section.

c • Focus on the task and the introductory and concluding paragraphs. Get SS to first choose individually which ones they think are best, and then to compare with a partner. Check answers, getting SS to explain why.

> The best introductory paragraph is the first one. It introduces the topic as specified in the title, and engages the reader's attention by posing the relevant question. Paragraph 2 is less suitable as all it does is spell out the structure of the essay, and paragraph 3 doesn't quite address the topic as stated in the title, but appears to be more of an introduction to an essay in favour of text messaging.

> The third conclusion is the best for the essay, as it sums up what has been said and gives the writer's overall opinion. Paragraph 1 is not appropriate because it comes down in favour of text-messaging, which does not reflect the content of the essay, and paragraph 2 is the same. It also includes a specific argument not mentioned in the rest of the essay.

• Now go through the **Introductions and conclusions** box with SS.

USEFUL LANGUAGE

d • Focus on the task and give SS time to complete the phrases individually or in pairs. Stress that not all the phrases are in the model essay. Check answers.

1 benefit	**8** favour
2 importantly	**9** result…; lead
3 disadvantage	**10** due
4 drawback	**11** balance
5 addition	**12** whole
6 more	**13** All…all
7 only	

• Remind SS that these phrases are all useful for writing this kind of essay.

PLANNING WHAT TO WRITE

a • Focus on the task. Tell SS, in pairs, to choose one of the titles and brainstorm the pros and cons. Get feedback by writing the titles on the board and then eliciting all the points for and against. Then elicit from the class which they think are the most important arguments on each side (they don't have to agree).

b • Set a time limit of about ten minutes for SS to write their introductory paragraphs.

c • Tell SS to compare their introduction with the partner they worked with in **a** and to write a final version together.

Extra idea

You could get all pairs who have chosen the first essay to read out their paragraphs and for the class to vote for the best one, and then do the same for the second title.

• Finally, go through the tips with SS.

WRITING

Go through the instructions and set the writing for homework.

Test and Assessment CD-ROM

CEFR Assessment materials

File 4 Writing task assessment guidelines

Lesson plan

In the first part of this lesson Adrian Hodges, a well-known UK-based screenplay writer, who wrote several episodes of the TV historical drama *Rome* is interviewed. He talks about various issues related to the making of historical films and TV dramas. In the second part of the lesson people in the street are asked in which historical period they would like to have lived and which historical figure they most admire.

Study Link These lessons are on the *New English File Advanced* DVD which can be used instead of the class CD (See Introduction *p.9*). SS can get more practice on the MultiROM, which contains more of the short street interviews with a listening task and scripts.

Optional lead-in (books closed)

* Set a time limit and get SS in pairs or small groups to brainstorm the main problems facing a film director and screenplay writer when making a historical film or drama.
* Get ideas from the class and write them on the board. After you have played the interview with Adrian Hodges the first time, get SS to see which of the problems he mentions and ask them about any others.

THE INTERVIEW

a ● Books open. Now focus on the task and on the glossary. Go through it with the class eliciting from them how to pronounce the words and phrases.

Extra support

You may want to pre-teach some other words and phrases before SS listen to the interview (see script 4.15).

b ● **4.15** Focus on the questions and give SS time to read them. Encourage SS not to write anything when they listen the first time. Tell them that they should listen and try to get the gist of what he is saying, and then discuss the questions with their partner.

● Play the CD once (**Part 1**). Give SS time to discuss the questions and tell each other what they understood. Then play the CD again pausing after each of Adrian's answers to give SS time to make notes and compare with their partner again. Play the recording again as necessary and check answers.

> 1 History is full of good stories which consequently make good films / dramas. As people often know something about the stories it may make them interested to see the film.
>
> 2 Achieving two things at the same time with one action, in this case when a film-maker not only tells a good story, but tells it in a way that makes it relevant to the present day.
>
> 3 Because you have to 'dress' the film. Actors have to be dressed in period costumes, and houses and furniture have to look authentic. Also scenes have to be shot very carefully to make sure there is nothing in them which gives away the period, e.g. a car or a plane. Often you need bigger crowds.

4.15 CD3 Track 5

(script in Student's Book on *p.128*)
I = interviewer, A = Adrian Hodges
I You've written a number of screenplays for historical dramas, for example, *Rome*, why do you think there is so much demand for historical drama and film?
A Well, film and TV is always about good stories. I know that seems a fairly obvious thing to say, but the thing about history is it's jam-packed full with good stories, many of which people know, part, or at least vaguely know. If you say, 'I'm going to do a film about Robin Hood', you know that part of your audience at the very least will already have some knowledge of that story and they will think, 'Oh yeah, I quite like that story, so maybe there's something in there that, for me in that film.' And there are many other examples, *Rome* is a, you know, is a canvas full of stories that have, you know, lasted for 2,000 years. So, you know, many people have vaguely heard about Julius Caesar, some of them know that story very very well, and so on and so on, or Caligula or whoever. So history is just an endlessly useful way of telling great stories from the past in a way that means something in the present. In a perfect world, you get a double hit, you, you tell a classic story, but you also tell it in a way that makes it resonate with the present.
I Are historical films necessarily any more expensive than films set in the modern day?
A Yeah, period is always more expensive. It's just something about the fact that you have to dress the film in a way that you don't have to dress a contemporary film. By 'dress' I mean, not just dress people who have to wear costumes that are authentic to the period. If your film is set in 1800, they all have to look as though they were, you know, dressed exactly as in that period. That all costs money. But 'dressed' also in terms of the way you make the houses look, the way you make all your decorations look, your furniture, everything has to be authentic to the period. You have to make sure there are no cars, no aeroplanes, every shot has to be weighed up to make sure that there's nothing in it which, which betrays the period. There's nothing more ridiculous than a period film where you see a glaring anachronism, some detail that's horrible wrong. So unfortunately, all of that costs money and you have to have bigger crowds in many cases. *Rome* was a case in point. We needed big crowds. In the Senate you have to have, a certain number of Senators, all of them have to be dressed in, you know, in togas and so on. So I'm afraid it is just an expensive way of making films, yeah.

c ● **4.16** Focus on the task and give SS time to read the questions. Play the CD once (**Part 2**) and tell SS just to listen. Then give SS time to discuss the questions and tell each other what they understood. Now play the CD again, pausing after each answer to give SS time to make notes and compare with their partner again. Play the recording again as necessary and check answers.

> 1 He thinks it's more important to make the drama mean something to a modern audience, rather than to be strictly accurate.
>
> 2 He thinks you can change details as long as you don't change so much as to make history ridiculous.
>
> 3 The more recent history is, the more difficult it is not to show it accurately, e.g. it is easier to change details about a drama set in ancient Rome than it is to change details of what happened in a recent war.

4 He thinks a writer only has a responsibility to be historically accurate if that was his intention, i.e. if you have told your audience that you are going to tell the true story of the murder of Julius Caesar. But if you are writing a fictional drama based on the murder of Caesar, then you do not have any obligation to be completely truthful.

5 If a historical film is the only thing that an audience sees on a particular subject, they may believe that it is the truth as people don't always make the distinction between films and reality. In that case it is dangerous if the film is very inaccurate.

6 The film *Spartacus* is the only one on the subject so most people's knowledge of this historical figure comes entirely from the film. In fact, very little is known about the real Spartacus (so presumably much of the detail in the film was invented).

7 *Braveheart* was a very inaccurate film as most of William Wallace's life was invented. Many people felt it was more about the notion of Scotland as an independent country than it was about historical authenticity. He believes it is a matter of personal taste and he personally enjoyed the film.

4.16   CD3 Track 6

(script in Student's Book on *p.129*)

I How important is historical accuracy in a historical film?

A The notion of accuracy in history is a really difficult one in drama because you know, it's like saying, you know, was *Macbeth* accurate, was a Shakespearean drama accurate. The thing is it's not about historical accuracy; it's about whether you can make a drama work from history that means something to an audience now. So I tend to take the view that in a way accuracy isn't the issue when it comes to the drama. If you're writing a drama, you have the right as a writer to create the drama that works for you, so you can certainly change details. The truth is nobody really knows how people spoke in Rome or how people spoke in the courts of Charles II or William the Conqueror or Victoria, or whoever. You have an idea from writing, from books, and plays, and so on. We know when certain things happened, what sort of dates happened. I think it's really a question of judgement. If you make history ridiculous, if you change detail to the point where history is an absurdity, then obviously things become more difficult. The truth is that the more recent history is, the more difficult it is not to be authentic to it.

In a way, it's much easier to play fast and loose with the details of what happened in Rome than it is to play fast and loose with the details of what happened in the Iraq War, say, you know. So it's all a matter of perspective in some ways. It's something that you have to be aware of and which you try to be faithful to, but you can't ultimately say a drama has to be bound by the rules of history, because that's not what drama is.

I Do you think the writer has a responsibility to represent any kind of historical truth?

A Not unless that's his intention. If it's your intention to be truthful to history and you put a piece out saying this is the true story of, say, the murder of Julius Caesar exactly as the historical record has it, then of course, you do have an obligation, because if you then deliberately tell lies about it, you are, you know, you're deceiving your audience. If, however, you say you're writing a drama about the assassination of Julius Caesar purely from your own perspective and entirely in a fictional context, then you have the right to tell the story however you like. I don't think you have any obligation except to the story that you're telling. What you can't be is deliberately dishonest. You can't say this is true when you know full well it isn't.

I Can you think of any examples where you feel the facts have been twisted too far?

A Well, I think the notion of whether a film, a historical film has gone too far in presenting a dramatized fictional version of the truth is really a matter of personal taste. The danger is with any historical film that if that becomes the only thing that the audience sees on that subject, if it becomes the received version of the truth, as it were, because people don't always make the distinction between movies and reality in history, then obviously if that film is grossly irresponsible or grossly fantastic in its presentation of the truth, that could, I suppose, become controversial. I mean, you know, I think that the only thing anybody is ever likely to know about *Spartacus*, for example, the movie, is Kirk Douglas and all his friends standing up and saying 'I am Spartacus, I am Spartacus', which is a wonderful moment and it stands for the notion of freedom, of individual choice and so on. So *Spartacus* the film, made in 1962, I think, if memory serves, has become, I think, for nearly everybody who knows anything about Spartacus the only version of the truth. Now in fact, we don't know if any of that is true really. There are some accounts of the historical Spartacus, but very very few and what, virtually the only thing that's known about is that there was a man called Spartacus and there was a rebellion and many people were, you know, were crucified at the end of it, as in the film. Whether that's irresponsible I don't know, I can't say that I think it is, I think in a way it's, *Spartacus* is a film that had a resonance in the modern era. There are other examples, you know, a lot of people felt that the version of William Wallace that was presented in *Braveheart* was really pushing the limits of what history could stand, the whole, in effect, his whole career was invented in the film, or at least, you know built on to such a degree that some people felt that perhaps it was more about the notion of Scotland as an independent country than it was about history as an authentic spectacle. But you know, again these things are a matter of purely personal taste. I mean, I enjoyed *Braveheart* immensely.

d ● **4.17** This exercise gives SS intensive listening practice in deciphering phrases where words are often run together, and introduces them to some common expressions and idioms used in spoken English. Focus on phrases 1–7 and give SS time to read them. Play the CD, pausing after the first phrase and replaying it as necessary. Elicit the missing words, and then the meaning of the whole phrase. Repeat for the other six phrases.

1 at **the very least** (= as a minimum amount, probably the number will be higher)

2 **weighed up** (= considered and looked at very carefully)

3 a **case in point** (= a clear example of the situation being discussed)

4 **and so on** (= etc., used at the end of a list to show that it continues in the same way)

5 **it comes to** (= when you are talking about)

6 **a matter of** perspective (= a question of)

7 know **full well** (= to be very aware of a fact and unable to deny or ignore it)

1 …you know that part of your audience at the very least
   will already have some knowledge of that story…
2 …every shot has to be weighed up to make sure that
   there's nothing in it which, which betrays the period.
3 *Rome* was a case in point. We needed big crowds.
4 …all of them have to be dressed in, you know, in togas
   and so on.
5 So I tend to take the view that in a way accuracy isn't the
   issue when it comes to the drama.
6 So it's all a matter of perspective in some ways.
7 You can't say this is true when you know full well it isn't.

Extra support

If there's time, get SS to listen again with the scripts on
pp.128–129, focusing on any new vocabulary, and getting
feedback on phrases SS didn't understand, e.g. because the
words were run together.

e ● Finally, focus on the two questions. For the second
    question you could suggest *El Cid*, *Lawrence of Arabia*,
    Gandhi. Get SS to answer in pairs and then get feedback
    from the whole class, or do this as an open-class
    discussion.

IN THE STREET

a ● **4.18** Focus on the task and play the CD once for SS
    to answer the questions. Get them to compare their
    answers with a partner and then elicit the answers onto
    the board. Leave the two questions the interviewer
    asked on the board as SS will use these later.

> **Questions**
> 1 If you could have lived in another historical period,
>   which period would you choose?
> 2 Which historical figure do you particularly admire?
> a) Tim (1960s and 70s)
> b) Mark (Ancient Greece)

(script in Student's Book on *p.129*)
I = **interviewer**, T = **Tim**, E = **Edmund**, M = **Mark**,
A = **Amy**, J = **Jerry**

Tim
I If you could have lived in another historical period, which
   period would you choose?
T I would have chosen the 60s and the 70s because of the
   music of that time. I thought the musical revolution, you
   know, you had the Beatles coming over to America. And,
   just the music, and it was a different culture at that time. I
   would have liked to experience that.
I Which historical figure do you particularly admire?
T Admire? I'd have to say Abraham Lincoln. He was pretty
   impactful on our country. You know, he had a lot of
   revolutionary viewpoints at that point in time that really
   put this country in a direction that I thought was pretty
   unique and necessary at the time.

Edmund
I If you could have lived in another historical period, which
   period would you choose?
E I think probably ancient Rome, probably the 1st, 2nd
   century AD, I think, because I'm most interested in that
   sort of period. And I quite like the idea of living in Italy,
   so…
I Which historical figure do you particularly admire?
E So many. I suppose I've always had a fondness for, sort of,
   the great generals, Alexander, or Wellington, or people
   like that, I suppose.

Mark
I If you could have lived in another historical period, which
   period would you choose?
M I think, sort of, ancient Greece quite appeals, I have to say.
   Sort of, I don't know, sitting around in a toga doing lots of
   thinking. Yeah, ancient Greece.
I Which historical figure do you particularly admire?
M I would say Leonardo da Vinci, principally because he
   is that archetypal Renaissance man. You know, a true
   polymath, genius really.

Amy
I If you could have lived in another historical period, which
   period would you choose?
A I think it would probably be the Victorian period because
   they always used to dress up so magnificently during the
   day and I just, I look around the streets nowadays and
   see people wearing jeans and that seems very normal so
   it would be very interesting to go back to a period like
   Victorian England where they dressed very elaborately
   and see if that's normal and what's casual and what's
   well dressed. I think that would be really interesting. So
   nothing historical.
I Which historical figure do you particularly admire?
A Gosh, I'm not really sure. I do very much admire
   Shakespeare. It's probably a very typical answer, but I
   think his writing's absolutely phenomenal and very much
   ahead of its time when he was writing it. So I would say
   that's the most influential person I can think of.

Jerry
I If you could have lived in another historical period, which
   period would you choose?
J I think maybe, maybe the 1950s. I wouldn't want to go
   very far back, maybe the 1950s.
I Why?
J I think it was quite a, at least in Britain, it was quite an
   optimistic time. I think society seemed to be progressing
   well and science seemed to be progressing well. And it
   seemed to be a time of hope, a sort of optimistic sort of
   time, unlike now, I think, where a lot of things like social
   developments and scientific developments seem more sort
   of ambivalent and unclear. I think that was a good time to
   be around.
I Which historical figure do you particularly admire?
J I've just read a book about Darwin, about Charles
   Darwin, and I think he was an amazing figure. I think
   to come up with an idea so simple and so brilliant and to
   have the courage to publish it. I think he was an amazing
   chap.

b ● Focus on the task. Play the recording again the whole
    way through and then give SS time to answer the
    questions. Then play it again, pausing after each speaker
    this time for SS to check and complete their answers.
    Play the recording as necessary and check answers.

> 1 **Abraham Lincoln** – he had a lot of impact on the
>   USA. His revolutionary viewpoints put the country
>   in the right direction.
> 2 **Alexander** (the Great) or (The Duke of) **Wellington**
>   – great generals
> 3 **Leonardo da Vinci** – the archetypal Renaissance
>   man, a genius
> 4 (William) **Shakespeare** – his writing is phenomenal
>   and very ahead of its time. He was very influential.
> 5 **Charles Darwin** – He came up with an idea which
>   was so simple and so brilliant and he had the
>   courage to publish it.

c ● **4.19** Focus on the phrases and give SS time to read them. Play the CD, pausing after the first phrase and replaying it as necessary. Elicit the missing words, and then the meaning of the whole phrase. Repeat for the other four phrases.

> 1 **coming over** (PV = travelling from one place to another, usually over a long distance and especially crossing seas or continents)
> 2 **like the idea of** (= I think I would enjoy)
> 3 **sitting around** (PV = spend time doing nothing very useful)
> 4 **absolutely phenomenal** (= extraordinary, impressive)
> 5 **come up with** (PV = to think of, to invent)

4.19	CD3 Track 9

1 …you know, you had the Beatles coming over to America.
2 And I quite like the idea of living in Italy, so…
3 Sort of, I don't know, sitting around in a toga doing lots of thinking.
4 I think his writing's absolutely phenomenal and very much ahead of its time…
5 I think to come up with an idea so simple and so brilliant…

Extra support

If there's time, get SS to listen again with the scripts on *p.129*, focusing on any new vocabulary, and getting feedback on phrases SS didn't understand, e.g. because the words were run together.

d ● Finally, get SS to ask each other the two questions that the interviewer asked the interviewees. Then get some feedback from the whole class.

HOMEWORK

Study Link **Workbook** *p.43*

4 REVISE & CHECK

For instructions on how to use this page, see *p.35*.

GRAMMAR

a		b	
1	b	1	to learn
2	a	2	would have enjoyed
3	a	3	travelling
4	b	4	pay
5	c	5	doesn't mind
6	a	6	would win
7	c	7	hadn't been wearing
8	a	8	to attend
9	c	9	Had…told
10	c	10	catching
		11	wouldn't be living
		12	have seen

VOCABULARY

a		b		c	
1	landline	1	broken		
2	casualties	2	get		
3	ceasefire	3	up		
4	voicemail	4	blow		
5	minded	5	out		
6	enquiries	6	up		
7	sighted			1	of
8	siege			2	on
9	worn			3	with
10	arrows			4	on
11	retreat			5	on
12	refugees				

Test and Assessment CD-ROM

File 4 Quicktest
File 4 Test

5
A

G permission, obligation, and necessity
V word formation: prefixes
P intonation in exclamations

Who's in control?

File 5 overview

This File begins, in **5A**, with a grammar focus on modal verbs and other expressions used to talk about permission, obligation, and necessity. SS also do further work on word building, adding prefixes to change the meaning of a word. In **5B** they look at verbs of the senses and related structures, with a vocabulary focus on prepositions of place and movement. Finally, in **5C**, the grammar focus is on more uses and types of gerunds and infinitives, and in vocabulary SS revise and expand their vocabulary related to health and medicine, and learn a set of health-related similes.

Lesson plan

The topic of this lesson is control. In the first part the focus is on the 'nanny state', i.e. policies where the state is characterized as being excessive in its desire to protect ('nanny') or control particular aspects of society or groups of people. SS read an article about new 'nanny state' laws in California, and then go into the grammar of permission, obligation, and necessity. They put the grammar into practice discussing the advantages or disadvantages of possible laws. The vocabulary focus is on prefixes which add meaning, e.g. anti-smoking. The angle of the topic then moves to control in education, and SS find out about the QI phenomenon, a TV quiz programme and series of books based on principles which the authors think should be applied to education, e.g. giving children control over their learning. The lesson ends with a pronunciation focus on intonation in exclamations such as *How ridiculous!*

Optional lead-in – the quote

- Write the quote at the top of *p.68* on the board (books closed) and the name of the author or get SS to open their books and read it. Get SS to discuss what they think it means (A bad law is an abuse of power).
- Point out that Edmund Burke (1729–1797) was also a Member of Parliament, and supported a lot of unpopular causes, e.g. he wanted to change the laws which prevented free trade with Ireland, and also to abolish laws which forbade Catholics from voting.
- Ask SS if they can think of any laws in their country which they would like to change or abolish.

1 READING & SPEAKING

a
- Write 'Nanny state' on the board and ask SS if any of them know what the expression refers to, or if they can guess. Help SS by asking what a *nanny* does (= take care of children, teach them how to behave).
- Then give SS a few minutes to read the definition and, with a partner, to summarize what it means.

Suggested answer
'Nanny state' is used to refer to laws passed by a government (central or local), which is trying to protect us from situations or our own behaviour, which the state considers harmful for us. (The implication is that the state knows best what is good and bad for us.)

b
- Focus on the title of the article and elicit from the class what they think it might be about ('Nannyfornia' is a play on words, combining *Nanny* and *California*, so it implies that the article will be something to do with California having 'nanny state' laws.).

c
- Focus on the task and the laws. Give SS time to go through them with a partner and discuss which ones they think may be true. Get feedback to find out which laws the majority of the class think really exist there.

Extra support

To help SS you might want to pre-teach *mandatory* and *age of majority*.

d
- Now set a time limit for SS to read the article and find out if they guessed correctly. Highlight that they have to mark some of the statements DS (doesn't say) as there are things not mentioned in the article.
- Check answers.

1	T
2	F ('Speed cameras remain unheard of')
3	T
4	T
5	T
6	DS
7	DS (the text implies that you are allowed to drive them but it doesn't specifically say so)
8	DS
9	F ('CCTV is rare')
10	T
11	T
12	DS

Digital extra idea

Ask SS to do some research on the Internet to find out whether any new nanny state laws have been passed recently in California.

LEXIS IN CONTEXT

e
- Focus on the task. Point out that some of these phrasal verbs have more than one meaning so SS should focus on the meaning of the verb as it is used in the article. Check answers.

pull up = (of a vehicle) to stop
wind sth down = (of a car window) to open
lean out = to bend or move from a vertical position so that you are partly outside, e.g. of a window
put sth out = (of a fire or cigarette) extinguish
hand sth out = to distribute sth to members of a group
bring sth in = to introduce
stub sth out = (of a cigarette) extinguish

f ● Focus on the instructions. Tell SS to start re-reading and stop when they come to the first phrase that they think shows the writer's attitude to the laws (*the most restrictive anti-smoking policy anywhere…* on line *12.*)

● Then get SS to continue on their own, and compare with a partner. Check which phrases they have underlined and elicit that the writer of the article is against many of the laws or considers them to be excessive.

Phrases that could be underlined (although sometimes this is open to opinion)
a frenzy of puritanical edicts (line *15*)
Other recent bans have challenged such monumental threats to human wellbeing as helium balloons (line *18*)
Of course, some of these things deserve to be discouraged. But criminalized? (line *23*)
California seemed to have avoided many of the worst examples of nanny-stateism inflicted on, say, Britain. (line *25*)
Tax on petrol isn't designed to punish you (line *27*)

g ● Focus on the task and get SS to go through the article with a partner, and discuss each law as it comes up (starting with the outdoor smoking ban on line *14*).

● Get feedback from the class as to which laws they think would be a good idea and why, and ask them what laws in their region they consider to be 'nanny state'.

Extra support

Ask SS to choose five other words or phrases they would like to learn from the article and get them to compare their choices. Get some feedback from the class as to the words or phrases they have chosen and deal with any vocabulary problems that arise.

2 GRAMMAR permission, obligation, and necessity

a ● Focus on the task and the pairs of sentences. Give SS time to discuss each pair with a partner. If necessary, remind them of the meaning of 'a difference in register', i.e. in the level of formality or informality.

1 The same in meaning but *It is not permitted* is more formal.
2 The same register but a slight difference in meaning: *you'd better* is stronger than *you ought to* and suggests that something negative may happen if you don't, i.e. *You'd better turn your mobile off in case it goes off in class. The teacher will be furious if it does.*
3 The same register but a slight difference in meaning: *We're supposed to speak English…* suggests that there is an obligation to speak English in class but that people don't always do it.
4 The same meaning and register.

5 The same register but completely different meaning:
I should have… = it was an obligation but I didn't do it.
I had to… = it was an obligation and I did it.

b ● Tell SS to go to **Grammar Bank 5A** on *p.148*. Go through each example and its corresponding rule with the class, or give SS time to read the examples and rules on their own, and answer any queries.

Grammar notes

● There are many different verbs in English, some of which are modal verbs, used to express permission, obligation, and necessity. The use of the most common ones should be revision for SS at this level. However, there are areas where there are small differences in meaning and register, e.g. between *have to* and *have got to*, or between *should* and *had better*, *don't need to* and *needn't*, etc. and this is the main focus of this section.

● Some SS may also still have ingrained basic errors such as confusing *mustn't* and *don't have to*.

● Focus on the exercises for **5A**. SS do the exercises individually or in pairs. If SS do them individually, get them to compare with a partner before checking answers. Check answers after each exercise.

a 1 supposed to park
  2 better put out that cigarette / put that cigarette out
  3 have lost my temper
  4 not permitted / forbidden / not allowed
  5 have to / must wear a seat belt
  6 allowed to swim
  7 have to wear a tie
  8 ought to / should get
  9 got to finish the sales report
  10 needn't bring your car /don't need to
b 1 have to pay
  2 is not permitted / allowed
  3 better not be
  4 needn't pay me
  5 shouldn't have said
  6 had to change
  7 ought to do
  8 allowed / supposed to use
  9 needn't have brought / taken / worn
  10 supposed to wear

● Tell SS to go back to the main lesson on *p.69*.

3 SPEAKING

a ● Divide SS into groups of three or four and focus on the task. Point out that some of the proposed laws in the exercise already exist in parts of the UK or USA. For example, the three proposed laws about education have been adopted as rules or guidelines by certain local councils in the UK. You may also want to elicit / explain the meaning of *units of alcohol* (= a fixed quantity; in the UK a unit of alcohol is 10 millilitres, e.g. one glass of wine is just over two units).

95

- You may want to set a time limit for each section to get SS to move on or to leave an argument where they strongly disagree. Remind them that they should back up their opinions with reasons.

⚠️ Some of these proposals may already be laws in your SS' country, in which case get them to discuss what they think of them.

- Monitor and correct, especially mistakes involving the bold verbs and phrases.

Extra support

You could discuss the laws in the first section with the whole class before getting them to continue in their groups.

- Get feedback by asking different groups which law they would most like to introduce from each section.

b • Focus on the task. Set a time limit, and tell SS if they can't think of a law they would like to introduce in one particular section, then they should move on to the next. One member of the group should write down the new 'law'.

- For each section write the proposed laws on the board. Get one person from the group that proposed the law to defend it to the other groups. Then have a class vote as to which law should be implemented.
- Continue with the other sections.

4 VOCABULARY word formation: prefixes

a • Focus on the task and the examples, and elicit that *anti* adds the meaning of 'against'. Highlight that sometimes there is a hyphen between *anti* and the next word (e.g. *anti-hero, anti-war*), but sometimes not (e.g. *anticlimax*).

- Elicit / explain that *out* here means *outside* and give more examples, e.g. an *outgoing* (= extrovert) person, an *outboard* motor, but warn SS that the prefix *out* has another meaning which they will see in the exercise below.

b • Focus on the instructions and give SS time to go through the sentences with a partner. Point out that *out* in sentence 1 has a different meaning from *out* in *outlaw*.

- Check answers, eliciting from SS what the sentence means.

1 exceeds, is larger than (There are more non-native than native speakers.)
2 too much (It is not as good as some people say it is.)
3 again (Waking up again a romance that had died)
4 wrongly (Portrayed in a way that wasn't accurate or truthful)
5 not enough (People do not value the importance of the translator enough.)
6 in favour of (Spending money in favour of society, i.e. on other people)
7 before (Her skin has aged earlier than is normal.)
8 lower (The value of the pound is lower than before.)

c • Set the task either for SS to do individually or in pairs. If they do it individually, get them to compare with a partner before checking answers.

1 misjudged
2 rewrite
3 antivirus
4 prearranged
5 outsells
6 Pro-government
7 demotivated
8 underprepared
9 overcharged
10 outdoor

5 LISTENING & SPEAKING

a • Divide the class into teams with at least four SS in each team. Focus on the task and the quiz questions. Set a time limit.

b • When the time limit is up, tell SS to go to **Communication** *QI quiz*. **A** on *p.117*, **B** on *p.119* to check their answers. Get feedback to find out which teams answered the most questions correctly, and which answers SS were surprised by.

c • **5.1** Focus on the task. Some SS may know about *QI* as the books have been translated into several languages.

- Give SS time to read the questions. Then play the CD once for SS to try to answer the questions. Get SS to compare answers. Then play the CD again. You could pause the recording where spaces have been inserted into the script to give SS more time. Check answers.

1 It stands for Quite Interesting and is IQ backwards (IQ = intelligence quotient, the numerical measurement of sb's intelligence).
2 Everything you think you know is probably wrong, and everything is interesting.
3 Goldfish have quite long memories; Julius Caesar was not born by Caesarean section.
4 Because human beings, especially children, are naturally curious and want to learn.
5 Because even the best schools can make an interesting subject boring by making SS memorize facts, and because SS only learn effectively when they do it voluntarily, so if they are forced to learn something, they will be less successful.

5.1   CD3 Track 10

(script in Student's Book on *p.129*)
Why is it that so many children don't seem to learn anything at school? A TV producer-turned-writer has come up with some very revolutionary ideas.
A few years ago TV producer John Lloyd thought up a formula for a new quiz show. The show is called *QI*, which stands for 'Quite Interesting', and which is also IQ backwards. It's a comedy quiz hosted by actor Stephen Fry, where panellists have to answer unusual general knowledge questions, and it's perhaps surprising that it's particularly popular among 15- to 25-year-olds. Along with co-author John Mitchinson, Lloyd has since written a number of QI books, for example *The Book of General Ignorance*, and these have also been incredibly successful.

Lloyd's basic principle is very simple: everything you think you know is probably wrong, and everything is interesting. The *QI Book of General Ignorance*, for example, poses 240 questions, all of which reveal surprising answers. So we learn, for example, that goldfish have quite long memories, that you're more likely to be killed by an asteroid than by lightning, or that Julius Caesar was not, in fact, born by Caesarian section.

The popularity of these books proves Lloyd's other thesis: that human beings, and children in particular, are naturally curious and have a desire to learn. And this, he believes, has several implications for education. According to Lloyd and Mitchinson, there are two reasons why children, in spite of being curious, tend to do badly at school. Firstly, even the best schools can take a fascinating subject, such as electricity or classical civilization, and make it boring, by turning it into facts which have to be learnt by heart and then regurgitated for exams. Secondly, *QI*'s popularity seems to prove that learning takes place most effectively when it's done voluntarily. The same teenagers who will happily choose to read a *QI* book will often sit at the back of a geography class and go to sleep, or worse still, disrupt the rest of the class.

d ● **5.2** Focus on the task and give SS time to read the statements. Play the CD once, and get SS to compare which suggestions they have ticked. Play the recording again as necessary. Check answers.

The following should be ticked
Learning should never feel like hard work.
Children should be able to decide on their own curriculum.
Children shouldn't be expected to learn to read until they actually want to.
Children shouldn't be made to go to school every day if they don't want to.
There should be no evaluation or assessment of children by teachers.
Children should learn theories through practical activities.
There should be no official school leaving age.

5.2   CD3 Track 11

(script in Student's Book on *p.129*)
So how could we change our schools so that children would enjoy learning? What would a 'QI school' be like? These are Lloyd and Mitchinson's basic suggestions.
The first principle is that education should be more play than work. The more learning involves things like storytelling and making things, the more interested children will become. Secondly, they believe that the best people to control what children learn are the children themselves. Children should be encouraged to follow their curiosity. They will end up learning to read, for example, because they want to, in order to read about something they're interested in.
Thirdly, they argue that children should be in control of when and how they learn. The QI school would not be compulsory, so pupils wouldn't have to go if they didn't want to, and there would be no exams. There would only be projects, or goals that children set themselves with the teacher helping them. So a project could be something like making a film or building a chair.
Fourthly, there should never be theory without practice. You can't learn about vegetables and what kind of plants they are from books and pictures; you need to go and plant them and watch them grow.
The fifth and last point Lloyd and Mitchinson make is there's no reason why school has to stop dead at 17 or 18. The QI school would be a place where you would be able to carry on learning all your life, a mini-university where the young and old could continue to find out about all the things they are naturally curious about.

e ● Focus on the points ticked in **d**, and get SS to first discuss them in pairs, and then go through the other suggestions (the ones they didn't tick).

Extra support

You could write on the board:
Do you think it's a good idea? Why (not)?
Do you think it's practical? Why (not)?

and get SS to answer the two questions for each suggestion.
Get feedback by finding out which of the suggestions SS both agree with and think could be put into practice, eliciting reasons.

Digital extra idea

Go to www.telegraph.co.uk/culture/qi/ to set some work for mini projects. Each group would look at one topic and feedback to the class. You would need a computer lab or it could be set as homework.

6 PRONUNCIATION intonation in exclamations

Pronunciation notes

When we make an exclamation, e.g. using *How* + adjective or *What* + adjective + noun, we usually give the adjective extra emphasis, with a rise-fall intonation. It is important to get the intonation right, because if the adjective is said with a flat or falling tone, it could sound as if you are uninterested or even being sarcastic.

a ● **5.3** Focus on the task. Play the CD, pausing for SS to write down **B**'s exclamation. Play the CD again as necessary. Check answers and write the exclamations on the board.

See **bold** exclamations in script 5.3

5.3   CD3 Track 12

A Did you know that in California schools they're not allowed to say 'Mom' and 'Dad' any more in case they offend someone from a one-parent family?
B **What a ridiculous idea**!

A Did you know that America was named after a British merchant called Richard Ameryk?
B **How interesting**! I'd always wondered where the name came from.

b ● Focus on the task and the questions. Then play the dialogues a couple of times more for SS to listen. Get them to discuss what they think and then check answers.

1 c
2 The /w/ sound. This is because *interesting* begins with a vowel, and when a word ending in *w* is followed by a word beginning in a vowel, the words are linked and a /w/ sound is inserted between them.

Extra support

A lot of SS (and even TT) find it difficult to identify intonation patterns. If this is the case with your SS, just focus on getting them to copy the pattern by playing the CD for them to repeat.

c ● Give SS time to practise saying the exclamations with a partner. Monitor and encourage them to get the right intonation.

d ● Sit SS in pairs, **A** and **B**, preferably face to face. Tell them to go to **Communication** *What a ridiculous idea!* **A** on *p.117*, **B** on *p.120*. Go through the instructions.

   ● Demonstrate the activity. Invent a piece of news, which should elicit one of the exclamations they have just practised. Tell it to them as convincingly as you can (*Did you know that…?*) and elicit an exclamation.

   ● Get SS to continue in pairs.

Extra photocopiable activities

Grammar
permission, obligation, and necessity *p.169*
Communicative
Mini debates *p.195* (instructions *p.180*)
Vocabulary
Word formation: prefixes *p.220* (instructions *p.206*)

HOMEWORK

Study Link Workbook *pp.44–46*

5
B

G verbs of the senses
V place and movement
P extra stress on important words

Just any old bed?

Lesson plan

In this lesson the topic is art. In the first half of the lesson the focus is on installations, or modern sculptures, things which many people find difficult to accept as art. SS try to identify which photos show works of art and which ordinary objects, and then listen to an expert explaining why these installations are art and what they are trying to convey. Then in the grammar focus SS work on verbs of the senses and the structures which follow them. The pronunciation focus is on giving extra stress to words (which may not normally be stressed) to convey meaning, and uses a poem about art to illustrate the point. In the second part of the lesson SS read a short story by Ray Bradbury, about a man who is obsessed with a famous painter. The lesson ends with a vocabulary focus on prepositions and adverbs of place and movement, and with the song *Vincent*.

Optional lead-in – the quote

● Write the quote at the top of *p.72* on the board (books closed) and the name of the author or get SS to open their books and read it.

● SS should know that the author of the quote, Pablo Picasso (1881–1973), was a Spanish painter and one of the greatest artists of the 20th century. He was a co-founder of the avant-garde art movement known as cubism.

● Get SS to discuss what they think it means. He seems to be saying that while some artists (perhaps inferior in his view) can paint a likeness of the sun, the best painters can convey the sun in a more imaginative way (perhaps through an impressionistic or abstract approach).

● You could ask SS for examples of painters whom they think 'can transform a yellow spot into the sun'.

1 LISTENING & SPEAKING

a ● Focus on the task and the photos, and give SS time to discuss them. Get feedback to find out which of the four objects most SS think are works of art, and why, but don't tell them the answer yet.

b ● Tell SS to go to **Communication** *Four works of art* on *p.118* to find out the answer to **a**, and some more information about the four works of art.

● Now ask SS what they think the artists are trying to communicate, and whether these are works of art in the same way that a painting or sculpture is.

c ● **5.4** Focus on the task and the questions, and give SS time to read them. You may want to point out the pronunciation of *sculpture* /ˈskʌlptʃə/, *portrait* /ˈpɔːtreɪt/, and *formaldehyde* /fɔːˈmældɪhaɪd/.

● Play the CD once all the way through and tell SS just to listen and not try to answer the questions yet.

● Then play the recording again, this time pausing (see spaces in the script) to give SS time to answer. Then get them to compare their answers with a partner.

d ● Play the recording as many times as necessary. Check answers.

1 a) Installations are mixed media artworks which take up a whole gallery or space.
   b) Modern sculptures are assemblies of objects which may take up a little less space than an installation, and which you would perhaps not think of as a traditional work of art at first sight.

2 In both cases the artist has an idea they want to communicate. They choose the medium (painting, sculpture, or an installation) which is most suitable to communicate that idea.

3 Because they might have received more training in how to make an installation than in how to draw.

4 They think that painting and drawing require expertise / skill whereas making an installation doesn't. They think, 'I could do that,' when they see an installation.

5 He had to research how the sheep could be preserved in formaldehyde and he had to arrange it in a particular way, so that it looks as if it's alive.

6 It's a kind of statement about death and life.

7 Because the objects on the bed (sheets, pillow, etc.) and on the floor (newspaper, slippers, water bottle, etc.) have been specially placed and arranged in a particular way, not at random, to communicate something.

8 The objects on the bed and on the floor represent her. It's like a self portrait – the story of her life and her relationships.

9 Because we can look at it and understand, as contemporary viewers, a lot about her life.

5.4   CD3 Track 13

(script in Student's Book on *p.129*)
I = interviewer, E = expert
I For most people, art for the last few centuries has meant paintings and sculptures, and suddenly there are all these new kinds of sculptures and installations, that for most people don't mean art. First of all, could you just explain exactly what these kinds of sculptures and installations are?

E Well, installations are really mixed-media artworks, which take up a whole gallery or space, and sculptures, these kind of modern sculptures, are assemblies of objects which may take up a little less space, but which you would perhaps not think of as a traditional work of art when you first saw them.

I So how would you explain to people that installations are also art?

E Well, an installation, or this new kind of modern sculpture, is really no different from a painting or a traditional sculpture if you think about where the artist starts from, and that is they have an idea about something they *want* to communicate, and then they decide *how* to communicate that idea, so that could be in paint, or it could be in stone, or it could be in wood or metal, or it could be through an installation, which could be this kind of assembly of different types of object. In all three methods, in all these different media, they would still be trying to say the same thing.

They would then choose the medium that was suitable for them, or for which they'd been trained in, or which was suitable for that particular idea they wanted to communicate. A lot of artists will have been trained in how to make an installation perhaps more than they will have been trained in how to draw today.

I But I think a lot of people would think that whereas drawing and painting requires an expertise, which the average person doesn't have, when people look at some installations, they think, 'Well, I could do that'. They don't see that there's any expertise involved at all.

E Well, it's just different skills. For example, take Damien Hirst and *Away from the Flock*, which is a sheep in some formaldehyde, in a case. First of all, he had to have the idea, and this was a very original idea, no-one had ever done anything like that before. He came up with the idea of an animal, a sheep, and it's isolated from its flock, and he came up with the idea of preserving this animal in formaldehyde, which is of course something that scientists have done, but artists haven't done. And then he had to research how this animal could be properly preserved in this substance, the formaldehyde, and how in ten or 20 years it would still be there and in good condition for people to look at, so there is a technical side to it as well. And then of course he had to arrange it in a particular way, this animal is in a particular pose, so that it looks as if it's quite alive, although of course we all know that it isn't. So it's a combination of an original idea and some very specific skills.

I And what is he trying to communicate to us through it?

E Well, as I said, the sheep looks alive, yet we all know it isn't, and so I think it's a kind of statement about death and life, just as lots of more classical kinds of art, paintings, are about life and death, and it's not really different from those, it's just that it's expressed in a different way. I think the important thing is what it gets the viewers to think about and to reflect on, and that's the same with all art. I mean there isn't really any difference.

I OK so I can understand that you need a certain amount of technical ability to create the sheep in formaldehyde, but what about the bed? I mean the bed is something that you look at and you think, 'Yeah, that looks like my bed in the morning'.

E Well, Tracey Emin's bed isn't actually her bed as it is in the morning when she gets up every day; it is a bed, and there are sheets and pillows, and lots of other objects, but she has assembled these objects to represent her self, this is an autobiographical piece just like a self-portrait, without her face or her body in it, but it still represents her. It's the story of her life, it's her relationship with all the men in her life and other people. You look on the floor and there are lots of bits of her, there are her slippers, her toy dog, and newspapers that she's read, and bottles of water. So it's a story of her life, and it's arranged in a very particular way, it's not random, not just like your bed or my bed, it's a bed that she's very specifically organized to communicate something about herself. I mean it's a different set of skills, from painting a self-portrait, but actually maybe it communicates a whole lot more to us, to viewers, than some self-portraits do, because actually we can look at it and understand, as contemporary viewers, a lot about her life. And incidentally, Tracey Emin is, in fact, very skilled at drawing, so if she'd wanted to say draw a self-portrait, she could have done that. But she chose this way of communicating her message.

Extra support

If there's time, get SS to listen again with the script on *p.129*, focusing on any new vocabulary, and getting feedback on phrases SS didn't understand, e.g. because the words were run together.

e • Put SS into small groups and go through the questions. Give them time to discuss the questions. Monitor and help with vocabulary.
  • Get feedback by asking different groups how they responded to the questions. You could also answer them yourself.

2 GRAMMAR verbs of the senses

a • (5.5) Focus on the task and get SS to do it individually or in pairs. Then play the CD for them to check their answers.

> See **bold** words in script 5.5

5.5   CD3 Track 14

1 When people **look at** some installations, they think 'Well I could do that', they don't **see** that there's any expertise involved at all.
2 And then of course he had to arrange it in a particular way, this animal is in a particular pose, so that it **looks as if** it's quite alive, although of course we all know that it isn't.
3 I mean the bed is something that you **look at** and you think 'Yeah, that **looks like** my bed in the morning'.

---

b • Focus on the questions. Get SS to answer them in pairs, and then check answers with the whole class. Alternatively, you could do this as a whole class activity.

1 *look as if* (or *as though*) is followed by a clause (*It looks as if it is alive*).
  It looks like is normally followed by a noun (*It looks like my bed in the morning*). However, in informal English it can also be followed by a clause (*It looks like it is alive*).
  look at = to turn your eyes in a particular direction. It is a conscious action. We look at a view, a photo, a person, etc.
  see = to become aware of sb / sth by using your eyes. It is not necessarily a conscious action – you can see something without looking at it.
  see can also be used like *watch*, e.g. + a match, a TV programme.
2 The other four senses are *smell*, *hearing*, *taste*, and *touch*.
3 Verbs associated with them are:
  smell: *smell, sniff*
  hearing: *hear, listen, sound* (*It sounds like thunder*)
  taste: *taste*
  touch: *touch, feel*

c • Tell SS to go to **Grammar Bank 5B** on *p.149*. Go through each example and its corresponding rule with the class, or give SS time to read the examples and rules on their own, and answer any queries.

Grammar notes

- The basic verbs related to the senses, *see*, *hear*, *smell*, *feel*, and *taste* do not work in quite the same way in English as in many other languages. They are not usually used in continuous forms and are normally preceded by *can* (e.g. *I can smell garlic* NOT ~~I smell garlic~~ or ~~I'm smelling garlic~~).

- The verbs which are used to describe the impression something or someone gives through the senses are the same for smell, taste, and feel (e.g. *It smells awful. They taste nice*, etc.) but for sight we use *look* (*You look exhausted*, etc.) and for hearing we use *sound* (*It sounds like thunder*, etc.).

- Focus on the exercises for **5B**. SS do the exercises individually or in pairs. If SS do them individually, get them to compare with a partner before checking answers. Check answers after each exercise.

> **a** 1 ✓
> 2 ✓
> 3 I actually heard the bomb explode.
> 4 It sounds like Beethoven's 7th
> 5 ✓
> 6 it feels more like plastic
> 7 ✓
>
> **b** 1 ✓   4 is looking
> 2 seems   5 look
> 3 seem
>
> **c** 1 like   5 of
> 2 seems   6 fishing
> 3 shut / close / slam   7 can't
> 4 if / though

- Tell SS to go back to the main lesson on *p.73*.

d • Focus on the questions and give SS a few minutes to read them. You could ask SS to choose one or two of the questions to ask you.

- Put SS in pairs and give them time to answer the questions together. Monitor and correct, especially mistakes with the verbs of the senses.

3 PRONUNCIATION extra stress on important words

Pronunciation notes

SS have always been taught that certain words (ones that convey information) are stressed more strongly in a sentence, and other words such as pronouns, articles, auxiliary verbs, etc. are not stressed. However, if we want to emphasize a particular aspect of meaning, almost *any* word in a sentence can be given extra emphasis.

a • **5.6** Focus on the poem. Point out that the poet Michael Swan is also a well-known grammar expert (author of *The Good Grammar Book, How English Works, Practical English Usage*) and SS are likely to have used one of his grammar books.

- Play the CD once for SS to read and listen. Then get SS to answer the questions in pairs, and then elicit answers from the class. You might want to elicit / explain who *Janus* is (= a Roman god with two faces or heads facing in opposite directions).

> 1 At an exhibition in an art gallery.
> 2 The directors of the gallery, or the people selling the works of art.
> 3 He buys the egg because he thinks it's a bargain and presumably will be a good investment.
> 4 He seems to be satirizing a certain kind of pretentious art connoisseur and their way of speaking. He shows how easy it is for them to fool someone, who knows very little about art, to pay a lot of money for something that may not really be worth the price they have paid.

> **5.6**   CD3 Track 15
> (See Student's Book)

b • Focus on the task. Play the poem again, this time with SS concentrating on the rhythm and stress. Elicit that the words are written in italics because they are words that are given extra stress when they are read aloud.

- Put SS in pairs, and get them to read the poem aloud together (**A** could read everything the buyer says and **B** read everything 'they' said), then get one or more pairs to read it aloud to the class.

c • **5.7** Go through the information box with SS. Then play the CD once the whole way through. Then play it again, pausing after each sentence for SS to match it to one of the continuations A–E. Get them to compare with a partner.

Extra challenge

You could ask SS to work out the different stresses before they listen to the recording.

> **5.7**   CD3 Track 16
> 1 I wanted to buy a flat in <u>London</u>.
> 2 I wanted to <u>buy</u> a flat in London.
> 3 <u>I</u> wanted to buy a flat in London.
> 4 I wanted to buy a <u>flat</u> in London.
> 5 I <u>wanted</u> to buy a flat in London.

d • **5.8** Play the CD for SS to check their answers. Elicit which word is stressed in each sentence.

> 1 D   2 E   3 A   4 B   5 C

> **5.8**   CD3 Track 17
> 1 I wanted to buy a flat in <u>London</u>, not in Liverpool.
> 2 I wanted to <u>buy</u> a flat in London, not rent one.
> 3 <u>I</u> wanted to buy a flat in London, but my wife didn't.
> 4 I wanted to buy a <u>flat</u> in London, but my wife wanted a house.
> 5 I <u>wanted</u> to buy a flat in London, but we couldn't afford one.

- Then get SS to practise saying the complete sentences, stressing the right word each time.

Extra support

Write a 'key' on the board so that SS remember which word has extra stress each time:

A stress on *I*, B stress on *flat*, C stress on *wanted*, D stress on *London*, E stress on *buy*

e ● Sit SS in pairs, **A** and **B**, preferably face to face. Tell them to go to **Communication** *Stressing the right word*. **A** on *p.118*, **B** on *p.120*. Go through the instructions.

● Demonstrate the activity. Write on the board: *She doesn't look 85.*

● Tell SS that they have to respond to what you're going to say with the sentence on the board, giving one word extra stress. Then say to the class *It was my mother's birthday yesterday. She was 85.* and elicit the response *She doesn't look 85.*

● Then get an **A** to say his / her first sentence (*That girl really looks like your sister*), and elicit from the **B**s *She is my sister.* Tell the **B**s to underline *is*.

● Now get SS to continue in pairs. **A** should read all his / her sentences first for **B** to respond, underlining the stressed word, and then vice versa.

● Finally, check that they have stressed (and underlined) the right words in the responses.

B 1 She is my sister.
2 No, I said she was Canadian.
3 No, it's the one before the traffic lights.
4 Personally, I still think she'd prefer that one.
5 I've bought it, but I haven't read it yet.
6 I told you to put it under my bed.
A 7 He's not my dog. He's my partner's dog.
8 Sorry, I asked for a tuna salad.
9 I gave him the money. He'd never be able to pay me back.
10 It looks expensive but actually it was really cheap.
11 I am going out. I haven't been out for ages.
12 They lost 2–1, you mean.

---

4 READING

● **5.9** Point out to SS that this is a short story by Ray Bradbury (1920–), a famous American writer whose most popular work is probably his science fiction novel *Fahrenheit 451*. The story here is quite challenging in terms of lexis, but SS should be motivated by the fact that they are reading an unsimplified piece of literature.

● This is a dramatized reading of the story, which encourages SS to all read at the same speed without getting stuck on unknown words, to help their understanding, and to increase their enjoyment. The title of the story is from a poem by the 19th century poet Wordsworth (*Ode: Intimations of Immortality*).

● Focus on the photo of Picasso and point out that although Pablo Picasso was Spanish, he lived for much of his life in the south of France. He often visited Biarritz, a seaside town in south-western France, which is where the short story is set.

● Focus on the story and the first section. Tell SS they are going to read and listen in sections, and then answer questions.

● Play the CD once for SS to listen and read. Then give them time to answer the questions in pairs. Check answers, and then deal with any other words or phrases that have caused problems.

---

1 George is an American art-lover, obsessed with Picasso. His wife is clearly not especially interested in Picasso, and perhaps is less well-educated than her husband. She seems to know her husband very well, and to be keeping a close eye on him.

2 *detrained* = got off the train
sprawled = lying with his arms and legs spread out in a lazy or awkward way
loomed = appeared as a large threatening shape
winced = made an expression with his face that showed that her mispronunciation pained or embarrassed him

---

5.9   CD3 Track 18

(See Student's Book)

● **5.10** Play the next section for SS to listen and read. Give SS time to answer the questions in pairs. Check answers, and then deal with any other words or phrases that have caused problems, e.g. *trudged* = walk very slowly with heavy steps.

---

3 To buy a painting from Picasso

4 *their bodies all lobster colours* = bright red like a lobster because they had stayed in the sun too long and they had got sunburnt
their wedding-cake hotels = white and with a lot of decoration, like a wedding cake
the shoreline stage was set = sth dramatic was going to happen on this piece of beach

5 He is quite short, well-built, and very suntanned with clear bright eyes, and his hair cut very short, as if it had been shaved (i.e. like Picasso in the photo).

5.10   CD3 Track 19

(See Student's Book)

● **5.11** Play the next section for SS to listen and read. Give SS time to answer the questions in pairs. Check answers, and then deal with any other words or phrases that have caused problems.

---

6 He picks up a stick from an ice cream, and starts drawing in the sand. George at first thinks it is just an old man playing around and finds it amusing (he chuckles), but when he gets closer, he suddenly realizes who it is and begins to tremble.

7 a) They are all words which describe ways of seeing:
glance = to look quickly at sth; *spy* = to suddenly see or notice sth; *gaze* = to look steadily at sth for a long time
b) They are all verbs which describe ways of drawing or writing:
sketch = to make a quick drawing of sth;
scribble = to write sth quickly and carelessly, or to draw marks that don't mean anything;
doodle = to draw lines or shapes, especially when you are bored or thinking of sth else

---

<table>
<tr><td>**5.11**</td><td>CD3 Track 20</td></tr>
</table>

(See Student's Book)

● **5.12** Play the next section for SS to listen and read. Give SS time to answer the questions in pairs. Check answers, and then deal with any other words or phrases that have caused problems, e.g. *slash* = to make a long cut with a sharp object, *frieze* = a long narrow picture, etc. You may want to demonstrate the verbs in question 9.

8 The artist is first surprised, and then amused by George's presence and his reaction. George is totally overwhelmed by the situation – he can't move or say anything.

9 *tremble* = to shake in a way you can't control, especially because you are very nervous or excited
slash = to make a long cut with a sharp object
draw back = to move backwards (*syn* withdraw)
shrug = to raise your shoulders and then drop them to show that you don't know or don't care about sth
stare = to look at sb or sth for a long time, especially with surprise or fear, or because you are thinking (*gaze* is more formal, and usually implies looking at sth with surprise or love)
blink = to shut and open your eyes quickly

10 If SS don't have any suggested answers (e.g. to bring sb else to see the drawings, to get a camera and photograph them, etc.), don't tell them now as they will find out later.

<table>
<tr><td>**5.12**</td><td>CD3 Track 21</td></tr>
</table>

(See Student's Book)

● **5.13** Play the next section for SS to listen and read. Give SS time to answer the questions in pairs. Check answers, (demonstrating the verbs if necessary) and then deal with any other words or phrases that have caused problems, e.g. *plaster-of-Paris* = a white powder that is mixed with water and becomes very hard when it dries, used especially for making copies of statues, *mould* = a container that you pour a liquid or soft substance into, which then becomes solid in the shape of the container, etc.

11 He doesn't know how to preserve the drawings, which are going to disappear with the tide. He considers digging a part up, getting someone to cast a mould with plaster, or taking photos of it. In the end he decides to walk round them and look at them for as long as possible, to imprint them in his mind, presumably because he realizes that the tide is coming in and there is no time to do anything else.

12 *grab* = to take sth with your hand suddenly or roughly
flick = to hit sth with a sudden, quick movement; to look at sth suddenly and quickly
whirl = to move around quickly in a circle
nod = to move your head up and down

<table>
<tr><td>**5.13**</td><td>CD3 Track 22</td></tr>
</table>

(See Student's Book)

● **5.14** Play the final section for SS to listen and read. Give SS time to answer the questions in pairs. Check answers, and then deal with any other words or phrases that have caused problems.

Suggested answers

13 Because he doesn't think she would understand or appreciate what he has experienced, or perhaps he thinks that she wouldn't believe him.

14 Probably sadness at the thought of the drawings being destroyed, but maybe also joy at having been the only person who saw them.

<table>
<tr><td>**5.14**</td><td>CD3 Track 23</td></tr>
</table>

(See Student's Book)

Extra challenge

Try to get a mini-discussion going on what SS think the author was trying to communicate with this story.

This story is very visual, in that there are a lot of descriptions and it paints images very clearly. Ask SS what images the story has left in their minds, and which image they think is the most powerful.

Extra support

You may want to ask SS to re-read the story at home and look up and record new vocabulary.

Digital extra idea

You could look at Ray Bradbury on YouTube – there are interviews and clips of his material.

5 VOCABULARY place and movement

a ● Focus on the sentences and instructions, and give SS a few moments to complete them.

1 onto, into, back, upon
2 towards, away, along
3 back, towards
4 round, back

b ● Tell SS to go to **Vocabulary Bank** *Place and movement* on *p.164*. Focus on exercise **a** and get SS to do it with a partner. Make sure SS write the words in the column on the right, not in the sentences so that they can test themselves later. Check answers, highlighting the relevant information after each group if SS need it.

⚠ Most of the words can be used as either adverbs or prepositions.

1 a above / over
  b over
  c above

above and *over* can both be used to describe a position higher than sth (sentence a). For movement from one side of sth to the other, you can only use *over* (sentence b). For a position above a minimum level or fixed point you can only use *above* (sentence c), e.g. *It's three degrees above zero.*

2 a under **b** below **c** under / below

below and *under* can both be used to describe a position lower than sth (sentence c). For movement from one side of sth to the other, you can only use *under* (sentence a). For a position lower than a minimum level or fixed point you can only use *below* (sentence b), e.g. *It's ten degrees below zero.*

3 a off **b** away **c** off / away

off and *away* can both be used to say at a distance from sth in space or time (sentence c); only *away* can be used + *from* + person / place (sentence b).

off (but not *away*) is also used to mean down from a higher place to the floor or ground especially after *fall*, *knock*, etc., e.g. *She knocked the glass off the table. He fell off his bike.*

4 a inside **b** into **c** in

We can use *in* or *inside* + a room or building, but we also use *inside* on its own as an adverb to mean in a building, e.g. *It's a bit cold on the terrace – let's eat inside.*

We use *into* (not *in*) + a place after a verb of movement, e.g. *Come into the living room* (sentence b). If no place is mentioned, we use *in*, e.g. *Come in.*

⚠ Nowadays you hear people say 'Come in the living room.'

5 a on **b** on top of **c** onto / on **d** on top

on is used with surfaces (sentence a), e.g. *Write your address on the envelope. It's on the first floor.*

on top of refers to the highest point of sth, e.g. on top of the mountain, or when sth covers sth else (sentence b), e.g. *I couldn't see my keys because I'd left my bag on top of them.*

Use *on top* when there is no following noun (sentence d).

onto is used with a verb and following noun to express movement (sentence c), e.g. *The actor walked onto the stage.* It can't be used on its own.

6 a out of **b** outside **c** out

outside can be a preposition (sentence b), e.g. *Wait outside the door*, or an adverb, e.g. *Wait outside.*

out of is used with a verb and a place or thing to express movement away from the inside of a place or thing, (sentence a), e.g. *She ran out of the room.*

Use *out* when there is no following noun (sentence c), e.g. *She ran out.*

7 a through **b** across **c** through / across

across means from one side to another (sentence b), e.g. *We swam across the river.* It can be used without a noun. *We reached the river and we swam across.* It is not normally used for closed spaces.

through means from one end or side to another, but is used for closed spaces or spaces with obstacles, e.g. trees (sentence a), e.g. *He climbed through the window. He pushed his way through the crowd.* It can be used without a noun.

For open spaces with some obstacles we sometimes use either *across* or *through* (sentence c).

8 a along **b** past **c** round

along is used to mean from one end towards the other (sentence a).

past is used to mean going to the other side of (sentence b), e.g. *They walked past us without saying hello.*

round means moving in a circle (sentence c).

⚠ *around* is used instead of *round* in NAmE, and is also used as an alternative to *round* in BrE.

9 a to **b** towards

towards means in the general direction of sth / sb (sentence b), e.g. *We drove towards the German border.*

to means that is your definite destination (sentence a), e.g. *I'm going to work.*

10 a at / in **b** in **c** at

at is used to say where sth or sb is or where sth happens (sentence c), e.g. *I waited half an hour at the bus stop. There's someone at the door.* It's also used for events, e.g. *See you at the party / concert*, and points on a journey, e.g. *We stopped at a station.*

in is used to say at a point inside an area, space, or building, i.e. when we are surrounded on all sides (sentence b), e.g. *We played in the street.*

⚠ With buildings *in* or *at* can sometimes be used, but with slightly different meanings:

We use *at* when we refer to the activity that is done in the place rather than the building itself, e.g. *Jane is at the cinema* (seeing a film); *When you called I was at the pub* (having a drink).

We use *in* when we are thinking much more about the building than its function, e.g. *It was really hot in the cinema. It was raining so we sheltered in the local pub.*

Frequently you can use either *at* or *in* with no real difference in meaning, e.g. *I saw Tom at / in the pub last night.* However, *in* the pub emphasizes *inside* whereas *at* the pub could be inside or outside, i.e. in the pub garden or on a terrace.

b ● Get SS to test themselves by covering the column on the right and trying to remember the missing words in the sentences.

Study Link SS can find more practice of these words and phrases on the MultiROM and on the *New English File Advanced* website.

● Tell SS to go back to the main lesson on *p.75*.

6 5.15 SONG ♫ *Vincent*

- This song, often known as 'Starry starry night', was written and recorded by Don McLean in 1971. *Vincent* in the title is Vincent Van Gogh. For copyright reasons this is a cover version. If you want to do this song in class, use the photocopiable activity on *p.236*.

5.15   CD3 Track 24

Vincent

Starry starry night
Paint your palette blue and grey
Look out on a summer's day
With eyes that know the darkness in my soul
Shadows on the hills
Sketch the trees and the daffodils
Catch the breeze and the winter chills
In colours on the snowy linen land

Chorus
Now I understand
What you tried to say to me
How you suffered for your sanity
And how you tried to set them free
They would not listen,
They did not know how
Perhaps they'll listen now

Starry starry night
Flaming flowers that brightly blaze
Swirling clouds in violet haze
Reflecting Vincent's eyes of china blue
Colours changing hue
Morning fields of amber grain
Weathered faces lined in pain
Are soothed beneath the artist's loving hand

Chorus

For they could not love you
But still your love was true
And when no hope was left in sight on that starry starry night
You took your life as lovers often do,
But I could have told you, Vincent
This world was never meant for one
As beautiful as you

Starry starry night
Portraits hung in empty halls
Frameless heads on nameless walls
With eyes that watch the world and can't forget
Like the strangers that you've met
The ragged men in ragged clothes
The silver thorn of bloody rose
Lie crushed and broken on the virgin snow

And now I think I know
What you tried to say to me
And how you suffered for your sanity
And how you tried to set them free
They would not listen
They're not listening still
Perhaps they never will

Digital extra idea

Type *Vincent* into YouTube and choose one of the clips of the song that has a slideshow of Vincent Van Gogh's paintings.

Extra photocopiable activities

Grammar
verbs of the senses *p.170*
Communicative
Spot the difference *p.196* (instructions *p.180*)
Vocabulary
Place and movement *p.221* (instructions *p.206*)
Song
Vincent p.236 (instructions *p.230*)

HOMEWORK

Study Link **Workbook** *pp.47–49*

5 C G gerunds and infinitives
V health and medicine; similes
P word stress

Trick or treatment?

Lesson plan

In this lesson the topic is health and medicine. The first part focuses on commonly held beliefs about health, and an expert talks about which are myths and which are true. SS revise and expand their vocabulary in this area, and learn some common similes. The grammar focus is on gerunds and infinitives, and SS look at perfect, continuous, and passive gerunds and infinitives, and some new uses. In the second part of the lesson the topic shifts to alternative medicine. There is a vocabulary and pronunciation focus on words related to alternative medicine, and SS then listen to some people's experiences and talk about their own. Finally, they read a review of a new book which questions the validity of alternative medicine.

Optional lead-in – the quote

- Write the quote at the top of *p.76* on the board (books closed) and the name of the author or get SS to open their books and read it.
- Point out that Voltaire lived from 1694 to 1778 and that his best known work today is probably *Candide*.
- Ask SS to what extent they think what Voltaire said was true at the time in which he wrote it, and if it is still true at all today.

1 SPEAKING & LISTENING

a • Focus on the quiz and set a time limit (e.g. five minutes) for SS to do it with a partner, or in groups of three.
  • Check answers, eliciting the meaning of the words and correcting pronunciation where necessary.

  Suggested answers
  1 **a** from a fall, being hit by sb, or knocking against sth, leaving you with a blue, brown, or purple mark
  b from walking a long way in uncomfortable shoes, or from wearing shoes that are too tight. It is a swelling on the skin filled with liquid.
  c as an allergic reaction to sth, or with certain children's illnesses like measles. It is an area of red spots on the skin.
  2 **a** to cover a cut that is not serious. It is a small piece of material which sticks to the skin.
  b to protect a part of the body that has been hurt, or after a sprain. It is a strip of cloth wound around a part of the body.
  c if you have a bacterial infection (but not for a virus). It is a kind of medicine, e.g. *penicillin*.
  d for a deep cut, or after an operation. It is a short piece of thread used with a needle to sew up a wound.
  e to check if a bone is broken. It is a photograph, which shows bones or organs in the body.
  f if you are pregnant to check the baby's progress, or to check muscles or internal organs, e.g. for back or joint problems. It is a medical test in which a machine produces an image on a computer screen.

3 **a** for any small medical problem, to get an appointment to see a specialist. GP = General Practitioner, i.e. a doctor who deals with general medical problems that don't require a specialist
  b because you have a medical problem that requires advice or treatment from a doctor who is an expert in that field
  c if you need to have an operation that involves cutting the body and often removing or replacing body parts. A surgeon is a doctor who does this.
4 **a** sneezing, coughing, a runny nose
  b same as for a cold but also with a temperature, and general aches and pains
  c vomiting / being sick and diarrhoea
  d chest pain, increased or irregular heart rate
  e coughing, especially at night, difficulty breathing
5 **a** you might faint
  b you might be sick, have a hangover
  c you might have an allergic reaction, get a rash, your hand might swell
  d you might get an electric shock / get electrocuted

b • Focus on the picture and statements 1–6. Tell SS that the information comes from a book of the same name, *Never Shower in a Thunderstorm*. Put SS into pairs or small groups and ask them to discuss each statement and say whether they think it is true or a myth, giving reasons and examples. Pre-teach the meaning of 'old wive's tale' (= an old idea or belief that has been proved not to be scientific).
  • Get feedback to find out what SS think, but don't tell them if they are right or not.

c • **5.16** Play the CD once for SS to see if they were right. Check answers, just finding out at this stage if the beliefs are true or myths, and how many SS guessed correctly.

| 1 myth | 3 true | 5 true |
| 2 true | 4 myth | 6 myth |

5.16 CD3 Track 25

(script in Student's Book on *p.130*)
I = interviewer, Dr = Doctor
I We have in the studio Dr Linda Blakey, who is helping us sort out the medical facts from all the myths and old wives' tales that are out there. So, first one, Linda, is there any truth in the belief that if you eat a large meal in the evening, you're more likely to put on weight than if you eat the same amount of food earlier in the day?
Dr Well, there's a clear answer there: if you're watching your weight, what matters is *what* you eat, not *when* you eat it. A calorie at midday is no different from a calorie at midnight, and the idea that your metabolism slows down in the evening is actually a myth. As a matter of fact, there is a medical condition called 'night-eating syndrome', which affects 2% of the population, and people who suffer from this eat very little during the day, but often wake up and eat during the night. These people on average are no more overweight than people who do not suffer from this syndrome.

I So I can go out for a big meal in the evening and not feel guilty about it?

Dr Absolutely – as long as you don't have a big lunch as well.

I Well, that's good.

The next one I'd like ask you about is catching colds. It's always seemed obvious to me that if you stay out in the cold and wind, you are more likely to catch a cold. But I also remember reading somewhere that this was a myth. What's the truth about this one?

Dr Well, colds, we know, are caused by viruses, which you catch from an infected person, for example, when they cough or sneeze. Now for many years doctors believed that the only reason why it was more common to catch a cold in the winter was because people stayed indoors more, and so they infected each other. But recent research has found that being exposed to cold temperatures does, in fact, lower our body's defences, so that means that if you get cold, you're more likely to become infected by a cold virus, or to develop a cold if you've already been infected. It's not a myth, it's true.

I OK. That all makes sense to me. Now something my parents used to tell me was that it was dangerous to have a bath or a shower during a thunderstorm, because I might get electrocuted. I've always thought this was crazy. Is this an old wives' tale?

Dr In fact, this one is quite true. Between ten and 20 people a year get an electric shock while having a bath or shower during a thunderstorm, and some of these die as a result. This is due to the fact that metal pipes are excellent conductors of electricity, as is tap water. So even though statistically it's not very likely to happen to you, especially if you live in a building with a lightning conductor, it is probably best to avoid showering during a storm.

I OK, I'll remember that! Now the next one is something I'm always saying to my children: 'Turn the light on. You can't possibly read in that light!' And they always tell me they can read perfectly well. But surely reading in dim light is bad for their eyes?

Dr Well, this is one that parents around the world have been telling their children for generations, but it actually has very little scientific backing. Reading in the dark or in bad light can cause a temporary strain on the eyes, but it rapidly goes away once you return to bright light.

I Well, now I know. Now the next one affects me directly. Every summer in the mosquito season I get really badly bitten, even when I put insect repellent on, but my husband never gets bitten at all. He says that mosquitoes don't like him. Is that possible?

Dr It is irritating, isn't it? As it happens, it seems to be true. Female mosquitoes, which are the ones that bite, are attracted to the carbon dioxide we exhale, our body heat, and certain chemicals in our sweat. But some lucky people produce chemicals which either prevent mosquitoes from detecting them or which actually drive them away. Unfortunately, I'm not one of those lucky people either, but your husband obviously is.

I The last thing I would like you to clarify for us is the idea that bottled water is purer than tap water. Now I know it's one thing to drink bottled water if you're travelling in a country where the water hasn't been treated and isn't safe to drink. But what about here in the UK, or in the States?

Dr We're all a bit suspicious of what comes out of our taps, and that's why sales of bottled water have risen so much over the last decade. But what many people don't realize is that bottled water, so-called mineral water, isn't subjected to the same regular testing that tap water is, and in some tests that were done in the United States, for example, a third of the samples of bottled water analysed were contaminated. In any case a quarter of all bottled water sold is just filtered tap water.

d ● Now play the CD again, pausing after each belief to give SS time to make notes (see spaces in script). Get SS to compare with a partner, and play the CD again as necessary. Check answers.

> 1 If you are watching your weight, what matters is <u>what</u> you eat, not <u>when</u> you eat it. A calorie at midday is no different from a calorie at midnight.
> 2 Being exposed to cold temperatures lowers our body's defences, so that means that if you <u>get</u> cold, you're more likely to become infected by a cold virus, or to develop a cold if you've already been infected.
> 3 Metal pipes are excellent conductors of electricity, as is tap water.
> 4 Reading in the dark or in bad light can cause a <u>temporary</u> strain on the eyes, but it rapidly goes away once you return to bright light.
> 5 Some lucky people produce chemicals which either prevent mosquitoes from detecting them or which actually drive them away.
> 6 Bottled water, so-called mineral water, isn't subjected to the same regular testing that tap water is, and in some tests that were done in the United States, for example, a third of the samples analysed were contaminated.

Extra support

If there's time, get SS to listen again with the script on *p.130*, focusing on any new vocabulary, and getting feedback on phrases SS didn't understand, e.g. because the words were run together.

LEXIS IN CONTEXT

e ● **5.17** Focus on the gapped sentences and give SS time to read them and see if they remember any of the missing words. Then play the CD, pausing after each sentence for SS to write the word. Check answers and elicit / explain exactly what the words or phrases mean.

> 1 **watching** your weight = trying not to put on weight
> 2 **viruses** = a microscopic organism which causes infectious diseases in people
> 3 **defences** = our body's mechanism for protecting itself
> 4 **syndrome** = a set of physical conditions that show you have a particular disease or medical condition, e.g. Down's syndrome
> 5 **strain** = an injury to a part of your body caused by working it too hard
> 6 **sweat** = drops of liquid that appear on the surface of your skin when you are hot or ill

<table>
<tr><th>5.17</th><th></th><th>CD3 Track 26</th></tr>
</table>

1 If you're **watching** your weight, what matters is what you eat, not when you eat it.
2 Colds, we know, are caused by **viruses**, which you catch from an infected person…
3 But recent research has found that being exposed to cold temperatures does, in fact, lower our body's **defences**.
4 As a matter of fact there is a medical condition called 'night-eating **syndrome**', which affects 2% of the population.
5 Reading in the dark or in bad light can cause a temporary **strain** on the eyes, but it rapidly goes away once you return to bright light.
6 …our body heat, and certain chemicals in our **sweat**.

f ● Do this as an open-class question, and tell SS what you think.

2 VOCABULARY similes

a ● Focus on the information box and go through it with SS. Elicit the pronunciation of *simile* /ˈsɪməli/ and then give SS time to complete the similes individually or with a partner.

Extra support

Go through the words in the list first to make sure SS know what they all mean. A *log* is a thick piece of wood. A *mule* is an animal which has a horse and a donkey as parents. A *post* is a piece of wood set in the ground vertically, e.g. a lamp post or sth to support a fence.

● Check answers, eliciting what each simile means.

1 mule (= very stubborn)
2 sheet (= very pale)
3 fish (= drinks a lot, usually refers to alcohol)
4 post (= can't hear at all)
5 log (= sleeps very well) (You may want to teach the alternative simile *sleep like a baby*.)
6 bat (= can't see at all)
7 gold (= very well-behaved)
8 dream (= works very well)
9 flash (= very quickly)
10 horse (= eats a lot)

b ● Give SS time to discuss the task with a partner and then get feedback. Try to elicit sb / sth for each simile.

3 GRAMMAR gerunds and infinitives

a ● 5.18 Focus on the task. Then play the CD, pausing after each verb to give SS time to write it in the right column. Get SS to compare with a partner. Tell them they should have 24 verbs or expressions altogether. Play the CD again as necessary.

<table>
<tr><th>5.18</th><th></th><th>CD3 Track 27</th></tr>
<tr><td>agree</td><td>imagine</td><td>pretend</td></tr>
<tr><td>avoid</td><td>involve</td><td>refuse</td></tr>
<tr><td>can't afford</td><td>it's not worth</td><td>regret</td></tr>
<tr><td>can't help</td><td>let</td><td>risk</td></tr>
<tr><td>can't stand</td><td>look forward to</td><td>suggest</td></tr>
<tr><td>deny</td><td>manage</td><td>tend</td></tr>
<tr><td>had better</td><td>miss</td><td>threaten</td></tr>
<tr><td>happen</td><td>practise</td><td>would rather</td></tr>
</table>

● Check answers.

+ *to* + infinitive	+ gerund	+ infinitive without *to*
agree	avoid	had better
can't afford	can't help	let
happen	can't stand	would rather
manage	deny	
pretend	imagine	
refuse	involve	
tend	it's not worth	
threaten	look forward to	
	miss	
	practise	
	regret	
	risk	
	suggest	

Extra support

To help SS after they have listened to the recording once, you could tell them how many verbs are in each column: column 1 has eight verbs, column 2 has 13, and column 3 has three.

b ● Now focus on the task and sentences. Get SS to do the exercise individually and then compare with a partner. Check answers.

1 ✓
2 being told
3 to have brought
4 ✓
5 to park
6 to last
7 worrying
8 to become

c ● Tell SS to go to **Grammar Bank 5C** on *p.150*. Go through each example and its corresponding rule with the class, or give SS time to read the examples and rules on their own, and answer any queries.

Grammar notes

At this level SS should be quite confident about whether they need to use a gerund or infinitive after many common verbs. Here SS look at some more complex gerund and infinitive constructions (e.g. passive gerunds and infinitives) and also some other uses of gerunds and infinitives not previously covered.

● Focus on the exercises for **5C**. SS do the exercises individually or in pairs. If SS do them individually, get them to compare with a partner. Check answers after each exercise.

a 1 to have followed
  2 to have been
  3 to be told
  4 running
  5 to be working
  6 to have saved
  7 committing / having committed
  8 to eat
  9 phoning
  10 to walk
  11 to sit down
b 1 haven't got / don't have enough eggs to
  2 hate being woken up
  3 Do you regret not having / not having had
  4 without having finished school
  5 'd love to have gone / would have loved to have gone / 'd have loved to have been able to go
  6 The children seem to be having a good time
  7 plan is not to redecorate the kitchen

- Tell SS to go back to the main lesson on *p.77*.
d - Sit SS in pairs, **A** and **B**, preferably face to face. Tell them to go to **Communication** *Guess the sentence*. **A** on *p.118*, **B** on *p.120*.
  - Go through the instructions with SS. As SS did a similar activity in lesson **4A**, the activity should not need as much demonstration although you could get a pair of SS to do the first two sentences to the whole class as a reminder.
  - If you did <u>not</u> do the activity in **4A**, see *p.79* for how to demonstrate the activity yourself. Write on the piece of paper:
    I would love to have gone to the concert last night but I couldn't get a ticket.
    Then write on the board:
    I would love _____ the concert last night but I couldn't get a ticket. (+)

4 VOCABULARY & PRONUNCIATION

Pronunciation notes

Although they may have similar looking words in their own language, SS will often find the terms used in English to refer to certain kinds of alternative medicine tricky to pronounce. There is also sometimes a stress change within a word family, e.g. *homeopath, homeopathy, homeopathic*.

a - Focus on the words for alternative medicine and give SS, in pairs, a few minutes to say what they think they all are.
b - 5.19 Play the CD once, pausing after each definition for SS to match it to the word. Get SS to compare with a partner, and then play the CD again if necessary. <u>Don't</u> check answers yet.

Extra support

You may want to pre-teach some of the vocabulary in the definitions if you think your SS won't know the words, e.g. *herbs, oils, rubbing, spine, joints, needles*.

5.19   CD3 Track 28

1 It's a kind of treatment that uses hypnosis, that is putting people into an unconscious state, to help with physical or emotional problems.
2 It's medicine or remedies made from herbs and plants.
3 It's a system of treating diseases or conditions using very small amounts of the substance that causes the disease or condition.
4 It's a technique which uses natural sweet swelling oils for controlling pain or for rubbing into the body during massage.
5 It's a type of alternative treatment in which somebody's feet are massaged in a particular way in order to heal other parts of the body or to make them feel mentally relaxed.
6 It involves treating some diseases and physical problems by pressing and moving the bones in a person's spine or joints.
7 It's the treatment of some diseases and physical problems by pressing and moving the bones and muscles.
8 It's a Chinese method of treating pain and illness which uses special thin needles which are pushed into the skin in particular parts of the body.

c - 5.20 Play the CD for SS to check their answers, and underline the syllable with the main stress in the words in **a**. Play the recording again as necessary. Check answers.

See script 5.20

5.20   CD3 Track 29

1 hypno<u>the</u>rapy   5 reflex<u>o</u>logy
2 <u>her</u>bal <u>me</u>dicine   6 <u>chi</u>ropractic
3 home<u>o</u>pathy   7 oste<u>o</u>pathy
4 aroma<u>the</u>rapy   8 <u>a</u>cupuncture

- Get SS to practise saying the words in **a**.
d - 5.21 Focus on the words in the list and get SS to use their instinct to underline the stressed syllables. Play the CD for SS to check.

See script 5.21

5.21   CD3 Track 30

an <u>a</u>cupuncturist
a <u>chi</u>ropractor
a <u>ho</u>meopath
homeo<u>pa</u>thic <u>me</u>dicine
hyp<u>no</u>sis
a hypno<u>the</u>rapist
an <u>os</u>teopath
a refl<u>ex</u>ologist

- Get SS to tell you in which word families the stress has shifted.

hypno<u>the</u>rapy – hyp<u>no</u>sis
home<u>o</u>pathy – a <u>ho</u>meopath – homeo<u>pa</u>thic medicine
oste<u>o</u>pathy – an <u>os</u>teopath

5 LISTENING & SPEAKING

a ● Do this as an open-class question, and elicit opinions.

b ● **5.22** Focus on the task. You could tell SS to copy the chart into their notebooks in order to have more room to complete it. Play the CD once, pausing after each person for SS to complete the chart. Play the CD again as necessary and get SS to compare their answers with a partner. Check answers.

Speaker A	acupuncture; he had lost his sense of taste and smell; yes
Speaker B	homeopathy; all kinds of illnesses, e.g. getting their voice back / losing their voice; yes
Speaker C	homeopathy / homeopathic medicine; childbirth; no
Speaker D	herbal medicine; to help him sleep; no

5.22   CD3 Track 31

(script in Student's Book on *p.130*)
I = Interviewer, Sp = speaker
Speaker A
I   Have you ever used alternative medicine?
Sp Yes.
I   What did you use?
Sp Acupuncture.
I   And did it work?
Sp Well, it did actually. I had a terrible time of, I lost my sense of taste and smell…
I   Wow!
Sp …which started off with a cold and I then completely lost my sense of taste and smell for about three or four months, and it was very debilitating, and it was really quite frightening.
I   I'm sure.
Sp You suddenly realize that there's no point in eating at all because it's just fodder, and all the beauty of life kind of goes, it's an extraordinary thing of not having one of your senses. And somebody recommended to me acupuncture, and I went along and I said, 'Do you think you can do anything about it?' and she said, 'Yes, I think I can.' She said, 'So, here's a rose', which was in her room.
I   Right…
Sp …and she said, 'Put your nose into it and tell me what you can smell.' I put my nose into it and I couldn't smell a thing at all, absolutely nothing at all. And she laid me down and half an hour of needles later, I got up and she said, 'Have a smell of the rose again', and I put my nose into it and there was this faint, faint odour of rose, which was quite the most beautiful thing I've ever smelled in my entire life.
I   It came straight away then?
Sp No, well, over the course of the next two weeks, very, very slowly it came back. I was walking down Old Compton Street and a woman walked past and I went 'Ooh perfume', and I literally turned and followed her, if she'd seen me, she would have thought I was rather weird because I was sort of, had my nose into her hair, so, and it all came back.
I   Wow!

Speaker B
Sp Er, ever since my children were born, well, even before my children were born, which is a very very long time ago now, we've used alternative medicine, or what, I like to call it complementary medicine, we use homeopathy. And none of my children ever had an antibiotic when they were growing up, and I think that's quite a good claim, actually. They have used them since they've been adult, for various things because of work and having to get their voices back, but apart from that no antibiotics, and I don't think I've had one in the last thirty-odd years.

Speaker C
I   Kate, have you ever taken alternative medicine?
Sp Well, the time I remember was when my second child, childbirth of my second, because my first was a pretty dramatic experience, so I thought I'd go and find out if I could make it easier, so I went to a homeopath who gave me a lot of pills, and said that when contractions started I should take one and then, you know, an hour later take another one, and an hour later take two, but within half an hour I'd taken all three bottles and was still in agony.
I   No.
Sp Yeah.
I   Not having done anything?
Sp No.
I   So did you call the person? 'These aren't working!'
Sp No, I never did, but I wouldn't recommend homeopathy for childbirth.
I   No, good conclusion.

Speaker D
I   So Adam, what's your take on alternative medicine, do you have any experience?
Sp One, just one, and I was taking a very long flight from London to Vancouver and I don't like flying, but I don't take anything for that, but when I got there I was only there for a very few days and I wanted to enjoy my waking hours, and the jet-lag was crazy so I bought some herbal sleeping pills.
I   Oh, right.
Sp So I didn't want to use really heavy, real sleeping pills, I've never used those, so I went to buy some herbal sleeping pills and put them in my bag and then I got there and I look at the, I look at the package and it says, 'Take eight half an hour before bedtime', so I thought that was quite a lot, but that's what it said, so I took eight, but it was a bit like having a lot of grass in my mouth, it was like swallowing a lot of grass before bed and then it made me a little windy, so it was like burping up, like a lot of grass and I was burping so I wasn't sleeping, so I wasn't really convinced about them.
I   So a great night's sleep.
Sp It was wonderful. A lot of grass.

c ● Focus on the sentences and go through them with SS. Then play the CD once or twice for SS to match the speakers and statements.

1 C	**2** D	**3** A	**4** A	**5** B	**6** D	**7** C	**8** B

Extra support

If there's time, get SS to listen again with the script on *p.130*, focusing on any new vocabulary, e.g. *fodder* (= food for horses and farm animals), and getting feedback on phrases SS didn't understand, e.g. because the words were run together.

d ● You may first like to tell SS about any experiences you have had with alternative medicine and whether they were successful or not. Then put SS in pairs or small groups to answer the questions.

● Get feedback about any good / bad experiences.

6 READING & SPEAKING

a • Focus on the title of the article, which is the title of a new book about alternative medicine being reviewed here. Elicit / explain that it is a play on words. At Halloween, celebrated on 31 October, especially in the United States, children dress up and go from house to house knocking on the doors saying 'Trick or treat?' to whoever opens the door, meaning give us a treat (usually sweets), or else we'll play a trick on you, e.g. throw flour or eggs at your door. Here instead of *Trick or treat?* the authors have called their book *Trick or treatment?* meaning *Is alternative medicine a trick or does it really work?*

• Now focus on the task. Set a time limit for SS to read the review once. Then give them time to answer the gist questions with a partner. Check answers.

> 1 In general, the authors believe alternative medicine is a trick.
> 2 They think there are some exceptions, e.g. some herbal medicine such as St John's Wort and osteopathy.
> 3 The reviewer does not entirely agree as he / she thinks that alternative medicine can be useful to prevent illnesses, rather than curing them.

b • Focus on the task. Tell SS to read the article again, and then go through the questions one by one, choosing the right answer. Get them to compare with a partner, justifying their choices to each other, and then check answers.

> 1 a   2 b   3 b   4 a   5 c   6 a

LEXIS IN CONTEXT

c • Focus on the task. Tell SS that the words they are looking for (the opposites) occur in the same order (1–7) in the text. Check answers, and get SS to underline the stressed syllable.

> 1 <u>main</u>stream
> 2 un<u>prov</u>en
> 3 inef<u>fec</u>tive
> 4 <u>use</u>less
> 5 sham
> 6 rip-off
> 7 mild

• You might want to highlight that:
  – *conventional* (adj) = following what is traditional or the way sth has been done for a long time
  – *mainstream* (adj) = the ideas and opinions that are thought to be normal because they are shared by most people
  – *sham* (noun and adj) = refers to sth which is not as good or true as it appears, e.g. *Their supposed happy marriage was a sham.*
  – *a bargain* = sth bought for less than the usual price
  – *a rip-off* (informal) = sth that is not worth what you pay for it
  – *mild* = not strong or severe, e.g. *The UK has a mild climate.*

• Deal with any other queries SS may have with the vocabulary in the text.

Extra support

Ask SS to choose five other words or phrases they would like to learn from the article and get them to compare their choices. Get some feedback from the class as to the words or phrases they have chosen and deal with any vocabulary problems that arise.

Extra challenge

Get SS to try to do the exercise first and then check with the text.

d • Finally, focus on the discussion points. With a small class you may want to have an open-class discussion. With large classes, divide SS into pairs or groups of three and give them time to discuss the points.

• Get feedback from different groups.

Extra photocopiable activities

Grammar
gerunds and infinitives *p.171*
Communicative
Medical vocabulary definitions game *p.197* (instructions *p.181*)
Vocabulary
Medical words and similes *p.222* (instructions *p.206*)

HOMEWORK

Study Link **Workbook** *pp.50–52*

Lesson plan

In this lesson the focus is on writing a report. The writing skills focus is on dividing a text into paragraphs with headings and using the right register, and the **Useful Language** section looks at common expressions for generalizing and making suggestions in a more formal register.

ANALYSING A MODEL TEXT

a • Focus on the text type (a report). Tell SS that being able to write a good report is a skill which they may find very useful in an English-speaking work context, as well as being a text type often set in school and international exams. The important thing to bear in mind with reports is that they are usually written for busy people, so making them clear and concise by dividing them into short sections with headings, is an important factor.
  • Focus on the **Key success factors** and go through them with SS.
  • Focus on the task, and get SS to read the report. Meanwhile write the headings on the board. Then get SS to close their books and try to remember the school's strengths and weaknesses in each area. You could elicit these from the class and write them on the board.

b • Focus on the task. Then get SS to cover the report, and try to rewrite the phrases from memory in a more formal style. Check answers, and elicit that this more formal style is appropriate for a report.

> 1 aim of this report
> 2 assess student satisfaction
> 3 rated the teachers very highly
> 4 As regards class sizes
> 5 the duration of classes
> 6 purchasing
> 7 The majority of students
> 8 the suggested changes are implemented

  • Highlight the use of *As for...* in 5 to refer to a topic you are going to discuss (*As for the duration of the classes...*) and remind SS of the other synonymous expressions they learned in **Discourse markers Grammar Bank 4A**, e.g. *Regarding / Regards / As far as...is concerned*

Extra support

If SS are having trouble remembering the phrases, allow them to quickly look back at the report.

Extra idea

Test SS on the phrases by saying the informal phrase and getting them to say the more formal one.

USEFUL LANGUAGE

c • Focus on the task. Point out that some, but not all, of these expressions are in the report. Get SS to do them with a partner and then check answers.

> 1 speaking   4 considered
> 2 general   5 Overall
> 3 view

d • Finally, focus on the sentences for making suggestions, and remind SS that this is usually a fundamental part of a report. Here they have practice in more formal ways of making suggestions. Get SS to do this individually and then compare with a partner. Check answers.

> 1 purchasing new computers
> 2 to improve the registration process
> 3 reducing class sizes
> 4 changing / that you change the opening hours
> 5 to last an hour

PLANNING WHAT TO WRITE

a • Focus on the task. Tell SS to read it carefully, and then to discuss 1, 2, and 3 with a partner.
  • Get feedback, writing SS' proposed headings on the board and getting SS to decide on the best ones, and eliciting all ideas for suggestions to improve the study trips.

> **Suggested headings**
> Accommodation
> The school
> Weekend activities / Weekend Cultural Programmes

b • Focus on the task.
  • Get feedback from SS.
  • Finally, go through the tips with SS.

WRITING

Go through the instructions and set the writing for homework.

Test and Assessment CD-ROM

CEFR Assessment materials
File 5 Writing task assessment guidelines

Lesson plan

In the first part of this lesson the person interviewed is Patricia Melvin, a New York-based artist. She talks about how she works and what influences and inspires her as an artist. In the second part of the lesson people in the street are asked whether they often go to art galleries, what kind of art they like, and whether they have a favourite painting or poster in their house.

Study Link These lessons are on the *New English File Advanced* DVD which can be used instead of the class CD (See Introduction *p.9*). SS can get more practice on the MultiROM, which contains more of the short street interviews with a listening task and scripts.

Optional lead-in (books closed)

- Revise the language of different kinds of paintings by reading these definitions and giving SS a couple of minutes to write the word. Get them to compare answers in pairs before checking answers.

  1 a painting of a view of the countryside (*a landscape*)
  2 a painting, drawing, or photograph of a person (*a portrait*)
  3 a painting that you do of yourself (*a self-portrait*)
  4 a painting of an inanimate object such as flowers or fruit (*a still life*)
  5 a painting which does not represent people or things in a realistic way, but expresses the artist's ideas about them (*an abstract*)

THE INTERVIEW

a • Books open. Now focus on the task and on the glossary. Go through it with the class eliciting from them how to pronounce the words and phrases.

Extra support

You may want to pre-teach some other words and phrases before SS listen to the interview (see script 5.23).

b • **5.23** Focus on the questions and give SS time to read them. Encourage SS not to write anything down when they listen the first time. Tell them that they should listen and try to get the gist of what she is saying, and then discuss the questions with their partner.

  • Play the CD once (**Part 1**). Give SS time to discuss the questions and tell each other what they understood. Then play the CD again, pausing after each of Patricia's answers to give SS time to make notes and compare with their partner again. Play the recording again as necessary. Elicit and check answers.

1 It is a magical place where anything is possible and everything seems to happen, 'New York is more of an event than a place'. Things are changing and becoming something new all the time.

2 Because the location is always changing. Things happen at different times (e.g. a bird flying past or a person walking in the street who uses a certain gesture), which might be perfect for the painting. In contrast a photo is static and flat.

3 Because things can change quickly, e.g. her view might suddenly get blocked by trucks. Also the seasons are constantly changing and nature changes daily, so it might be hard to finish the painting in a different season or even later in the same season.

4 Anything from a few hours to a few years. (She often leaves a painting and comes back to it a year later when the season and light is right.)

5 The city is geometric and she loves drawing angles and different geometric shapes. The countryside is more difficult because you don't have the perspective of the streets. She had to learn how to make the eye move across a field as opposed to down a street.

6 Because she's usually alone there and doesn't get distracted by passers-by.

7 She finds it hard to find someone who will sit for her for a few hours and she doesn't like painting from photographs.

5.23 CD3 Track 32

(script in Student's Book on *p.131*)
I = interviewer, P = Patricia Melvin

I What is it about New York that inspires you?

P I was born here and raised nearby and so I have memories of New York City from my early childhood and to me it was always a magical place. Anything is possible here and everything seems to happen here. As my aunt once said to me, she said, 'People who live in New York, even if they've only been here for one year, they feel like they own the place,' and I think that it's because New York is almost more of an event than a place, where everything's changing and becoming something new all the time, and I think that's why it draws creative people and it's very inspiring.

I Do you always paint in situ or do you sometimes use photos?

P I always paint in situ, almost always. I use sketches and I work a little from memory and from sketches. I touch things up a little in the studio sometimes or finish things. But I like to be in the location because it's always changing and I take pieces of the scene, things that happen at different times, a bird flying by might be very beautiful or a person walking in the street and assuming a certain gesture or pose that's perfect for the composition. Things like that happen over the course of a painting and they can be just perfect. But a photo is very static and kind of flat and it doesn't interest me to work from that.

I Does that mean you have to work very fast?

P Actually I do, I have learnt to work very fast because there are so many things that change on the street including being blocked by trucks and I do often work very fast, the seasons are constantly changing. People think of the four seasons but really nature changes almost every day, or every day so if I started painting at one point, it's hard to finish it later in a different season or later on in the same season.

I   What techniques do you use?
P   I use traditional technique. I use oil paint and brushes and canvas.
I   How long does it normally take you to finish a painting from start to finish?
P   Oh, there, every painting is different, they can take a few hours or a few years. I've worked on some paintings for years and years and sometimes I'll come back to a painting the following year when the season and the different light is right for that painting.
I   As well as the city pictures, you also paint outside New York in the countryside. What similarities and differences are there in painting the city and painting the countryside?
P   The city is very geometric and I love, I happen to love geometry, I love angles criss-crossing on the composition and different shapes, geometric shapes but the countryside, when I first started painting it was very difficult for me for that reason, because you don't have the perspective of the streets and the angles of the roofs and so on to lead your eye through the painting. It's, it was wonderful experience to learn how to make your eye move across a grassy field as opposed to down a street where it is so clear and easy kind of, to figure out.
I   So what are the advantages and disadvantages of painting in the country and the city?
P   The countryside is a wonderful place for me to paint. I love it because I'm usually alone, pretty much alone there and I'm not distracted by passers-by. In New York City there are just so many distractions with people coming up to me and they're usually well-meaning but it's just an interruption, it's a distraction from my work. And the countryside is so beautiful that I love painting there.
I   Do you ever paint portraits?
P   I do occasionally. I love painting portraits, but it's very rare to find someone who will sit for a few hours, for a couple of sessions, and I don't like to do portraits from photos. I've tried it and I don't like the results.

c   ● **5.24** Focus on the task and give SS time to read the questions. Play the CD once (**Part 2**) and tell SS just to listen. Then give SS time to discuss the questions and tell each other what they understood. Now play the CD again pausing after each answer to give SS time to make notes and compare with their partner again. Play the recording again as necessary. Elicit and check answers.

1 She grew up on the banks of the Hudson River, which is very beautiful in different lights and seasons. It was an important influence on her becoming a landscape painter.
   Her parents loved art and had lots of painting in their house. Her mother painted pictures. These things were also an influence on her.
2 It's her favourite time of day for painting although she doesn't always get up in time.
3 Just before spring (in March) the air is clear and there aren't leaves on the trees so she can really see the streets. It's also a very magical time. During spring there is the blossom when the trees come out, which is also a magical time though short.
4 She'd love to paint in the ancient and older cities such as Paris, Amsterdam, Florence, and Venice. Also many places in Sicily, Greece, Turkey, and the Mediterranean. Anywhere where there is antiquity and water or mountains.

5 You have to make big sacrifices in your social life because you constantly have to change plans you have made with people because the weather is suddenly right to go and work on a particular painting. You also have to make a sacrifice in financial terms as it's hard to earn money and be a dedicated painter at the same time.

5.24   CD3 Track 33
(script in Student's Book on p.131)
I   What kind of things have influenced you as an artist?
P   I think one of the greatest influences on me was growing up on the banks of the Hudson, which is such a beautiful place in the different light and different times of year. I think that was a main influence on me to want to be a landscape painter. Also there were lots of paintings in the house where I grew up and my parents loved painting very much and also my mother painted some, so I, especially after we all grew up, she painted, so, there were a lot of influences on me.
I   What's your favourite time of day for painting?
P   Actually my favourite time of day is sunrise, but I don't always get up in time for that, so early morning and also late afternoon.
I   Do you have a favourite time of year or season?
P   Yes, I do actually. I love to paint just before the spring when the air is so crisp and clear, and there aren't yet any leaves on the trees, so that I can really see down the streets, so there's something magical in New York about that time of year, around March and then of course, when spring comes and the blossoms and the trees start to come out, it's just magical, but it lasts a very short time.
I   Are there any other cities that you'd like to go and paint in?
P   Oh, there are thousands of cities I'd love to go and paint in, the ancient cities, the older cities, Paris, Amsterdam, Florence, Venice, many places in Sicily, in Greece, I'd love to go to Turkey and paint on the Mediterranean and any place where there's antiquity and where there's water or mountains. But it is hard to travel and paint, it's much better to go to one place and settle in and paint for a while in one place to get to really know the landscape. That's what I prefer to do.
I   What do you think are the pros and cons of an artist's life?
P   I think to be an artist usually it requires a lot of sacrifice and I know that sounds like a cliché, but it's true. Because it requires an enormous amount of time, it requires being free to suddenly change your plans at a moment's notice. For example, being a landscape painter is completely insane, I could be going out the door with one painting under my arm to work on it and the weather could change and I'd be working on a different painting, or I could have plans with someone and suddenly change them, or drop the plans because the weather's right for a particular painting, and that's a real big sacrifice in terms of your social life and also, of course, finances, if, as I do, I tend to put painting before anything else. So I'm not, well it's hard to earn money and be a dedicated artist at the same time, I think. They contradict one another to some degree.

d   ● **5.25** This exercise gives SS intensive listening practice in deciphering phrases where words are often run together, and introduces them to some common expressions and idioms used in spoken English. Focus on phrases 1–5 and give SS time to read them. Play the CD, pausing after the first phrase and replaying it as necessary. Elicit the missing words, and then the meaning of the whole phrase. Repeat for the other four phrases.

5.25 | CD3 Track 34

1 I touch things up a little in the studio sometimes or finish things.
2 ...as opposed to down a street where it is so clear and easy kind of, to figure out.
3 I love it because I'm usually alone, pretty much alone there and I'm not distracted by passers-by.
4 ...and that's a real big sacrifice in terms of your social life...
5 They contradict one another to some degree.

Extra support

If there's time, get SS to listen again with the scripts on *p.131*, focusing on any new vocabulary, and getting feedback on phrases SS didn't understand, e.g. because the words were run together.

e ● Finally, focus on the question. Get SS to answer in pairs and then get feedback from the whole class.

IN THE STREET

a ● **5.26** Focus on the task and play the CD once for SS to answer the questions. Get them to compare their answers with a partner and then elicit the answers onto the board.

Questions

1 Do you often go to art galleries?
2 What kind of art do you like?
3 Do you have a favourite painting or poster in your house?

Ian goes to art galleries the most ('fairly often'), Jerry goes the least ('almost never').

5.26 | CD3 Track 35

(script in Student's Book on *p.131*)
I = interviewer, J = Jason, Je = Jerry, A = Amy, Ia = Ian

Jason
I Do you often go to art galleries?
J I try to, yeah.
I What kind of art do you like?
J I like a lot of different art. My favourite is probably landscapes. Things involving the ocean.
I Do you have a favourite painting or poster in your house?
J Do I have a favourite? I have a Kandinsky that I'm quite fond of.
I Can you describe it?
J It's hard to describe and I don't even know the name of it, but it's just, it's beautiful and colourful and it's in motion.

Jerry
I Do you often go to art galleries?
Je No, almost never in fact. Almost never.
I What kind of art do you like?
Je Not, well, not one kind I don't think. I like art which has a sort of emotional effect on me, I suppose. But it could be anything. I mean it's not a particular style, it's more, a sort of, what I see in it. If it means something to me, then I think I appreciate it.
I Do you have a favourite painting or poster in your house?
Je Most of the art in my house is actually painted by my father. I've got, I must have 20 or 30 paintings by him. He paints, I take holiday snaps and he sort of improves them and paints them, you know, a photograph of Florence, say, and he'll take out some buildings and invent some replacements, and I, you know, I rather like that. It's almost like a sort of version of holiday photos, but with his personality superimposed, which is quite interesting.

Amy
I Do you often go to art galleries?
A I don't go as often as I should actually. A lot of my friends go quite a bit and I never seem to find the time. It might be because I'm outside London. I think if you live in London, you spend more time, or it's more available for you to go to them. So I don't go as much as I should.
I What kind of art do you like?
A I like art that feels very accessible, that you can understand. So portraiture and photography as well. Travel photography I find really interesting.
I Do you have a favourite painting or poster in your house?
A I do actually and it's in my parents' house. It's a painting that my best friend did for our family because she's an artist by profession. And she painted a picture of my mum and I, a photo that we took when I was very young and painted it as if from the point of view of the person taking the picture and it's a really interesting picture and she set it on the cliffs in Cornwall, which is where our family used to spend a lot of time. And it's a really lovely picture that she painted for us as a gift. So, yeah, that's it.

Ian
I Do you often go to art galleries?
Ia Yeah, fairly often, whenever I'm in a new town and there's a good gallery there I'll try and go. Yeah, I'm quite keen.
I What kind of art do you like?
Ia Generally 20th century and generally not figurative, not representational, a bit abstract I quite like, yeah.
I Do you have a favourite painting or poster in your house?
Ia Gosh! I have a Rothko poster that I really like, yes.
I Can you describe it?
Ia It's blocks of colour basically, sort of large blocks of a sort of magenta and grey. Very stark, but I like it, yeah.

b ● Focus on the task and give SS time to read statements 1–5. Play the recording again the whole way through and then give SS time to try and match the statements to the speakers. Then play the recording again, pausing after each speaker this time for SS to check their answers. Play again as necessary and check answers.

1 Ian (speaker 4)
2 Jerry (speaker 2), Amy (speaker 3)
3 Jerry (speaker 2)
4 Jason (speaker 1)
5 Jason (speaker 1), Ian (speaker 4)

c ● **5.27** Focus on the phrases and give SS time to read them. Play the CD, pausing after the first phrase and replaying it as necessary. Elicit the missing words, and then the meaning of the whole phrase. Repeat for the other three phrases.

1 **quite fond of** (= like or feel affection for)
2 **say** (= for example)
3 **quite a bit** (= informal way of saying *often*)
4 **a sort of** (= a kind of, used to describe something in a not very exact way)

| 5.27 | | CD4 Track 2 |

1 I have a Kandinsky that I'm quite fond of.
2 …you know, a photograph of Florence, say, and he'll take out some buildings and invent some replacements…
3 A lot of my friends go quite a bit and I never seem to find the time.
4 …sort of large blocks of a sort of magenta and grey.

Extra support

If there's time, get SS to listen again with the scripts on *p.131*, focusing on any new vocabulary, and getting feedback on phrases SS didn't understand, e.g. because the words were run together.

d ● Finally, get SS to ask each other the three questions that the interviewer asked the interviewees. Then get some feedback from the whole class.

HOMEWORK

Study Link Workbook *p.53*

For instructions on how to use this page, see *p.35*.

GRAMMAR

a 1 to apologize / to have apologized
  2 being told
  3 to have seen
  4 to be going out
  5 to sit down
  6 go
  7 phoning
  8 to be seen
  9 to use
  10 bring
b 1 ✓
  2 I can hear
  3 ✓
  4 You should have listened
  5 is not permitted
  6 ✓
  7 tastes like
  8 don't need to
  9 I needn't have taken
  10 as if

VOCABULARY

a 1 under
  2 plaster
  3 log
  4 blister
  5 scribbled
  6 mule
  7 osteopath
  8 along
  9 glanced
  10 post
b 1 self-portrait
  2 blink
  3 installation
  4 acupuncture
  5 tremble
  6 hypnotherapy
  7 doodle

c 1 misunderstood
  2 demotivated
  3 outnumbered
  4 overrated
  5 anti-war
  6 undercharged
  7 pre-paid
  8 rearranged
d 1 out
  2 up
  3 out
  4 out of
  5 down
  6 in

Test and Assessment CD-ROM

File 5 Quicktest
File 5 Test

6A

G expressing future plans and arrangements
V travel and tourism
P homophones

A moving experience

File 6 overview

The first lesson in this File, **6A**, focuses on the grammar of expressing future plans and arrangements and SS expand their knowledge of vocabulary related to travel and tourism. In **6B** the grammar focus is on ellipsis and substitution, with a vocabulary focus on the natural world. Finally, in **6C**, the grammar focus is on cleft sentences (emphasizing one part of a sentence) and the vocabulary focuses on words which are often confused.

Lesson plan

The topic of this lesson is travel and tourism. SS begin by reading a newspaper article, which questions the value of visiting famous tourist sights. This leads to vocabulary, where SS learn new travel-related words and phrases, and then to speaking, where they do a questionnaire to find out what kind of traveller they are. The pronunciation focus is on homophones (words pronounced the same but spelt differently, e.g. *site* and *sight*). In the second half of the lesson the topic shifts to extreme commuting (people who travel long distances to work every day) and the grammar, language for expressing future plans and arrangements, is presented through an article and a listening about a British extreme commuter. Finally, SS listen to a radio programme where a well-known orchestral conductor describes a memorable journey.

Optional lead-in – the quote

- Write the quote at the top of *p.84* on the board (books closed) and the name of the author or get SS to open their books and read it.
- Point out that Mark Twain (1835–1910) is best known as the author of *The Adventures of Huckleberry Finn* and *The Adventures of Tom Sawyer*, but in his time was also known as a great humorist and was a popular public figure.
- Tell SS that this quote comes from the novel *Tom Sawyer Abroad*. Ask them in what way the sentence is ungrammatical (*ain't* = non-standard English for *isn't / aren't / am not* and *no surer way* = a double negative).
- Then ask SS if they agree and elicit reasons why (not) and any relevant experiences SS might have had.

1 READING & SPEAKING

a • Think of five places, sights, or monuments that you would consider 'Wonders of the World' and write them on the board. Tell SS that they are your personal 'Wonders of the World' and find out if SS have seen them (either on TV, in books, etc. or have actually been there) and if they were impressed or not.
- Now get SS to make their own list, and then, in groups of three, compare their list with other SS.
- Get feedback.

b • Focus on the article and the photo, and elicit / explain that the mountain in the photo is called Uluru, or Ayers Rock, and is one of the most famous sights in Australia. Set a time limit for SS to read the article once for gist, and then give them time to discuss the question with a partner.

> Because the author thinks that the Wonders of the World, or what makes a place special, are the small details of life, not the main sights, and that there are probably thousands of them.

c • Focus on the task. Set a time limit and tell SS to read the article again and then go through the questions and answer them with a partner.
- Check answers.

> 1 In the way tourists to Uluru are supposed to behave. It is clear from the ironic tone ('glass full of Château Somewhere') that the writer does not approve.
> 2 Exhaustion, emptiness, boredom
> 3 Because she has realized that she doesn't really enjoy these experiences, partly because she gets angry with other tourists who are filming everything.
> 4 Tourists who photograph or film beautiful buildings and views instead of looking at them with their own eyes and enjoying them.
> 5 Copies of guide books such as *1,000 Places to See Before You Die*. So that they can visit the places and then tick them to show that they've been there.
> 6 'A duty visit to a dull relative', i.e. going to see a rather boring relative because you feel you ought to, not because you really want to. She makes this comparison because she thinks that most tourists don't really enjoy these sights, but just go there because they feel it's expected of them.
> 7 It blamed or criticized us for not wanting to visit it.
> 8 The waterproof banknotes, the surfers who refused to leave the beach after a tsunami warning, and the warning at the hand luggage machine at Alice Springs airport. They all told her a lot about the Australian people, their personality, and the way they live.

Extra support

Ask SS to choose five other words or phrases they would like to learn from the article and get them to compare their choices. Get some feedback from the class as to the words or phrases they have chosen and deal with any vocabulary problems that arise. SS may not be familiar with the use of *folks* here (a friendly, informal way of addressing a group of people).

d • Focus on the task and go through it with SS.
- Divide SS into groups of three, and give them time to discuss the questions.
- Get feedback and tell SS what you think.

6A

Digital extra idea

Type *Wonders of the world* into Wikipedia. This site shows the Seven Wonders of the Ancient World, Wonders of the Medieval World, and Wonders of the Modern World.

2 VOCABULARY & SPEAKING travel and tourism

a ● Focus on the task, and give SS a few minutes to find the words. Check answers. Elicit the meaning of the phrases from the class.

Extra support

You could tell SS, to save time, that 1 is in the second paragraph; 2, 3, and 4, are in the fifth paragraph, and 5 is in the last paragraph.

1	backpacker	4	itinerary
2	sight	5	scenery
3	destination		

b ● Tell SS to go to **Vocabulary Bank** *Travel and tourism* on *p.165*. Focus on section **1 Nouns and noun phrases** and get SS to do the exercises individually or with a partner. If they do them individually, get them to compare with a partner. Check answers and elicit / model the pronunciation of tricky words as necessary.

> **a 1** City break (= short stay in a city, typically over a weekend)
> **2** package holiday (= a holiday that is organized by a company at a fixed price which includes cost of travel, hotel, etc.)
> **3** stop-over (= short stay between two parts of journey, normally used when you break a long journey by air, e.g. *We had a 24-hour stop-over in Hong Kong on the way to Australia.*)
> **4** day trip (= a trip or visit completed in one day)
> **5** guided tour (= a tour that is led by sb who works as a guide)
> **6** site (= place where a building is or was located, or where sth happened, e.g. *the site of the battle of Gettysburg*. Also a *campsite* = a place where you can camp.)
> **7** low-cost (= an airline offering cheap fares, usually by not offering traditional passenger services, e.g. numbered seats, free meal, newspapers, etc.)
> **8** long-haul (opp. *short-haul*) flight (= a long distance plane journey, usually inter-continental)
> **b 1** trip **2** journey **3** travel

● Remind SS that *travel* is an uncountable abstract noun and cannot be used instead of *trip* or *journey*, e.g. ~~It was a difficult travel~~. *Travel*, of course, can also be a verb.

● Now focus on section **2 Verb phrases** and get SS to do it individually or with a partner. If they do it individually, get them to compare with a partner. Check answers and elicit / model the pronunciation of tricky words as necessary. You might want to highlight that the *t* in *postpone* /pəˈspəʊn/ is silent.

1	take out	5	go on
2	set off / set out	6	postpone / put off
3	cut short	7	cancel
4	go		

● Now focus on section **3 Adjectives and phrases to describe places** and get SS to do it individually or with a partner. If they do it individually, get them to compare with a partner. Check answers and elicit / model the pronunciation of tricky words as necessary. Highlight that:
  – *breathtaking* = so beautiful or spectacular it takes your breath away, i.e. it leaves you unable to breathe
  – *touristy* is usually used in a negative sense. Compare: *This is a tourist town* (factual statement) and *This town is very touristy* (implied criticism).
  – *off the beaten track* comes from the idea that the *beaten* (i.e. flattened by thousands of footsteps) *track* is the road where many people walk. A place which is *off the beaten track* is away from where most people go and is therefore more remote, unspoilt, etc.

1	overrated	6	off the beaten track
2	dull	7	crowded
3	touristy	8	breathtaking
4	spoilt	9	picturesque
5	lively		

● Finally, focus on the instruction 'Can you remember the words on this page? Test yourself or a partner.'

Testing yourself

For **1 Nouns and noun phrases** SS can cover the gaps and try to remember the words. For **2 Verb phrases** and **3 Adjectives and phrases to describe places**, they can cover the columns while looking at the collocates and definitions, and try to remember the missing words.

Testing a partner

See **Testing a partner** *p.18*.

> **Study Link** SS can find more practice of these words and phrases on the MultiROM and on the *New English File Advanced* website.

● Tell SS to go back to the main lesson on *p.85*.

c ● Focus on the questionnaire and the **Expressing preferences** box. Elicit what *'d* stands for (*would*) and remind SS that *would prefer* is followed by *to* + infinitive (as opposed to *prefer* + gerund for general preferences), but *would rather* is followed by infinitive without *to*. Highlight also that as they will be discussing hypothetical situations, they will mainly be using the conditional tense (*I'd go / spend / stay, I wouldn't rent / go on*, etc.).

● Now focus on the questionnaire and put SS in pairs. Encourage them to discuss each option saying why they would / wouldn't want to do it, and making one final choice for each section. Monitor and help.

d ● Elicit some adjectives to describe different types of travellers and write them on the board, e.g. *adventurous, conservative, well-organized, active*, etc.

● Then get SS to swap books. They look at each other's answers and then decide what sort of traveller they think their partner is.

● Get feedback from different pairs.

3 **6.1** **SONG** ♫ *I Wish I Could Go Travelling Again*

- This song was written and recorded by Stacey Kent in 2007. For copyright reasons this is a cover version. If you want to do this song in class, use the photocopiable activity on *p.237*.

6.1   CD4 Track 3

I Wish I Could Go Travelling Again

I wish I could go travelling again
It feels like this summer will never end
And I've had such good offers from several of my friends
I wish I could go travelling again

I want to sit in my shades, sipping my latte
Beneath the awning of a famous café
Jet-lagged and with our luggage gone astray
I wish I could go travelling again

I want a waiter to give us a reprimand
In a language neither of us understand
While we argue about the customs of the land
I wish I could go travelling again

I want to sit in traffic anxious about our plane
While your blasé comments drive me half insane
I want to dash for shelter with you through the tropical rain
I wish I could go travelling again

I want to be awakened by a faulty fire alarm
In an overpriced hotel devoid of charm
Then fall asleep again back in your arms
I wish I could go travelling again

But how can I ever go travelling again
When I know I'll just keep remembering again
When I know I'll just be gathering again
Reminders to break my heart?

I wish I could go travelling again, etc.

---

4 PRONUNCIATION homophones

Pronunciation notes

Homophones are words with different meanings but the same pronunciation (e.g. *wait* and *weight*). Even at this level SS often doubt whether two words are pronounced exactly the same when their spelling is different. Homophones may also occasionally cause confusion for SS when they hear one word, but imagine that they have heard the other.

a • Focus on the information box and go through it with SS, stressing that the pronunciation of the words is identical.

- Then focus on the exercise. Do number 1 with the whole class, getting them to spell the word to you (*weight*). Then get SS to continue in pairs. Check answers, getting SS to spell the words. Make sure SS know the meaning of all the bold words. They may not know, e.g. *source* and *quay*.

2	board	5	peace	8	waste	11	cereal
3	brake	6	caught	9	sweet	12	wood
4	fare	7	sauce	10	key		

b • Focus on the task. Demonstrate by asking a student for two meanings and spellings of /weɪt/. Then get SS to continue in pairs.

Extra challenge

You could ask SS if they know any more homophones, e.g. *sent / cent / scent*; *flower / flour*; *whether / weather*; *through / threw*; *new / knew*; *aloud / allowed*, etc.

5 GRAMMAR expressing future plans and arrangements

a • Focus on the questions. You could answer them yourself first, and then get SS to answer them with a partner.

b • Focus on the title of the article and ask SS what 'extreme commuting' means (travelling a very long way each day to work and back, i.e. more than 90 minutes each way). Then set a time limit for SS to read the article and answer the question with a partner. Check answers.

Pros: He doesn't have to relocate, and his family are happy in the place where they live. He has time on his own so while he's travelling he can to listen to music or radio programmes that his family don't like.
Cons: He has to get up very early every day (at 'the crack of dawn'). He has to travel for six hours every day, and put up with traffic. He has very little time to relax when he gets home.

---

c • **6.2** Focus on the task. Play the CD once or twice and elicit answers to the questions.

---

1 At 5.40.
2 He cycles, takes the underground ('the tube'), gets a bus, and walks.
3 8.30 (the bus arrives at 8.20 and it's a ten-minute walk)

6.2   CD4 Track 4

It's 5.15. I'm in bed in my house in Woolwich in south-east London and the alarm has just gone off.
Ten minutes later. I've had a shower and I'm trying to eat a bowl of cereal – I'm not that hungry, but I have to eat something. I'll be leaving home very shortly.
It's now 5.40 and I'm about to get on my bike to cycle to the tube station. It takes me about half an hour to get to North Greenwich underground station.
It's now 6.10 and I've just caught a Jubilee Line train, which takes me to Baker Street. The bus to Oxford leaves at 6.40, so I should make it with time to spare. It's due to arrive in Oxford at 8.20, but it depends a bit on the traffic.
I just caught it, which was a relief because I need to be on time today – I'm meeting a client at nine o'clock.
On time today, thank goodness. So I've now just got a ten-minute walk and then I'll be there. I desperately need a coffee.

---

d • **6.3** Focus on the sentences and give SS time to read them. Then play the CD, pausing after each sentence to give SS time to complete them. Check answers (see bold words in script 6.3) and elicit that all the phrases are forms or structures that are used here for future plans or arrangements.

6.3   CD4 Track 5

1 **I'll be leaving** home very shortly.
2 I'm **about to** get on my bike to cycle to the tube station.
3 My bus **leaves** at 6.40.
4 It's **due to** arrive at 8.20, but it depends a bit on the traffic.
5 I need to be on time today – I'**m meeting** a client at nine o'clock.

---

e ● Tell SS to go to **Grammar Bank 6A** on *p.151*. Go through each example and its corresponding rule with the class, or give SS time to read the examples and rules on their own, and answer any queries.

Grammar notes

SS should be very familiar with the different verb forms used to express future plans and arrangements. Here they are pulled together and contrasted. Other ways of expressing this aspect of the future such as *be due to* and *be about to* may be new for SS.

● Focus on the exercises for **6A**. SS do the exercises individually or in pairs. If SS do them individually, get them to compare with a partner. Check answers after each exercise.

a 1 ✓   6 ✓
  2 I'll be having   7 I'll be wearing
  3 going to watch   8 ✓
  4 going to pay me   9 ✓
  5 ✓

b 1 no difference
  5 no difference
  6 *is due to arrive* is more formal
  8 *is to open* is more formal
  9 *I'm going to see John* implies you have planned it. *I'll be seeing* implies it's sth you know will happen, but that you have probably not planned yourself.

c 1 We're about to go out
  2 Our head of department is due to be promoted
  3 Will you be going to the canteen at lunchtime
  4 The ministers are on the point of signing
  5 I'll be seeing James

● Tell SS to go back to the main lesson on *p.86*.

6 LISTENING & SPEAKING

a ● **6.4** Focus on the instructions and on the advert for the radio programme. You could ask SS if they know of anyone who has used an air taxi and why.

● Focus on the first part of the listening task and get SS to look at the questions.

● Play the recording once (**Part 1**) and get SS to answer the questions and compare them with a partner. Then play the CD again for SS to complete their answers. Check answers 1–4 and elicit responses to question 5.

Extra support

You may want to pre-teach *rehearsal* and *to make it* (= to arrive somewhere in time) if you think SS won't know them.

1 From Warsaw to Berlin and back, for rehearsals.
2 Because it was the only way to get there and back in time.
3 The weather was too bad for them to leave.
4 The plane was quite old and there was a hole by the door where air was coming through.

6.4   CD4 Track 6

(script in Student's Book on *p.131*)
I was in Warsaw in Poland for a week because I had rehearsals and a concert there, but on the Wednesday, Thursday, and Friday of that week I also had to do rehearsals in Berlin. I needed to be able to have the rehearsal in Warsaw in the morning, then fly to Berlin for the rehearsal there in the late afternoon, and then straight back to Warsaw late at night in time for the next morning rehearsal. The only way to get to Berlin and back in time was to fly. So I hired an air taxi.
As soon as I left the rehearsal, there was a car waiting to take me to the airport, and when I arrived at the airport my heart sank because the weather was not so good, and the operations manager said, 'Look, I'm terribly sorry. We can't fly at the moment because of the weather.' Finally, the weather cleared and they said we could fly, so I was still hoping to make it in time for my rehearsal. However, we got into the plane and I didn't have a very good impression of it: it looked a bit old, and there was a little hole where the air was coming through where the door had been shut on my side.

b ● **6.5** Focus on the task. Play the CD once (**Part 2**) and give SS time to take notes and compare with a partner. Then play the CD again for them to complete their notes. Check answers.

The weather was very bad (a storm, rain).
It was very cold and noisy (there were no headphones).
The co-pilot's door wasn't shut properly. He tried to shut it properly by opening it and closing it (as you would with a car door), but because of the air pressure, he couldn't shut it and so the plane door stayed open.
The co-pilot would have fallen out if he hadn't had his seat belt on.
The plane started going up and down (presumably because of the bad weather or perhaps because the door was open and air was coming in).

6.5   CD4 Track 7

(script in Student's Book on *p.132*)
I thought, 'Well, never mind,' and I put on my seat belt and finally we took off.
The weather was not good, and after about five or ten minutes I was terribly cold and I thought, 'Well, I know it can be cold' – and it was also very noisy – normally they give you headphones but for some reason they didn't, so the noise was very loud and it got very very cold, and then to my horror I realized that the co-pilot's door wasn't shut properly! By this point the co-pilot himself had realized that the door wasn't shut, so he turned to me and said 'Problema' and then he started gesticulating to the pilot, who was already having difficulties because the weather was very bad and it was raining very hard and there was a bit of a storm. I was feeling extremely uncomfortable by now, wishing that I was on the ground, but then came the real drama because the pilot was trying to indicate to the co-pilot how to shut the door properly. Now what do you do if you're driving a car and you realize that you haven't shut the door properly? You usually stop, open the door again and then shut it with a bang or sometimes you don't even stop, you just while you're driving slowly, you do that. Anyway, this idiotic co-pilot, he proceeded to do precisely that. He then opened the door completely, in order to shut it properly, and I was just behind them, as this is a small plane, so right in front of me was just open air, this open door – I was absolutely terrified, cold air rushing in, and then he tried to shut it properly, but presumably because of the pressure or the cold I don't know what, he couldn't do so, and had he not had his seat belt on, he would have fallen out of the plane, so he was holding on, partly for dear life, partly to try and shut it, unsuccessfully.

The pilot was shouting at him but he couldn't correct the situation because, you know, he had to keep the plane in the air, which was now extremely precarious and the plane was going up and down.

c ● **6.6** Focus on the questions for part 3. Play the CD once. Get SS to discuss the questions. Then play the CD again. Check answers to 1 and 3, and elicit opinions for 2.

> 1 The plane landed but they were not in Berlin, they were in another town. He eventually arrived late for the rehearsal (but luckily it wasn't a real problem).
>
> 3 He used the same company on the way back; this time, despite their promises to go quickly, they had to go very slowly because the aircraft was running out of fuel.

6.6   CD4 Track 8

(script in Student's Book on *p.132*)
Then suddenly I felt that we were going right down and I prayed that we were going to land.
To my relief we landed in one piece, so at least my life was no longer in danger, but as far as the rehearsal was concerned, I realized with horror that because of this emergency in the air the pilot had had to land at the nearest town, which was still quite a long way from Berlin. I had to phone the rehearsal people to say I was going to be late and I was feeling thoroughly miserable. However, we eventually took off and arrived in Berlin and I did my rehearsal, and fortunately it had been the type of rehearsal where my lateness had not caused a real problem.
Then on the way back, the pilots were waiting for me at the airport – this was now about ten o'clock at night or 9.30. So this time we took off, and I said, 'Are you quite sure the door is properly shut? Quite sure?' and they said, 'Yes, yes,' and I said, 'We're very late now, I want you to get back to Warsaw as fast as possible,' and they said, 'Yes, the wind is in our favour, this aircraft can go very fast, we should be back soon in Warsaw, don't worry, everything will go fine,' so we took off, and things were… well, nothing was going particularly wrong, but I noticed that they were going rather slowly, but it was still so noisy that I couldn't communicate with them and ask, 'Why are you going so slowly?' Eventually when we landed I said, 'Why were you going so slowly? I told you to go as fast as possible,' and the pilot said, 'I'm terribly sorry, I didn't know this plane very well and we were having a fuel problem, we were running out of fuel.' So on the way there I'd nearly fallen to the ground through an open door and now we'd been in danger of falling to the ground because of lack of fuel.

● You may want to tell SS that the next day, when the conductor had to make the same journey again, he used a different company – which was much more efficient!

Extra support

If there's time, get SS to listen again with the scripts on *pp.131–132*, focusing on any new vocabulary, and getting feedback on phrases SS didn't understand, e.g. because the words were run together.

LEXIS IN CONTEXT

d ● Focus on the task and the expressions. Get SS to discuss what they mean with a partner, and to try to remember roughly how the sentences continue. Check answers (sentence continuations in brackets).

> 1 my heart sank = I immediately felt sad / depressed (the weather was not so good)
>
> 2 to make it in time = to get there in time (my rehearsal)
>
> 3 to my horror = feeling horror, i.e. great shock / fear (the door wasn't shut properly.)
>
> 4 by this point = now (the door wasn't shut)
>
> 5 presumably = used to say that you think that sth is probably true (he couldn't do so)
>
> 6 to my relief = feeling pleased that sth bad hadn't happened (in one piece)
>
> 7 on the way back = on the return journey (waiting for me at the airport)
>
> 8 nothing was going particularly wrong = everything was happening as it should (they were going rather slowly)

e ● Focus on the task and give SS time to try to think of a journey and make a few notes.

● If you have a good story, tell the SS. Then put them in groups and get them to tell each other their stories. Encourage SS to listen 'actively' and interact with the person telling the story with exclamations and further questions.

Extra photocopiable activities

Grammar
expressing future arrangements and plans *p.172*
Communicative
Travel roleplays *p.198* (instructions *p.181*)
Vocabulary
Travel and tourism *p.223* (instructions *p.206*)
Song
I Wish I Could Go Travelling Again p.237 (instructions *p.231*)

HOMEWORK

Study Link) **Workbook** *pp.54–56*

G ellipsis and substitution
V the natural world
P weak and strong pronunciation of auxiliary verbs and *to*

Pets and pests

Lesson plan

The topic of this lesson is animals, as pets in the first part, and as pests in the second, where the topic opens up for SS to discuss various controversial issues relating to animals. In the first half of the lesson SS read a newspaper article about how pets and their owners become more alike as time passes. This is followed by a grammar focus on ellipsis and substitution, and a focus on the weak and strong pronunciations of auxiliary verbs and *to*. SS then expand their knowledge of vocabulary related to animals and the natural world. They listen to extracts from two radio programmes, which focus on problems which have arisen firstly because of the re-introduction of wolves into an area of the French Alps and secondly because of the protection of foxes in a residential area of London.

Optional lead-in – the quote

- Write the quote at the top of *p.88* on the board (books closed) and the name of the author or get SS to open their books and read it. Elicit / explain the meaning of *loathe* (= really hate) and *haven't got the guts* (= don't have the courage).
- Point out that August Strindberg (1849–1912) is considered one of the fathers of modern theatre. He was a hypersensitive and neurotic character, as one might perhaps guess from the quote.
- Ask SS what they think Strindberg might have meant by the quote. Then ask SS how they feel about dog owners.

1 READING

a • Focus on the photos and the task.

b • Focus on the article and the gist question. Set a time limit for SS to read the article once and answer the question with a partner. Check answers.

> Possibly the dog owner, because he says they also look alike (which the others don't), but accept any well argued opinions.

c • Now focus on the multiple matching task. Remind SS that this task involves reading the questions and scanning the article to find the answers. Set a time limit again. Get SS to compare with a partner, and then check answers.

1 F		3 F		5 D		7 D		9 B
2 C		4 B		6 R		8 R		10 C

Extra support

To help SS you might want to pre-teach *subliminal* (= affecting your mind even though you are not aware of it), *harass* (= to annoy or worry sb), and *snuggle up* (= to get into a warm comfortable position, esp close to sb).

LEXIS IN CONTEXT

d • Focus on the task and give SS time to find the words, and then check with a partner. Check answers and elicit / model and drill pronunciation where necessary. Make sure SS are clear about where the stress falls in the multi-syllabic words.

Extra challenge

See if SS can remember some of the words without looking back at the text.

1	a<u>like</u>	6	se<u>rene</u>
2	trait	7	smart
3	<u>grum</u>py	8	<u>lu</u>natics
4	<u>to</u>lerant	9	ec<u>cen</u>tric
5	<u>fu</u>ssy	10	a <u>show</u>-off

Extra support

Ask SS to choose five other words or phrases they would like to learn from the article and get them to compare their choices. Get some feedback from the class as to the words or phrases they have chosen and deal with any vocabulary problems that arise.

e • Do this as an open-class question, and give your opinion too.

2 GRAMMAR   ellipsis and substitution

a • Focus on the task and get SS to compare answers with a partner. Check answers.

Extra challenge

Get SS to complete the sentences first and then check with the article.

> **1** is   **2** does   **3** am   **4** do   **5** do
> They are replacing a whole phrase, which is not said, but which is understood by the listener from the context, e.g. *...and so is he* replaces the full phrase *...and so is he becoming more bad-tempered.*

b • Tell SS to go to **Grammar Bank 6B** on *p.152*. Go through each example and its corresponding rule with the class, or give SS time to read the examples and rules on their own, and answer any queries.

Grammar notes

SS at advanced level will already have an instinctive feel for the aspects of substitution and elision covered here, but they probably will not have totally assimilated them into their own English. The emphasis in this lesson is to look overtly at the theory thus making SS feel more confident when they speak.

- Focus on the exercises for **6B**. SS do the exercises individually or in pairs. If SS do them individually, get them to compare with a partner. Check answers after each exercise.

a	**(these words should be crossed out)**		
	1	like it	5	come to dinner, come
	2	win	6	go
	3	taken it	7	be able to go
	4	I	8	we
b	1	is	5	would
	2	will	6	must / should
	3	am	7	can't
	4	didn't	8	does
c	1	hope not	4	'll try to
	2	used to	5	guess so
	3	suppose not	6	've always wanted to

- Tell SS to go back to the main lesson on *p.89*.

3 PRONUNCIATION weak and strong pronunciation of auxiliary verbs and *to*

Pronunciation notes

Encouraging SS to distinguish between strong and weak forms of the auxiliary and *to* in the infinitive form is a clear and motivating way of improving their pronunciation at this level.

a ● **6.7** Focus on the instructions and the dialogues. Give SS time to do the task with a partner. Encourage them to read the dialogues out loud to decide when the auxiliary verbs or *to* are stressed.

- Play the CD once for SS just to listen. Then play it again, pausing after each dialogue for SS to check their answers.

- Then get SS to practise saying the dialogues stressing the right words.

See underlined words in script 6.7

Extra support

You could play the recording line by line and get the class to copy the stress and sentence rhythm.

6.7 CD4 Track 9

A <u>Do</u> you like dogs?
B No, I <u>don't</u> but my husband <u>does</u>.
A So does mine. We have three Alsatians.

A I went to Iceland last summer.
B Lucky you. I'd love to go there. <u>Did</u> you see any whales?
A No. I wanted <u>to</u>, but I get seasick, and you have to go on a boat.

A Allie <u>doesn't</u> have any pets, <u>does</u> she?
B She <u>does</u> have a pet. She has a hamster.
A Ugh. I <u>don't</u> like hamsters.
B Neither do I. They're too much like mice.

---

b ● Give SS a few minutes to answer the questions, using the underlined words in the dialogues to help them.

1 S (stressed) in question tags, short answers, negative sentences, when they are used for emphasis, and when they come as the last word in a sentence.
U (unstressed) in *wh-* questions and with *so* and *neither*.

⚠ The auxiliary verb in *yes / no* questions, e.g. *Did you see her? Do you like it?* can be stressed or unstressed depending on how fast the person is speaking.

2 The sound /ə/. The exceptions are *did*, which is pronounced /dɪd/ even when it's unstressed, and *do* in the phrases *So do I* and *Neither do I* where it is pronounced /duː/.

3 a) /tə/ b) /tuː/

4 When it is used in ellipsis (e.g. *I don't have a pet but I want to*) and if it is the last word in a sentence (e.g. *I'm not sure who I spoke to*) or question (e.g. *Which restaurant are you going to?*).

c ● Sit SS in pairs, **A** and **B**, preferably face to face. Tell them to go to **Communication** *Match the sentences* **A** on *p.118*, **B** on *p.120*. Go through the instructions. You could get a strong pair to demonstrate the activity. Get **A** to say his / her first sentence *Have you ever been to Canada?* for **B** to find the correct response *No, but I'd love to if I ever got the chance.* Correct **B**'s pronunciation if necessary.

- Get SS to continue in pairs. Monitor and correct any pronunciation errors. When they have finished, SS can repeat the exercise concentrating on correct pronunciation of auxiliaries and *to*.

Extra support

You could elicit the matched pairs of sentences from the class before getting them to practise the dialogues for a final time.

4 VOCABULARY the natural world

a ● Focus on the quiz. Set a time limit for SS to do it in pairs or small groups. Check answers. Model and drill pronunciation where necessary.

1	**a**	puppy
	b	kitten
	c	foal
	d	calf (pl. calves)
2	**a**	birds
	b	bees
	c	horses
	d	dogs
	e	fish or reptiles
	f	hamsters, birds, etc. and captive animals, e.g. in a zoo
3	**a**	mice
	b	dogs
	c	horses
	d	cats
	e	lions, tigers
	f	pigs

Extra idea

Elicit / Point out that the words in **3** are onomatopoeic, and find out what the corresponding words are for these sounds in SS' L1.

b • Tell SS to go to **Vocabulary Bank** *The natural world* on *p.166*. Focus on section **1 Animals, birds, and insects** and get SS to do the exercises individually or in pairs. Get them to compare with a partner if they did them individually. Check answers and elicit / model the pronunciation of tricky words as necessary.

> **a 1** claws
> **2** fins
> **3** fur
> **4** horns
> **5** wings
> **6** a shell
> **7** a beak
> **8** a tail
> **9** paws
> **b a** dog, mosquito, etc.
> **b** bee, wasp
> **c** cat, etc.
> **d** horse, donkey, mule
> **e** camel, llama

• Now focus on section **2 Issues relating to animals** exercise **a**. First, get SS to read the sentences, and then ask them to say what the bold words mean and elicit the pronunciation.

> **a 1 protect** = look after, defend
> **environment** = the conditions in a place that affect the behaviour and development of sb / sth
> **animal charities** = organizations which collect money to help animals, e.g. the World Wildlife Fund
> **2 animal activists** = people who demonstrate, often violently, for animal rights, e.g. against animal experiments
> **3 treated cruelly** = handled in a cruel or violent way
> **4 live in the wild** = live in their natural habitat, not in zoos, etc.
> **5 endangered species** = kinds of animals that are in danger of becoming extinct, e.g. the tiger, the polar bear
> **6 hunted for sport** = killed for enjoyment rather than for food, e.g. foxes in the UK, wild boars and birds in the Mediterranean countries
> **7 bred in captivity** = kept in order to reproduce
> **8 battery hens** = hens which are kept in tiny cages joined together and never allowed out

• Focus on **b**, and get SS to answer in pairs. Get feedback.

Extra support

Ask the questions to the whole class and elicit examples.

• Now focus on section **3 Animal idioms**, highlighting that many common English idioms involve animals. Get SS to do exercise **a** with a partner. Encourage them to read each sentence and try to guess the meaning from the context. Then they should try to find the meaning from A–O.

• Check answers. Highlight that:
  - the origin of the idiom *water off a duck's back* is because water runs off a duck's back without affecting or bothering it, in the same way that criticism does not affect or worry certain people.
  - although the full expression is *Don't count your chickens before they are hatched*, we usually just say the first part.
  - the expression *dark horse* originates from horse racing. A 'dark horse' was a horse which was unknown to people betting on the race.
  - the origin of the idiom *to be in the doghouse* is when you send a dog to his kennel to sleep (because he has been naughty). *Doghouse* is used in American English instead of *kennel* but the idiom is used in both American and British English.
  - only the first part of *the last straw* (*which breaks the camels back*) is used. Its origin is the story of a camel being laden very heavily with straw until the addition of one final piece of straw breaks it backs.

1	B	4	H	7	F	10	J	13	M
2	D	5	A	8	L	11	N	14	K
3	O	6	G	9	I	12	E	15	C

• Focus on exercise **b** and elicit similar idioms from SS.
• Finally, focus on the instruction 'Can you remember the words and phrases on this page? Test yourself or a partner.'

Testing yourself

For **1 Animals, birds, and insects** SS can cover the words, look at the pictures and say the words. For **3 Animal idioms** get SS to look at A–O and try to remember the idioms. Then for each one, ask them if they have an equivalent idiom in their L1.

Testing a partner

See Testing a partner on *p.18*.

Study Link SS can find more practice of these words and phrases on the MultiROM and on the *New English File Advanced* website.

• Tell SS to go back to the main lesson on *p.90*.
c • Focus on the circles and give SS time to read them. Demonstrate the activity by telling SS about people you know. Then get SS to do the activity in pairs.
• Get some feedback from the class by saying, e.g. *Who knows somebody who has been attacked by a wild animal? What happened?*, etc.

5 LISTENING

a ● Do this as an open-class question, eliciting the meaning of *pests* = animals or insects which destroy plants, food, other animals, etc., e.g. *rodents (mice, rats), foxes*, etc.

b ● **6.8** and **6.9** Focus on the instructions. Play the CD once. Get SS to compare what they think the stories have in common. Play again as necessary.

> They are both about animals, which the local authorities are protecting but which are causing problems for local residents.

6.8   CD4 Track 10

(script in Student's Book on *p.132*)
And finally wolves or dogs? Which is more dangerous to mountain walkers?
Jean-Luc Renaud was on a mountain-walking holiday in the French Alps when he saw a bloodstained man staggering towards him. The man's shorts were torn, he had been bitten badly in both buttocks, and he was in a state of complete shock.

The man, who was a tourist from Belgium, had been attacked by a notoriously ferocious breed of mountain dog, Le Chien de Montagne des Pyrénées or the Pyrenean Mountain dog. This breed is white and fluffy, and looks like a cuddly family pet – but it is anything but. Fearless and ferocious, it can weigh up to 60kg and will fight to the death against wolves and bears to save a flock of sheep.

So why are there so many of these dogs around? They've been brought into the French Alps to defend sheep from wolves. Wolves were re-introduced into the Alps in 1992 and there are now about 150 of them. They're protected by European Union law, but Alpine farmers say that they've killed thousands of sheep and are a threat to their livelihoods.

In an attempt to pacify the farmers, the EU has spent millions of euros on fences and sheep dogs. The plan appeared to be working. The arrival of about 1,000 Pyrenean Mountain dogs in the Alps coincided with a sharp fall in the number of sheep deaths.

But it has also brought about an alarming rise in attacks on holidaymakers by these dogs. The attacks are driving tourists away and are further splitting the community, who were already divided over the re-introduction of the wolf in France. To add to the controversy, several shepherds have been taken to court by holidaymakers who have been attacked, and 17 dogs have been poisoned in the Maurienne region of the Alps.

6.9   CD4 Track 11

(script in Student's Book on *p.132*)
P = presenter, C = Carol
P And to finish the local news for London today, what's your view on foxes? Are they pests or should they be a protected species? There are now approximately 10,000 foxes living in London parks, squares, and gardens, and in Hampstead in North London, their barking is keeping the residents awake at night. Carol Martin is one such sufferer. What happened to you last week, Carol?

C Well, I came down in the morning after *another* bad night's sleep and I saw a large fox on my lawn, which didn't look very well at all – it had bits of fur hanging off it. I was worried that it might have some infectious disease, so I phoned the local council.

P And what did they say?
C Well, first I asked for pest control, and they said, 'What pest?' And I said, 'A fox', but the woman from the council told me that foxes aren't pests, and she put me through to the 'fox project' department.

P 'The fox project department'? So then what happened?
C Well, the man from the fox project asked me to find out if the fox was really ill, and he said that once they knew what was wrong with it, they could supply me with some medicine. So I said that, first of all I didn't speak fox language, and secondly I had no intention of going anywhere near it. I said that I would like the fox dead and the only medicine I was interested in was poison.

P I see – and how did they respond to that?
C Well, the fox project man got a bit annoyed, and told me that this was not a caring attitude at all, and he suggested that it might be best to send an ambulance to take the animal to a vet or, if it wasn't seriously ill, to take it to the country and release it back into the wild.

P That's what the man from the council suggested?
C Those were his very words. At this point I couldn't believe what I was hearing. Luckily, when I looked out of the window again, the fox had disappeared, so I hung up. It does seem absolutely ridiculous to me. Camden Council have problems getting ambulances to sick people, because of staff shortages, but they *are* able to provide ambulances to take sick foxes to the vet.

P Well, thank you Carol. Incredible! So, does anyone else have a story about foxes in London? Do give us a ring…

c ● Focus on the two summaries. Get SS to read the first text, and focus on the gaps seeing if they can remember any of the missing information. If they can, they could write it in pencil.
● Play the first news story again, pausing the recording (see spaces in the script) to give SS time to write. Get SS to compare answers and then play the CD again without pausing. Check answers and then repeat the whole process for the second news story.

> **1** **1** blood
>   **2** Pyrenean mountain
>   **3** 60 kilos
>   **4** sheep
>   **5** wolves
>   **6** 150
>   **7** EU
>   **8** fences
>   **9** sheep dogs
>   **10** holidaymakers / tourists
>   **11** court
>   **12** poisoned
> **2** **1** 10,000
>   **2** sleeping
>   **3** ill / unwell
>   **4** pest control
>   **5** fox project
>   **6** really ill
>   **7** medicine
>   **8** kill
>   **9** an ambulance

d ● Ask SS who they sympathize with most in each story. Then ask the questions to the whole class and elicit examples and opinions.

6 SPEAKING

a ● **6.10** This exercise focuses on how we frequently collocate certain adverbs with other words when we give our opinion, e.g. *I feel very **strongly** about this* or *I'm **totally** / **completely** against hunting. I'm **quite** sure that…*, etc.

- Focus on the task and give SS time to read the phrases. Play the CD for SS to complete the gaps, playing the recording again as necessary. Check answers. Remind SS that *I don't entirely agree* is used when you partly but not completely agree.

- Highlight that *quite* in the phrase *I'm quite sure* = completely, and is another very common collocation. You might also want to highlight the use of 'Well…' used here by several of the speakers to give themselves time to think.

- Play the recording again for SS to focus on the rhythm and intonation of the phrases. Elicit / Point out that the adverbs are stressed more strongly. Get them to practise saying the phrases.

Extra support

Play the recording again for SS to copy the rhythm and intonation.

6.10   CD4 Track 12

1 Now this is something I feel **very strongly** about…
2 Well, I don't feel **particularly strongly** about it either way…
3 I have to say I am **completely** against zoos nowadays…
4 Oh no, I **totally** disagree with you there…
5 Well, I couldn't disagree with you **more**.
6 Well, I don't **entirely** agree with you…
7 Well, I'm **absolutely** convinced that the animal does not want to be there…
8 Well, I'm **quite** sure that kids could get the same amount of pleasure from seeing animals in the wild.

---

b ● Divide the class into groups of three or four. Focus on the instructions and the debate issues. Tell SS in each group to choose the issues they are going to talk about, and then to agree with the other members of their group so that each student opens the debate on a different issue.

- Give SS time to make notes, helping with vocabulary where necessary.

c ● Set a time limit for each debate. Then tell one student from each group to start.

- Monitor and make a note of any mistakes you think it would be useful to deal with when they have finished the debates.

- Get feedback to find out which issues created the most controversy in each group, and which ones everybody generally agreed about.

Extra idea

If a group finishes much earlier than the others, get them to discuss some of the other topics from the list.

Extra support

Go through some of the mistakes you picked up while you were monitoring the debates.

Extra photocopiable activities

Grammar
ellipsis and substitution *p.173*
Communicative
Four fables *p.199* (instructions *p.181*)
Vocabulary
Animal idioms *p.224* (instructions *p.206*)

HOMEWORK

Study Link **Workbook** *pp.57–59*

6
C

G adding emphasis (2): cleft sentences
V words that are often confused
P intonation in cleft sentences

The promised land?

Lesson plan

The topic of this lesson is immigration. The lesson begins with a Polish woman and a British man who emigrated abroad talking about their experiences. In the grammar section SS work on the grammar of clauses or phrases which emphasize one part of a sentence, sometimes called cleft sentences. In pronunciation, they work on the intonation patterns in these kinds of sentences. In the second half of the lesson SS read and discuss an extract from a well-known novel, *The Joy Luck Club* by Amy Tan, about first and second generation Chinese immigrants in the United States. Finally, the vocabulary focus is on words which are often confused, e.g. *foreigner* and *stranger*.

Immigration is very much a part of the modern world but may be a sensitive topic in some teaching situations. Although the lesson does not encourage SS at any point to talk about immigration to their own country, teachers should be alert to this possibility, especially if there are immigrants in the class, and be ready to prevent any insensitive opinions being aired.

Optional lead-in – the quote

- Write the quote at the top of *p.92* on the board (books closed) and the name of the author or get SS to open their books and read it.
- Point out that Theodore Roosevelt (1858–1919) was president of the USA from 1901 to 1909, a period when there was a great deal of emigration to the USA, especially from Europe.
- Elicit / explain the meaning of *allegiance* (= a person's continued support) and get SS in pairs to say whether they agree with Roosevelt's view.

1 LISTENING & SPEAKING

a • Do this as an open-class question and elicit reasons. Find out what proportion of the class can imagine themselves going to live in another country.

b • Focus on the questions and put SS in pairs to discuss them. Get feedback. You could write the two headings on the board and list the pros and cons underneath them.

c • **6.11** and **6.12** Focus on the chart and the task. You could tell SS to copy a simplified chart (with the number of each question and the names of the two speakers) into their notebooks in order to have more room to complete it. Play the interview with Renata once all the way through. SS can begin to make notes in the chart. Point out that SS should just write down the main points and refer briefly to examples the speakers give (but without writing down all the details).

- Then play the recording again, this time pausing to give SS time to complete their notes (see spaces in scripts).

6.11 CD4 Track 13

(script in Student's Book on *p.132*)
I = interviewer, R = Renata

I Why did you decide to come to Spain?
R Well, it's a bit complicated. It was a bit of a fluke really. In fact, it was my husband who first came up with the idea of moving here. He's from Peru, and when I met him he was studying catering in Poland, in Poznan where I live, and he could sort of speak a bit of Polish, but not very well. So it would have been very difficult for him to get a job in Poland. Not to mention the paperwork, which would have been very complicated too. At that time, when we got married I mean, I'd just finished university, where I'd studied Spanish, and I'd got a job teaching Spanish in a school. So we thought about what we were going to do because if we'd stayed in Poland, I would have to be the one that worked. So as I spoke Spanish, and of course he did too, we decided to try living in Spain.

I When was this?
R About four years ago. We came with nothing, with just a bit of money and two suitcases – and that was it. But bit by bit, we managed to find jobs and somewhere to live. We were very lucky, the guy who rented us our first flat was a chef and he gave my husband a job, and I managed to get a job teaching Spanish to Polish immigrants here.

I What's the plus side for you about living in Spain?
R What I like best is that if you're prepared to work hard, you can get what you want, you can get a good standard of living quite easily. Then the weather is nice, it's not as cold as in Poland – though actually I really miss the snow. Here in Valencia it never snows. Another good thing here is that you have the sea and mountains quite close by, which we didn't have in Poznan.

I What about the downside?
R The traffic. I absolutely hate driving here, nobody obeys the traffic rules, they drive really crazily. And what else? The food is different, but it's OK. My husband would say the noise, the people here are so noisy. In Peru people aren't nearly as noisy – they live in their houses – if you want to see someone, you go to their house – they're not in the street all the time like they are here. I agree with him. And I think people gossip a lot here too. They're always talking about what everyone else is doing, and I don't like that.

I There must be things you miss about Poland.
R Of course – loads of things! The food! My family and my friends. The little corners of my town that I love, my favourite cafés and cinemas. That's what I miss most.

I Might you go back to Poland one day?
R I personally would love to go back, but I'm not sure if we ever will. It would be very difficult, especially for my husband. But you never know – or maybe we'll end up in Peru!

- Now repeat the process for Andrew.

6.12   CD4 Track 14

(script in Student's Book on *p.132*)
Andrew

I've been living in Milan for just over 15 years now. The reason why I first came here was because I'd always wanted to go and live abroad. I'd always had this picture in my mind of me having aperitifs at a café on some exotic seafront promenade in the south of France or somewhere like that, although I must admit I never imagined staying abroad for so long. Even when I married my Italian girlfriend, I always thought we'd eventually go back to the UK.

You see, what I like best about living here is that in some way I'm still 'living the dream'. Even though I have a demanding job with a multinational company, and a young child, both of which have their own stresses, somewhere in my brain there's a little voice that reminds me that I'm living abroad as I always wanted to be. Something which I think is very true is what another Brit said to me some time ago – he said, 'Despite everything, it's almost as if you are still on holiday'. And although Milan isn't half as exotic as people might imagine – I mean it's a bit grey and industrial, it's a bit like Manchester in that way – the food is a million times better, and you're only 40 kilometres of motorway away from the Alps, and about 130 from the Mediterranean.

The problems I have here are mainly to do with the bureaucracy, which can be incredibly frustrating. For instance the other day, the doctor told me I needed a chest X-ray and just to *book* the appointment involved me queuing in two different places for an hour and a half! The practicalities of life can be frustrating too. Socially, Italy has changed enormously in the last 15 years, but the state hasn't realized it yet. Most Italian women work these days, but nursery schools are still only open from 8.30 in the morning till about 4.00 in the afternoon. So who goes to pick your child up when both parents work full-time?

The things I miss most about the UK are the countryside, and the BBC – I find the Italian news too politically biased. But I can't really see myself going back. I'm a foreigner here, but I think I'm also a foreigner in the UK now too. When I go back to the UK, and that's maybe twice a year, and watch the TV, I understand the language, but the words or constructions are not what I would say. It isn't just language, though; it's the way of life. The UK has changed a lot and I can't say that I like it. It seems a much more violent place than it used to be, and it seems too, well, it's too politically correct. For example, on the news I notice they never say 'actress' now for women because it's supposed to be sexist – they say 'actor' for both men and women. I think it's all getting a bit out of hand. Italy still hasn't gone too far down that road, thank goodness!

d ● Give SS time to compare their answers with a partner before checking answers, eliciting as much information as possible.

RENATA
1 It was her husband's idea. He is Peruvian so it's difficult for him to work in Poland (language / paperwork). Both speak Spanish.
2 4 years
3 If you work hard, you get a good standard of living. Weather nice Close to sea and mountains
4 The traffic, anarchic way people drive People are noisy and gossip about you.
5 Misses family / friends, snow, food, 'little corners of her town'
6 Unlikely to go back because difficult for her husband

ANDREW
1 Always wanted to live abroad. Had idealized picture of exotic lifestyle.
2 15 years
3 He is living abroad as he always dreamed He feels as if 'still on holiday' Food much better than in UK Near Alps and Mediterranean
4 Bureaucracy, e.g. queuing for hours to book an X-ray, Practicalities, e.g. nurseries close at 4.30. Who collects children?
5 Countryside and BBC. Italian news too politically biased.
6 No. Feels like a foreigner in the UK. Language changing, more violent than before, too politically correct, e.g. can't say 'actress'.

LEXIS IN CONTEXT

e ● Focus on the task and give SS, in pairs, time to go through the phrases and answer the two questions.

Extra support

Finally, get SS to read both scripts on *p.132* and deal with any other vocabulary queries or problems.

1 She is referring to going to live in Spain. *a bit of a fluke* = unplanned, an accident
2 She is referring to her husband staying in Poland. *the paperwork* = the bureaucracy, e.g. getting work permits, etc.
3 She is referring to the time when they had just arrived in Spain. *bit by bit* = gradually
4 She is referring to what she misses about Poland. *loads of things* = an informal expression meaning *lots of things*
5 He is referring to living in Italy / abroad. *living the dream* = living as you have always dreamed
6 He is referring to the Italian news. *politically biased* = not neutral, either very pro- or anti-government
7 He is comparing Italy to the UK as regards being politically correct. *hasn't gone too far down that road* = hasn't gone too far in that direction

f ● Focus on the questions and get SS to answer with a partner. Then get feedback from the whole class.

2 GRAMMAR adding emphasis (2): cleft sentences

a ● Focus on sentences 1–4 and give SS time to try to complete them with a partner, preferably in pencil or on another piece of paper.

b ● ▶ **6.13** Play the CD for SS to check, pausing and playing again as necessary. Then get SS to compare the sentences.

> See script 6.13

● Elicit that the second versions give more emphasis to a particular part of the sentence, e.g. In the first sentence *It was my husband who...* gives more emphasis to her husband than *In fact my husband....* In the second sentence, putting *What I like best...* at the beginning gives more emphasis to this than when it was at the end.

> **6.13**   CD4 Track 15
>
> 1 In fact, it was my husband who first came up with the idea of moving here.
> 2 What I like best is that if you're prepared to work hard, you can get what you want.
> 3 The reason why I first came here was because I'd always wanted to go and live abroad…
> 4 The things I miss most about the UK are the countryside, and the BBC.

c ● Tell SS to go to **Grammar Bank 6C** on *p.153.* Go through each example and its corresponding rule with the class, or give SS time to read the examples and rules on their own, and answer any queries.

Grammar notes

When we want to focus attention on or emphasize one part of a sentence, we can do this by adding certain words or phrases to the beginning of the sentence as a kind of introduction or build-up. For example, *What I most enjoyed about the film was...* or *The reason I was late was....* These kinds of sentences are often referred to in grammar books as 'cleft' sentences (from the old-fashioned verb 'to cleave' = to cut), because the sentence is divided into two parts.

● Focus on the exercises for **6C**. SS do the exercises individually or in pairs. If SS do them individually, get them to compare with a partner. Check answers after each exercise.

> **a** 1 It   5 All
>   2 What   6 place
>   3 reason   7 What
>   4 happens   8 me
>
> **b** 1 The reason why she left her husband was because
>   2 The place where we stopped for lunch
>   3 What happened was (that)
>   4 What really annoyed me was (that)
>   5 It was a girl from my town who
>   6 All I said was
>   7 The person I like best of all my relatives
>   8 What happens is (that)
>   9 What you need to do right now is
>   10 The first time I met Serena was

● Tell SS to go back to the main lesson on *p.93.*

3 PRONUNCIATION & SPEAKING intonation in cleft sentences

Pronunciation notes

Cleft sentences have a specific intonation pattern, which SS should be made aware of. Encourage them to imitate it, as this will make their English sound more natural. If they find the technical expressions (fall-rise tone, etc.) difficult to understand, tell them not to worry and to simply try to copy the intonation on the CD.

a ● ▶ **6.14** Focus on the information box and go through it with SS. Play the example sentences twice for them to listen to and try to grasp the two different intonation patterns.

> **6.14**   CD4 Track 16
>
> 1 What I hate about my job is having to get up early.
> 2 The reason why I went to France was because I wanted to learn the language.
> 3 It was her mother who really broke up our marriage.
> 4 It's the commuting that I find so tiring.

b ● ▶ **6.15** Play the CD pausing after each sentence for SS to listen and repeat. Play the recording again as necessary.

> **6.15**   CD4 Track 17
>
> (See Student's Book)

c ● Focus on the task and give SS time to complete the sentences. Monitor and help.

● Then get SS to take turns to read their sentences to each other. Monitor and check their intonation, correcting it where necessary.

Extra idea

Make up some sentences of your own for SS to listen to your intonation.

4 READING & SPEAKING

a ● Focus on the photo and the book cover, and find out if any SS have read the book or seen the film. Then focus on the pre-reading questions and get SS to answer them with a partner.

● Get feedback from the class and tell SS what you think.

b ● Focus on the gist questions. Set a time limit for SS to read the extract once. Check answers.

> Waverly seems to be experiencing an identity crisis because she had always wanted to be seen as American, not as Chinese, but now that she wants to visit China she feels unhappy that, according to her mother, Chinese people will see her as an outsider because she cannot speak the language and is clearly 'all American-made'.
>
> Her mother feels responsible. She wanted her children to have the best of both worlds, having the benefits of living in the USA while retaining their Chinese character, but she now realizes that this is impossible.

c ● Focus on the task. Get SS to read the extract again and then answer the questions, referring back to the text. Get them to compare with a partner, justifying their choices, and then check answers.

> 1 b   2 d   3 a   4 c   5 b

LEXIS IN CONTEXT

d ● Focus on the task and give SS time to find the verbs in the text and guess their meaning. They can do this in pairs or individually and then compare with a partner. Check answers.

> **blend in** = to look similar to other people, so that you don't stand out / look different
> **sue** = make a claim against sb in court about sth they have said or done to harm you
> **obey** = do what sb has told you
> **pursue** = follow sth in order to catch or acquire it
> **polish** /ˈpɒlɪʃ/ = make sth shine by rubbing it with a cloth, e.g. *I polished the car*, (metaphorically) to improve sth by making changes, e.g. *We need to polish our performance before the show on Friday.*
> **flash around** = (disapproving) to show sth you have to other people in order to impress them, e.g. *He flashes his money around.*
> **stick to** = become fixed (in her mind)

e ● Do this as an open-class question and elicit opinions.

Extra support

Deal with any other vocabulary queries and problems SS may have. You may want to point out that there are a couple of phrases in the text which do not sound totally English and are probably used by the author to convey the idea that the mother's English is perhaps influenced by Chinese, e.g. *the way you carry your face, put your feelings behind your face*, etc.

You could ask SS to choose five other words or phrases they would like to learn.

5 VOCABULARY words that are often confused

a ● Focus on the task. Get SS to compare their answers with a partner. Check answers, eliciting the exact meaning of each word.

> **a foreigner** is sb from another country
> **an outsider** is sb who is not accepted as a member of a society or a group
> **a stranger** is sb you don't know; sb who is in a place they haven't been to before

b ● Give SS time to complete their sentences and then compare with a partner. Check answers, eliciting the pronunciation of both words. Emphasize in each case that the word which is right in one sentence cannot be used in the other.

> **1 a** suite = a set of rooms, esp. in a hotel, usually with a bedroom, a living area, and a bathroom
> **b** suit = a jacket with matching trousers or skirt
> **2 a** besides = in addition to, apart from, e.g. *What sports do you like besides football?*
> **b** beside = next to or at the side of sb / sth, e.g. *Come and sit beside me.*

> **3 a** lie = put yourself in a horizontal position (past *lay*, past participle *lain*)
> **b** lay = put sth or sb in a particular position or put sth down on sth (past *laid*, past participle *laid*), e.g. *He laid his hand on my arm.*
> ⚠ *lie (down)* does not have an object; *lay sth / sb (down)* needs an object.
> **4 a** currently = at the moment
> **b** actually = in fact, to tell the truth
> **5 a** announce = tell people sth officially, e.g. *The government has announced that it is going to lower the school leaving age.*
> **b** advertise = tell people about a product or service to encourage them to buy or use it
> **6 a** affect = verb meaning to produce a change in sb or sth
> **b** effects = noun meaning the consequences of an action
> **7 a** embarrassed = shy or awkward especially in a social situation
> **b** ashamed = feeling bad about sth you have done
> **8 a** deny = say you have not done sth
> **b** refused = say you will not do sth
> **9 a** compromise = an agreement between two parties or groups in which each side gives up some of the things they want so that both sides are happy at the end. It can also be a verb, e.g. *We had to compromise.*
> **b** commitment = a promise to do sth or to behave in a particular way. It is also a verb, e.g. *The company is committed to providing quality at a reasonable price.*
> **10 a** economical = money-saving
> **b** economic = related to the economy, e.g. *There is a serious economic crisis.*

c ● Focus on the task and give SS a few moments to complete the sentences. Check answers.

> | 1 affect | 4 advertised |
> |---|---|
> | 2 embarrassed | 5 actually |
> | 3 commitment | 6 refuse |

● Put SS in pairs and get them to discuss whether they think the sentences are more true of men or of women. Get feedback.

Extra photocopiable activities

Grammar
adding emphasis (2) *p.174*
Communicative
Celebrity immigrants *p.200 (instructions p.181)*
Vocabulary
What's the difference? *p.225 (instructions p.206)*

HOMEWORK

Study Link Workbook *pp.60–62*

6 WRITING: DISCURSIVE ESSAY (2): TAKING SIDES

Lesson plan

In this lesson the focus is on the second type of discursive essay, where SS decide to either argue in favour or against a statement (the balanced approach was covered in **Writing 4**). The writing skills focus is on topic sentences and using synonyms, and the **Useful Language** section covers common expressions for giving personal opinions, and for expressing opposite arguments and refuting them.

ANALYSING A MODEL TEXT

a • Focus on the text type (a discursive essay where you take one side). Remind SS of the balanced approach, which they covered in **Writing 4**. Point out to them that sometimes an essay title simply asks them if they agree with a statement or not. As an alternative to the balanced approach they can argue strongly in favour or against the statement rather than giving both sides of the argument. They can also include a typical counter argument which they then refute (prove that it is wrong), although this may not always be necessary or appropriate.

• Focus on the **Key success factors** and go through them with SS.

• Focus on the task, and give SS time to discuss the essay title and decide whether, generally speaking, they agree or disagree with it. Get feedback to find out what the majority of the class think.

b • Focus on the task. Go through the **Topic sentences** box with SS. Then give SS time to read A–F and in pairs discuss how the paragraphs are likely to continue.

> A We expect the rest of the paragraph to give examples of this, e.g. better public transport, better water systems, etc.
> B We expect the paragraph to develop this argument and give more examples, e.g. overcrowding, excess traffic, etc.
> C We expect some information about tourism in general.
> D We expect specific examples of this such as drunkenness, noise, etc.
> E We expect specific examples of what governments are doing and the results of this, e.g. creating conservation areas.
> F We expect the paragraph to elaborate on this statement, e.g. hundreds of jobs are created in hotels and restaurants.

c • Now focus on the essay. Tell SS to read it though once, and then to read it again, completing each paragraph with the appropriate topic sentence. Get SS to compare with a partner and then check answers.

> 1 C 2 F 3 A 4 E 5 B

d • Focus on the task and the information box. Give SS time to discuss the questions. Check answers.

> 1 In the introduction and the conclusion
> 2 Three
> 3 To give an opposing opinion, and then refute it

e • Focus on the **Using synonyms and richer vocabulary** box (this was also focused on in **Writing 2**) and the task. Tell SS to look for the synonyms in the topic sentences as well as the paragraphs. Check answers.

> 1 holidaymakers, visitors
> 2 influences
> 3 for instance
> 4 to gain from

• Point out that the verb *benefit* could also be used as a synonym in 4. It can be used in an active way, as it is in the essay, (A benefits B) or in a passive way (B benefits from A), and the passive way is a synonym for *profit from*.

USEFUL LANGUAGE

f • Finally, focus on the expressions. Get SS to complete them individually and then compare with a partner. Check answers.

> | 1 feel | 5 Personally | 9 may have |
> |---|---|---|
> | 2 believe | 6 argue | 10 flaws |
> | 3 view | 7 claimed | 11 case |
> | 4 opinion | 8 those | |

PLANNING WHAT TO WRITE

a • Focus on the task. Tell SS to read the titles and decide which side they take and why, and make notes of as many reasons as possible.

• After they have noted down reasons, get them to choose the three most important ones, and also to think if there is a typical opposing argument.

b • Now tell them to share their ideas with a partner, but point out that they don't have to agree.

• Get feedback from individual SS finding out if they agree or disagree, what their reasons are, and if they can refute a typical opposing argument.

c • Now get SS to decide which essay they are going to write, and to write topic sentences for the introduction and the main paragraphs.

• Then get them to compare with a partner and comment on, and improve where possible, each other's sentences.

Extra support

If a pair has chosen the same essay title and agreed with each other when they discussed it, they could write the topic sentences together.

• Finally, go through the tips with SS.

WRITING

Go through the instructions and set the writing for homework.

Test and Assessment CD-ROM

CEFR Assessment materials

File 6 Writing task assessment guidelines

Lesson plan

In the first part of this lesson the person interviewed is Peter Jinman, who is a vet (short for *veterinary surgeon*), and President of the British Veterinary Association. He works in Herefordshire, a county in the west of England. He talks about his job and also gives his opinion on several animal related issues. In the second part of the lesson people in the street are asked what animals they are afraid of and if they have ever had a frightening experience involving an animal.

Study Link These lessons are on the *New English File Advanced* DVD which can be used instead of the class CD (See Introduction *p.9*). SS can get more practice on the MultiROM, which contains more of the short street interviews with a listening task and scripts.

Optional lead-in (books closed)

- Set a time limit. Get SS, in pairs, to brainstorm the good side and bad side of being a vet. Feedback ideas onto the board and leave them there during the listening activity. The first time SS listen they can see how many of these points the vet himself mentioned.

THE INTERVIEW

a • Books open. Now focus on the task and on the glossary. Go through it with the class eliciting from them how to pronounce the words. Also focus on the photos of the animals and elicit how the words are pronounced.

Extra support

You may want to pre-teach some other words and phrases before SS listen to the interview (see script 6.16).

b • **6.16** Focus on the questions and give SS time to read them. Encourage SS not to write anything down when they listen the first time. Tell them that they should listen and try to get the gist of what he is saying, and then discuss the questions with their partner.

- Play the CD once (**Part 1**). Give SS time to discuss the questions and tell each other what they understood. Then play the CD again pausing after each of Peter's answers to give SS time to make notes and compare with their partner again. Play the recording again as necessary. Elicit and check answers.

1 Because he didn't want to teach and the Professor of Zoology pointed out that 80% of Zoology students become teachers. The Professor suggested becoming a vet instead.

2 It involves him driving around nice countryside and meeting people on their farms (rather than in a surgery).

3 Because he hasn't had much experience of them so he is not familiar with their anatomy and peculiarities, or how medicines will react. In these cases he needs to consult a book or somebody who knows more about them.

4 This is a situation when someone comes into his surgery with an animal in a cardboard box and the vet has no idea what is in it. He describes the cardboard box as 'dreaded' (= causing fear) because this is a moment which all vets fear.

5 The way they get sheep in (i.e. into the pen) and sort them out, the way they work with cattle.

6 Best thing is birth. The worst is having to put an animal down (i.e. kill an animal that is very old or sick, usually by injecting it with a drug).

6.16   CD4 Track 18

(script in Student's Book on *p.133*)
I = interviewer, P = Peter Jinman
I What made you decide to become a vet?
P I was always interested in animals and originally when I was at school, I was hoping to become a zoologist. I wanted to study animals and their behaviour. And because my father was working at a university at the time, I said to him, 'Do you know anybody there that I can go and talk to in the zoology department?' and he arranged for me to meet the Professor of Zoology, and I went to the university and he said to me, 'Do you want to teach?' and I said, 'No, I don't think I do.' He said, 'Well, 80% of the people who do the zoology course teach. Have you ever thought of being a vet?' And I thought that's a rather good idea.
I Do you prefer treating farm animals or pets?
P Personally I'm, I do probably a little bit more with the farm work but I don't mind, I like treating them all. I like being involved with them all. And I'm in general practice, so I don't have a specialization in one particular species or one particular discipline within that.
I So why do you tend to prefer farm animals?
P I quite like meeting the people on the farm, I'm living in the countryside, where we are today, in this surgery, we're right in a little village in the countryside on the border of England and Wales and if you look around and look out there, you'd understand why it's nice to be able to go round and drive round a bit of that country and see the animals there.
I What's the most difficult animal to treat?
P It's surprising what people turn up with in the surgery. So some time, most of the animals that we would see belong to a certain group, say dogs, cats, maybe rabbits, guinea pigs, hamsters, ferrets. But now we're starting to see cameloids. That is llamas – certainly we've got llamas locally – and other members of that same group. Those suddenly present a challenge because you're looking at an animal that you haven't really dealt with and is different because every species is different. Even within a species, we sometimes have variations between breeds. So the most difficult is really just one that you're not used to and you suddenly find yourself thinking, 'What are the peculiarities, what's the anatomy, what's the anatomical variation, how will particular medicines react, what is the dosage?' And you sincerely hope that either you've got a book or there's something somewhere or somebody you can ring up and find out. But I can assure you that when somebody brought a tarantula spider in one day, I did have a moment there where I thought to myself, 'Now what are we going to do with that?' It's the dreaded cardboard box. Somebody comes in with a little cardboard box and they put it down very proudly on the table and you're waiting in expectation and then they open it up and you look at it and go, 'Ah, very interesting. Now what is that?'

I What do you think is the most intelligent animal of all the ones you treat?

P I suppose when we're dealing with intelligence it's a question that you can have intelligent animals within a particular species. So I've met some extremely intelligent dogs, particularly collies, working collies. They are amazing, how they get the sheep in, how they sort them out or work with the cattle. Marvellous! People always say pigs are very intelligent and I had a professor at college who always maintained that why do we keep dogs and cats; we should keep pigs as pets. He reckoned they were very clean and they were wonderful animals to have as a pet – highly intelligent.

I What's the best and worst thing about your job?

P I think the best is always birth. It doesn't matter what species, birth is brilliant, amazing every time it happens, one marvels at it, whatever the species. I suppose the worst is always having to put an animal down, put it to sleep.

---

c ● **6.17** Focus on the task and give SS time to read the questions. Play the CD once (**Part 2**) and tell SS just to listen. Then give SS time to discuss the questions and tell each other what they understood. Now play the CD again, pausing after each answer to give SS time to make notes and compare with their partner again. Play the recording again as necessary. Elicit and check answers.

1 He says the principle in the UK is to try to reduce the number of animals used, but he can see no other way of testing particular substances. However, he feels uncomfortable with the idea of testing substances which are not medicines such as cosmetics. He does not think this is a good use of animals.

2 He says all dogs can be dangerous. Deaths involving babies or small children have sometimes been caused by small dogs. He thinks the problem is really dog owners, who don't look after their dogs properly. Children should never be left alone with dogs.

3 He says that you need to assess the risk of all animals you are dealing with and take suitable precautions as even cows and pigs can be dangerous, for example when they are looking after their young.

4 His son has a snake which he uses to terrify visitors, especially young ladies. It escaped once but was recaptured.

5 Clients use the Internet to research what they think is wrong with their pet and then bring the information to the vet. Often when the vet examines the pet he finds that it does not have the illness that they have researched.

6.17   CD4 Track 19

(script in Student's Book on *p.133*)

I How do you feel about animals being used in experiments?

P Well, the whole principle of using animals in experiments has been reviewed certainly in this country very, very strongly. And the principle has been to try to reduce the number of animals used. Now unfortunately, there seems to be no other way of achieving always the result that we require in testing a particular substance. I do find myself a little bit uncomfortable with the wish that there is to test substances other than medicines. When we start to get testing cosmetics and things that are somewhat ephemeral in the needs of the human population, I'm not sure that's a good use of animals.

I How do you feel about people having large dangerous dogs as pets?

P All dogs can be dangerous. If you look at where deaths have occurred in babies and small children, it's surprising, sometimes it's been very small dogs that have been involved. It hasn't always been the big dogs. Unfortunately, it's not really the dog's problem and fault, it's usually the owner's problem and fault. And so if the owner can't restrain, keep control, have a proper care of that animal, then any dog can become more dangerous. And the principle of leaving children with dogs is one that should not on any occasion occur, no matter how good anybody believes a particular dog is. Dogs can be dangerous.

I Are there any animals or insects you are afraid of?

P I suppose that 'afraid' is one word, 'being extremely cautious of', is another. I've been attacked by cows, not uncommonly unfortunately over the years, picked up and thrown across the room and so on. Now everybody thinks cows are rather nice creatures and so on but when they've got a calf at foot, they are very protective and they can be extremely dangerous. A sow with its piglets will be very dangerous and possibly one of the most dangerous species that we deal with. I've treated tigers, I've treated chimpanzees, and in their own right those are extremely dangerous, so I think it's a question of assessing the animal, the risk, and taking the suitable precautions, because sometimes it's the small ones that bite you when you're not thinking about it rather than the big one that you are watching and thinking was going to be dangerous.

I Do you have any pets yourself?

P Yes, over the years we've had various animals. At the moment we've got a dog, 40 sheep, a couple of ponies and a snake. And it sits in its, in its vivarium on the landing at home, and it's my son's snake and I think he uses it purposely to terrify some of the young ladies who visit and others, and my daughter's boyfriend, is not at all keen on it and walks round the landing to try and avoid it.

I Has it ever escaped?

P On one occasion it did escape briefly, but was rapidly recaptured I hasten to add.

I Would you recommend becoming a vet?

P Yes, I think it's been a good life. I certainly have enjoyed it. It's meant it's very challenging, very demanding. You never stop learning and, in fact, you can't stop learning because medicine – whether it be veterinary medicine or human medicine – the changes are immense over the years. So you're constantly having to be kept up to date by reading, attending lectures, talking to colleagues, and also by your clients. Because these days with the Internet, they very often will come in with a whole sheaf of papers and say, 'We think our dog has got so and so. Here you are Mr Vet, look at all this information.' And you then sort of go, 'Thank you very much,' and put it gently to one side and have a look at the animal and decide that this extraordinary disease that they've just found on the Internet doesn't have any relation to what's in front of you. But that's one of the challenges of today.

---

d ● **6.18** This exercise gives SS intensive listening practice in deciphering phrases where words are often run together, and introduces them to some common expressions and idioms used in spoken English. Focus on phrases 1–6 and give SS time to read them. Play the CD, pausing after the first phrase and replaying it as necessary. Elicit the missing words, and then the meaning of the whole phrase. Repeat for the other five phrases.

1 **turn up with** (= arrive with)
2 **can assure you** (= to tell sb that sth is definitely true or is definitely going to happen, especially when they have doubts about it)
3 **put** an animal **down** (= to kill an animal, usually by giving it a drug, because it is old or sick)
4 **no matter how** good (= it doesn't matter how good the dog is)
5 **up to date** (= having or including the most recent information)
6 **so and so** (= used to refer vaguely to a person or thing when you don't give the exact name)

6.18   CD4 Track 20

1 It's surprising what people turn up with in the surgery.
2 But I can assure you that when somebody brought a tarantula spider in one day…
3 I suppose the worst is always having to put an animal down, put it to sleep.
4 And the principle of leaving children with dogs is one that should not on any occasion occur, no matter how good anybody believes a particular dog is.
5 So you're constantly having to be kept up to date by reading, attending lectures…
6 We think our dog has got so and so.

Extra support

If there's time, get SS to listen again with the scripts on *p.133*, focusing on any new vocabulary, and getting feedback on phrases SS didn't understand, e.g. because the words were run together.

e ● Finally, focus on the questions. Get SS to answer in pairs and then get feedback from the whole class, or do this as an open-class discussion.

IN THE STREET

a ● **6.19** Focus on the task and play the CD once for SS to answer the questions. Get them to compare their answers with a partner and then elicit the answers onto the board.

Questions

1 Are there any animals or insects that you are afraid of or feel uncomfortable with?
2 Have you ever had a frightening experience involving an animal?

6.19   CD4 Track 21

(script in Student's Book on *p.133*)
I = interviewer, P = Priti, S = Sheila, J = Jerry
Priti
I Are there any animals or insects that you are afraid of or feel uncomfortable with?
P Mosquitoes, just they bite me a lot and I'm really really allergic to their bites.
I Have you ever had a frightening experience involving an animal?
P There was one time in India on a tiger safari and we were in an open 4x4 going down this steep hill when we came across a tiger in the middle of the path coming up towards us so we had to try and reverse up whilst this tiger was stalking towards us. That was pretty scary.

Sheila
I Are there any animals or insects that you are afraid of or feel uncomfortable with?
S Snakes. I hate them.
I Have you always felt like this?
S Yes, I think so. I've seen a few snakes in the wild and really don't like them. I have had a boa constrictor put around my neck, but I didn't like it very much.
I Have you ever had a frightening experience involving an animal?
S A few! The elephant was probably the most frightening. I was on safari with my husband and we were having lunch in the camp and he said, 'Oh, I'm just going to pop up to the office', there's a little office in a hut, because they can charge your batteries at certain times of the day. So he said, 'I'll just pop up and get my battery for the camera' and off he went. Five minutes later he came running back into the lunch area and said, 'There's an elephant out there. Come on, come and have a look!' So the guy in therestaurant said, 'Just be careful, don't get too close,' and he didn't say what he meant by 'don't get too close' so out we went, and we walked around the corner and we looked up the pathway and there was a massive elephant. And it saw us and it just came charging towards us. Thank God, behind us the waiter had come out and we were just about to turn and run, because the elephant was very very close, probably about 10, 15 feet away. We were just about to run and the waiter said, 'Whatever you do, don't run!' So we just stood our ground and the elephant swung its trunk a bit and walked away. But my heart was beating so fast. It really was quite frightening.

Jerry
I Are there any animals or insects that you are afraid of or feel uncomfortable with?
J I'm afraid of spiders, I must confess. I mean above a certain size I'm afraid of them. Small ones I can cope with, larger ones I don't like very much. Even pictures of spiders in a book, you know, or a magazine. If I turn a page and see a picture of a spider, I kind of, a little shudder of fear passes through me.
I Have you always felt like this?
J Yeah, yeah, I mean it's getting better, but when I was a child it was really quite bad. You know, I'd run screaming from the room. I don't do that any more.
I Have you ever had a frightening experience involving an animal?
J I've had an encounter with a bear in a national park in California, where I was having, camping with a friend and we were eating dinner round a campfire and he looked over my shoulder and said, 'Jerry, there's a bear behind you,' and it was standing up on its hind legs about ten feet away so we had to withdraw and it ate our dinner and then walked off. So there was no damage done, but it was quite frightening.

b ● Focus on the task and give SS time to read questions 1–6. Play the recording again all the way through and then give SS time to try and answer the questions. Then play it again pausing after each speaker this time for SS to check their answers. Play again as necessary and check answers.

1 Sheila (speaker 2)	4 Sheila (speaker 2)
2 Jerry (speaker 3)	5 Priti (speaker 1)
3 Priti (speaker 1)	6 Jerry (speaker 3)

c ● **6.20** Focus on the phrases and give SS time to read them. Play the CD, pausing after the first phrase and replaying it as necessary. Elicit the missing words, and then the meaning of the whole phrase. Repeat for the other four phrases.

1 **came across** (PV = meet or find by accident)
2 **pop up** (PV informal = go somewhere quickly)
3 **off** he **went** (= informal and more dramatic way of saying *he went off / he left*)
4 **the guy** (= informal way of saying *the man*)
5 **no damage done** (= informal way of saying nobody was hurt, nothing bad happened)

6.20	CD4 Track 22

1 …when we came across a tiger in the middle of the path coming up towards us…
2 So he said, 'I'll just pop up and get my battery for the camera'…
3 …and off he went.
4 So the guy in the restaurant said, 'Just be careful, don't get too close,'…
5 So there was no damage done, but it was quite frightening.

Extra support

If there's time, get SS to listen again with the scripts on *p.133*, focusing on any new vocabulary, and getting feedback on phrases SS didn't understand, e.g. because the words were run together.

d • Finally, get SS to ask each other the two questions that the interviewer asked the interviewees. Then get some feedback from the whole class.

HOMEWORK

Study Link **Workbook** *p.63*

6 REVISE & CHECK

For instructions on how to use this page, see *p.35*.

GRAMMAR

a 1 –
2 but ~~she~~ didn't speak to him
3 or ~~I~~ go for
4 and then ~~he~~ immediately
5 –
6 –
7 –

b 1 back
2 point
3 was
4 has
5 so
6 to
7 to
8 will / must / should
9 so
10 not

c 1 reason why I didn't bring any sunscreen is /was
2 is due to begin
3 The person I spoke to was
4 about to leave (any minute now)
5 What I don't like about my boss is the way
6 'll be wearing a white suit
7 All I said was (that)
8 It was a boy from my school who

VOCABULARY

a 1 refused
2 claws
3 trip
4 lying
5 stung
6 embarrassed
7 track
8 off
9 affect
10 low-cost

b 1 shell
2 breathtaking
3 species
4 package
5 fins
6 off / out
7 haul
8 activists
9 site

c 1 take the bull by the horns
2 made a real pig of myself
3 his bark is far worse than his bite
4 a dark horse
5 count my chickens
6 kill two birds with one stone

Test and Assessment CD-ROM

File 6 Quicktest
File 6 Test

7A

G nouns: compound and possessive forms
V preparing food
P -ed adjective endings and linking

A recipe for disaster

File 7 overview

The first lesson in this File, **7A**, covers the grammar of compound and possessive nouns, and expands SS' vocabulary related to food and cooking. In **7B** the grammar focus is on the use of *so* and *such*, and in vocabulary SS practise making nouns and verbs from common adjectives, e.g. *strong, strength, strengthen.* In the final lesson, **7C**, SS revise and extend their knowledge of expressions for making comparisons, and learn a vocabulary set related to humour.

Lesson plan

The topic of this lesson is cooking. In the first half of the lesson SS begin by expanding their knowledge of verbs and utensils related to preparing food and in Pronunciation they revise *-ed* endings and linking. They then listen to four people talking about cooking disasters, and in Speaking they plan a meal with a set of ingredients, and talk about aspects of cooking. In the second half of the lesson SS focus on the grammar of compound and possessive nouns. They then read a magazine article about what famous chefs would eat for their last meal, which turns out to be far simpler food than what one would perhaps expect.

Optional lead-in – the quote

- Write the quote at the top of *p.100* on the board (books closed) and the name of the author or get SS to open their books and read it. Elicit / explain *exasperating* (= extremely annoying).
- Point out that Robert Frost (1874–1963) is one of the best known American poets. His most famous poems are probably *Stopping by Woods on a Snowy Evening* and *The Road Not Taken* (which in a recent poll was voted America's favourite poem).
- Ask SS what they think of the quote, and ask them if they know anyone who can't cook well but insists on trying.

1 VOCABULARY preparing food

a • Focus on the instructions and give SS time to read the menu and make their choices.

- Get SS to compare their choices with a partner. Get feedback and elicit / explain any vocabulary SS ask about.

- You may want to point out that:
  - *cobb salad* is a garden salad. Its main ingredients are iceberg lettuce, tomato, bacon, chicken breast, hard-boiled egg, avocado and Roquefort cheese (blue cheese).
  - *gravy* is a brown sauce made by adding flour to the juices that come out of meat while it's cooking.
  - *parsley* is a plant with curly green leaves used in cooking and to decorate food.
  - *jasmine rice* is a long grain rice with a nutty flavour used in Thai cooking.

- *haddock* is a white fish very common in the UK, which is often smoked.
- *hollandaise sauce* is a French sauce made with butter, egg yolks, and lemon juice or vinegar.
- *basmati* is a variety of long grain rice grown in India and Pakistan. It has a distinctive fragrance.
- *pecorino* is a hard Italian cheese made from sheep's milk.
- the difference between a *pie* and a *tart* is that a pie has pastry on top and a tart has pastry on the bottom.
- *custard* is a sweet yellow sauce made from milk, sugar, eggs, and flour.
- *Amaretto* is an almond-flavoured Italian liqueur often used in cooking.

b • Focus on the instructions and get SS to complete the chart individually or with a partner. Check answers by writing the chart headings on the board and completing with SS' suggestions. Model and drill pronunciation as necessary.

Ways of preparing food
grilled, steamed, stir-fried, mashed, poached, baked, stuffed

Vegetables
avocado, rocket, peppers, onions, potatoes, French beans, aubergines

Fruit
raspberry, plum, apple, blackberry

Sauces, etc.
vinaigrette, gravy, hollandaise, custard

Fish, etc.
mussels, sardines, haddock

c • In a monolingual class, do this as an open-class question, and teach SS any words they didn't know. In a multilingual class, get SS to talk in small groups.

  ⚠ Names for fish and some more unusual types of seafood are notoriously difficult to translate. Get SS to do some research on the Internet or with dictionaries.

d • Tell SS to go to **Vocabulary Bank** *Preparing food* on *p.167*. Focus on the exercise and get SS to do it with a partner. Check answers and model and drill pronunciation where necessary.

1	a chopping board	17	steamed mussels
2	stir (a sauce)	18	spices
3	pour	19	turkey breast
4	a baking tray	20	minced beef
5	drain (the pasta)	21	scrambled eggs
6	frying pan	22	roast lamb
7	heat (sth in the microwave)	23	grated cheese
8	mix (the ingredients)	24	peeled prawns / shrimps
9	an oven	25	herbs
10	simmer	26	sliced bread
11	beat (eggs)	27	chopped onions
12	a saucepan	28	poached eggs
13	shellfish	29	toasted sandwich
14	baked figs	30	whipped cream
15	melted chocolate	31	stuffed peppers
16	mashed potatoes	32	pork ribs

- You may want to highlight some of the following information:
  - common herbs include parsley, rosemary, thyme, basil
  - common spices include pepper, cinnamon, curry, cumin
  - *beat* and *whip* describe similar movements but *whip* is used mainly with cream and egg whites, and means *beat until stiff*
  - with meat and potatoes we usually say *roast*, not *roasted*.
  - *baked* and *roasted* are similar (both mean cooked in the oven) but *roast* = with fat, e.g. oil or butter.
- Finally, focus on the instruction 'Can you remember the words and phrases on this page? Test yourself or a partner.'

Testing yourself
Get SS to cover the words, and look at the pictures and say what each one is.

Testing a partner
See **Testing a partner** *p.18*.

Study Link SS can find more practice of these words and phrases on the MultiROM and on the *New English File Advanced* website.

- Tell SS to go back to the main lesson on *p.100*.

2 PRONUNCIATION *-ed* adjective endings and linking

Pronunciation notes

- Even at this level the pronunciation of the *-ed* endings for adjectives (and of past forms and past participles) can still cause problems. SS typically will often doubt which of the two similar endings /t/ and /d/ is required, and may also struggle to produce the sounds correctly. When the adjective is used in conjunction with a noun this does not usually cause a communication problem, but it may when the adjective is used on its own.

- In this exercise SS also revise two of the rules for linking they have learnt, i.e. when one word ends with a consonant sound and the next one begins with a vowel sound, e.g. *baked apples*, and when the second word begins with the same consonant sound that the previous word ended with, e.g, *chopped tomatoes*. The exercise also recycles the vocabulary the SS have just learnt.

a • Focus on the task and give SS, in pairs, time to write the words in the right column. Tell SS that saying the words aloud will help them.

Extra support
Elicit the pronunciation of the words in the list first to remind SS of the pronunciation.

b • **7.1** Play the CD for SS to check their answers. Remind SS of the rules for the pronunciation of *-ed* endings and that of course the same rules apply to past tense verb forms and past participles as well as adjectives:
  - words which end in an unvoiced sound (made without using the voice box), i.e. which finish with the sound /f/, /k/, /p/, /s/, /tʃ/, and /ʃ/ are pronounced /t/ when you add *-d* or *-ed*, e.g. *baked, chopped*
  - words which end in a voiced sound (sounds which are made using the voice box – you can feel the sound vibrate if you touch your throat) are pronounced /d/ when you add *-d* or *-ed*, e.g. *boiled, scrambled*
  - words which end in the sound /t/ or /d/ are pronounced /ɪd/ when you add *-d* or *-ed*, e.g. *grated, melted*

7.1		CD4 Track 23
/t/	/d/	/ɪd/
baked	boiled	grated
chopped	grilled	melted
mashed	peeled	toasted
minced	scrambled	
sliced	steamed	
stuffed	stir-fried	
whipped		

c • **7.2** Focus on the phrases and highlight that they are all linked. Get SS to practise saying them, and then play the CD for SS to check they were saying them correctly. Elicit answers to the question *Why are the words linked?*

They are linked because the first word ends in a consonant sound and the second word begins with a vowel sound.

Extra support
Play the recording again, pausing after each phrase for SS to copy the pronunciation.

7.2	CD4 Track 24
(See Student's Book)	

7 A

d ● **7.3** Get SS to practise saying the phrases, and then play the CD for SS to check their answers.

- Then elicit / explain that these words are linked in the first phrase (*chopped tomatoes*) because the first word ends in the same consonant sound (/t/) that the second word begins with. Highlight that the /t/ sound of the *ed* ending is not pronounced, but the /t/ of *tomatoes* is.

- In the next two phrases (*stir-fried tofu, grilled tuna*) the words are linked because the two sounds (/d/ and /t/) are very similar. The /d/ sound of *fried* and *grilled* is dropped, but the /t/ sound at the beginning of the next word is pronounced.

Extra support

Play the recording again, pausing after each phrase for SS to copy the pronunciation.

> **7.3**   CD4 Track 25
>
> (See Student's Book)

e ● This exercise is to give more practice in the pronunciation of *-ed* endings. Try to elicit an adjective, e.g. *fried* or a phrase, e.g. *fried eggs*. Do this as an open-class question.

3 LISTENING

a ● **7.4** Focus on the chart and the task. Highlight to SS that sometimes they will need to infer the answers from what the speakers say.

- Play the CD once the whole way through for SS to listen. Elicit what each dish was (*spaghetti bolognese, roast meat*, and *bruschetta*). Then play it again, pausing after the first speaker to give SS time to write. Then get them to compare with a partner. Repeat for the other two speakers. Check answers from the chart.

Extra support

Pre-teach *bin* (= where you throw rubbish) and *bruschetta* (= an Italian starter of toasted bread with olive oil and different toppings, e.g. tomatoes) if you think SS won't know them.

> **Speaker 1** her boyfriend and a colleague; green peppers, green chilli peppers; it was much too hot / spicy; they threw it away
> **Speaker 2** friends; meat; he put on the grill instead of the oven so the meat was not cooked properly and the top was burnt; they sent for a takeaway
> **Speaker 3** her family; bread, tomatoes, garlic; she used too much garlic; they couldn't eat it so they threw it away

> **7.4**   CD4 Track 26
>
> (script in Student's Book on *p.133*)
> 1 Just after I left drama school, I was cooking supper for my boyfriend and another bloke who we were working with in the theatre, and I was going to do spaghetti bolognese and I wanted some green peppers. And I didn't realize then that there was a difference between green peppers and green chilli peppers and so I cooked the spaghetti bolognese and I couldn't quite understand why my, underneath my nails was burning so terribly, but I just kept washing my hands and ignored it. And then we sat down to eat and Jeff, the friend who'd come, took one mouthful of the spaghetti bolognese before either of us did and fell off his chair onto the floor. And I'm afraid the whole lot had to go into the bin, it was the most horrendous experience.
>
> 2
> I Have you had any awful, memorable disasters in the kitchen?
> Sp One particular one when I'd just bought a new oven, and I'd invited some friends round and I was going to cook a piece of roast meat, and I put it in my new oven, and turned it on, and left it for an hour to cook and when I opened the oven door, I realized that I'd put the grill on, not the oven, so that the top of the meat was completely charred, and underneath it was completely raw, so the meal was completely ruined. So I had to send out for a takeaway.
> I Ah, that's a shame.
>
> 3
> I Katie, have you had a bad cooking experience?
> Sp Um, well it didn't really involve cooking as such, but it was certainly a bad, preparing food experience. My family, we went to Italy, and everybody in my family enjoyed the antipasti, the bruschetta, so I thought when I came home that I would re-invent this, it's very simple, basically it's little bits of bread with lovely tomato sauce on top and garlic. And I'd asked an Italian waiter and my Italian isn't very good, so I thought that I'd interpreted well what he said. However, you're supposed to rub the garlic on the bread, the sort of slightly toasted bread, just a little on one side. However, I went mad and was rubbing for a minute on both sides of the bread and I put the tomato sauce on and handed it to my family, and they all spat it out. It was inedible.
> I So did you, did you recycle it or did you throw it away?
> Sp Um, I think we threw it away.

LEXIS IN CONTEXT

b ● **7.5** Focus on the extracts and see if SS can remember any of the missing words. Play the CD, pausing after each one. Check answers, and elicit exactly what the words mean.

> See **bold** words in script 7.5

> **7.5**   CD4 Track 27
>
> 1 ...and Jeff, the friend who'd come, took one **mouthful** of the spaghetti bolognese before either of us did...
> 2 ...so that the top of the meat was completely **charred**, and underneath it was completely **raw**...
> 3 ...you're supposed to **rub** the garlic on the bread.
> 4 ...and I put the tomato sauce on and handed it to my family and they all **spat** it out. It was **inedible**.

c ● Put SS in groups to answer the question. Get feedback, and tell them of any cooking disasters you have had.

4 SPEAKING

a ● Focus on the task. You may want to tell SS that there is a UK TV programme called *Ready Steady Cook*, where celebrity chefs have to improvise a meal from a set of ingredients chosen by a member of the public.

● Tell SS they can use basic store cupboard ingredients like flour, sugar, oil, salt, pepper, etc. You can decide whether or not you want SS to be able to use rice or pasta as well.

● Now put SS in groups and set a time limit for them to come up with a menu.

Extra challenge

Tell SS they have to make a starter, a main course, and a pudding. Point out that where the words next to the illustrations are plural, they can choose the quantities; however, if the word is singular, they can only have one.

● Get feedback from each group to see what they are going to cook and get SS to vote for the best menu.

b ● Focus on the questions, and get SS to answer them in their groups.

● Get some feedback by asking the groups who they think is probably the best cook in each.

Digital extra idea

You could watch a clip of *Ready Steady Cook* on YouTube.

5 GRAMMAR nouns: compound and possessive forms

a ● Focus on the task and give SS time to go through the phrases individually, and then compare with a partner. Check answers.

> 1 a recipe book
> 2 a tuna salad
> 3 children's portions
> 4 Both are possible but with a different meaning:
>   *a coffee cup* = a cup used for coffee, probably empty;
>   *a cup of coffee* = a cup with coffee in it
> 5 a chef's hat
> 6 a tin opener
> 7 Both are possible and mean the same, but the second is more common.
> 8 a friend of John's

b ● Tell SS to go to **Grammar Bank 7A** on *p.154*. Go through each example and its corresponding rule with the class, or give SS time to read the examples and rules on their own, and answer any queries.

Grammar notes

● This is a complicated area of grammar where SS will still have doubts as to when they should use a possessive 's or use an *of* structure (*the film's name* or *the name of the film*) and when both are possible.

● Your SS' own language might use an *of* or *for* structure where English uses a compound noun, e.g. *a recipe book*, or a possessive noun like *children's portions*.

● Focus on the exercises for **7A**. SS do the exercises individually or in pairs. If SS do them individually, get them to compare with a partner. Check answers after each exercise.

> **a** 1 ✓
> 2 ✓
> 3 the end of the film
> 4 the wife of my friend who lives in Australia
> 5 a colleague of my sister's
> 6 a bottle of milk
> 7 photo of the house
> 8 story book
> 9 glass table
> 10 ✓
> 11 ✓
> **b** In 1, *my friend's children* = the children of a friend of mine; *my friends' children* = the children of several friends of mine
> In 2 and 10 there is no difference in meaning.
> In 11 *a wine glass* = a glass for wine, empty; *a glass of wine* = a glass with wine in it
> **c** 1 bottle opener
> 2 Alice and James' wedding / Alice and James's wedding
> 3 wine list
> 4 woman's film
> 5 marketing manager
> 6 garage door
> 7 sea view
> 8 government's proposal
> 9 cats' bowls

● Tell SS to go back to the main lesson on *p.102*.

6 READING

a ● Focus on the task and the introduction to the text. Set a time limit for SS to read the introduction once and answer the three gist questions with a partner. Check answers.

> 1 A game where people choose what they would want to eat for their last supper on earth.
> 2 Some of the world's best-known chefs.
> 3 Photographs of the chefs (taken by Melanie Dunea)

b ● Get SS to read the introduction again and then give them time to discuss the questions together. Tell SS not to worry about words they don't know, as they will be dealt with later. Check answers, and elicit SS' opinions.

> 1 Because they have eaten all kinds of food from all over the world, including the most expensive things like truffles and caviar.
> 2 Because most of them choose simple, rustic, and unpretentious food.
> 3 That they are difficult people to work with: 'loud obsessive dominating control freaks'.
> 4 Cooking is about control, manipulating people, and ingredients. Eating is about letting go, i.e. being relaxed, and surrendering yourself to the food.

c • Focus on the photo of one of the chefs (Lidia Bastianich), and ask SS what the photographer is communicating (that her main choice would be pasta), and then focus on the questions and answers. Set a time limit for SS to read, and get feedback from individual SS.

⚠ You don't want to go into too much detail at this stage, as SS will be answering the questions themselves later.

d • Focus on the sentences, and set a time limit again for SS to read the answers again and complete the sentences with a partner. Encourage them to use their own words. Check answers.

> **Suggested answers**
> 1 they choose elaborate meals with several courses (whereas the others choose much simpler meals).
> 2 at the chef's home.
> 3 have any music playing (he wants background TV).
> 4 she would make the occasion more light-hearted, because Russians are very good at dealing with death and the grieving process (i.e. the time when you feel very sad because sb has died).

LEXIS IN CONTEXT

e • Now focus on the instructions and give SS time to underline the words, compare with a partner, and check with a dictionary if they are not sure what they mean, or with you if they don't have a dictionary. Elicit / explain that many foreign words are used when talking about food, but some have been completely assimilated into English, e.g. *pasta*, *baguette*, whereas others haven't and these may not be in SS' dictionaries.

• Check the words SS have underlined and their meanings.

> *vin ordinaire* = French for table wine
> **truffle** (here) = an expensive type of fungus that grows underground
> **beluga** = a type of caviar (fish eggs)
> **prosciutto** = Italian for cured ham
> **linguine** = Italian for a type of pasta like spaghetti but flat
> **clam** = a kind of shellfish
> **spaghetti all'arrabbiata** = spaghetti with a spicy sauce made from tomatoes and chillies
> **rice pudding** = a dessert made from rice cooked with milk and sugar
> **oysters** = a large flat shellfish, some of which produce pearls
> **foie gras** = goose liver (French, the term commonly used in English)
> **rib eye steak** = a steak from the beef rib
> **mackerel** = a sea fish with greenish blue bands on its body that has oily flesh
> **broccoli** = a dark green vegetable with a thick stem and flower heads
> **saucisse de Morteau** = type of French smoked pork sausage
> **Gruyère** = a type of strong-flavoured Swiss cheese

f • Focus on the task and give SS time to find the words. Get them to compare with a partner and check answers. At this point you can deal with any other vocabulary queries.

1	nibble	4	crave	7	pot
2	skewer	5	crust	8	tasting menu
3	edible	6	ripe	9	dine

g • Finally, focus on the questions again and get SS to answer them with a partner.
• Get feedback to see whether SS chose simple or elaborate food, and tell them your own answers too if you like.

Extra photocopiable activities

Grammar
nouns: compound and possessive forms *p.175*
Communicative
Two recipes *p.201* (instructions *p.182*)
Vocabulary
Preparing food *p.226* (instructions *p.207*)

HOMEWORK

Study Link Workbook *pp.64–66*

7
B

G *so* and *such*
V word building: adjectives, nouns, and verbs
P homographs

Sport on trial

Lesson plan

This lesson focuses on two different angles on sport. In the first half SS read a newspaper article, *Battle of the workouts*, which compares similar activities (aerobics and running, yoga and Pilates), which people might decide to take up if they want to get fit, and looks at the pros and cons of each. Then there is a focus on word-building, forming nouns and verbs from common adjectives, e.g. *strong, long, deep*, etc. In the second part SS look at some statements from a controversial new book criticising sport, called *Foul Play*, and listen to a well-known British sportsman and psychoanalyst, Mike Brearley, give his opinion on these issues. SS then work on grammatical structures involving *so* and *such*. The lesson ends with a pronunciation focus on homographs, words which are spelt the same but pronounced differently according to the meaning, e.g. *row*.

Optional lead-in – the quote

- Write the quote at the top of *p.104* on the board (books closed) and the name of the author or get SS to open their books and read it.
- Point out that Heywood Broun (1888–1939) was a well-known male journalist, sports writer, and newspaper editor.
- Ask SS what they think it means and if they agree with it, and elicit specific examples (referring to sports and players) of how character is revealed through playing sport.

1 READING & SPEAKING

a • Focus on the photos and the questions, and elicit answers from the class. Some SS may not be familiar with Pilates /pɪˈlɑːtiːz/. You could elicit / explain that it is a physical fitness system (developed by Joseph Pilates in the early 20th century) which focuses on the core postural muscles which help keep the body balanced and which are essential to providing support for the spine. Point out that it always has a capital *P* as it is named after someone.

Digital extra idea

Google the sports, yoga, Pilates, and aerobics to make sure SS know exactly what they are. YouTube has some clips too.

b • Now focus on the article and the questions. Set a time limit and tell SS to scan the article to find the answers. If they can't find the answer to one of the questions, tell them to go on to the next one, and return to the one they couldn't answer at the end. Get SS to compare with a partner and then check answers.

1	aerobics and yoga	7	aerobics
2	Pilates	8	aerobics
3	running and aerobics	9	Pilates
4	running and Pilates	10	yoga
5	running	11	Pilates
6	yoga	12	running

c • Focus on the task. Explain that in the original article for each pair of activities, one was declared the winner by a sports expert. Get SS to read each pair of activities carefully and guess which was judged the winner. Elicit opinions before giving the answer.

> The winners were running and Pilates.

LEXIS IN CONTEXT

d • Focus on the definitions and see if SS can remember any of the words. Then set a time limit for them to find the others in the article. Get SS to compare their answers with a partner. Check answers.

1	stride	4	prone	7	press-ups
2	spine	5	joint	8	sit-ups
3	a workout	6	stretch	9	trunk

e • Focus on the task. Get SS to do it without looking back at the article, and then to check back. Check answers and elicit the meaning of each phrase.

> master the postures = to learn to do sth completely
> challenge yourself more by entering fun runs = to test your abilities / skills. Remind SS of the phrase they learnt in File 1 *a challenging job*.
> attain a sense of unity = a more formal way of saying *reach*, e.g. *a particular level*.
> perform six press-ups = more formal way of saying *do*
> set personal targets (= to give yourself or others sth to try and do successfully, e.g. *Our teacher set us a target of reading three books this term.*); achieve a target or goal (= succeed in reaching a goal or standard)
> burn calories = use food to produce energy
> *achieve* and *attain* are similar in meaning

Extra support

Ask SS to choose five other words or phrases they would like to learn from the article and get them to compare their choices. Get some feedback from the class as to the words or phrases they have chosen and deal with any vocabulary problems that arise.

f • Focus on the task and give SS time to prepare their answers. If you have SS who know little or nothing about sport, put them with a student who does, who can 'teach' them about a particular sport. Then put them in pairs to describe their chosen activity. Get feedback by asking some pairs to talk about their chosen sport.

2 VOCABULARY word building: adjectives, nouns, and verbs

a • Focus on the task. Elicit that in the first sentence a verb is needed, and in the second a noun. Get SS to complete the sentences. Check answers.

1 strengthen		**2** strength	

b • Elicit that with *strong*, the verb is formed by adding *-en* to the noun. Point out that with the other words in the chart sometimes the verb is formed from the adjective, and sometimes from the noun, and they should try out both ways to see which sounds right. Give SS time to complete the chart with a partner and check answers.

Adj	Noun	Verb
strong	strength	strengthen
long	length	lengthen
deep	depth	deepen
short	shortness	shorten
wide	width	widen
high	height	heighten
weak	weakness	weaken
thick	thickness	thicken
flat	flatness	flatten

⚠ Point out that *heighten* doesn't mean *to make sth higher*, but *to intensify or increase sth*, e.g. *heighten the awareness of sth*.

c • Focus on the sentences and get SS to complete them with words from the chart. They can do this in pairs or individually and compare answers with a partner. Check answers, eliciting pronunciation.

1 shorten		**5** depth		**9** widening	
2 length, width		**6** thicken		**10** shortness	
3 height		**7** flatten			
4 weaken		**8** weaknesses			

3 SPEAKING & LISTENING

a • Focus on the task and the six points. *Foul play* is used mainly to refer to actions in sport which are against the rules, and the word *foul* can be used as a noun and verb, e.g. *The defender committed a foul. The forward fouled the goalkeeper.*

• Give SS time to read and tick or cross the points, and to think of reasons why they agree / disagree.

b • Now put SS in groups of three or four to debate each point. Monitor and help where necessary, making notes of any recurring problems or errors to deal with afterwards.

• Get feedback, asking SS whether as a whole they agreed or disagreed with the statements.

c • **7.6** Focus on the photo of Mike Brearley and the task. Some SS may be unfamiliar with cricket, a popular summer sport in the UK, which has some similarities to baseball. SS sometimes confuse *cricket* with *croquet*. Point out that Mike Brearley was a very successful captain of the England cricket team and since retiring works as a psychoanalyst and motivational speaker.

• Play the CD, pausing after each answer, for SS to mark the statements A if they think he basically agrees with the statement, D if they think he basically disagrees, or PA if they think he partially agrees. Play again as necessary. Check answers and find out if Mike Brearley's opinions (i.e. agreeing or disagreeing with the statements) coincide with what SS decided in **b**.

1 D		**2** PA		**3** A		**4** D		**5** PA		**6** D	

7.6 CD4 Track 28

(script in Student's Book on *p.134*)
I = interviewer, M = Mike Brearley

I There's a deeply held belief that sport teaches us valuable lessons about life and ultimately makes us better people. In your view, is there any justification for that?

M Some, it can do. Sport involves, well, there are two types of sport, there's team sport and individual sport, but team sport most clearly involves both competition and cooperation and the advantages of cooperation, you can't do it well without the support of other people. The football striker can't score goals if he doesn't get passes. And the whole team relies on each other, and part of building up a good team is building up a good sense of cooperation.

Now, secondly, in individual sport as well as team sport, there are all sorts of individual qualities that you have to have to be good at sport, you have to have guts, you have to have persistence, you have to overcome difficulties, loss, bad form, injury, you have to overcome or deal with your fear of success and your fear of failure.

So there's a terrific number of qualities there, that people in general would respect and would like to develop in themselves. And sport, it seems to me does develop them.

I On balance would you say that sport brings about more happiness or unhappiness in the world?

M I saw a picture in *The Observer* some years ago of someone scoring a goal, and the picture was taken so that behind the netting you could see the crowd, and there must have been a hundred faces in this crowd, and every single one of them was totally, intently observing the point where the ball was, which was, I don't know if it was in the picture, I can't remember, and it seems to me that that kind of intensity, of attention and focus is something that the crowd shares with the players, and has a passion for and I would say that, it may not increase happiness, I mean happiness is a very difficult concept anyway, but it certainly increases living one's life to the full in the moment. And I would say that sport is like a mass form of art, certainly of culture.

Sport has its ways of bringing unhappiness too. Some people can become too depressed at losing or not doing well, or losing their form, some people find it very hard to move on from sport, say they're professionals, into another form of life. But nevertheless, I would say it increases happiness, it increases living in the moment, it increases, it develops a passionate interest which goes beyond success and failure.

I Do you think there is a sense that sport has replaced religion in modern society?

M It can become a religion in a bad sense for people, and it can become, as it were, the thing that gives meaning to life, and if something is the only thing that gives meaning to life, I think it's rather disappointing. It can become a religion in the sense of a sort of tribal, partisanship, which the worst forms of religion have. Religion has been the source of many disastrous conflicts, but it's also brought out the best in people, and I'd say the similar thing is true in sport.

I Do you think there is any difference between using new technology to gain an advantage, for example hi-tech swimming suits, and doping, I mean taking performance-enhancing drugs?

M It seems to me there is a, a radical difference, between say, having a good diet, training better, getting better shoes and, on the one hand and taking performance-enhancing drugs on the other, which seems like a form of cheating, it seems like a form of, well, the word 'artificial', artificial transformation of the body into a different shape or outcome without the necessary work that usually goes into it. If you're going to build muscles, you have to work at it. If you build muscles by steroids, you don't work at it, it's sort of magical and it's, it's something that it goes against the idea, which is only partially true in sport, the idea is that success is related to hard work, you don't achieve anything without hard work.

I We seem to expect athletes to be positive role models in society, is there any reason that we should?

M We hope that they're going to be role models on the field of play, that's what they're especially gifted at. Now as to off the field, if they play for England or Manchester United, they are going to be in the public eye, and if they do something that an ordinary person does at the same age, stupid, gets drunk, is late out at a night club, is found to be gambling, you know those kinds of things, the focus on him's going to be much higher than it is on most people. And that's something that they have to learn to accept. They get the benefits of being celebrities, but there are disadvantages too. And it seems to me that it is hard to expect them to be much better than the rest of us, but we do and they have to know that they're going to pay a heavier price if they're caught out. So I think it's part of the coach's job, or the senior players' job, to warn people, to guide people, to encourage them, but you, again you can't expect, it's wrong to expect too much.

I I've noticed this morning that the result of last night's football match is all over the front pages of the newspaper as well as the back pages. Does that suggest that we may have lost a sense of proportion when it comes to sport?

M You have to think that sport actually, whether you like it or not, matters a very great deal to a lot of people today and it gets a great deal of publicity and it's a talking point for many, many people. People will be talking about that match at work today, the Manchester United versus Barcelona match, they'll be fed up about it, they'll be critical, they'll be disappointed, they'll have their theories, they'll have arguments about it, it will be a talking point of a major kind. Now if you have something that's a talking point of a major kind, you're going to get extreme coverage of it, and if you get extreme coverage of it, you're going to have more of a talking point, so it's a kind of a circle that goes round and round. And in a way, it's crazy, in another way it's inevitable, and if people are so passionately involved, then it's reflected by the newspapers.

d ● Focus on the task. Play the CD again, pausing after Mike Brearley talks about the first statement to give SS time to make notes (see spaces in the script). Get SS to compare notes with a partner and then check answers. Ask SS whether they agree with what he says. Repeat the process for the other statements.

1 He says that team sport teaches you the advantages of cooperation, and in individual sports you can develop guts, persistence, and learn how to overcome fear of success or failure.

2 He thinks that although it's true that some people get depressed when their team loses, and sportspeople tend to get depressed when they retire, he also thinks that sport helps you to 'live in the moment' (i.e. enjoy certain moments very intensely), and to develop a passionate interest for something.

3 He agrees because he says for some people it is the only thing that gives meaning to life; it can become a religion in a sort of tribal partisanship (the worst aspect of religion) but can, like religions, bring out the best in people.

4 He thinks using technology, such as better shoes, still requires athletes to train hard, but using performance enhancing drugs (doping) is a form of cheating as you are making your body stronger artificially. This goes against the idea that success is related to hard work.

5 He thinks that while athletes can be expected to be role models on the field of play, it is wrong to expect them not to do the same crazy things off the field, e.g. drinking too much, that ordinary young people do. However, we do expect good behaviour from them, so coaches need to warn and guide young players.

6 He says that sport matters a great deal to a lot of people, and it is a major talking point for them, so he thinks that it is inevitable that it gets a lot of press coverage whether we think it is a good thing or not.

Extra support

If there's time, get SS to listen again with the script on *p.134*, focusing on any new vocabulary, and getting feedback on phrases SS didn't understand, e.g. because the words were run together.

4 GRAMMAR *so* and *such*

a ● Focus on the sentences and get SS to complete them individually, and then compare with a partner. Check answers.

1 such	3 such a	5 so much
2 so	4 so, so	6 such an

Extra challenge

Elicit from SS what the rules are governing *so* and *such* before they go to the **Grammar Bank**.

b ● Tell SS to go to **Grammar Bank 7B** on *p.155*. Go through each example and its corresponding rule with the class, or give SS time to read the examples and rules on their own, and answer any queries.

Grammar notes

So and *such* was only dealt with as a 'mini grammar' point in *New English File Upper-intermediate*. Here it is dealt with more thoroughly, and some new uses are introduced.

- Focus on the exercises for **7B**. SS do the exercises individually or in pairs. If SS do them individually, get them to compare with a partner. Check answers after each exercise.

a	**1**	so, so much	**6**	such a
	2	so	**7**	so
	3	so many	**8**	such an
	4	such	**9**	so many
	5	so much		

b 1 It was such a windy day.
   2 I have such a lot of things to do
   3 The water was so dirty
   4 I have such fantastic colleagues (that)
   5 The match was so gripping
   6 There was so much noise
   7 such as sailing and windsurfing
   8 He drives so dangerously

- Tell SS to go back to the main lesson on *p.107*.

5 PRONUNCIATION homographs

Pronunciation notes

- Homographs (words with different meanings which have the same spelling but different pronunciation) cause problems as in many cases SS are not even aware that a word like *row* has more than one possible pronunciation.

- This exercise focuses on some common homographs and you should encourage SS to note down any others they come across.

- ⚠ SS should already be aware of one kind of homograph, i.e. two-syllable words which can be verbs or nouns, and where the stess shifts, e.g. <u>con</u>tract (verb) and con<u>tract</u> (noun).

a ● Focus on the information box and go through it with SS.
b ● Focus on the task. Get SS in pairs to try saying the two pronunciations first and then match them to the correct sentence.
c ● **7.7** Play the CD for SS to check answers. Pause after each pair of sentences and elicit the answer. Then move on to the next sentence.

close	1 b	2 a	
row	3 b	4 a	5 a
minute	6 b	7 a	
tear	8 a	9 b	
content	10 b	11 a	
wound	12 b	13 a	
use	14 a	15 b	

7.7   **CD4 Track 29**

1 It was a really close finish, and they had to use a video replay to see who won the race.
2 What time does the ticket office close? We need to get our tickets for the match on Saturday.
3 The coach had a row with one of his players, and threw a boot at him.
4 We were sitting in the front row so we could almost touch the players.
5 People who row tend to have very well-developed biceps.
6 He was disqualified because they found a minute quantity of a banned substance in his blood sample.
7 He scored a goal just one minute before the referee blew the final whistle.
8 If you tear a muscle or a ligament, you may not be able to train for six months.
9 As she listened to the national anthem play, a tear rolled down her cheek.
10 Football players never seem content with their contracts. They're always trying to negotiate better conditions.
11 The content of the programme was a two-hour analysis of the match.
12 He wound the tape tightly round his ankle to prevent a sprain.
13 You could see his head wound bleeding as he was taken off the pitch.
14 If you use a high-tech swimsuit, you will be able to swim much faster.
15 It's no use complaining; the umpire's decision is final.

- Finally, get SS in pairs to practise saying the sentences.

Extra support

If your SS seem to have particular problems with some of the pairs of words, you could use the recording to model and drill the different pronunciations and get SS to say the sentences.

6 **7.8** SONG ♫ *Eye of the Tiger*

- This song was originally a hit for the American rock group, Survivor in 1982. It was the theme song for the film *Rocky III* and is often played at sporting events. For copyright reasons this is a cover version. If you want to do this song in class, use the photocopiable activity on *p.238*.

7.8   **CD4 Track 30**

Eye of the Tiger
(See photocopiable *p.238*)

Extra photocopiable activities

Grammar
so and *such p.176*
Communicative
Sports quiz *p.202* (instructions *p.182*)
Vocabulary
Word building race *p.227* (instructions *p.207*)
Song
Eye of the Tiger p.238 (instructions *p.231*)

HOMEWORK

Study Link Workbook *pp.67–69*

7C

G comparison
V humour
P *augh* and *ough*

The funniest joke in the world?

Lesson plan

The topic of this final lesson is humour. Although this can be a tricky subject due to the fact that what is considered funny varies from country to country and person to person, the first half of the lesson actually exploits this fact by featuring an online survey that was done to find 'the funniest joke in the world'.

SS listen to and read five jokes from the survey, one of which was voted the funniest joke, and then listen to a journalist talking about the results of the survey and the differences it showed up between different nationalities and the genders regarding sense of humour. SS then learn specific words and expressions related to humour, which are practised in a speaking activity. The pronunciation focus is on the different pronunciations of *augh* and *ough*. SS then revise and extend their knowledge of structures used for comparison, and finally read three different kinds of humorous texts: some of Winston Churchill's famous 'put-downs', an extract from the TV series *Yes Minister*, and a poem by Wendy Cope.

Optional lead-in – the quote

- Write the quote at the top of *p.108* on the board (books closed) and the name of the author or get SS to open their books and read it.
- Point out that Ian Hay (1876–1952) was a Scottish novelist and playwright. The quotation is a line from one of his plays.
- Elicit that *funny* has two meanings, *strange* (what Hay calls 'funny peculiar') and *amusing* ('funny ha ha'), and that we sometimes use these expressions, coined by Ian Hay, to make it clear which use we mean on a particular occasion.

1 LISTENING

a ● **7.9** Focus on the introduction to the jokes and emphasize that this refers to a real survey that was done and which was given a lot of publicity at the time on TV and in the press.

- Highlight that the point of the survey was to try and find a joke which the largest number of people in different countries found amusing. Point out that SS may not find any of the jokes funny but that does not matter.
- Play the CD for SS to read and listen. Then get SS to re-read each joke and score it 1–5, and then compare their scores with a partner.
- Get feedback, to find out which joke SS found funniest.

> **7.9**   CD4 Track 31
>
> (See Student's Book)

b ● **7.10** Now focus on the task, and give SS time to read the questions. Play the CD once for SS just to listen. Then play the recording again for SS to make notes of the answers, pausing the CD to give them time to answer (see spaces in the script). Get SS to compare their answers with a partner. Play again as necessary and then check answers.

> 1 They create a sense of superiority in the person reading or hearing the joke.
> 2 Because it is a way of getting revenge on them.
> 3 The English about the Irish, the Mexicans about the Americans, and the French about the Belgians. They feel good when they laugh at how stupid they think they are.
> 4 That we laugh at things that are subconsciously making us feel anxious.
> 5 Jokes about people getting older.
> 6 A play on words, as in the cereal killer joke.
> 7 Women prefer jokes involving wordplay while men favour jokes which involve an element of aggression or sex. They both find jokes about the opposite gender more amusing than ones about their own.
> 8 No. For example, the British prefer jokes based on wordplay, the Americans and Canadians prefer jokes with a sense of superiority, and the Europeans often enjoy surreal jokes.

> **7.10**   CD4 Track 32
>
> (script in Student's Book on *p.134*)
> **I = interviewer, J = journalist**
> **I** What was the purpose of Professor Wiseman's research? Was it simply to find the funniest joke?
> **J** No, it was much more than that. He wanted to take what he calls 'a scientific look' at what makes us laugh and this included finding answers to questions like 'Do people from different countries find the same things funny?' or 'Do men and women laugh at different types of jokes?'
> **I** And could you tell us something about the results of his research?
> **J** Well, the first thing that came out clearly was that the jokes which people generally found the funniest had one thing in common – they create a sense of superiority in the person hearing or reading the joke, usually because the person in the joke appears to be stupid. This is clearly illustrated in the Sherlock Holmes joke, where Watson is the one who is shown to be stupid.
>   Generally speaking, the more superior a joke makes us feel, the more we laugh. And it seems that we especially enjoy jokes where people in authority are made to look stupid, which is why there are so many jokes all over the world about policemen.
> **I** And is there an explanation for this?
> **J** Yes, there is. According to Professor Wiseman, telling this kind of joke is simply our way of getting our own back on people in authority, people who have power over us in our daily lives.

I What about the jokes people tell about other nationalities being stupid?

J Well, again this is the superiority theory in action. The English traditionally tell jokes about the Irish, the Mexicans make fun of the Americans, the French laugh at the Belgians, etc., etc., and in each case, it's a question of one group of people trying to make themselves feel good at the expense of another, by laughing about how stupid they are.

I I think it was Sigmund Freud who said that we laugh at things which are subconsciously making us feel anxious. Is this true?

J Well, Professor Wiseman's research definitely supported this theory. For example, older people tend to find jokes about the problems of getting old much funnier than young people do. Everybody worries to a greater or lesser extent about getting an incurable illness, which is why we laugh at the joke about the man who has an incurable disease, which of course in reality is not a laughing matter. And for the same reason there are many many jokes about loveless marriages, family problems, and even death.

I Why do we find wordplay funny?

J Professor Wiseman's research found that wordplay was enjoyed by many nationalities. The joke about the 'cereal killer' is an example of the most basic kind of joke, what we call 'a pun', where we play with words which have different meanings, or different words which are pronounced the same. It seems that we find puns funny because the first line of the joke usually sets up a situation; then the second line (the 'punchline') at first seems strange, but then suddenly we get the joke, we understand it, and this feeling of surprise makes us laugh. Surprise is a very important element in humour.

I Do men and women laugh at the same things?

J Apparently not. Generally speaking, women find jokes with wordplay more amusing, whereas men often prefer jokes which involve some element of aggression or sex. Perhaps not surprisingly, women find jokes about men being stupid far funnier than jokes about women being stupid. And of course the opposite is true. So for example a woman will probably find the joke about the man doing the jigsaw funnier than the man does. That's the superiority theory in action again.

I Do different nationalities find the same kind of jokes funny?

J Well, the answer it seems is no. Professor Wiseman's research found clear differences between different countries and cultures as to what they found amusing. For example, people from Britain, Ireland, and Australia enjoyed jokes based on wordplay. Whereas Americans and Canadians preferred jokes where there was a strong sense of superiority – either because a character looks stupid, or is made to look stupid by someone else. And many European countries preferred jokes which were more surreal.

c ● **7.11** Focus on the task and get SS to read the questions. Play the CD and get SS to answer the questions, comparing what they heard with a partner. Play the recording again as necessary. Check answers.

> **1** The joke about the two hunters (joke 5) because it was universal – it appealed to both sexes, different nationalities, young and old, etc. It also had three classic elements of humour: it makes us feel superior, it makes us laugh at an anxiety provoking situation (an accident and death), and it has a strong element of surprise.
> **2** A British psychiatrist. He sometimes tells it to his patients to make them feel better.
> **3** No. He thinks there is no such thing – there is no one joke that will make everybody laugh.

7.11 CD4 Track 33

(script in Student's Book on p.135)

I So which joke *was* voted the funniest?

J Well, in second place was the joke about Sherlock Holmes and the tent. But in first place was the joke about the two hunters. This joke won because it was universal – it appealed to people in many countries, to men and women, and young and old people alike. And it also combined the classic three elements of humour – it makes us feel superior, it makes us laugh at an anxiety-provoking situation – an accident and death, and it has a strong element of surprise.

I Who submitted the winning joke?

J It was sent in by a British psychiatrist from Manchester. Apparently, he told Professor Wiseman that he sometimes tells it to his patients to make them feel better 'because it reminds them that there's always someone who is doing something more stupid than they are.'

I And did Professor Wiseman think that he really had found the world's funniest joke?

J No, he didn't. According to him, the funniest joke in the world doesn't exist. In the conclusion to his research, he said, 'If our research into humour tells us anything, it's that different people find different things funny. Women laugh at jokes in which men look stupid; the elderly laugh at jokes about memory loss or hearing difficulties; people who don't have power laugh at those who are in power. There is no <u>one</u> joke that will make everyone laugh.'

Extra support

If there's time, get SS to listen again with the scripts on *pp.134–135*, focusing on any new vocabulary, and getting feedback on phrases SS didn't understand, e.g. because the words were run together.

● Ask SS if anything in the research surprised them or if there was anything they disagreed with and why.

2 VOCABULARY & SPEAKING humour

a ● Focus on the task and give SS time to go through the questions, eliciting the meaning of the bold words, and focusing on the prepositions in some of the phrases, e.g. *make fun of, laugh at*, etc. Check answers, and model and drill pronunciation where necessary. Explain / elicit that:

– *make fun of* = laugh at sb or make others laugh at sb in an unkind way
– *comedian* = an entertainer who makes people laugh by telling jokes
– *comedy series* = a set of TV programmes with a humorous content
– *witty* = able to say or write clever or amusing things
– *political cartoon* = an amusing drawing, often with a caption in a newspaper
– *cartoonist* = person who draws cartoons
– *amusing* = funny (ha ha)
– *laughing at themselves* (opp. *taking themselves seriously*)
– *get a joke* = understand it
– *black humour* = dealing with unpleasant or terrible things in a humorous way
– *surreal humour* = very strange humour, more like a dream than reality
– *slapstick* = the type of humour that is based on simple actions such as people falling over or hitting each other
– *irony* = the use of words that say the opposite of what you really mean, often as a joke and with a tone of voice that shows this, e.g. *England did well last night!* (when they lost 6–0)
– *hilarious* = very funny
– *laugh out loud* = laugh, making a loud noise as you do it
– *burst out laughing* = suddenly start laughing loudly

b ● Now get SS to ask and answer in pairs.
   ● Finally, get some feedback as a whole class.

Extra idea

You could get the class to choose five of the questions to ask you first.

3 PRONUNCIATION *augh* and *ough*

Pronunciation notes

These two combinations of letters cause problems because they can be pronounced in several different ways although by this stage SS should be clear about most of the common examples. It is important to highlight that there are not that many words with this combination of letters, and that SS can easily learn them, so they should not feel frustrated by this slightly 'anarchic' aspect of English pronunciation. This exercise also practises using phonetics to check pronunciation, which is the best guide when confronted with a new word with this spelling.

a ● Focus on the question and elicit that all irregular past verbs with these letters are pronounced /ɔː/.

b ● Focus on the information box and go through it with SS. Then focus on the task, and tell SS to read the definition for each one, and look at the phonetics and write the words. Check answers, getting SS to spell the words out to you.

> See script 7.12

c ● **7.12** Tell SS to focus on the phonetics and practise saying the words. Then play the CD for them to check.

7.12				CD4 Track 34
1	laugh	5 through	9	doughnut
2	enough	6 although	10	cough
3	draught	7 rough	11	plough
4	drought	8 tough	12	thorough

Extra support

You could use the CD recording to model and drill the pronunciation of the words or pause the recording, elicit the pronunciation and then play the word.

d ● Focus on the task. Put SS in pairs. **A** (book open) chooses six definitions to read to **B** for him / her to say the words. They then swap roles.

e ● **7.13** Focus on the task. Play the CD once the whole way through. Then play it again, pausing after each sentence to give SS time to write. Get them to compare with a partner and then play the CD again.
   ● Check answers by writing (or getting SS to write) the sentences on the board.

7.13	CD4 Track 35
1 There's no doubt there'll be a drought.	
2 Don't laugh at my scarf!	
3 I haven't got enough stuff.	
4 It was his cough that carried him off.	
5 If you go through, you'll see the view.	
6 Although it's going to snow, it won't be cold.	

4 GRAMMAR comparison

a ● Focus on the task. Get SS to do it individually and then compare with a partner. Check answers.

1	…the more we laugh
2	✓
3	…a few more votes
4	✓
5	…many more jokes
6	…the better
7	✓

b ● Tell SS to go to **Grammar Bank 7C** on *p.156*. Go through each example and its corresponding rule with the class, or give SS time to read the examples and rules on their own, and answer any queries.

Grammar notes

SS at this level should be confident with basic comparative and superlative adjectives and adverbs. They should also have seen the *the…the…* structure before, though may well not use it with great fluency. Here they revise this structure and look at common modifiers used with comparative and superlative structures.

- Focus on the exercises for **7C**. SS do the exercises individually or in pairs. If SS do them individually, get them to compare with a partner. Check answers after each exercise.

a	1	**the** more you laugh	**b**	1	as
	2	**by** far the best meal		2	✓
	3	just **as** good a player		3	by far
	4	**a** lot funnier		4	The sooner the better
	5	**as** late for work		5	twice as much as
	6	the cheaper **it** is		6	the worse I do it
	7	far **more** laid-back		7	easier and easier
	8	**a** bit bigger		8	a few more
	9	easily **the** most intelligent		9	many more

- Tell SS to go back to the main lesson on *p.110*.
- **c** • Focus on the task, and put SS in groups of three. Tell them to start, and then when two minutes are up, say 'Stop' for them to move onto the next topic.
- Get feedback by finding out whether groups agreed or not with the statements.

5 READING

- Focus on the instructions. Tell SS that as this is the last reading in the book the idea is that they should read purely for pleasure without doing any exercises.
- Focus on the three texts and highlight this information:

  Famous put-downs

  Tell SS that all these are true comments made by the people mentioned.

  Yes, Minister

  This was one of the most popular BBC comedy series in the 1970s. Politicians particularly found it funny, even though it was making fun of them – Margaret Thatcher, the conservative Prime Minister of the time, said it was her favourite programme.

  First date

  Wendy Cope is one of the most popular poets at the moment, and is famous for her witty poems often about love and personal relationships.

- Let SS read at their own speed. Monitor, helping with any vocabulary queries. Then get them to discuss with a partner which text they enjoyed the most / least and why.
- Get feedback, dealing with any vocabulary problems.

Digital extra idea

You could watch a clip of *Yes, Minister* on YouTube. We recommend one called 'The speech'.

Extra photocopiable activities

Grammar
comparison *p.177*
Communicative
Joke telling *p.203* (instructions *p.182*)
Vocabulary
Revision: describing game *p.228* (instructions *p.207*)

HOMEWORK

Study Link **Workbook** *pp.70–72*

Lesson plan

In this lesson SS write a letter or email complaining about a product or service. SS have already written a formal letter / email of application in **Writing 1**, so here the focus is on the specific language relating to a letter of complaint. Although this is something SS may have looked at in previous years (for example, there was a letter of complaint in *New English File Upper-intermediate*), this text type often comes up in advanced exams, and the language SS would be expected to use is more sophisticated. The writing skills focus is on getting the right style and register, and the writing task involves expressing information in a more formal way.

ANALYSING A MODEL TEXT

a • Focus on the text type (a complaint). Remind SS of the importance of being able to write a formal letter or email in English, and point out to them that one context in which they may need to write one is if they have had a problem while travelling, e.g. with an airline or a hotel. A letter of complaint is also a common exam question.

• Focus on the **Key success factors** and go through them with SS.

• Focus on the questions, and either get SS to discuss them in pairs or have an open-class discussion.

b • Now focus on the letter, and set a time limit for SS to read it. Tell them to ignore the gaps. Then elicit that it is a complaint about an entertainment programme which was part of a package holiday to Scotland.

c • Set a time limit for SS, in pairs, to read the letter again and choose the best phrase for each gap. Check answers, eliciting why one phrase is better than the other.

> 1 b (avoid using contractions)
> 2 a (avoid emotional language)
> 3 a (more formal verb)
> 4 b (formal fixed phrase)
> 5 b (more precise, less vague)
> 6 a (use of passive is less confrontational)
> 7 a (formal phrase)
> 8 b (avoid informal idioms)
> 9 a (passive is less personal and confrontational)
> 10 a (less aggressive and demanding)

• Highlight the use of the passive rather than the active in 6 and 9, which is often used in a letter of complaint as it is less accusatory and distances the complaint from any individual.

Extra idea

Test SS on the phrases by saying the informal phrase and getting them to say the more formal one.

USEFUL LANGUAGE

d • Focus on the task. Get SS to read the letter again and then cover it, and with a partner try to remember the five phrases that were used. Check answers.

> 1 I am writing to complain…
> 2 According to your website…
> 3 Not only was the comedian not funny at all, but he…
> 4 I feel strongly…should be changed…
> 5 I look forward to hearing your views on this matter.

PLANNING WHAT TO WRITE

a • Focus on the email. Tell SS to read it carefully, and then to discuss the questions with a partner. Check answers.

> 'Board first' is a service where, for €20 extra per person, you board the plane before other passengers.
> Because they were taken to the gate by bus, she ended up boarding after most of the other passengers, and her family couldn't sit together.

b • Focus on the task and give SS time to discuss it with a partner. Get feedback. Accept all reasonable suggestions for compensation, e.g. free flights or a refund of the €60. As regards the threat to contact the Air Transport Users Council, in real life many people would include this as it is often the only way to elicit a response. Tell SS that if they do decide to include it, it should not be expressed in an aggressive way, but simply in a firm, matter of fact way, e.g. *If I do not hear from you in the very near future, I will take up this matter with the ATUC.*

• Details that SS should include in their letter would be:
  – the date and time
  – the airport the flight left from, the destination, and the flight number
  – the number of people travelling together, and the children's ages

• Finally, go through the tips with SS.

WRITING

Go through the instructions and set the writing for homework.

Test and Assessment CD-ROM

CEFR Assessment materials
File 7 Writing task assessment guidelines

7 COLLOQUIAL ENGLISH
COOKING ROUND THE WORLD

Lesson plan

In the first part of this lesson the person interviewed is Chantelle Nicholson, who is sous-chef at the Marcus Wareing restaurant. The restaurant, one of the top establishments in London, is run by the chef Marcus Wareing who SS read about in **Lesson 1A**. Chantelle talks about how she came to be working in the UK, what it is like working as a top chef, and finally answers the question 'What would be your last meal on earth?', picking up on the text in 7A. In the second part of the lesson, people in the street are asked if they think that people in their country are good cooks, how healthy they think the cuisine is in their country, and what other cuisines they like.

SS may find the interview with Chantelle to be the most challenging in the book as she is from New Zealand, and has quite a distinctive accent. For example, she often pronounces the letter *e* as /ɪ/, e.g. pronouncing *chef* as /ʃɪf/ as opposed to /ʃef/. Point out to your SS that at this level it is important for them to be exposed to different varieties of English, even if it requires more effort for them to understand her. SS may also notice that Chantelle makes frequent use of the colloquial phrase 'kind of', which is largely redundant in terms of meaning.

Study Link These lessons are on the *New English File Advanced* DVD which can be used instead of the class CD (See Introduction *p.9*). SS can get more practice on the MultiROM, which contains more of the short street interviews with a listening task and scripts.

Optional lead-in (books closed)

● Get SS to go to *p.4* and re-read text 3 about Marcus Wareing. Tell them that he is now one of the best-known chefs in the UK, and that they are going to listen to an interview with someone who works at one of his restaurants.

THE INTERVIEW

a ● Books open. Focus on the task and elicit that the person in the photo with Chantelle is Marcus Wareing. Go through the glossary with the class, eliciting from them how to pronounce the words and phrases, and use the second photo to show them what *scallops* are.

Extra support

You may want to pre-teach some other words and phrases before SS listen to the interview (see script 7.14).

b ● **7.14** Focus on the questions and give SS time to read them. Encourage SS not to write anything down when they listen the first time. Tell them that they should listen and try to get the gist of what she is saying, and then discuss the questions with their partner.

● Play the CD once (**Part 1**). Give SS time to discuss the questions and tell each other what they understood. Then play the CD again pausing after each of Chantelle's answers to give SS time to make notes and compare with their partner again. Play the recording again as necessary. Elicit and check answers.

1 Her parents.
2 She had to submit a menu for a three-course meal, and talk about the food.
3 He offered her a job at The Savoy Grill, working for Marcus (Wareing).
4 He is a perfectionist, with a real eye for detail, he has a very good business sense and oversees the whole operation. In that sense he is a good mentor. He wants all the guests at the restaurant to be treated well and have an amazing experience, however much they are spending.
5 Following Marcus Wareing's beliefs, they use traditional techniques and they try to get the maximum flavour out of all ingredients.

7.14　　　　　　　　　　　　　　　　CD4 Track 36

(script in Student's Book on *p.135*)
I = interviewer, C = Chantelle Nicholson
I Who taught you to cook?
C It would probably be my parents when I was younger. It was more, it was always something that I was interested in from an early age and I used to be in the kitchen quite a lot.
I How did you end up as a chef in London?
C One kind of afternoon when I was reading the, a foodie magazine in New Zealand, and it mentioned the Gordon Ramsay scholarship and we had to submit a menu kind of a three-course menu and talk about the food, talk about what you'd done, so I thought, 'Well, why not give that a go?' So I submitted an entry and then got a phone call kind of six weeks later saying I'd got into the semi final, which was basically 12 people, 11 of them all chefs, so I kind of felt a bit like a fish out of water, but anyway, whilst I was there I met Josh Emmet, who was the head chef at the Savoy Grill, which was run by Marcus, and at the end of it he said, 'Well, you know, there's a job at the Savoy Grill if you want one,' and it was just a, too good an opportunity to turn down, so it all kind of happened relatively quickly because I thought well, I can't turn this opportunity down. I was kind of at a point in my career where I was looking for another job anyway. So I just thought, 'Well, I'll do it.'
I Top chefs have a reputation of being difficult. What's Marcus Wareing like to work for?
C He is very, he's quite, I mean I wouldn't want to work for any other chef of that high calibre really. He's a very, he's a person that's very, he's got a real eye for detail and a perfectionist. But he's also got a very good business sense, which is a great thing to learn from as well, because he oversees the whole operation. So in that sense he's a great kind of mentor, I guess. I mean if he gets upset with people, it's because of what's going on on the plate or in the restaurant. There's no kind of, there's no ego there at all, it's all about what goes out on the plate and what happens, and how the guests are treated, he's very much a person that people, when people come to the restaurant he wants them to have an amazing experience, no matter if they're kind of buying a £30 bottle of wine or £3,000 bottle of wine.
I Is this restaurant into the new tendencies in cooking, using science in the kitchen and things like that?
C We are more, not traditional but we use traditional techniques, classic techniques. We, I guess in a sense, we're more about, Marcus, Marcus is a person that's very respectful of ingredients and basically treats, you know, will treat a carrot the same way as a piece of foie gras in the sense they're both great things that need to be looked after and treated in the right way to get the maximum kind of flavour out of them and I guess we're more about making a carrot taste like a carrot as opposed to making a carrot taste like a beetroot, which, in a sense, I think some people get a little carried away with.

c • **7.15** Focus on the task and give SS time to read the questions. Play the CD once (**Part 2**) and tell SS just to listen. Then give SS time to discuss the questions and tell each other what they understood. Now play the CD again, pausing after each answer to give SS time to make notes and compare with their partner again. Play the recording again as necessary. Elicit and check answers.

⚠ You may want to highlight how for question 4 she uses 'a' and 'b' to highlight the two reasons when she gives this answer.

1 A sous-chef is the 'second chef' who works under the head chef.
2 She works very long hours, from 7.00 a.m. to 12.00–1.00 a.m. the following morning.
3 When a lot of people all arrive at the same time and they have to try not to keep people waiting, when they cook something that's not right and they have to begin again, and the long hours – because when people are tired they get more stressed.
4 Because she's not at home very much, and because she finds it a bit difficult cooking in her kitchen which is small and doesn't have the sort of equipment that she has at work.
5 She would start with foie gras, then have scallops, then beef rib as a main course, then cheese, and then pear tarte Tatin for dessert.

7.15	CD4 Track 37

(script in Student's Book on *p.135*)
I = interviewer, C = Chantelle Nicholson
I You are the sous-chef here. Can you tell us what exactly is the difference between a chef and a sous-chef?
C Basically a sous-chef is, it basically translates to a second chef, so you have the head chef and then you have the sous-chefs under the head chef, so they run the kitchen in the head chef's absence.
I How many hours do you work?
C We, they are long days for most people. I mean, we start at about 7.00 in the morning and we normally finish, kind of, between 12.00 and 1.00 in the morning, so it's a long day, but in a sense it's something that you get used to the more you do it.
I Does it get very stressful in the kitchen?
C It can do. The biggest thing is organization. It can be, it makes a big difference, kind of the way diners come in as well, if they all come in at once then it does get a bit, because you, you're always conscious of the fact that you don't want to keep people waiting too long but you don't want to, in the other sense just push out the food because they're here for the experience. So it can get stressful in some situations and when, if you cook something and something, and it's not right and you can't serve it, the time it takes to kind of begin the whole process again, a) for those, the guests that have ordered that particular dish, they have to wait a long time, but also it creates a backlog in a sense, so it can get stressful but again it's something that's managed and if you're organized and kind of a bit forward-thinking and always one step ahead then it becomes, it minimizes the stress completely.
I And presumably the long hours don't help?
C Again the hours don't, don't help the stress because obviously the more tired people are then the more stressed they can get. But in a sense the people that work here are quite, very focused, very, very passionate about what they do, you kind of have to be to be able to put in the time that we all put in. So the stress is, I think it's something that can be managed.

I Do you cook at home, if so what kind of food?
C Ah, not much, I don't cook at home much, a) because I'm not really there a huge amount and b) when you have what we have here to go to a kind of small, small kitchen it's a bit, I find it a bit difficult, in a sense because you're used to having such great equipment and kind of ovens, and everything around you and then you go back to a little flat and kind of trying to do it it's just not quite the same. But when I have time off if I'm on holiday or something like that, I of course enjoy kind of going to a market or even a supermarket and getting kind of local ingredients and doing it that way.
I What would you have as your last meal on earth?
C Wow, it's a big question, probably would start with, something like foie gras, because it is such a kind of delicacy and then a seafood, probably scallops, main course would probably be some beef, a rib of beef with some beautiful vegetables, seasonal vegetables, then I'd definitely have to have cheese, I because I'm a big fan of cheeses, especially the European cheeses, they're just, that's one thing that I really love about the, kind of, the UK and Europe and then probably to finish, probably a pear tarte Tatin.

d • **7.16** This exercise gives SS intensive listening practice in deciphering phrases where words are often run together, and introduces them to some common expressions and idioms used in spoken English. Focus on phrases 1–6 and give SS time to read them. Play the CD, pausing after the first phrase and replaying it as necessary. Elicit the missing words, and then the meaning of the whole phrase. Repeat for the other five phrases.

1 **give** that a **go** (= try to do something)
2 to **turn down** (PV = to reject, say no to)
3 get a little **carried away** with (= idiomatic way of saying to get very excited or lose control of your feelings)
4 **at once** (= all at the same time)
5 it creates **a backlog** (= a quantity of work – in this case meals being cooked – that should have been done already, but has not yet been done)
6 **one step** ahead (= idiom meaning you have predicted what needed doing and have already done it)

7.16	CD4 Track 38

1 …so I thought, 'Well, why not give that a go?'
2 …and it was just a, too good an opportunity to turn down…
3 …as opposed to making a carrot taste like a beetroot, which, in a sense, I think some people get a little carried away with.
4 …it makes a big difference, kind of the way diners come in as well, if they all come in at once…
5 …the guests that have ordered that particular dish, they have to wait a long time, but also it creates a backlog in a sense…
6 …and if you're organized and kind of forward-thinking and always one step ahead…

Extra support

If there's time, get SS to listen again with the scripts on *p.135*, focusing on any new vocabulary, and getting feedback on phrases SS didn't understand, e.g. because the words were run together.

e • Finally, focus on the questions. Get SS to answer in pairs and then get feedback from the whole class, or do this as an open-class discussion.

IN THE STREET

a ● **7.17** Focus on the task and play the CD once for SS to answer the questions. Get them to compare their answers with a partner and then elicit the answers onto the board. Leave the three questions the interviewer asked on the board as SS will use these later.

> **Questions**
>
> 1 Do you think in general that people from your country are good cooks?
> 2 How healthy do you think the cuisine in your country is?
> 3 What other cuisines do you like?
>
> Naomi is the most positive about the cuisine in New Zealand and Liz (the USA) is the least positive. Thai is the most popular foreign cuisine mentioned.

7.17   CD4 Track 39

(script in Student's Book on *p.135*)
I = interviewer, S = Sheila, L = Liz, N = Naomi
Sheila
I   Do you think in general people from your country are good cooks?
S   I think there are some fantastic cooks in the UK, but if we talk about people in general, there are some pretty bad cooks as well. So it's, I think people are getting better. I think people are taking a lot more interest in cooking, there's a lot of cooking programmes, and we are leading the world in some respects, in being adventurous about our cooking. So people are getting more interested, but still there's a long way to go before we can say, in general people in the UK are good cooks.
I   How healthy do you think the cuisine in your country is?
S   There's a balance I think. Again, people are trying to be healthier or are being encouraged to be healthier, but if you go to a restaurant, there'll be a great selection of healthy and non-healthy foods on the menu. But there are also an awful lot of really awful fast food outlets encouraging you to eat junk. So it's a balance and I think the balance tips towards junk food rather than healthy food.
I   What other cuisines do you really like?
S   Thai food is my favourite. I also love Italian, but Thai most definitely up at the top there.
I   Why is that?
S   Because there are so many different flavours. Even in one dish, you can taste a variety of flavours and it's all very fresh, so Indian food is spicy, but it's made with a lot of dried spices so sometimes it feels very heavy and you can taste the spices afterwards, and you can smell the spices afterwards. But with Thai food, it's very very fresh and zingy and you don't feel full or heavy afterwards, you just feel exhilarated.
Liz
I   Do you think in general people from your country are good cooks?
L   I think so, yeah.
I   How healthy do you think the cuisine in your country is?
L   In general, not very healthy at all.
I   Why is that?
L   Because people eat a lot of fast food and it's very processed, and full of fat, and salt, and all that kind of stuff.
I   What other cuisines do you really like?
L   What other cuisines do I like? I like, well, I'm a vegetarian so I like vegetables and fruit and fresh food, and I like Italian, I like Thai, I like a lot of stuff.
I   What do you like about Thai food?
L   Thai, I like how spicy it is, I like the curries, and I like, I really like the curried vegetables.

Naomi
I   Do you think in general people from your country are good cooks?
N   Yeah, I think so. New Zealand's had a sort of a food revolution. It used to be very English in its food style. But over recent years, it's taken on a strong Asian feel and it's quite eclectic so I think people in New Zealand do like to cook and experiment with food. And they enjoy food.
I   How healthy do you think the cuisine in your country is?
N   I think it's pretty healthy. We are an outdoor country, lots of fruit and vegetables and home-grown things. So, yeah, I think overall, it's a pretty healthy place.
I   What other cuisines do you really like?
N   I really like Indian, but also all types of curries, so Malaysian, Thai, Indonesian curries. I like the heat and the flavour that you get in those sorts of cuisines.

b ● Focus on the task and give SS time to read questions 1–7. Play the recording again all the way through and then give SS time to try and answer the questions. Then play it again, pausing after each speaker this time for SS to check their answers. Play again as necessary and check answers.

> 1 There are a lot of cooking programmes on TV and the UK leads the world in some respects in being adventurous about cooking.
> 2 More people eat junk food than healthy food.
> 3 Indian food is very spicy but is made with lots of dry spices and you can feel heavier after eating. Thai food is very fresh and exciting (zingy) and doesn't leave you feeling heavy, just exhilarated.
> 4 A lot of it is fast food, very processed and full of fat and salt.
> 5 Liz is a vegetarian. As a result she likes vegetables, fruit, and fresh food so she likes Italian and Thai food (particularly curried vegetables.)
> 6 It has taken on an Asian feel.
> 7 Heat. i.e. spicy, and flavour.

c ● **7.18** Focus on the phrases and give SS time to read them. Play the CD, pausing after the first phrase and replaying it as necessary. Elicit the missing words, and then the meaning of the whole phrase. Repeat for the other three phrases.

> 1 there's a **long way to go** (= a lot more progress needs to be made)
> 2 an **awful lot of** (= informal way of saying a large number of)
> 3 all that **kind of stuff** (= informal way of saying 'and other similar things', i.e. unhealthy things in this case)
> 4 **overall** (= in general, taking everything into consideration)

7.18   CD4 Track 40

1 …still there's a long way to go before we can say, in general people in the UK are good cooks.
2 …there are also an awful lot of really awful fast food outlets encouraging you to eat junk.
3 …and full of fat, and salt, and all that kind of stuff.
4 So, yeah, I think overall, it's a pretty healthy place.

Extra support

If there's time, get SS to listen again with the scripts on *p.135*, focusing on any new vocabulary, and getting feedback on phrases SS didn't understand, e.g. because the words were run together.

d ● Finally, get SS to ask each other the three questions that the interviewer asked the interviewees. Then get some feedback from the whole class.

HOMEWORK

Study Link **Workbook** *p.73*

7 REVISE & CHECK

For instructions on how to use this page, see *p.35*.

GRAMMAR

a 1 ✓
    2 a tin opener
    3 such awful weather
    4 ✓
    5 ✓
    6 such a good film
    7 ✓
    8 a glass of wine
    9 darker and darker
    10 …second-largest city in the UK.
b 1 the main causes of poverty
    2 photo album
    3 ✓
    4 children's bedroom
    5 ✓
    6 a bit
    7 ✓
    8 such
    9 as
    10 by far
    11 a few
    12 The end of the book

VOCABULARY

a 1 chopping board   **b** 1 heat
    2 simmer   2 beat
    3 stir   3 burst
    4 stuff   4 take
    5 melted   5 turned
    6 draught   6 make
    7 spine   7 burn
    8 hilarious   8 Set
    9 ripe

c 1 cartoonist
    2 strength
    3 shorten
    4 height
    5 lengths
    6 comedians
    7 whipped

Test and Assessment CD-ROM

File 7 Quicktest
File 7 Test
Progress Test 4–7

CONTENTS

GRAMMAR ACTIVITY ANSWERS   155

GRAMMAR ACTIVITY MASTERS   157

COMMUNICATIVE ACTIVITY INSTRUCTIONS   178

COMMUNICATIVE ACTIVITY MASTERS   183

VOCABULARY ACTIVITY INSTRUCTIONS   204

VOCABULARY ACTIVITY MASTERS   208

SONG ACTIVITY INSTRUCTIONS   229

SONG ACTIVITY MASTERS   232

DEPENDENT PREPOSITIONS   239

Photocopiable material

- There is a Grammar activity for each main (A, B, and C) lesson of the Student's Book.
- There is a Communicative activity for each main lesson of the Student's Book.
- There is a Vocabulary activity for each main lesson of the Student's Book.
- There are seven Song activities. These can be used as part of the main lesson in the Student's Book or in a later lesson. The recording of each song can be found in the main lesson on the Class CD.
- There are two pages of dependent prepositions.

Using extra activities in mixed-ability classes

Some teachers have classes with a very wide range of abilities, where some SS finish activities much more quickly than others. You could give fast-finishers a photocopiable activity (either Communicative, Grammar, or Vocabulary) while you help the slower SS. Alternatively, some teachers might want to give faster SS extra oral practice with a communicative activity while slower SS consolidate their knowledge with an extra grammar activity.

Tips for using Grammar activities

The Grammar activities are designed to give SS extra practice in the main grammar point from each lesson. How you use these activities depends on the needs and abilities of your SS and the time you have available. They can be used in the lesson if you think all of your class would benefit from the extra practice, or you could set them as homework for some or all of your SS.

- All of the activities are divided into two stages: Consolidation and Activation.
- Consolidation is a writing stage, and provides SS with controlled practice of the language point. If you use this stage in class, get SS to work individually or in pairs. Allow SS to compare before checking the answers.
- Activation is an optional stage which gives SS freer practice to produce the target language. This is either in the form of a written or spoken exercise. It can be used as immediate follow-up to Consolidation, or as a warmer or cooler in a subsequent lesson.
- If SS are having trouble with any of the activities, make sure they refer to the relevant Grammar Bank in the Student's Book.
- Make sure that SS keep their copies of the activities and that they review any difficult areas regularly. Encourage them to go back to activities, and cover and test themselves. This will help with their revision.

Tips for using Communicative activities

- We have suggested the ideal number of copies for each activity. However, you can often manage with fewer, e.g. one copy per pair instead of one per student.
- When SS are working in pairs, if possible get them to sit face to face. This will encourage them to really talk to each other, and also means they can't see each other's sheet.
- If your class doesn't divide into pairs or groups, take part yourself, get two SS to share one role, or get one student to monitor, help, and correct.
- If some SS finish early, they can swap roles and do the activity again, or you could get them to write some of the sentences from the activity.

Tips for using Vocabulary activities

The Vocabulary activities are designed to reactivate the lexis in each lesson, and to help SS to learn the new words and phrases.

- The activities include lexis from the Vocabulary Banks, Vocabulary exercises, and Lexis in context exercises from the Student's Book. There are pair work communicative activities (such as split-crosswords and games involving word definition) which can only be done in class. There are also vocabulary races and quizzes which can either be done in class or set for homework.
- The Vocabulary activities can be used either immediately after the Student's Book lesson for consolidation, or later in the course for revision.
- We have suggested the ideal number of copies for each activity. However, with some activities such as vocabulary races and quizzes, you could use fewer, e.g. one copy per pair instead of one per student.
- When SS are working in pairs, if possible get them to sit face to face. This will encourage them to really talk to each other, and also means they can't see each other's sheet.
- If SS are having trouble with any of the activities, make sure they refer to the relevant Vocabulary Bank or Vocabulary exercise in the Student's Book.
- Make sure that SS keep their copies of the activities for revision later.

1A discourse markers (1)

2 consequently   3 so as not to   4 in case   5 though
6 Although   7 but   8 As a result   9 so that
10 However   11 Despite   12 As   13 so as to
14 so that   15 because of

1B have

a 2 I've been reading   3 ✓   4 to have escaped
5 Don't you have   6 already have   7 I'll be having
8 didn't have to   9 have it dry cleaned   10 ✓

b 2 I've been having / I've had   3 has this been going on
4 having my hair cut   5 I've seen   6 doesn't have / hasn't
got   7 Do you have / Have you got   8 I have / I've got

1C pronouns

a 2 It's   3 themselves   4 it's   5 you   6 you   7 there's
8 their   9 themselves   10 one another   11 they
12 there's

b 2 there   3 they   4 one   5 It   6 you   7 they
8 yourself   9 they   10 you   11 there   12 it

2A past: narrative tenses, *used to* and *would*

2 had been living / had lived   3 looked   4 used to frown
/ would frown / frowned   5 used to wash / would wash /
washed   6 was playing   7 remembered   8 had told
9 jumped   10 was passing / passed   11 had made
12 was awaiting / awaited   13 heard   14 always got off /
would always get off / always used to get off

2B distancing

a 2 It seems that men are more at risk…
3 It appears that she has changed her mind…
4 It seems that you are unable to deal…
5 It seems that the weather is improving.
6 It appears that the robbers were wearing…

b 2 A spokesman is expected to make an announcement…
3 More than half of the population are believed to suffer
from headaches.
4 St Petersburg is said to be one of the…
5 At least 70 people are thought to have been injured…
6 The economy is expected to grow…

c The following expressions should be underlined:
according to, do not appear to have been used, apparently,
there are said to be, it has been suggested, may have
broken down

2C get

a 2 ✗ get to the point   3 ✗ got broken   4 ✗ get the bus
5 ✓   6 ✗ get paid   7 ✓   8 ✗ get Gareth to look
9 ✗ got the kitchen painted by a decorator
10 ✗ got to the nearest petrol station

b 2 Paying a lot to get your hair cut is a waste of money.
3 The best way to get rich is to work hard.
4 Getting hurt is usually a learning experience.
5 People get wiser as they get older.
6 Cheating is fine provided you don't get caught.
7 Giving presents is better than getting them.
8 School doesn't help you to get anywhere in life.

3A speculation and deduction

a 2 can't be   3 must be   4 might be doing / could be doing
5 can't have been   6 must have been   7 might have gone
8 might not have thought   9 should be

b 2 the disease **is** likely to   3 you **will** probably be able
4 is unlikely **to** be   5 we **are** bound to   6 it's very
unlikely that   7 she's bound **to** be   8 she **will** definitely

3B adding emphasis (1)

a 2 only   3 when   4 have   5 did   6 sooner
7 when   8 will

b 2 Not until two hours later did the plane finally take off.
3 Rarely have I seen such breathtaking countryside.
4 Not only was she well dressed, but she was also
beautiful.
5 Hardly had I switched on my laptop when the battery
ran out.
6 Not until we got home did we realize (that) we had
been robbed.
7 Only when you go abroad can you understand your
own country.
8 No sooner had we found our seats than the show started.

3C past simple and past perfect: unreal uses

2 c   3 b   4 b   5 a   6 c   7 a   8 b   9 b   10 c   11 a
12 b   13 b   14 a   15 c

4A discourse markers (2)

2 Obviously   3 That is to say   4 Besides
5 in other words   6 By the way   7 Anyway   8 Basically
9 On the one hand   10 To sum up

4B verb + object + infinitive or gerund

a 2 to take   3 to be offended   4 ✓
5 for Jack to attend   6 you to feel   7 ✓
8 for our children to go   9 ✓

b 2 to retake   3 do   4 taking   5 being able
6 stopping   7 using   8 to leave   9 not to arrive
10 to get

4C conditional sentences

a 2 could provide   3 lacks   4 won't be   5 had built
6 might not have lost   7 would still be working
8 hadn't messed up   9 were   10 would have noticed
11 aren't   12 will call

b 2 If I had saved some money, I wouldn't be broke.
3 You can borrow my laptop on condition that you look
after it.
4 I'm going to the party whether I'm invited or not.
5 Supposing you hadn't found your passport, what would
you have done?
6 Your exam will be fine providing (that) you do enough
revision.
7 I'm in favour of contact sports as / so long as nobody
gets seriously injured.
8 I would never wear fur, even if the weather was very
cold / it was very cold.
9 You can go out tonight provided (that) you're back by
midnight.

5A permission, obligation, and necessity

a 2 ✗ had better not   3 ✓   4 ✗ mustn't download
5 ✓   6 ✗ ought to   7 ✓   8 ✓   9 ✗ ought to have thought of

b 2 ✓   3 ✓   4 had better   5 should   6 can't
7 ✓   8 ✓

c 2 no difference   3 no difference   7 *must* is stronger
8 *had better* is more urgent

5B verbs of the senses

2 smells like garlic   3 as if she had   4 been hearing good
things about you   5 ice cream really tastes of   6 see
anyone leave the house   7 sounds like a violin   8 to have
changed much   9 heard the bomb go off   10 looks as if
he didn't sleep very well   11 as though she was delighted
12 heard the couple arguing

5C gerunds and infinitives

a 2 ✓   3 ✗ being spoken to   4 ✗ to have been able
5 ✗ to understand   6 ✓   7 ✗ inviting   8 ✓
9 ✗ to be trying   10 ✓

b 2 feeling   3 being told   4 have been informed
5 to do   6 to be searching   7 to be / to have been
8 not having been contacted

Activation
1 h   2 e   3 a   4 c   5 f   6 g   7 b   8 d

6A expressing future arrangements and plans

a 2 ✓   3 ✗ we're going / we're going to go / we'll be going
4 ✗ due to go   5 ✓   6 ✓   7 ✗ are you and Jennifer
doing / going to do / will you and Jennifer be doing   8 ✓
9 ✗ they're going to lose / they'll lose   10 ✓   11 ✗ I'm
going to paint

b The following should be underlined:
is to face, what is going to be, I'm about to become, I'm
going to show him, begins

6B ellipsis and substitution

a No ellipsis or substitution is used.

b Nicky's father gave her his phone number and said she
could contact him whenever she wanted (to). She said
goodbye, and then hung up. At first, she was angry that
he had got in touch, and wished that he hadn't. But a few
weeks later she called and arranged to see him, because
she felt they needed to talk. She got on well with him,
though she hadn't expected to. Nicky decided that she
wanted them to meet regularly, and her father promised
that they would. Five years later, when she got married,
no one imagined that her father would be leading her up
the aisle, but he was.

c 2 I'm afraid that we haven't got any batteries **not**.
3 I guess I'll go skiing **so**, though…
4 I suspect that they won't accept it **not**.
5 I don't imagine that they will come **so**.
6 I suppose that he won't be interested in taking part **not**.

6C adding emphasis (2)

a 2 The reason (why) he married her was for her money.
3 The person she loves more than anyone in the world is
her niece.
4 The last time I saw her was in October.
5 The person who really understands how I feel is my
sister.
6 The reason (why) we retired early was in order to have
time to enjoy life.

7 The place where I relax most is (in) the garden.
8 The first time I met David was just after the military
coup.

b 2 What my son is really crazy about is skateboarding.
3 All they want to do is to lie on a beach and relax.
4 What I'm desperate for is a nice cup of tea.
5 It was the atmosphere that made the restaurant special
rather than the food. / It was the atmosphere rather
than the food which made the restaurant special.
6 What I don't want is to be late for work tomorrow.
7 All she asked for was a glass of water.
8 It was Alec who was a professional footballer when he
was young, not Darren.

7A nouns: compound and possessive forms

2 ✗ other people's business   3 ✓   4 ✗ a bottle opener
5 ✗ the flatmate of my cousin Jane, who works for the city
council   6 ✓   7 ✓   8 ✗ the high point of her career
9 ✓   10 ✗ kitchen cupboard   11 ✗ wine glasses   12 ✓
13 ✗ the middle of the room   14 ✓

Activation
Possible answers:
chocolate cake, birthday cake, lemon cake, etc.
coffee cup, tea cup, egg cup, etc.
bread knife, paper knife, fish knife, etc.
CD player, DVD player, football player, etc.
sewing machine, coffee machine, running machine, etc.
city centre, health centre, sports centre, etc.
surf board, chopping board, message board, etc.
story book, cheque book, physics book, etc.
car key, house key, back door key, etc.
mineral water, sea water, tap water, etc.
credit card, birthday card, identity card, etc.
picture frame, photo frame, window frame, etc.

7B so and such

2 She was **so** tired…   3 …so **much** snow…   4 …so
many vases…   5 …such **a** nasty look…   6 Valuable
items **such** as watches…   7 …such **an** amazing
performance…   8 She speaks **so** quickly…   9 There's
such **a** lot of rubbish…   10 …with **such** great
determination…   11 He said **such** hurtful things to
her…   12 **So** thick was the fog all around us…

Activation
1 h   2 d   3 f   4 b   5 g   6 a   7 e   8 c

7C comparison

2 more money people have, the more time   3 nearly the
tallest girl   4 louder and louder   5 a little more snow
6 as expensive as   7 is much the best   8 Far more
students passed   9 The bigger the car you have, the
higher the road tax   10 more and more difficult
11 as much as   12 The longer we waited, the angrier

Consolidation

● Complete the texts with the discourse markers from the list.

~~so~~	as a result	consequently	as	because of	so as to	so as not to
so that (x2)	in case	but	however	although	though	despite

I would say that the most challenging period in my career so far was my first junior management position in the company where I still work today. I had always wanted to be an account manager, [1] _so_ I was thrilled when I got the job, but little did I know what was waiting for me on my first day. The office environment wasn't exactly organized, and to make matters worse, my boss was completely unsupportive towards me. For some reason, he just refused to take any responsibility for dealing with the clients, and I was [2]_____ forced to deal with all the problems by myself, which wasn't easy. I used to stay late in the office almost every night [3]_____ miss any of the clients' deadlines. It seems ridiculous now, but I was so stressed that I used to check my emails every couple of hours, even at weekends, [4]_____ there was an urgent message asking me to sort something out. It was worth it in the end [5]_____, because eventually my boss was sacked and I was promoted in his place!

The toughest time I've ever had was definitely my first term here at university. [6]_____ I really love student life now, but it wasn't so easy at the beginning. My bad luck started on the very first day. My parents had just dropped me off with all my stuff when some of the guys whose rooms were on the same corridor as mine suggested going to play basketball in the park nearby. I don't know exactly how it happened, [7]_____ somehow, during the game, I tripped and fell very hard on my right arm and broke it. Apart from not being able to do any sports for weeks, it was especially annoying because my injury meant I wasn't able to write properly. [8]_____, I got really behind with my essays and I had to take extra classes later in the year [9]_____ I could catch up. On top of that, it wasn't as easy as I had expected to find friends, and I was pretty homesick for quite a while. [10]_____, things got better eventually. Once my arm was better, I managed to get into the first basketball team and made loads of new friends. I can look back now and laugh, but at the time things didn't seem so funny.

Most people can't wait until the day they give up working, but I can tell you it's not quite as simple as you might think. [11]_____ all the free time, retirement isn't just a question of enjoying yourself and feeling delighted that you never have to work again. My husband Frank had terrible trouble adjusting to the new lifestyle when he retired after forty rewarding years as a lawyer. [12]_____ he had always been committed to his career, it wasn't easy just to give it up overnight. We decided to move to the countryside [13]_____ be nearer to our daughter and her family, but when we arrived, we found that they were all so busy with their own lives that they didn't have much time for us. Of course, we did babysit for her sometimes [14]_____ she could go out in the evenings, but somehow it wasn't the life we had imagined. Just when we were feeling really down, a friend of ours invited us along to a ballroom dancing class in the village. Frank wasn't keen at first, as dancing isn't really his thing, but once we got there, we had a wonderful time. Now we go three times a week and it's changed our lives. We keep fit and we've met so many fantastic people. And it's all [15]_____ the dance club. I don't know what we would have done without it!

Activation

● Write your own paragraph about a challenging experience you have faced. You could write about your work, studies, or family. Explain what the challenge was, and how you survived it. If you can't think of anything from your life, write about a friend or relative.

In your paragraph, make sure you use at least five of the discourse markers from the list.

When you have finished, swap paragraphs with a partner, and check the discourse markers. Has your partner used them correctly?

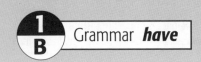
Consolidation

a Circle the correct form. Tick (✓) if both are possible.

1 You should definitely catch that movie if you **hadn't seen it** / **haven't seen it** already.

2 **I've been reading** / **I've read** the same book for three months and I still haven't finished it.

3 I'm not going to her wedding because I **don't have** / **haven't got** anything to wear.

4 The thieves are thought **to escape** / **to have escaped** after the robbery.

5 **Don't you have** / **Haven't you** a TV? I thought everyone had one these days.

6 Don't give them a toaster as a present because they **already have** / **are already having** one.

7 Don't call me after seven because **I'll be having** / **I'll have** dinner.

8 Once the kids were older we **hadn't got to** / **didn't have to** drive them to school.

9 If you want to get rid of the stain on your jacket, you'll have to **have it dry cleaned** / **have dry cleaned it**.

10 I need to leave work early tonight. **I've got to** / **I have to** go to the dentist.

b Complete the dialogue with a suitable form of the verbs in brackets.

PSYCHOLOGIST   So, why ¹ *have* you *come* (come) to see me today?

PATIENT   Well, I ²_____ (have) a really weird dream.

PSYCHOLOGIST   I see. How long ³_____ this _____ (go on)?

PATIENT   About a month now, on and off. It's driving me crazy!

PSYCHOLOGIST   Can you describe the dream for me?

PATIENT   I'm in the middle of ⁴_____ my hair _____ (cut), and suddenly I realize that the man doing my hair isn't Paul, my usual hairdresser...

PSYCHOLOGIST   Go on...

PATIENT   He's the strangest hairdresser I ⁵_____ (see) in my life.

PSYCHOLOGIST   Can you describe him?

PATIENT   Well, he's really tall with little round glasses and he ⁶_____ (not have) much hair.

PSYCHOLOGIST   ⁷_____ you _____ (have) any idea who this person might be?

PATIENT   Yes. I ⁸_____ (have) a horrible feeling it might be you!

Activation

● Complete the following sentences about yourself. Compare your answers with a partner.

• I'm really proud of the fact that I've...

• My worst characteristic is that I have a tendency to...

• One thing I often have to do which I'd rather avoid is...

• When I really want to have fun I...

New English File Teacher's Book Advanced
Photocopiable © Oxford University Press 2010

Consolidation

a Read the following email and circle the correct pronouns.

New Message

To: Giovanna Rossi

From: Aileen Campbell

Subject: Visiting Glasgow!

Hi Giovanna!
Great to hear that you and Alessandro are going to be visiting Glasgow over the summer. I'm sure you're going to love it. As far as I'm concerned, ¹(there's)/ it's nowhere in the world quite like it.
² **It's / There's** the people in Glasgow who really make the city something special. I think the whole way they express ³ **them / themselves** is quite different from other parts of the UK. For example, ⁴ **there's / it's** not uncommon to exchange a few words with the person sitting next to ⁵ **yourself / you** on the bus or waiting in a queue, and ⁶ **you / one** sometimes end up having a laugh with them as well! It's part of the city's outgoing spirit and sense of humour.
You told me you're feeling a bit nervous about understanding the Glasgow accent, but I don't think you need to worry too much about that. Of course ⁷ **there's / it's** the problem that the city has its own dialect, but everyone I know who's visited has been able to manage, and to find ⁸ **his / their** way around or go shopping by ⁹ **themselves / himself**.
And you might be interested in listening out for some of the expressions some Glasgow people use to address ¹⁰ **one another / themselves**. For example, if someone calls you 'hen', don't be offended, because ¹¹ **they / you** aren't trying to say you look like a chicken! In fact it's quite an affectionate local greeting for women.
Finally, ¹² **it's / there's** so much to see and do in Glasgow. I know you're passionate about art and architecture, so I think you'll really appreciate the grand buildings and famous museums and galleries. And when you're done with that, there are some excellent places to eat as well.
Have a great time!
Aileen

b Complete the following email with a suitable pronoun in each space.

New Message

To: Katya Kabanova

From: Andy Fordham

Subject: RE: Oxford

Hello Katya,
What an excellent idea to take some time off from your job to study English in Oxford. For anyone who wants to improve ¹ _their_ language skills, I don't think ² _____ can be anything better than spending some time surrounded by the language.
³ _____ say that one always learns something when ⁴ _____ goes to Oxford. ⁵ _____ can't be denied that although the city is small, it is a centre for many kinds of learning, with its two universities and numerous schools and colleges where ⁶ _____ are able to study everything from astrophysics to English grammar!
Anyone who arrives in Oxford will soon realize that ⁷ _____ are in a truly international city. Most of the people who work in the shops and restaurants in town are used to dealing with visitors so I don't think you'll have much trouble making ⁸ _____ understood. As for the way people interact, well, I find that in general, they're very polite. I mean, if you accidentally bump into someone in the street, ⁹ _____ are actually quite likely to say sorry to you, not the other way round! However, people who don't know ¹⁰ _____ are less likely to start up conversations just to pass the time.
You'll find that ¹¹ _____'s no shortage of historical and cultural attractions in Oxford, from the picturesque river Thames to the beautiful old colleges. What's more, ¹² _____'s only a short train ride from London, so you can easily link it in with other destinations in the UK.
Hope this is of some use. All the best for your trip,
Andy

Activation

● Write your own email to a visitor from abroad, telling them what to expect when they visit the place where you live. In your email, try to use at least six of the pronouns from **a** and **b** above.
When you have finished, swap emails with a partner and check the pronouns. Has your partner used them correctly?

● Read the story and put the verbs in the right form. There is sometimes more than one possibility.

When Tom turned twelve, his family
¹ *moved* (move) out of their flat in the city
to a huge semi-detached house in the
suburbs, near a park. Tom thought that he
was the luckiest boy alive. The one less
attractive feature of Tom's new home was
the inhabitant of the house next door. He
was an extremely serious and strict middle-
aged dentist who ²_____ (live) in
the street for decades. Dr Scorey, or, as Tom
used to call him, 'Dr Scary', ³_____
(look) uncomfortably like Dracula and he
⁴_____ (frown) threateningly at
his new neighbours whenever he saw them.
Tom was absolutely terrified of him. The
only thing Dr Scorey seemed to care about
was his BMW sports car, which he
⁵_____ (wash) every Saturday
without fail.

One afternoon during the summer
holidays, Tom ⁶_____ (play)
football in the park when he suddenly
⁷_____ (remember) that his
mother ⁸_____ (tell) him to
come home earlier than usual for dinner.
He ⁹_____ (jump) onto his bike
to cycle home as fast as he could. However,
just as he ¹⁰_____ (pass)
Dr Scorey's BMW, he somehow lost control
of his bike, crashed into the side of the car,
and fell off. After picking himself up, he
noticed to his horror that his bike
¹¹_____ (make) deep scratches all
down one side of the car! Tom was afraid
to tell anyone, and spent all night
imagining what horrible punishment
¹²_____ (await) him at the hands
of his neighbour. In the end, he told his
father, who went straight round to Dr
Scorey's and arranged to pay for the
damage. Tom never ¹³_____
(hear) anything more about it, but from
that day onwards he ¹⁴_____
(always get off) his bike at a very safe
distance from Dr Scorey's car, just in case.

● Think of a time in your childhood when you did something wrong, and either
got punished or managed to get away with it. Write a paragraph describing
the incident. Swap paragraphs with a partner.

2/B Grammar **distancing**

a Rewrite the sentences using *It seems / appears + that + clause.*

1 The government appears to be planning to raise taxes.

It appears that the government is planning to raise taxes.

2 Men seem to be more at risk from this disease than women.

3 She appears to have changed her mind since I last spoke to her.

4 You seem to be unable to deal with this problem effectively.

5 The weather seems to be about to improve.

6 The robbers appear to have been wearing face masks.

b Rewrite the sentences using subject + passive verb + *to* + infinitive.

1 It is thought that the finance minister is about to resign from his post.

The finance minister is thought to be about to resign from his post.

2 It is expected that a spokesman will make an announcement later today.

3 It is believed that more than half of the population suffer from headaches.

4 It is said that St Petersburg is one of the most majestic cities in the world.

5 It is thought that at least seventy people have been injured as a result of the explosion.

6 It is expected that the economy will grow over the next six months.

c Read the news report and underline all the distancing expressions.

Concern is growing about a thirty-year-old man who has been missing from his Yorkshire home for more than a week. It seems that Dan Glayver was last seen when he left his office at around six p.m. last Thursday. According to his partner, he did not return home that evening. Mr Glayver's credit cards and mobile phone do not appear to have been used since Thursday and his sudden disappearance is apparently completely out of character. Furthermore, there are said to be several inconsistencies in his partner's version of events, and the police are continuing to question her. It has been suggested by neighbours that the couple's relationship may have broken down in recent months.

You are a TV newsreader. Use the following pieces of gossip to prepare an official news report about a famous actress. Be careful to distance yourself from the people's claims using a range of structures from **a–c** above.

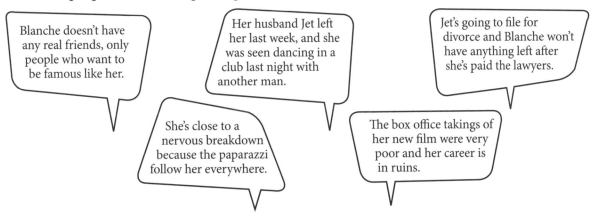

Blanche doesn't have any real friends, only people who want to be famous like her.

Her husband Jet left her last week, and she was seen dancing in a club last night with another man.

Jet's going to file for divorce and Blanche won't have anything left after she's paid the lawyers.

She's close to a nervous breakdown because the paparazzi follow her everywhere.

The box office takings of her new film were very poor and her career is in ruins.

Actress Blanche Devoy was said to be close to a nervous breakdown last night.
It has been suggested that…

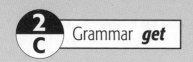
a Right (✓) or wrong (✗)? Correct the mistakes in the highlighted phrases.

1 She was so exhausted that she got the children to cook while she relaxed. ✓

2 We're now starting to get the point where we just can't cope.

3 Quite a few of our things got to break when we were moving house.

4 Look online to find out where you can get to the bus into town.

5 It can take a long time to get used to a new neighbourhood.

6 Top managers often get pay substantial bonuses at the end of the year.

7 She was in the middle of getting her legs waxed so I said I'd call her back.

8 I was wondering if you could get Gareth looked at the figures for me.

9 We got painted the kitchen by a decorator.

10 By the time they got the nearest petrol station, night had fallen.

b Order the words to make sentences.

1 the always women men same paid get should as
Women *should always get paid the same as men.*

2 a lot a to paying of waste cut hair your is money get
Paying _____.

3 get to the work to is rich way best hard
The _____.

4 experience hurt a getting usually is learning
Getting _____.

5 older people get as they wiser get
People _____.

6 provided fine get is you caught don't cheating
Cheating _____.

7 than them better presents giving getting is
Giving _____.

8 in you help anywhere school doesn't get life to
School _____.

● Discuss the sentences in **b** with a partner. Do you agree with them?

New English File Teacher's Book Advanced
Photocopiable © Oxford University Press 2010

a Complete the dialogue. Rewrite the phrases in the list with *must, can't, may, might,* or *should,* and a verb in the correct tense.

---

1 it's possible that he's having   **2** almost certainly isn't   **3** I'm almost sure he is
4 it's possible that he's doing   **5** I'm almost sure it wasn't   **6** he was almost definitely there
7 perhaps he went   **8** perhaps he didn't think   **9** will probably be

---

JOY   Pam, why are you crying? What's wrong?

PAM   It's Derek. I think ¹ *he might be having* an affair.

JOY   Come on, Pam, that ²_____ true. He ³_____ one of the most reliable partners in the world. How can you possibly think that he ⁴_____ something behind your back?

PAM   That's what I thought. Until a friend saw him coming out of a nightclub with another woman!

JOY   It ⁵_____ him. Derek's never been a late-night person.

PAM   No, Joy, it was definitely him. I found this ticket in his pocket, so he ⁶_____ there that night.

JOY   Well, he ⁷_____ there with a group of colleagues from work. He ⁸_____ it was important enough to tell you about it.

PAM   What do you mean, not important enough?

JOY   Look, don't you think it would be a good idea to talk to him about it? Everything ⁹_____ fine once you give him a chance to explain. You'll see.

b Add one word in the right place to make the sentences correct.

1 The traffic is heavy today, so they're sure **to** be late for the meeting.

2 Medical experts say that the disease likely to spread all over the world.

3 With an experienced guide you probably be able to get to the top in four or five hours.

4 The company is unlikely be in a position to make a profit this year.

5 If we play as badly as we did last week, we bound to lose in the semi-final.

6 It's very that you'll win anything. I'd say there's only a 2% chance.

7 With her presentation skills she's bound be able to convince the company to diversify.

8 If Sophie doesn't get to the gate before it closes, she definitely miss the flight.

Prepare a two-minute presentation for the class about how you think life might be in 20 years' time. Try to use the grammar from **a** and **b**. Choose two or three of these topics:

---

family and friends   shopping   the environment   work   entertainment
the economic situation in your country   technology   transport

---

'First of all, I think **it's very likely** that 20 years from now I'll still have a small group of very close friends, although if I am married I **might not see** them as often as I do now. People will **definitely** still want to meet each other face-to-face, and I don't believe that email or talking online will ever replace that. Families are **bound to** become smaller in the future as nowadays people are having fewer children and I think that the tradition of large extended family **is likely to** disappear, etc.'

a Read these people's emphatic comments, taken from reviews on a local restaurant guide website. Complete the comments with one word from the list.

~~Never~~	when	only	did	sooner	have	will	when

REVIEWS

★☆☆☆☆ **1** '_Never_ have I had such an unpleasant dining experience.'

★★☆☆☆ **2** 'Not _____ was the restaurant in need of cleaning, it was also overcrowded.'

★☆☆☆☆ **3** 'Hardly had we sat down at our table _____ the waiter told us we had to move again.'

★★☆☆☆ **4** 'Rarely _____ I been treated so rudely by staff in a restaurant.'

★★☆☆☆ **5** 'Not until two full hours later _____ our meal finally arrive.'

★☆☆☆☆ **6** 'No _____ had we started eating than we noticed that our chicken was uncooked.'

★☆☆☆☆ **7** 'Only _____ we threatened to leave without paying did the manager pay any attention.'

☆☆☆☆☆ **8** 'Never again _____ my husband and I return to this so-called 'restaurant'.'

---

b Rewrite the sentences using inversion.

1 I have never been so insulted in all my life.
   Never in all my life have I been so insulted.

2 It wasn't until two hours later that the plane finally took off.

3 I have rarely seen such breathtaking countryside.

4 She was not only well dressed, but she was also beautiful.

5 I had hardly switched on my laptop when the battery ran out.

6 We didn't realize we had been robbed until we got home.

7 You can only understand your own country when you go abroad.

8 As soon as we had found our seats the show started.

Write a short review (just a paragraph) for a restaurant or travel website about an unpleasant dining or travelling experience you have had. In your paragraph, use one or two inverted sentences to emphasize your point.

Consolidation

● Circle the correct answer.

1 That boyfriend of yours is useless. Isn't it time _____ a new one?
  a you found
  b you find
  c you had found

2 If only our neighbours _____ a dog, life would be much quieter.
  a wouldn't have
  b don't have
  c didn't have

3 What a lovely view. I wish _____ my camera.
  a I brought
  b I'd brought
  c I've brought

4 I'm too tired to go out tonight. I'd rather _____ at home.
  a to stay
  b stay
  c stayed

5 If only you _____ Mike the car, we'd be able to drive there.
  a hadn't lent
  b lent
  c didn't lend

6 Come on, children! It's time _____ to bed now.
  a you go
  b you must go
  c you went

7 I'd rather _____ your shoes off at the door, if you don't mind.
  a you took
  b you take
  c you to take

8 I'd love to be able to sing in a choir. If only _____ a better voice!
  a I'd have
  b I had
  c I have

9 As soon as I said it, I wished _____.
  a I wouldn't
  b I hadn't
  c I didn't

10 Diane thinks it's time her daughter _____ married.
  a get
  b to get
  c got

11 Those children look freezing. I bet they wish _____ indoors.
  a they were
  b they are
  c they can be

12 As you're busy, _____ we postponed the meeting?
  a had you rather
  b would you rather
  c would rather

13 I'd wear these jeans more often if they _____ so tight.
  a were
  b weren't
  c wouldn't be

14 If only those people in the front row _____ talking. I can't hear the film!
  a would stop
  b stopped
  c will stop

15 I've just had a text from Ann. She'd rather we _____ at 6.30, as she's running late.
  a meet
  b to meet
  c met

Activation

● Write a short dialogue between two people who are arguing. For example, the argument could be between a strict parent and a rebellious teenager.

In your dialogue, try to use some of the structures from the exercise above. When you have finished, check the grammar with a partner. Then perform the dialogue for the class.

Don't you think it's high time you started studying for your exams?

New English File Teacher's Book Advanced
Photocopiable © Oxford University Press 2010

Consolidation

● Complete the presentation with the discourse markers from the list.

~~in fact~~   that is to say   by the way   obviously   in other words
to sum up   anyway   on the one hand   basically   besides

Hi, everyone. The historical figure I've chosen for my mini-presentation is Oliver Cromwell. You may not have heard of him before, but ¹ *in fact* he was one of the most influential figures in the history of the British Isles. ²_____, I don't have time to give you all the details about his life in only five minutes, but let's start with some dates…

…Cromwell did not accept the absolute power of the King. ³_____, he strongly believed that his country should be governed not only by the King, but also by Parliament. After joining the army as a soldier, he eventually became a commander and led his troops in the Civil War which ended in the defeat and execution of the King. ⁴_____ this, Cromwell also led military campaigns in Ireland and Scotland. He was later named as Lord Protector of England, or, ⁵_____, the absolute leader of the country…

…⁶_____, you might be interested in finding out more about the English Civil War. It was a very violent and unstable period in the country's development, during which thousands of people were wounded or killed. ⁷_____, to get back to the main subject of my presentation, Cromwell…

…⁸_____, there are two contrasting opinions about Oliver Cromwell. ⁹_____, some people believe that he was a great hero who liberated his country by overthrowing the King. On the other hand, he is regarded by many as a violent dictator whose actions led to the oppression and death of many people…

…¹⁰_____, I believe that Oliver Cromwell was an extremely important figure in British history, whatever you think about him. Thank you for listening. Does anyone have any questions? I'm not the world's greatest expert on British history, but I'm happy to try to answer…

Activation

● Give a five-minute mini-presentation to the class about a famous historical figure who interests you. If you need to find information, try searching on the Internet in English. When you give your mini-presentation, use the discourse markers from the exercise above.

a Circle the correct form. Tick (✓) if both are correct.

1 Cathy taught us **that we should check / to check** new words in a dictionary. ✓

2 Mark begged us **that we took / to take** him to the nearest village.

3 I didn't mean you **be offended / to be offended**. I'm very sorry.

4 Luckily the doctor didn't advise **me to change / that I should change** my lifestyle.

5 We have arranged **for Jack to attend / Jack to attend** to attend the meeting.

6 I would hate **you to feel / that you feel** uncomfortable about the proposed changes.

7 Having an extra team member helped us **complete / to complete** the project ahead of schedule.

8 We'd always planned **our children to go / for our children to go** to university.

9 Phil persuaded me **that I should give up / to give up** extreme sports.

b Complete the sentences with the verbs in brackets in the infinitive (with or without *to*) or the gerund.

1 I'm afraid I can't let you _check_ (check) in until I see proof of your identity.

2 Any student who fails will be made _____ (retake) the test.

3 Dad would always make us _____ (do) our homework before watching TV.

4 Fortunately her injury won't prevent her _____ (take) part in the competition.

5 I'm sure I don't remember her _____ (be able) to swim!

6 I really dislike people _____ (stop) me in the street to ask for money.

7 Any task which involves my mother _____ (use) a computer makes her panic.

8 We strongly advise guests _____ (leave) their valuables in the hotel safe.

9 Nigel reminded everyone _____ (not arrive) late for the welcome tour.

10 It shouldn't take you more than five minutes _____ (get) here. We're just round the corner.

AIRPORT-CHECK-IN

Discuss these questions with a partner.

• Does the Internet make people more sociable, or does it isolate them?

• Do you mind musicians playing music in the street?

• Should we really expect students to be responsible for their own learning?

• Should local governments force people to use public transport in cities where there is a traffic problem?

• How can governments encourage people to respect the environment?

• Can you imagine yourself living the rest of your life in another country?

Consolidation

a Complete the dialogue with the correct form of the verbs in brackets.

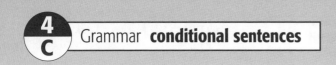

MR STACKFORD   Well, I think we're all agreed that your department is in a very difficult situation. Am I right?

MARTIN + EMMA   Yes, Mr Stackford.

MR STACKFORD   Well, I ¹ *'d be* (be) delighted if one of you ²_____ (can / provide) me with an explanation.

MARTIN   I must say I think Emma made mistakes with marketing. Everyone knows the rule that if a company ³_____ (lack) a clear marketing strategy, it simply ⁴_____ (be) able to keep up with the competition.

EMMA   Come on, Martin. If you ⁵_____ (build) a better relationship with our clients, we ⁶_____ (might / not lose) that important account last month.

MARTIN   That's ridiculous. We ⁷_____ (still work) for them if you ⁸_____ (not mess up) that presentation.

EMMA   How can you say that? If you ⁹_____ (be) as experienced as I am in dealing with clients you ¹⁰_____ (notice) from their reaction that they absolutely loved it.

MR STACKFORD   Right, that's it! I've had enough of you two arguing. You're both sacked! If you ¹¹_____ (be) out of the building in half an hour, I ¹²_____ (call) security.

b Rewrite the sentences using the word in **bold**.

1 Had we been aware of the situation, we would have changed our plans. **IF**
   We would have changed our plans if we had been aware of the situation.

2 I didn't save any money. Now I'm broke. **IF**

3 You can borrow my laptop provided you look after it. **CONDITION**

4 I'm going to go to the party. It doesn't matter if I'm invited or not. **WHETHER**

5 What would you have done if you hadn't found your passport? **SUPPOSING**

6 Your exam will be fine as long as you do enough revision. **PROVIDING**

7 I'm in favour of contact sports providing nobody gets seriously injured. **LONG**

8 I would never wear fur, even in very cold weather. **IF**

9 So long as you're back by midnight, you can go out tonight. **PROVIDED**

Activation

Write a paragraph on one of the following topics:

• Supposing the government decided to cut off all electricity supplies for one day, how would your life be affected? Give examples.

• If people in the past had been more careful with our planet's resources, the environment would be in a better state than it is today. Do you agree? Explain, giving one clear example.

• If everybody earned the same amount of money, do you think the world would be a happier place today?

a Right (✓) or wrong (✗)? Correct the mistakes in the highlighted phrases.

1 These jeans are too tight. I should have tried them on before buying them. ✓

2 Emma's still very upset about her divorce, so you hadn't better ask her about it.

3 The invitation said we didn't need to wear formal clothes, so we wore jeans.

4 Employees don't have to download any software as it's against company rules.

5 We're supposed to finish early on Fridays, but always end up staying late.

6 If you want to be sure of passing your exam, you really ought study more.

7 The boss is in a bad mood today so you'd better watch out.

8 You don't need to show your passport for domestic travel within the UK.

9 We ought to think of that solution earlier. It's too late now.

b Circle the correct alternative in each pair. Tick (✓) if both are possible.

BECKY Hi, I'm Becky. I'm Amanda's new personal assistant.

MATT Well, you ¹(can't)/ needn't sit on that chair because it's mine. The assistants sit over there.

BECKY I'm so sorry.

MATT You ² needn't / don't have to apologize. And incidentally, never apologize to the boss. Amanda says we ³ mustn't / aren't allowed to ever say sorry, just do the job and do it well. Have you met her yet, by the way?

BECKY Only briefly, at my interview.

MATT Well, you ⁴ had to / had better get ready for a shock. By the end of today you'll be wondering if you ⁵ should / must have accepted this job.

BECKY What do you mean?

MATT Let's just say that you ⁶ can't / don't have to relax when she's around. Oh, and you ⁷ must / should have her carrot juice ready by 11 a.m. and it's already three minutes past. You ⁸ should / had better hurry up!

c Look at the pairs you have ticked. Is there any difference in meaning?

Imagine you are the mayor of your town. Write ten rules for citizens to follow which you think would improve life there. Use the grammar from **a** and **b** above.
Example:
*Cyclists are **not allowed** to ride on the pavement, and will be fined on the spot if caught doing so.*

Consolidation

● Rewrite the second sentence using the word in **bold**.

1 The situation sounds worse than had been expected.

   THOUGH   It sounds *as though the situation is worse* than had been expected.

2 This herb has a similar smell to garlic, but it isn't.

   LIKE   This herb _____, but it isn't.

3 I could see that she had probably been crying.

   IF   She looked _____ been crying.

4 Your manager has been telling me good things about you.

   HEARING   I've _____ from your manager.

5 You can really taste the almonds in this ice cream.

   TASTES   This _____ almonds.

6 The neighbour says that no one left the house after nine p.m. that night.

   SEE   The neighbour says she didn't _____ after nine p.m.

7 A viola makes a noise similar to a violin, but its range is lower.

   SOUNDS   A viola _____, but its range is lower.

8 It seems as though the city hasn't changed much since I left.

   HAVE   The city doesn't seem _____ since I left.

9 The bomb went off at exactly eight o'clock.

   HEARD   I _____ at exactly eight o'clock.

10 Adam seems not to have slept very well judging by the amount he's yawning.

   LOOKS   Adam _____ judging by the amount he's yawning.

11 She seemed to be delighted with the outcome of the meeting.

   THOUGH   It seemed _____ with the outcome of the meeting.

12 According to neighbours, the couple were arguing for more than an hour.

   HEARD   Neighbours _____ for more than an hour.

Activation

ⓐ Read the following poem.

Sitting in my kitchen

I can	see	sunbeams dancing on the curtains.
The birds outside	sound	as if they're having a serious conference today.
The air	smells	of the coffee I've just made.
The cup	feels	warm in my hand,
And the coffee	tastes	deliciously sweet.

ⓑ Now write your own poem about any place you like or dislike. Write a title and five lines, one for each of the senses, paying particular attention to the grammar in the exercise above. Use this frame to help you:

(your title)		
I can	see	
	sound(s)	
	smell(s)	
	feel(s)	
	taste(s)	

170

Consolidation

a Right (✓) or wrong (✗)? Correct the mistakes in the highlighted phrases.

1 I expect to have finished the report by Friday afternoon. ✓

2 It's no use sitting around talking about it. We need actions, not words.

3 Your remarks offended me. I will not put up with speaking to like that.

4 We would love to be able to stay longer in Rome, but it just wasn't possible.

5 She's very narrow-minded so it's difficult for her understanding your point of view.

6 I wasn't aware of having been introduced to her before.

7 There's no point to invite George because he never goes to parties.

8 Having studied abroad will certainly be an advantage when you come to apply for a job.

9 What's that noise? Someone seems to try to open the door.

10 We enjoyed the holiday, but we would rather have stayed at home.

b Complete the second sentence with a gerund or infinitive so that it means the same as the first.

1 We can't get a taxi because we don't have enough cash.

We don't have enough cash _to get_ a taxi.

2 It won't do you any good to feel guilty about what happened.

It's no good _____ guilty about what happened.

3 He was fed up with his girlfriend telling him what to wear.

He was fed up with _____ what to wear by his girlfriend.

4 It would have been better if the director had informed me personally.

I would rather _____ by the director in person.

5 He's unsure about what he should do after he graduates.

He's unsure about what _____ after he graduates.

6 It is thought that the police are searching the whole area.

The police are thought _____ the whole area.

7 She was the first female prime minister.

She was the first woman _____ elected prime minister.

8 I'm concerned that I haven't been contacted yet.

I'm concerned about _____ yet.

Activation

c Match **1–8** with **a–h** to make questions, and then discuss with a partner.

1 How easy is it for you	**a** to have achieved by the end of your life?
2 Do you think there is any point in	**b** have spent your last holiday differently?
3 What do you hope	**c** telling a white lie is ever justifiable?
4 Do you think	**d** dedicating their whole life to their career but neglecting their family?
5 What would it have been like	**e** regretting something after you've done it?
6 Do you mind	**f** to have lived 100 years ago?
7 Would you rather	**g** being asked about your age?
8 Would you admire someone for	**h** to tell people how you really feel?

a Right (✓) or wrong (✗)? Correct the mistakes in the highlighted phrases.

KEITH So, what [1] are you and Wendy doing this weekend? ✓

GAVIN Well, the school holidays [2] start on Friday and [3] we will go to the seaside with the kids. We can't stay away for long, though. Wendy's [4] due go into hospital on Monday.

KEITH Really? [5] Is she having an operation?

GAVIN Yes, but it's nothing too serious. It's only her wrist. [6] She'll be home again in the evening. What [7] do you and Jennifer do this weekend?

KEITH Sadly, Jennifer is working all weekend. Her company [8] is about to be taken over by a big multinational so everyone is worried [9] they're losing their jobs. So it looks like [10] I'll be spending the weekend on my own. I've decided that [11] I'm painting the outside of the house if the weather stays fine.

GAVIN That doesn't sound like much fun! Have a good weekend.

b Read the news report and underline six different structures used to express the future.

One of the most talked-about matches in the history of tennis is due to take place this afternoon in New York. Current world number one Arturo Villa is to face his long-term rival Bill Everard in what is going to be a long and tough struggle for the top spot, according to commentators. Their last match was a narrow defeat for Everard. 'I have worked so hard to come this far, and this time I'm 100% sure I'm about to become the most highly-ranked player in the world,' he commented in a pre-match press conference. When asked about his predictions for the match, Villa replied: 'I've never been on better form and I'm going to show him who's the boss, just like last time.' The match begins at five p.m. local time.

Use the information below to write another news report in one paragraph about a visit from the President. Use some of the structures from **a** and **b**.

9 a.m.	Arrival of President and First Lady in Lynnburg by helicopter, greeted by mayor.
10 a.m.	Press conference at City Hall; First Lady time to meet the public.
11.30 a.m.	Visit to new city hospital; spend time with patients.
1 p.m.	Formal lunch at City Hall with local officials and community leaders.
2 p.m.	President: meeting with business leaders at city hall. First Lady: speech at local high school, followed by theatrical performance by students.
3.30 p.m.	Tour of newly redesigned city gardens for President and First Lady.
5 p.m.	End of visit; departure from Lynnburg by helicopter.

'The President and his wife **are due to** arrive in town by helicopter at nine a.m. and **are to be** greeted by the mayor. At ten o'clock, the President **will be giving** a press conference at City Hall, while the First Lady...'

New English File Teacher's Book Advanced
Photocopiable © Oxford University Press 2010

a Read the story. What differences in style do you notice between the two paragraphs? Talk to a partner and explain why.

Ever since she had been a small girl, Nicky had wanted to get to know her father, but she had never been able to. Whenever Nicky used to ask about him, her mother would shake her head and look angry. Every year on her birthday Nicky used to hope that he would come to visit, but he never did. Nicky's mother told her he was always busy working abroad, but Nicky didn't believe he was. She was constantly talking about him, even though her mother begged her not to. Although Nicky had never met her father, she always felt that one day she would. Sometimes she used to close her eyes and pray that he would contact her. But when he finally phoned on her 21st birthday and asked her if she wanted to see him, Nicky wasn't sure if she did.

Nicky's father gave her his phone number and he said she could contact him whenever she wanted to contact him. Nicky said goodbye, and then she hung up. At first, she was angry that he had got in touch and she wished that he hadn't got in touch. But a few weeks later, she called him and she arranged to see him because she felt they needed to talk. She got on well with him, although she hadn't expected to get on well with him. Nicky decided that she wanted them to meet regularly, and her father promised that they would meet regularly. Five years later, when Nicky got married, no one imagined that her father would be leading her up the aisle, but he was leading her up the aisle.

---

b Rewrite the second paragraph leaving out repeated words where possible, and substituting where necessary. When you have finished, swap paragraphs with a partner. Have you left out the same words?

c Make substitutions in the following sentences using *so* or *not*.

1 **A** Will classes start at the normal time next week?

   B I presume ~~they will start at the normal time~~ **so**. Otherwise the director would have mentioned it.

2 **A** Have you got any batteries?

   B I'm afraid that we haven't got any batteries. We sold the last packet yesterday.

3 **A** Are you going to go skiing at Easter?

   B I guess I'll go skiing, though I'm not very keen on it.

4 **A** Do you reckon they'll accept the contract as it is?

   B I suspect that they won't accept it. They'll ask us to change some sections.

5 **A** Do you think Chris and Angie will come tomorrow?

   B I don't imagine that they will come. They're very busy at the moment.

6 **A** John won't be interested in taking part, will he?

   B I suppose that he won't be interested in taking part. He has other plans for the summer.

Think about the following topics and then discuss them with a partner.

• If you strongly disagree with someone's opinion, is it always a good idea to say so?

• Do you know anyone who has a talent, but doesn't make good use of it?

• Is there anything you'd love to be able to do, but can't?

• Can you remember a time when you gave in to temptation, even when you promised yourself you wouldn't?

• When was the last time you accepted an invitation even though you secretly didn't want to?

Consolidation

a Rewrite these sentences starting with *The person, The place, The first / last time,* or *The reason.* Keep the emphasis on the **bold** phrase.

1 I've always wanted to visit **Istanbul** more than anywhere else.

   The place I've always most wanted to visit is Istanbul.

2 He married her **for her money**.

3 She loves **her niece** more than anyone else in the world.

4 I saw her for the last time in **October**.

5 It's **my sister** who really understands how I feel.

6 We retired early **in order to have time to enjoy life**.

7 I relax most in **the garden**.

8 I met David for the first time **just after the military coup**.

b Complete the second sentence so that it emphasizes the **bold** part.

1 **His unhealthy diet** really worries me.

   What *really worries me is his unhealthy diet.*

2 My son is crazy about **skateboarding**.

   What _____.

3 They just want **to lie on a beach and relax**.

   All _____.

4 I'm desperate for **a nice cup of tea**.

   What _____.

5 The restaurant was made special by **the atmosphere** rather than the food.

   It _____.

6 I don't want **to be late for work tomorrow**.

   What _____.

7 She only asked for **a glass of water**.

   All _____.

8 **Alec** was a professional footballer when he was young, not Darren.

   It _____.

Activation

● Guess this information about your partner and complete the sentences. Then discuss your predictions together.

• The reason you're learning English is _____.

• What you most like about your English class is _____.

• The thing that bothers you most in the cinema, theatre, or at a concert is _____.

• The person you spend most time with is _____.

• What really annoys you on trains, planes, or buses is when people _____.

• When you're on holiday, all you want to do is _____.

New English File Teacher's Book Advanced
Photocopiable © Oxford University Press 2010

Consolidation

● Right (✓) or wrong (✗)? Correct the mistakes in the highlighted phrases.

1 There's a small garden at the back of the house . ✓
2 She's always sticking her nose into other peoples' business .
3 We're going to be at Paula and James' house for dinner tonight.
4 Does anyone have a bottles opener ? It's time to open the wine.
5 Nick is my cousin Jane who works for the city council's flatmate .
6 Mrs Thwaite has always been a very dear friend of my aunt's .
7 Have you got a coat hanger ? This jacket creases easily.
8 This painting is regarded as her career's high point .
9 Opticians usually sell accessories like glasses cases and cleaning products.
10 Please put the sugar back in the kitchen's cupboard after use.
11 Be careful when you wash the glasses of wine , as they're very fragile.
12 I'm just going round to the newsagent's . Do you want anything?
13 To play this game, we need to form a circle in the room's middle .
14 His partner is a physics teacher at one of the local high schools.

Activation

● Try to think of at least two nouns that collocate to make compound nouns with the **bold** words.

traffic				
street	} **lights**			} **board**
	} **cake**			} **book**
	} **cup**			} **key**
	} **knife**			} **water**
	} **player**			} **card**
	} **machine**			} **frame**
	} **centre**			

175

● Add <u>one</u> word in the right place to make the sentences correct.

1 They had so **many** pets that they couldn't count them all.

2 She was tired that she fell asleep at her desk after lunch.

3 There was so snow outside that we couldn't go to school.

4 I've never seen so vases. You must have at least a hundred of them!

5 She gave her ex-boyfriend such nasty look that he didn't even dare say hello.

6 Valuable items as watches and cameras should be left at reception.

7 It was such amazing performance that the crowd were screaming for more.

8 She speaks quickly that I never understand a word she's saying.

9 There's such lot of rubbish on TV these days that I never bother to watch it.

10 He approaches his job with great determination that he always succeeds.

11 He said hurtful things to her that night that she never called him again.

12 Thick was the fog all around us that we had absolutely no idea where we were.

● Match **1–8** with **a–h** to make questions. Then discuss the questions with a partner.

1 Have you ever felt so ☐
2 Do you think it's fair that there's such ☐
3 Why do so ☐
4 Why has the Internet become so ☐
5 Why do the media pay so ☐
6 Is it right that some sportspeople receive such ☐
7 Do people such ☐
8 Do you agree that modern life is so ☐

a massive salaries in comparison to other hard-working people?

b popular in the short time since it was invented?

c stressful that most people find it difficult to relax?

d a big difference in TV coverage between men's sport and women's sport?

e as politicians and TV stars make good role models for young people?

f many people choose their partner by how they look?

g much attention to the private lives of celebrities?

h worried or excited about something that you couldn't sleep?

Consolidation

● Complete the second sentence using the word in **bold**.

1 I used to be much stronger than I am now.

 HALF   I'm not _half as strong as_ I used to be.

2 When people have money, they spend a lot of time worrying about it.

 MORE   The _____ they spend worrying about it.

3 Only one girl in the class is taller than her.

 NEARLY   She's _____ in the class.

4 As we approached the house, the noise became increasingly loud.

 AND   The noise became _____ as we approached the house.

5 This year we had slightly less snow than last year.

 LITTLE   Last year we had _____ snow than this year.

6 Our holiday was cheaper than we had expected.

 AS   Our holiday was not _____ we had expected.

7 Taking regular exercise is by far the best way to lose weight.

 MUCH   Taking regular exercise _____ way to lose weight.

8 Far fewer students failed the exam than had been expected.

 PASSED   _____ the exam than had been expected.

9 If you have a big car you have to pay higher road tax.

 BIGGER   The _____ you have to pay.

10 It's getting harder and harder to find job security nowadays.

 DIFFICULT It's getting _____ to find job security nowadays.

11 The average house in this area is worth more than mine.

 MUCH   My house isn't worth _____ the average house in this area.

12 Our anger grew as we waited.

 LONGER   The _____ we became.

Activation

● Write a short paragraph comparing the lifestyles of people in your country nowadays and when your grandparents were young. Use the grammar from the exercise above. You could write about some of the following topics:

• education and jobs
• free time
• transport
• entertainment
• family life
• life expectancy and health

'When my grandparents were young, most people had a **much harder** life than they do now, because they didn't have **nearly as many** technological devices **as** our generation, for instance cars and washing machines which make life **a lot easier**. However, it's not necessarily true that **the more** gadgets people have, **the happier** they become. For example…'

1 A Have I got the job?

A job interview roleplay

SS take the roles of interviewers or applicants in a series of quick job interviews. Copy one sheet per 12 SS. Cut off the candidate's role card and make five more copies of this. Then cut up all the cards.

| LANGUAGE | Question formation, Work vocabulary |

- Divide the class in half. One group will be interviewers and the others candidates. If you have an uneven number, double up on one of the interviewers. With a very large class you may want to get interviewers to work in pairs, interviewing individual candidates together.

- Give each interviewer (or pair of interviewers), and each candidate, a role card. Give them five minutes to prepare their questions and answers. Interviewers should think of questions to elicit whether candidates fit the profile of the ideal candidate.

- Arrange the class so that the interviewers for the different jobs aren't sitting too close together. They should have an empty chair opposite or next to them for the candidates.

- Send one candidate to each interviewer or pair of interviewers, and tell them to start. Remind interviewers to take notes to help them to remember the strengths / weaknesses of each candidate. After exactly four minutes, stop the interviews and get the candidates to move on for another interview. Continue until each candidate has been interviewed for all the jobs, or until you run out of time.

- Give the interviewers time to decide who they thought was the best candidate, and get the candidates to discuss which job they think they would prefer.

- Finally, get the interviewers to say who they would like to offer the job to. The chosen candidate must say if he / she will accept the job or not. If a candidate is offered more than one job, he / she must choose between them, and the interviewer should select another candidate for the job.

 1 B The family

A pairwork photo description and discussion

SS describe and compare photos, and then discuss family-related issues. Copy one sheet per pair and cut into **A** and **B**.

| LANGUAGE | Describing photos, agreeing and disagreeing |

- Put SS in pairs, ideally facing each other, and give out the sheets. Focus on instruction **a**. Tell SS when they describe their photo they should not just comment on what they can see, but say what they think of the photo, and what the image communicates.

- Set a time limit (e.g. two minutes) for **A** to describe his / her photo. Then give **B** two minutes to describe his / hers, and then tell them to discuss what the photos have in common and how they are different.

- Finally, focus on rubric **b**, and set a time limit.

Extra support Get SS to look at the phrases for agreeing, half-agreeing and disagreeing on *p.11* in the Student's Book and encourage them to use these phrases.

 1 C Language quotes

A pairwork information gap activity

SS complete quotes about language and then discuss them. Copy one sheet per pair and cut into **A** and **B**.

| LANGUAGE | Explaining what something means, giving opinions. |

- Put SS in pairs, ideally facing each other, and give out the sheets. Focus on **a**, and give SS time to read the quotes and complete the gapped ones. Monitor and help SS with vocabulary where necessary.

  Extra support Get each **A** to work with another **A** and each **B** with another **B** to complete the quotes. Then partner each **A** with a **B**.

- Focus on **b**, and give SS time to discuss the quote. **A** may want to write down what the original continuation was.

- Focus on **c**, and get SS to continue alternately telling each other how they had completed the quote, and discussing it.

- Finally, get feedback to find out if there were any quotes that SS had completed in a similar way to the original, and also to see which quote they liked best.

2 A Childhood questionnaire

A pairwork questionnaire

SS choose six questions from a questionnaire about childhood to ask each other. Copy one sheet per student.

| LANGUAGE | narrative tenses, *used to / would* + infinitive |

- Put SS in pairs and give out the questionnaires. Focus on **a**, and give SS time to read the questions and choose six. Elicit the meaning of *chores* in 7 (small jobs in the house like washing up) and *look up to* in 8 (admire or respect sb).

- Then get SS to ask and answer questions alternately. **B** should turn his / her sheet face down when **A** asks the first question. Highlight that most of the questions have one or two follow-up questions, and SS should ask the first one, wait for their partner to answer it, and then ask the follow-up questions.

- Monitor, correcting particularly any mistakes in the use of tenses, and helping with vocabulary. Feedback from SS.

 2 B Time: Proverbs and sayings

Proverbs for SS to discuss

SS read ten proverbs related to time, and discuss what they mean. Copy one sheet per student.

| LANGUAGE | Paraphrasing meaning |

- Put SS in pairs and give out the sheets. Focus on the instructions, and on the first proverb. Elicit from the class what it means (*that sb who takes the earliest opportunity to do sth will gain an advantage over others*). Then ask SS if they have a similar proverb in their L1, and how it compares to the English proverb.

- Get SS to continue in pairs, helping them with any vocabulary that is causing problems.

- Get feedback for each proverb. Then ask SS which one they think is the most useful advice.

Meaning of the proverbs

2 If you act quickly when something goes wrong, it will save time later, because the problem will get worse if you leave it.

3 Make good use of an opportunity while it lasts.

4 People will naturally take advantage of the absence of someone in authority to do what they like.

5 It isn't worth making a fuss about a misfortune that has happened and can't be changed or reversed.

6 You can't make people change their ways when they are past a certain age.

7 Don't treat sth that hasn't happened yet as a certainty.

8 When you are impatient for sth to happen, it seems to take longer.

9 We'll deal with the problem when and if it arises, rather than worry about it beforehand.

10 Make use of an opportunity immediately as soon as it occurs (in case it later disappears).

Extra idea Ask SS to write a short story (100–120 words) illustrating one of the proverbs. Then read the stories to the class and ask them which proverb it illustrates.

2 C Reconciliation?

A roleplay activity

A free-speaking activity to promote fluency in which SS role play a conversation between a couple who have split up, but are considering getting back together again. Copy one sheet per pair and cut into **A** and **B**.

LANGUAGE	Arguing and persuading

- Put SS in pairs, ideally facing each other, and give out the sheets. Try to pair SS with someone of the opposite sex. If you have an uneven gender split, get women to play men or vice versa. **Make sure SS can't see each other's sheets.** If you have odd numbers, take part in the roleplay yourself, or ask the extra student to act as 'counsellor' for one pair, to mediate and advise after they have discussed each point.

- Give SS time to read their instructions. SS should think about their role and what they are going to say. Tell them to decide on their priorities, and if there is anything they are not prepared to give way on.

- When SS are ready, get them to sit face to face, and tell them to imagine that they have just arrived at a café. They are going to discuss the four areas on the sheet (remind them of the difference between *discuss* and *argue*.) Set a time limit (but be flexible depending how the conversations are going), and highlight the instruction **Try to keep calm and don't lose your temper**.
  Emphasize that SS should go through the areas one by one, first giving their own points of view, and then trying to reach agreement. Encourage SS to discuss all the points.

- Finally, get feedback from some pairs and if they have reached any kind of agreement or reconciliation.

3 A Sound or noise?

A pairwork survey activity

SS mark different sounds / noises according to how they feel about them, and compare with a partner. Copy one sheet per student.

LANGUAGE	Sounds and the human voice

- Put SS in pairs and give out the sheets. Focus on **a**, and give SS time to tick or cross the sounds. Use the drawing to explain what *crickets* are in the third sound from the bottom (insect noise on a hot summer night).

- Now set a time limit, e.g. ten minutes, for SS to compare and explain their answers.

- Get feedback on which sounds SS loved / hated.

3 B Who wrote it? A man or a woman?

A reading and discussion activity

SS read extracts from novels, all of which describe women, and decide whether they think they were written by a man or by a woman, and why. Copy one sheet per student.

LANGUAGE	Giving reasons

- Put SS in pairs and give out the sheets. Focus on **a**, and tell SS to read extracts and mark them **M** for man or **W** for woman. They could underline specific parts which made them think they were written by a man or a woman.

- Focus on **b**, and give SS time to compare and discuss.

- Now check answers. For each extract, first find out what most SS think and why, and then tell them whether it was written by a man or a woman. Then write the name of the book and author on the board. Find out if SS have read any of the books.

1 M From *Promise me*, by Harlan Coben
2 W From *The Palace of Strange Girls*, by Sallie Day
3 M From *Beware of Pity*, by Stefan Zweig
4 W From *Spellbound*, by Jane Green
5 W From *Sex in the City*, by Candace Bushnell
6 M From *In the Company of Cheerful Ladies*, by Alexander McCall Smith
7 W From *Bridget Jones' Diary*, by Helen Fielding
8 M From *The Girl with the Dragon Tattoo*, by Stieg Larsson

3 C Money questionnaire

A pairwork questionnaire

SS interview each other with a questionnaire to find out about their attitude to money. Copy one sheet per student.

LANGUAGE	Money vocabulary: *savings, stock market*, etc.

- Put SS in pairs and give out the questionnaires.

- Focus on the instructions. Give SS time to read the questions and to choose **two** from each section to ask their partner.

- Tell **B** to put his / her questionnaire face down. **A** interviews **B**, then swaps roles.

- Get feedback from SS to find out which questions they found most interesting.

4 A Historical films quiz

A group quiz

SS revise history and warfare vocabulary through a film quiz. Copy one sheet per group of three or four.

LANGUAGE	History and warfare vocabulary

- Put SS in groups of three or four, and give each group a quiz sheet face down. Set a time limit, and tell SS to answer as many questions as possible.

- Tell SS to turn over the sheet and start. When the time is up, say 'Stop' and check answers. The group with the most right answers is the winner.

1 **a** Roman times   **b** Before, during, and after the Russian Revolution   **c** The Second World War   **d** The American Civil War   **e** The Middle Ages
2 **a** Alexander the **Great**   **b** Robin Hood: **Prince** of Thieves   **c** Full **Metal** Jacket   **d** The Boy in the **Striped** Pyjamas   **e** **Saving** Private Ryan
3 **a** Titanic   **b** Life of Brian   **c** The Diary of Anne Frank   **d** Cyrano de Bergerac   **e** Chariots of Fire   **f** Lawrence of Arabia   **g** Gandhi   **h** Frost/Nixon   **i** Dances with Wolves   **j** El Cid
4 **a** Che Guevara   **b** Wolfgang Amadeus Mozart   **c** Adolf Hitler   **d** Idi Amin   **e** John Fitzgerald Kennedy
5 **a** Virginia Woolf   **b** J.M. Barrie   **c** Isak Dinesen   **d** Mary Shelley   **e** C.S. Lewis
6 **a** Cate Blanchett   **b** Elizabeth Taylor   **c** Emily Blunt   **d** Judi Dench   **e** Kirsten Dunst

4 B Do you think you could possibly…?

A mingle activity

A free-speaking activity to practise the language of persuasion and the techniques SS read about in the lesson. Copy and cut up one sheet per 16 SS.

LANGUAGE	Language of requests and persuading, and polite intonation

- Tell SS they are going to be given a situation in which they need to find sb to do sth for them. They must talk to as many SS as possible, and try to find at least two people who will do what they need. Also, they must agree to help two other SS, but only if another student convinces them.
- Give out the cards. Let SS swap cards if the request is more suited to a male / female. Give SS time to read and memorize their request, and to think of some persuasive reasons. Elicit different ways of making polite requests, e.g. *Could you…?*, *Do you think you could possibly…?*, *Would you mind…?*, etc. Remind them to use polite intonation. You could also elicit the two tips for persuading they read about in 4B, i.e. to always give a reason, and that asking for a little can help.
- Set a time limit and then get SS to stand up and mingle.
- When the time is up, find out how many SS managed to convince two people to help them.

4 C Case studies

A pairwork evaluating activity

SS read some case studies about people with obsessions and rate them 1–5 according to their seriousness. They then compare their scores with a partner. Copy one sheet per student.

LANGUAGE	Language related to obsession, e.g. *obsessed by, can't cope with, incessantly*, etc.

- Give out the sheets and focus on **a**. Tell SS that all these are based on real cases, although the names have been changed. Set a time limit for SS to read the case studies and mark them from 1–5.
- When time is up, put SS in pairs, and set another time limit for SS to compare their scores and explain why they gave them.
- Get feedback by finding out which cases SS found most / least serious and why.

5 A Mini debates

A roleplay activity

SS debate proposed new laws each from the perspective of a different role. Copy and cut up one sheet per three SS.

LANGUAGE	Verbs + gerund or infinitive (with or without *to*)

- Put SS into groups of three. If you have uneven numbers, have a group or groups of four, and give one of the role cards to two SS. Explain that SS are going to debate a proposed new law for their area. They will each have a role, and must prepare arguments according to the role card.
- Give out the role cards and allow SS a few minutes to prepare their arguments. When SS are ready, set a time limit for the debates. They should speak in the order of the numbers on their role cards, first explaining who they are, and at the end have a group discussion responding to the other people's arguments.

  Extra support Write the phrases from the Student's Book for emphasizing that sth is your own opinion on *p.13* and for agreeing and disagreeing on *p.11* to help SS.

- When the time is up, stop the debates. Tell SS to now imagine that they had been watching the debates as themselves (not as their roles) and to say how they would have voted and why.
- If time, give each group another of the proposals to debate.

5 B Spot the difference

A pairwork information gap activity

SS describe their pictures to each other to find 11 differences. Copy one sheet per pair and cut into **A** and **B**.

LANGUAGE	Place and movement: *towards, out of, off…*

- Revise / pre-teach any words for things in the painting that you think SS may not know, e.g. *bucket, tavern, market stall*, etc.
- Put SS in pairs, ideally facing each other, and give out the sheets. **Make sure SS can't see each other's sheets.**
- Focus on the instructions and explain that they both have the same picture, but it has been changed so that there are 11 differences. Encourage SS to try to be as accurate as possible when they are describing place and movement.
- Tell SS to fold their sheet in half vertically and then open it out again so they have the left and right side clearly defined or draw a line dividing the page in half.
- Get **A** to start by describing what is happening on the left of the picture, e.g. *there's an open window on the 1st floor of the house on the left. A woman is at this window throwing out some water from a bucket down into the street.* **B** should listen, and ask questions if necessary, to see if there are any differences. Then **B** describes what is happening on the right-hand side.
- When SS have described the whole picture and found the differences they can finally show each other the pictures to make sure they have identified the differences correctly.
- Check the differences orally with the class, correcting any mistakes with prepositions / adverbs of place and movement.

Differences clockwise from left to right:
2 **Picture A:** A man is under the window at the exact moment the woman is throwing out the water.
  Picture B: There is no one under the window.
3 **Picture A:** There is an open window on the second floor of the house, above the woman with the bucket.
  Picture B: A woman is looking out of the window on the second floor.

4 **Picture A:** Four children are jumping over each other. **Picture B:** The children are jumping over a rope (i.e. skipping).

5 **Picture A:** There's a market with four stalls. At the stall on the right the stallholder has taken a bottle off the shelf and is showing it to a customer. **Picture B:** The stallholder is putting down / picking up a bottle.

6 **Picture A:** There is a tavern in the square. Three men are staggering towards it. **Picture B:** The men are staggering away from the tavern.

7 **Picture A:** An elegant lady is riding past the tavern, towards the left, i.e. coming into the square. **Picture B:** The lady is riding towards the right of the picture, i.e. going out of the square.

8 **Picture A:** Two men are standing next to a cart, lifting a barrel of beer. **Picture B:** One man is standing on the cart.

9 **Picture A:** There's a river on the right of the picture. A man is rowing a boat across. **Picture B:** The man is rowing a boat along the river, parallel to the bank.

10 **Picture A:** Some of the houses have shops on the ground floor. On the right-hand side, a boy is running into the baker's shop. **Picture B:** The boy is not running but is standing outside the baker's.

11 **Picture A:** Three dogs are chasing each other round a tree. **Picture B:** One of the dogs is running away.

5 C Medical vocabulary definitions game

A pairwork activity

SS revise and extend their knowledge of medical vocabulary by describing medical-related words to each other and teaching each other new words. Copy one sheet per pair and cut into **A** and **B**.

> LANGUAGE   Medical vocabulary: *crutches, hiccups, scar…*

- Put SS in pairs **A** and **B** and give out the sheets. Explain that SS have half the things in their picture labelled, and the other half not (their partner will have these labelled). Tell them to make sure they can pronounce all their words.

- **B** now starts by asking **A**, e.g. *What do you call the things that you use to help you walk when you've got a broken leg?* **A** should identify the image that **B** is describing and then tell him / her what the word is, giving both the spelling and pronunciation. **B** then writes the word down. They then swap roles.

- SS continue until they have labelled all their pictures. They can then compare their sheets to make sure they have spelled the words correctly. Check answers.

6 A Travel roleplays

A pairwork roleplay

SS roleplay being a dissatisfied tourist with a complaint, and a travel agency representative responding to a client's complaints. Copy one sheet per pair and cut into **A** and **B**.

> LANGUAGE   Making complaints, travel and tourism vocabulary

- Put SS in pairs and give out the sheets. Focus on Roleplay 1 and give SS time to read their instructions and make some notes about what they are going to say.

Extra support You could write the following phrases on the board to help SS.
Making complaints *I'm very unhappy about / dissatisfied with…   I think this is unacceptable / outrageous…*
Responding to complaints *I see what you mean / I understand what you're saying / I can see why you feel like this but…   I'll do my best to…*

- Set a time limit for SS to have the first roleplay. Monitor and make a note of any problems to deal with later.

- When time is up, stop the roleplay and find out what agreement, if any, was reached. Monitor and feedback to class.

- Now repeat the process for Roleplay 2.

6 B Four fables

A group reading and retelling activity

SS in groups read and retell four fables, and decide what the moral of each story is. Copy and cut up one sheet per four SS.

> LANGUAGE   narrative tenses or dramatic present

- Put SS into groups of four. Give each student a different fable. Highlight that they have all been taken from *Aesop's Fables*. Elicit / teach the meaning of *fable* (a traditional short story that teaches a moral lesson, especially one with animals as characters).

- Tell SS that they are each going to read and retell a fable to the other members of the group. After each person has told his / her fable, the group should decide what the moral of the story is. Tell them that the morals are all related to aspects of friendship.

Extra support Suggest that SS begin their retelling by saying 'My fable is called….' They can then explain what the animals are, in case the other group members don't know the words.
Alternatively, you could pre-teach / elicit the names of all the animals that occur in the fables before SS start: *hare, bull, goat, calf, bat, beasts* (= old-fashioned word for wild animals), *bat, fox, stork, lion,* and *mouse.*

- Give SS a few minutes to read their fables. Tell them that they can retell their stories either using narrative tenses (as they are written), or using the present tense, as if they were describing the plot of a book or film.

- Tell SS with card **1** to start. They should place their card face down and try not to refer to it at all, but retell the fable from memory. When they have finished, the group decides on the moral of the story. Then SS with card **2** tell their fable, etc.

- When all SS have told their fables and decided on the morals, check answers, and find out which one the class thinks is best.

6 C Celebrity immigrants

A group game

SS read and retell short biographical details about famous immigrants for other SS to identify. Copy one sheet per group of four and cut into cards.

> LANGUAGE   Biographies, reduced relative clauses

- Put SS in groups of four and give them a set of cards face down. Tell SS they are going tell each other about famous people who emigrated to the USA.

- When you say 'Start', one student takes a card, and reads aloud the information on his / her card. The group should then try to agree who the person is, and write down the number of the card and the name of the person. Then another student picks a card.

- When the groups have finished, check answers. The group who identified the highest number of people is the winner.

> 1 Harry Houdini   2 Antonio Banderas
> 3 Arnold Schwarzenegger   4 Anna Kournikova
> 5 Ang Lee   6 Joseph Pulitzer   7 Salma Hayek
> 8 Levi Strauss   9 Cary Grant   10 Max Factor
> 11 Gloria Stefan   12 Isaac Asimov

Non-cut alternative Make one copy per pair. Give out the sheets and set a time limit for SS to read about the 12 people and try to name them.

7 A Two recipes

A pairwork activity

SS use a picture recipe to explain to each other how to make perfect scrambled eggs and perfect roast potatoes. Copy one sheet per pair, and cut into **A** and **B**.

LANGUAGE	Preparing food and cooking vocabulary

- Put SS in pairs and give out the sheets.
- Focus on **a** and give SS time to look at their recipe. At this point they can ask you for any words they have forgotten, or check in Vocabulary Bank *Preparing food*.
- Focus on **b**. Tell **A** that he / she is going to explain his / her recipe to **B**, who will take notes. Tell **A** to start, and set a time limit for explaining the recipe.
- When **A** has finished, **B** explains his / her recipe.
- When both SS have finished, get them to compare their notes with the pictures to check that they understood how to make each dish.

7 B Sports quiz

A group quiz

Quiz to revise and extend the vocabulary of sport. Copy one sheet per group of three or four.

LANGUAGE	Sport vocabulary

- Put SS in groups of three or four and give out the quiz sheets. Set a time limit. Check answers, and get SS to make a note of any vocabulary they didn't know. Where there is more than one answer, try to elicit as many items as possible.

> 1 **a** Switzerland, tennis   **b** Romania, gymnastics
> **c** USA, swimming   **d** Ukraine, pole vault
> **e** Mexico, football
> 2 **a** football, rugby, hockey, ice hockey   **b** rugby
> **c** tennis, football   **d** tennis, table tennis, squash, badminton, volleyball   **e** football, basketball, hockey
> **f** basketball
> 3 **a** football (when a player hits the ball with his / her head)   **b** tennis, badminton, squash, etc. (when a player returns the ball softly so that it drops after going over the net)   **c** golf (a score for a particular hole which is one less than par, i.e. the standard score for that hole)   **d** yoga (a sitting position with crossed legs)   **e** gymnastics (a movement where sb turns over completely with their feet over their head, on the ground or in the air)
> **f** basketball (when a player jumps up high and puts the ball into the basket with great force)
> 4 **a** running, motor racing (a race track)   **b** boxing, wrestling   **c** tennis, squash, badminton, basketball, handball, volleyball   **d** ice skating   **e** skiing

> 5 **a** horse riding (the seat you put on a horse)
> **b** badminton (feathered object you hit)   **c** hockey (protective pieces of thick material players wear inside their socks or to cover their legs)   **d** snooker (stick with which you hit the ball)
> **e** swimming (plastic glasses swimmers wear)
> 6 **a** goalkeeper   **b** umpire   **c** coach (or sometimes *manager* in British English)   **d** referee   **e** caddy
> 7 **a** a racket (or racquet)   **b** a bat   **c** a stick   **d** a club
> 8 **a** unfair or cruel   **b** deeply asleep   **c** in trouble
> **d** give up   **e** give a detailed account
> All the idioms come from **boxing** (explanations below):
> **a** To punch sb below the waist is against the rules and considered a foul blow.
> **b** A boxer is 'out for the count' if he is knocked down and the referee counts to ten, during which time he must get up and continue fighting. If he doesn't, then the other boxer is declared the winner.
> **c** A boxer is 'on the ropes' if he is trapped with his back to the ropes surrounding the ring, putting him in a very vulnerable position, as he can be more easily hit by his opponent.
> **d** If a boxer is getting beaten by his opponent, and is taking a lot of blows, particularly to the head, his coach may 'throw in the towel', i.e. throw the boxer's towel into the ring to show that he is giving up. In this way the coach prevents his boxer getting seriously injured.
> **e** A 'blow by blow' account or commentary of a boxing match is a very detailed account, describing every action and punch.

7 C Joke telling

A pairwork retelling activity

SS in groups of four read and retell jokes. Copy one sheet per group and cut into four.

LANGUAGE	dramatic present

- Put SS in groups of four, and give each student a joke. Tell SS that they each have a joke which they are going to tell the rest of the group. Tell SS to try to memorize their joke. They should make a special effort to memorize the punchline, but the rest of the joke they can tell in their own words.
- When they have had time to memorize, SS in turn tell their jokes.
- Finally get each group to decide which joke they found the funniest. Get feedback.

Role cards for interviewers

1

You are interviewing for a part-time librarian post. It will be a short-term contract to cover maternity leave.
Profile of the ideal candidate:
• Book lover
• Prepared to work flexible hours
• Previous experience not essential, but desirable
• Able to work well alone
• Organized

You have three minutes to speak to the interviewees. You have to decide who you would like to employ. At the end of the interviews, you'll be asked to explain who you chose, and <u>why</u>. Before you begin, think about and write down the questions you are going to ask.

2

You are interviewing for a tele-marketing post for a well-known mobile phone company. It is a three-month, non-renewable contract. Basic salary with commission.
Profile of the ideal candidate:
• Good interpersonal skills and telephone manner
• No experience necessary, but experience in sales or marketing a bonus
• Determination and drive essential
• Able to work well under pressure

You have three minutes to speak to the interviewees. You have to decide who you would like to employ. At the end of the interviews, you'll be asked to explain who you chose, and <u>why</u>. Before you begin, think about and write down the questions you are going to ask.

3

You are interviewing for a toy shop supervisor post. Three-month trial period leading to permanent, full-time contract. Job share possible.
Profile of the ideal candidate:
• Proven team leader
• Excellent organizational skills
• Basic accounting knowledge
• Some knowledge of what toys are popular at the moment would be appreciated

You have three minutes to speak to the interviewees. You have to decide who you would like to employ. At the end of the interviews, you'll be asked to explain who you chose, and <u>why</u>. Before you begin, think about and write down the questions you are going to ask.

4

You are interviewing for a car park attendant post. Full-time job which sometimes includes 24-hour shifts. Permanent contract.
Profile of the ideal candidate:
• Would suit a solitary person who isn't easily bored
• Numerate
• Able to take on-the-spot decisions
• Able to deal with difficult or aggressive customers
• Physically fit

You have three minutes to speak to the interviewees. You have to decide who you would like to employ. At the end of the interviews, you'll be asked to explain who you chose, and <u>why</u>. Before you begin, think about and write down the questions you are going to ask.

5

You are interviewing for a job as a messenger for a company which uses bikes and motorbikes to deliver letters and packages. Six-month contract with possibility of extension. Some Saturdays.
Profile of the ideal candidate:
• Able to ride motorbike (licence required) or bike in city centre
• Reliable and trustworthy with confidential documents
• Organized and punctual
• Good knowledge of city

You have three minutes to speak to the interviewees. You have to decide who you would like to employ. At the end of the interviews, you'll be asked to explain who you chose, and <u>why</u>. Before you begin, think about and write down the questions you are going to ask.

6

You are interviewing for the post of care assistant at an old people's home. Alternate morning / evening shifts. One weekend a month.
Profile of the ideal candidate:
• Caring personality, with experience of older people
• First aid knowledge an advantage
• Ability to take decisions on own
• Must be a team player
• Available to work overtime

You have three minutes to speak to the interviewees. You have to decide who you would like to employ. At the end of the interviews, you'll be asked to explain who you chose, and <u>why</u>. Before you begin, think about and write down the questions you are going to ask.

Role card for candidates

You are out of work and desperate for **any** job (you really need the money). You are going to be interviewed for some of following jobs:
• Care assistant at old people's home
• Bike messenger
• Car park attendant
• Assistant librarian
• Toy shop supervisor
• Tele-marketing post

The interviews will last three minutes each. You really want to sell yourself well at the interview! Think about the following questions you might be asked and make some notes. You can use real information about yourself, or invent some. Once you have decided on your answers, you mustn't change them.
• What do you consider your main skills?
• What previous work experience do you have?
• How physically fit are you?
• What kinds of contract would you prefer (part time / full time / temporary / permanent?)
• Are you prepared to work overtime and at weekends?

New English File Teacher's Book Advanced
Photocopiable © Oxford University Press 2010

A **a** Describe your photo to **B** in detail. Then listen to **B** describe his / her photo. Discuss what the photos have in common and in what way(s) they are different.

b Discuss the following statements with **B**, giving reasons for your opinions. Do you agree or disagree?

1 It's very important for families to have at least one meal together per day without the TV on.

2 It's impossible for a man to either look after a child or do housework as well as a woman.

3 Children should be encouraged to leave home once they've turned 18.

4 One parent should stay at home and look after the child until he / she is of school-starting age.

5 Children need a male and female parent as a role model.

B **a** Listen to **A** describe his / her photo. Then describe your photo to **A** in detail. Discuss what the photos have in common and in what way(s) they are different.

b Discuss the following statements with **A**, giving reasons for your opinions. Do you agree or disagree?

1 It's very important for families to have at least one meal together per day without the TV on.

2 It's impossible for a man to either look after a child or do housework as well as a woman.

3 Children should be encouraged to leave home once they've turned 18.

4 One parent should stay at home and look after the child until he / she is of school-starting age.

5 Children need a male and female parent as a role model.

A

a Read the quotes below. Then complete the gapped quotes in your own words.

b Now tell **B** what you wrote for quote 1. **B** will tell you what the original quote was. Discuss the quote, saying what you think it means, and whether you agree with it.

c Now **B** will tell you how he / she completed quote 2. Tell **B** what the original was, then discuss it as above. Continue with the other quotes.

---

1 One language sets you in a corridor for life. Two languages _____.
Frank Smith

2 Americans who travel abroad for the first time are often shocked to discover that many foreign people **still speak in foreign languages**.
David Barry

3 If you talk to a man in a language he understands, that goes to his head. If you talk to him in his own language, _____.
Nelson Mandela

4 Learn a new language and get a new **soul**.
Czech proverb

5 Any tool has multiple uses. Language, for example, can be either **a bridge or a barrier**.
Shane Tourtellotte

6 It is of interest to note that while some dolphins are reported to have learned English, no human being _____.
Carl Sagan

7 Language is the roadmap of a culture. It tells you where its people **came from and where they are going**.
Rita Mae Brown

8 When you go to a country, you must learn how to say two things: _____, and _____.
Louis L'Amour

9 A man who speaks three languages is trilingual. A man who speaks two languages is **bilingual**. A man who speaks only one language is **English**.
Claude Gagnière

10 Talking is silver, while staying silent is _____.
Proverb

B

a Read the quotes below. Then complete the gapped quotes in your own words.

b **A** will tell you how he / she completed quote 1. Tell **A** what the original quote was, and discuss the quote, saying what you think it means, and whether you agree with it.

c Now tell **A** what you wrote for quote 2. **A** will tell you what the original quote was. Discuss it as above. Continue with the other quotes.

---

1 One language sets you in a corridor for life. Two languages **open every door along the way**.
Frank Smith

2 Americans who travel abroad for the first time are often shocked to discover that many foreign people _____.
David Barry

3 If you talk to a man in a language he understands, that goes to his head. If you talk to him in his own language, **that goes to his heart**.
Nelson Mandela

4 Learn a new language and get a new _____.
Czech proverb

5 Any tool has multiple uses. Language, for example, can be either _____.
Shane Tourtellotte

6 It is of interest to note that while some dolphins are reported to have learned English, no human being **has been reported to have learned 'dolphinese'**.
Carl Sagan

7 Language is the roadmap of a culture. It tells you where its people _____.
Rita Mae Brown

8 When you go to a country, you must learn how to say two things: **how to ask for food**, and **to tell a woman that you love her**.
Louis L'Amour

9 A man who speaks three languages is trilingual. A man who speaks two languages is _____. A man who speaks only one language is _____.
Claude Gagnière

10 Talking is silver, while staying silent is **golden**.
Proverb

New English File Teacher's Book Advanced
Photocopiable © Oxford University Press 2010

ⓐ Read the questionnaire and choose six questions to ask a partner.

ⓑ Ask the questions and answer the ones your partner asks you.

1 Are there any clothes you had as a child that you particularly loved or hated? Did you have to wear clothes that used to belong to your older brothers or sisters?

2 Were there any favourite places where you liked going to play? Did you go alone or with your friends? What did you do there?

3 What was your favourite toy? Can you describe it? Why do you think you liked it so much?

4 Were you ever a member of a youth club or organization, e.g. the Scouts? How long did you belong to it for? Did you enjoy it?

5 Who were the people you felt closest to as a child? What do you remember about them?

6 Did you get pocket money? How much? Did you use to spend it immediately or did you sometimes save it? What for?

7 Did you have to do any chores while you were growing up? What were they? How did you feel about having to do them?

8 As you were growing up, was there anybody you really looked up to or wanted to be like?

9 Who was the oldest member of your immediate or extended family when you were a child? What do you remember about him / her?

10 As a child, what did you want to be when you grew up? Do you still have the same ambition or did you change your mind? Why?

11 What were your typical family meals like? Did you all eat together? Where? Who used to cook?

12 Did your parents use to read you a story / book before you went to sleep or did you read stories yourself? What was your favourite story?

13 If you did something naughty, how did your parents punish you? Can you remember which type of punishment was the most effective?

14 As a child, what was your favourite special occasion, e.g. birthday, Christmas? How did you use to celebrate it?

New English File Teacher's Book Advanced
Photocopiable © Oxford University Press 2010

Read the proverbs, which are all related to time. Discuss with a partner what you think they mean. Are there any similar proverbs in your language?

1 The early bird catches the worm.

2 A stitch in time saves nine.

3 Make hay while the sun shines.

4 When the cat's away the mice will play.

5 It's no use crying over spilt milk.

6 You can't teach an old dog new tricks.

7 Don't count your chickens before they're hatched.

8 A watched pot never boils.

9 We'll cross that bridge when we come to it.

10 Strike while the iron is hot.

A Nicole

You're Nicole and you went out with Steve for two years. About six months ago you **mutually** agreed to split up but you have kept in touch. Recently, you've discussed the possibility of getting back together again. You've agreed to meet to talk through the reasons why you broke up, and to see whether solutions can be found to make a reconciliation possible.

1 **His appearance**
When you first started going out, Steve always looked fantastic. Over the two years you were together, you felt he'd started to let himself go, e.g. he stopped going to the gym with you, put on a lot of weight, and started to wear any old thing – this wasn't the man you first fell in love with!

2 **Helping in the house**
You know that your way of doing things is the best way. It used to drive you mad when Steve did things his way (the wrong way), e.g. when he was preparing a meal or doing the washing up. So, when you saw him doing things incorrectly, you'd try and put him right. Steve used to get very annoyed by this, but you can't see why. It's your area of expertise after all.

3 **Your friend Max**
One of the main reasons why you split up was because Steve was jealous of your friendship with Max – your ex-partner. Although you get on really well with Max and he's one of your closest friends, you certainly don't have any romantic feelings for him any more. You meet Max about once a month for a drink, or to see a film (you and Max have the same taste in cinema, unlike Steve).

4 **The spoilt child**
When you met Steve he told you that he had an nine-year-old daughter (Nina) from his previous marriage. You didn't see that as a problem because you like children. He has Nina for a weekend once a fortnight. You think Nina is immensely spoilt, manipulative, and badly-behaved. Initially, you spent time as a threesome, but you felt this wasn't working so you used to go away with friends for the weekends when Steve had Nina.

> **Talk to Steve about these problems and try to find a way forward. Remember you want to get back together with him, so try to keep calm and don't lose your temper!**

B Steve

You're Steve and you went out with Nicole for two years. About six months ago you **mutually** agreed to split up, but you have kept in touch. Recently, you've discussed the possibility of getting back together again. You've agreed to meet to talk through the reasons why you broke up to see whether solutions can be found to make a reconciliation possible.

1 **Appearance**
You think that when you're in a relationship, you need to be able to be yourself, and that includes your appearance, but Nicole is always going on about the clothes you wear and the fact that you aren't in such good shape as you used to be. Nicole still looks great, but you think she is rather obsessed with the gym, and that she spends a fortune on clothes.

2 **Unwanted advice**
You've managed to survive perfectly well all these years cooking and cleaning in your own way. One of the reasons you split up with Nicole was because she was always telling you a 'better' way of doing things (i.e. her way) when you hadn't asked her for advice, and it used to really get on your nerves.

3 **Her ex**
Nicole's ex-boyfriend is called Max. They often go out to the cinema, talk on the phone, and have a drink together. You don't understand why she still needs him in her life. You're not jealous of Max, it's just that you don't like him and you really don't think it's healthy for Nicole to stay in touch with him.

4 **Your daughter**
You have a nine-year-old daughter (Nina) from a previous relationship who you have every other weekend. Nina can be a bit difficult at times, and you know that you do tend to spoil her and need to be stricter – but that's only because you see her so little. You're aware that Nicole didn't get on with Nina, but you don't think she is very good with children and she didn't really give Nina a chance. She just started going off with friends when Nina was around. It is really important for you that Nina and Nicole get on.

> **Talk to Nicole about these problems and try to find a way forward. Remember you want to get back together with, her so try to keep calm and don't lose your temper!**

New English File Teacher's Book Advanced
Photocopiable © Oxford University Press 2010

a Look at the list of sounds. Mark each one with:

   ✓✓   I love the sound.

   ✓   I quite like it.

   o   It doesn't bother me.

   ✗   I find it irritating.

   ✗✗   I can't stand the sound. It drives me mad.

b Compare your list with a partner and explain your marks.

- birds chirping
- loud party music
- church bells ringing
- children splashing in a swimming pool
- a rotating ceiling fan
- the crash of thunder
- a stormy sea
- the wind whistling at night
- dogs barking
- a tennis ball being hit by a racket
- the bang of a balloon bursting
- the 'music' coming from the mp3 player of a person sitting next to you
- audience laughter during a TV or radio comedy programme
- a TV on in the background
- fireworks going off
- someone sniffing
- a foreigner speaking your language
- a hairdresser snipping at your hair with scissors
- a fly or a bee buzzing
- a fountain
- cars in a Formula 1 race
- football commentary on the radio
- opera
- people chewing gum and blowing bubbles
- insect noise on a summer night, e.g. crickets
- a cock crowing
- flamenco dancing

Communicative **Who wrote it? A man or a woman?**

New English File Teacher's Book Advanced
Photocopiable © Oxford University Press 2010

a You're going to read eight extracts from novels, all of which describe women or women's attitudes to life in some way. Four of the extracts are written by men, and four are written by women. Decide which you think are by whom and write **M** or **W** in the boxes.

b Compare with a partner and explain your reasons, and try to convince your partner where you disagree.

---

1 You fall in love with a man because he is everything your father isn't. He is strong and tough and you like that. He sweeps you off your feet. You don't even realize how much he takes over your life, how you start to become merely an extension of him, rather than a separate entity or as you dream, one grander entity, two becoming one in love, like out of a romance novel. You acquiesce on small things, then large things, then everything. Your laugh starts to quiet before disappearing altogether. Your smile dims until it is only a facsimile of joy, something you apply like mascara.

---

2 She puts the white stilettos she has been carrying since she reached the sands under her chair, opens her handbag and pulls out a pink enamelled compact decorated with the silhouette of a black poodle. She checks her lipstick in the mirror first, using a brightly varnished nail to wipe away the inevitable smudges of matching pink lipstick from the corners of her mouth. Snapping the compact smartly shut, she flashes Jack a brilliant smile. In present company Irene may have both youth and beauty on her side, but still she regards Ruth with a careful eye.

---

3 By my side sat the brown-eyed, proud beauty, the pretty niece, who had after all, it appeared, noticed my admiring gaze in the patisserie, for she smiled at me kindly as at an old acquaintance. Her eyes were like coffee-beans, and, when she laughed, they really did seem to crackle like roasting beans. She had charming, translucent little ears beneath luxuriant dark hair; like pink cyclamen nestling in moss, I thought. She had bare arms, soft and smooth; they must be like peeled peaches to the touch.

---

4 Alice strides ahead, loving that she's not dressed up, that when she's with Emily she doesn't have to put on an act, she can wear her oldest, most casual, comfortable clothes, and really be herself. Her jeans may be Earl, but today she's wearing her gym sneakers, a Gap sweatshirt and a baseball cap pulled down tight over hair scraped back into a ponytail. She can really walk in these clothes, can sit with her legs apart, resting her elbows on her knees, can run and play games with Humphrey, scooping him up for a cuddle without worrying that he might be getting mud on – heaven forbid – a Chanel jacket or a shearling coat.

---

5 Camilla was the first to arrive. Five feet ten, pale white skin, big lips, round cheekbones, tiny nose. Camilla is twenty-five but says she 'feels old.' She began modelling at sixteen. When I first met her, months ago downtown, she was doing her duty as a 'date' to a well-known television producer, which meant she was smiling and speaking back when someone asked her a question. Other than that, she was making very little effort, except to occasionally light her own cigarettes.

---

6 What attracted men? Good looks? Certainly if a girl was pretty, then she tended to get the attention of men; that was beyond any doubt at all. But it was not just prettiness that mattered, because there were many girls who did not look anything special but who seemed to find no difficulty in making men notice them. These girls dressed in a very careful way; they knew which colours appealed to men and they knew how to walk and sit down in a way which would make men sit up and take notice. The walk was important: it should not be a simple walk, with one leg going forward, to be followed by the other; no, the legs had to bend and twist a bit, almost as if one were thinking of walking in a circle.

---

7 I looked at her wistfully, her vast, bulbous bottom swathed in a tight red skirt with a bizarre three-quarter-length striped waistcoat strapped across it. What a blessing to be born with such Sloaney arrogance. Perpetua could be the size of a Renault Espace and not give it a thought. How many hours, months, years, have I spent worrying about weight while Perpetua has been happily looking for lamps with porcelain cats as bases around the Fulham Road? She is missing out on a source of happiness, anyway. It is proved by surveys that happiness does not come from love, wealth or power but the pursuit of attainable goals: and what is a diet if not that?

---

8 She had a wide mouth, a small nose, and high cheekbones that gave her an almost Asian look. Her movements were quick and spidery, and when she was working at the computer her fingers flew over the keys. Her extreme slenderness would have made a career in modelling impossible, but with the right make-up her face could have put her on any billboard in the world. Sometimes she wore black lipstick, and in spite of the tattoos and the pierced nose and eyebrows she was… well…attractive. It was inexplicable.

New English File Teacher's Book Advanced
Photocopiable © Oxford University Press 2010

Choose two questions from each section to ask a partner.

Saving money

1 Would you say you are good at saving money? Why (not)?
2 Do you have any strategies for saving money, e.g. when you are shopping?
3 Are you saving for anything at this moment in time? What for?
4 What factors might influence your decision to keep your money in a specific bank?

Losing and winning money

Do you know anyone who…
1 has been a victim of credit card fraud?
2 found that money had been mistakenly paid into their bank account?
3 lost or made a large amount of money on the stock market?
4 won a substantial amount of money in the lottery?

Earning money

1 Did you have a Saturday job or a holiday job when you were younger?
   What kind of work did you have to do?
2 Do you have any skills which could bring you extra income if you needed it?
3 How would you feel about earning a lot less than your partner?
4 In what jobs do you think you can justify people earning huge salaries?

Spending money

1 When you go shopping do you prefer paying cash or by credit card?
2 Do you prefer spending money on things (e.g. clothes, gadgets) or
   experiences (e.g. holidays)?
3 Is there anything you feel guilty about spending money on? Why?
4 Have you ever bought something which you now think was a complete
   waste of money?

Giving money

1 Do you give money to any charities or non-governmental organizations?
   Which ones? Why did you choose them?
2 Where and when do you tend to give tips? What factors influence your decision to
   give a tip or not?
3 Do you ever give money to people begging in the street?
4 Do you often give money as a present, e.g. for a birthday or wedding present?
   Do you prefer being given money yourself, or would you rather have an
   actual present?

Borrowing or lending money

1 Do you think it's better to borrow money from friends or family?
2 Have you ever lent someone some money and never been paid back?
3 Do you currently have a bank loan or a mortgage? What for?
4 Do you think the government should give young people loans for higher
   education, or grants (which they don't have to pay back)?

New English File Teacher's Book Advanced
Photocopiable © Oxford University Press 2010

1 **In which historical period were the following films set?**

a *Gladiator*

b *Dr Zhivago*

c *Pearl Harbor*

d *Cold Mountain*

e *The Name of the Rose*

2 **Correct these film titles by changing one word.**

a *Alexander the Huge*

b *Robin Hood: King of Thieves*

c *Full Velvet Jacket*

d *The Boy in the Checked Pyjamas*

e *Helping Private Ryan*

3 **Which historical film do these quotes come from? Match the quotes with the films below.**

a 'I'm the King of the world.'

b 'He's not the Messiah. He's a very naughty boy!'

c 'I still believe, in spite of everything, that people are really good at heart.'

d 'My nose precedes me by about 15 minutes.'

e 'I believe God made me for a purpose, but he also made me fast.'

f 'I pray that I may never see the desert again.'

g 'An eye for an eye only ends up making the world blind.'

h 'Are you really saying that the President can do something illegal?'

i 'As I heard my Sioux name called out over and over I knew who I really was.'

j 'You risk having no Spain at all!'

Chariots of Fire

Cyrano de Bergerac

Dances with Wolves

El Cid

Frost/Nixon

Gandhi

Lawrence of Arabia

Life of Brian

The Diary of Anne Frank

Titanic

4 **Which historical figure do you associate with these films?**

a *The Motorcycle Diaries*

b *Amadeus*

c *The Great Dictator*

d *The Last King of Scotland*

e *JFK*

5 **Which famous authors are these historical films about? Match the films with the authors.**

a *The Hours* — C.S. Lewis ☐

b *Finding Neverland* — Isak Dinesen ☐

c *Out of Africa* — J.M. Barrie ☐

d *Gothic* — Mary Shelley ☐

e *Shadowlands* — Virginia Woolf ☐

6 **Who played the following famous queens? Match the films with the actresses.**

a Queen Elizabeth I in *Elizabeth the Golden Age (2007)*

b Cleopatra in *Cleopatra (1963)*

c Queen Victoria in *The Young Victoria (2009)*

d Queen Elizabeth I in *Shakespeare in Love (1998)*

e Marie Antoinette in *Marie Antoinette (2006)*

Elizabeth Taylor ☐

Judi Dench ☐

Kirsten Dunst ☐

Cate Blanchett ☐

Emily Blunt ☐

1

You need someone to help you translate a 20-page instruction booklet from English into your language.

Think of some persuasive reasons why you need this favour done, and try to convince them to do it!

2

You need someone to look after your pet snake for the weekend. It is not poisonous.

Think of some persuasive reasons why you need this favour done, and try to convince them to do it!

3

You need someone to give you a lift to the airport tomorrow morning – the flight departure time is 6.45 a.m. so you'll need to be there at 5.45 a.m. at the latest.

Think of some persuasive reasons why you need this favour done, and try to convince them to do it!

4

You've just had a big row with your partner and want to be on your own. You need someone to let you stay in his / her spare room for a couple of nights.

Think of some persuasive reasons why you need this favour done, and try to convince them to do it!

5

You need to find someone to look after your three-year-old nephew for the day. You had promised your sister to do it, but now can't.

Think of some persuasive reasons why you need this favour done, and try to convince them to do it!

6

You need someone to help you to get rid of a sofa and two armchairs you don't want any more. You live in a second-floor flat with no lift.

Think of some persuasive reasons why you need this favour done, and try to convince them to do it!

7

You're new in the city and don't know many people yet. You want someone to come with you to a speed-dating evening.

Think of some persuasive reasons why you need this favour done, and try to convince them to do it!

8

You need someone to sit down with you for a couple of hours and go over the finer points of the present perfect, as you have an exam next week.

Think of some persuasive reasons why you need this favour done, and try to convince them to do it!

9

You need someone to go round to your house and sort out some problems you're having with your computer.

Think of some persuasive reasons why you need this favour done, and try to convince them to do it!

10

You need someone who has good dress sense to spend a day with you helping to choose an outfit for a wedding.

Think of some persuasive reasons why you need this favour done, and try to convince them to do it!

11

You need someone to go along with you to the dentist's tomorrow (and take you home). You're having two teeth taken out.

Think of some persuasive reasons why you need this favour done, and try to convince them to do it!

12

You need someone to let you download some films on his / her home PC tomorrow night. It may take a few hours. Your Internet connection isn't working.

Think of some persuasive reasons why you need this favour done, and try to convince them to do it!

13

You need someone to come over and cook you one meal a day for at least a week – you've got a broken wrist and it's in plaster.

Think of some persuasive reasons why you need this favour done, and try to convince them to do it!

14

You need someone to come to your house and help you colour your hair.

Think of some persuasive reasons why you need this favour done, and try to convince them to do it!

15

You need someone to sponsor you on a charity marathon run. The money you raise will go to a cat protection charity.

Think of some persuasive reasons why you need this favour done, and try to convince them to do it!

16

You need someone to pretend to be your partner at a family get-together this weekend.

Think of some persuasive reasons why you need this favour done, and try to convince them to do it!

a Read the case studies. Rate each one from 1–5 (1 = not very serious, 5 = very serious) according to the impact you think the obsession might have on their life.

b Compare your score with a partner and try to justify it.

Case study 1

Mark, 23, is obsessed with his partner Alison who he's been going out with for over three years. Alison is very attractive and since the start of their relationship he's always worried that she'll leave him for someone more interesting and better-looking. He sends her about 30 text messages a day and calls her incessantly on her mobile. He admits to having hired a private detective a couple of months ago to make sure she wasn't cheating on him. Mark says, 'I really love her.'

Case study 2

Karen, 19, has been obsessed with 'single food eating' for the last three years. Basically, this means she can only eat one certain food type at a time – that's to say she can't mix textures or flavours, and she has to brush her teeth after each different food she eats. So, for example, if she has chicken, potatoes, and peas, she will eat all the peas first, then all the potatoes, and finally the chicken.

Case study 3

Phil, 29, has an 'order' obsession. He puts all the books on his bookshelves in strict order according to their publication date. Similarly, all the magazines in the rack at his home have to be chronologically ordered. He admits to feeling 'seriously stressed' if someone takes out a book or magazine and then puts it back in the wrong place.

Case study 4

Helen, 41, is obsessed with the stage show *Mamma Mia*. Since it opened in London in 1999 she has been to see the show more than five hundred times, always sitting in the first five rows of the theatre. She spends all her money on buying tickets and has not had a holiday for years. Helen says 'Abba's music gives me such a high. I can't live without it.'

Case study 5

Amanda, 25, has an obsession with germs. She is unable to shake hands with anyone, as she knows that is how germs are transmitted from person to person. She can't even cope with holding her child's hand, or her partner's. She cleans the bathroom and kitchen twice a day from top to bottom, and won't have carpets or rugs in her house as she believes that this is where germs breed. She also disinfects all her daughter's toys every evening to prevent her catching anything.

Case study 6

Sean, 18, has had an obsession with car number plates since he was five or six years old. Whenever he sees a car, he automatically looks at the number plate, and starts adding up the digits. 'I find it impossible to watch a car go by without trying to see the number plate and adding up the numbers,' he says.

Case study 7

Simon, 36, is obsessed with Arsenal, the football team he supports. He goes to all their home games and travels all over the country to see them when they play away. All the rooms in his house are painted in red or white, the Arsenal colours, and there are pictures of all the players, past and present, on all the walls. His two young boys are named after famous Arsenal players. His wife likes football and is an Arsenal fan, but only goes to some of their home games. 'Arsenal are my life,' says Simon.

Case study 8

Maria, 28, is obsessed with going to the gym and healthy eating. She works on a night shift at a call centre. She sleeps during the morning and then spends every afternoon at the gym, six days a week. She works out in the weights room and also does aerobics or spinning. She weighs herself three times a day. 'If I've put on any weight, I have to spend another hour at the gym,' says Maria.

Proposal 1

The city centre should be car-free every Saturday from 9 a.m. until 1 p.m.

Role 1

- You're a local shop owner with a very successful business in the city centre. Most of your customers come to your shop at weekends.
- Decide if you are happy or not with this proposal. Think of at least two reasons why / why not.
- Prepare what you are going to say and then have a discussion with the other two people in your group. Remember you don't have to agree!

Proposal 1

The city centre should be car-free every Saturday from 9 a.m. until 1 p.m.

Role 2

- You're a parent and your daughter has music lessons in the city centre on Saturday mornings. You don't live in the city centre, and you usually drive her in, although there is a bus and train service from your village to the city.
- Decide if you are happy or not with this proposal. Think of at least two reasons why / why not.
- Prepare what you are going to say and then have a discussion with the other two people in your group. Remember you don't have to agree!

Proposal 1

The city centre should be car-free every Saturday from 9 a.m. until 1 p.m.

Role 3

- You're a keen cyclist and you are also a member of an ecology group.
- Decide if you are happy or not with this proposal. Think of at least two reasons why / why not.
- Prepare what you are going to say and then have a discussion with the other two people in your group. Remember you don't have to agree!

Proposal 2

Bars and pubs in town centres should close at 10.30 p.m. every day of the week.

Role 1

- You're an office worker who has to get up for work very early in the morning. The block of flats where you live in the centre of town has a bar underneath it.
- Decide if you are happy or not with this proposal. Think of at least two reasons why / why not.
- Prepare what you are going to say and then have a discussion with the other two people in your group. Remember you don't have to agree!

Proposal 2

Bars and pubs in town centres should close at 10.30 p.m. every day of the week.

Role 2

- You're a student and you live in a village with your parents. Most of your friends live in town so that's where you usually meet up with them.
- Decide if you are happy or not with this proposal. Think of at least two reasons why / why not.
- Prepare what you are going to say and then have a discussion with the other two people in your group. Remember you don't have to agree!

Proposal 2

Bars and pubs in town centres should close at 10.30 p.m. every day of the week.

Role 3

- You're a bar owner who has a bar in the centre of town with a terrace which does really well in the summer months.
- Decide if you are happy or not with this proposal. Think of at least two reasons why / why not.
- Prepare what you are going to say and then have a discussion with the other two people in your group. Remember you don't have to agree!

Proposal 3

People who live in city centres shouldn't be allowed to own dogs.

Role 1

- You're a dog owner who lives in the town centre. You always clean up after your dog and your dog has no anti-social tendencies.
- Decide if you are happy or not with this proposal. Think of at least two reasons why / why not.
- Prepare what you are going to say and then have a discussion with the other two people in your group. Remember you don't have to agree!

Proposal 3

People who live in city centres shouldn't be allowed to own dogs.

Role 2

- You're a vet with a surgery in town. Some of your clients who live in flats have big dogs.
- Decide if you are happy or not with this proposal. Think of at least two reasons why / why not.
- Prepare what you are going to say and then have a discussion with the other two people in your group. Remember you don't have to agree!

Proposal 3

People who live in city centres shouldn't be allowed to own dogs.

Role 3

- You're a mother of two who loves going to the town park with her children in the afternoons. One of your children is scared of dogs and lots of dogs are always off their leads.
- Decide if you are happy or not with this proposal. Think of at least two reasons why / why not.
- Prepare what you are going to say and then have a discussion with the other two people in your group. Remember you don't have to agree!

New English File Teacher's Book Advanced
Photocopiable © Oxford University Press 2010

A

B

A

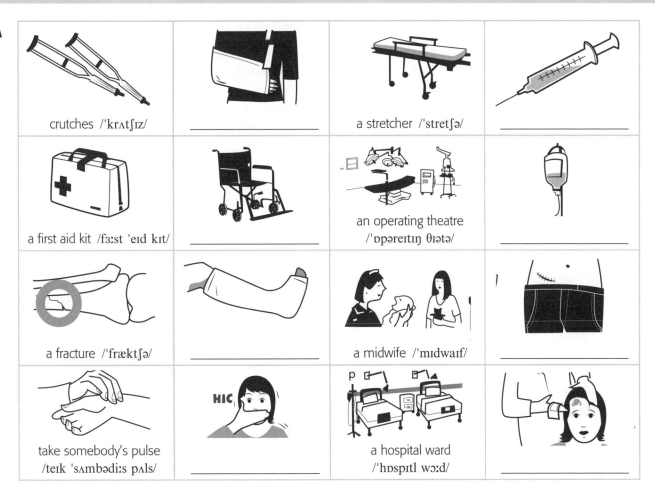

crutches /ˈkrʌtʃɪz/	_____	a stretcher /ˈstretʃə/	_____
a first aid kit /fɜːst ˈeɪd kɪt/	_____	an operating theatre /ˈɒpəreɪtɪŋ θɪətə/	_____
a fracture /ˈfræktʃə/	_____	a midwife /ˈmɪdwaɪf/	_____
take somebody's pulse /teɪk ˈsʌmbədiːs pʌls/	_____	a hospital ward /ˈhɒspɪtl wɔːd/	_____

B

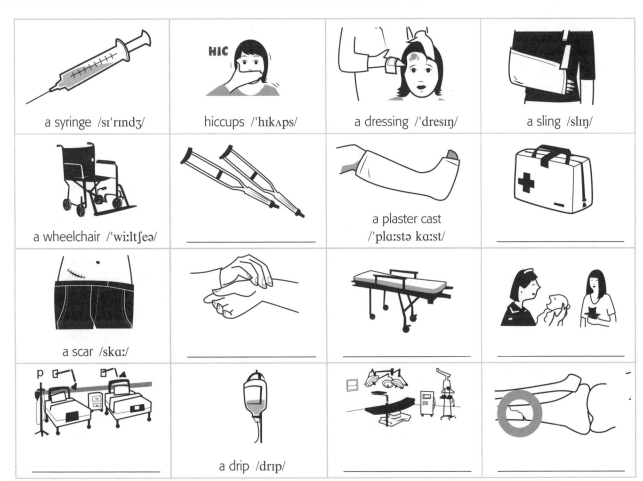

a syringe /sɪˈrɪndʒ/	hiccups /ˈhɪkʌps/	a dressing /ˈdresɪŋ/	a sling /slɪŋ/
a wheelchair /ˈwiːltʃeə/	_____	a plaster cast /ˈplɑːstə kɑːst/	_____
a scar /skɑː/	_____	_____	_____
_____	a drip /drɪp/	_____	_____

A Roleplay 1

You're a travel agency representative at a popular tourist resort on the coast. The resort has several hotels, all of which are full because it's peak season. All hotels have swimming pools and cater for families.
It's your first week in this job. You want to make sure you don't get anything wrong, and that you are quite clear about any problems clients may have, so that there aren't any misunderstandings later on. You've been trained to use the customer's first name wherever possible in a conversation to personalize things more. You don't have much authority as yet – especially not when it comes to promising refunds.

B is a client who arrived at one of the resort's hotels last night and has asked to speak to you.
- You begin. Introduce yourself by your first name (Mark / Sandra) and ask what **B**'s first name is.
- Remember to use it throughout the conversation! Ask how you can help **B**.
- Listen to **B**'s complaints and ask for more specific details. Then rephrase and repeat the information back to **B** (to show you fully understand).
- Try to think of solutions, but under no circumstances promise any kind of discount or refund.

Roleplay 2

You're a tourist on a one-week city break. Your trip was expensive and included transport, a four-star hotel and various excursions. You were not satisfied with the hotel and asked to be moved on the first day, which eventually you were.
However, you are still unsatisfied for the following reasons:
- The restaurant at the new hotel is not very good (why?).
- There is no wi-fi in the hotel.
- The excursion to the castle was very unsatisfactory (why?).

B is the local travel agency representative. You don't feel that he / she was particularly sympathetic with your original problem with the first hotel, and today you're determined to make him / her take you seriously. You're not going to be satisfied with vague promises. You arranged to speak to him / her a few moments ago and you want to have a long conversation.
- You begin. Inform **B** of your three new complaints, giving as many details as possible.
- Insist on **B** providing concrete solutions.
- Try to prolong the conversation as much as possible, and only accept the solutions you think are convincing.

B Roleplay 1

You're a tourist (Barry / Sophie Appleton). You arrived last night with your family at a popular tourist resort, and there are already three complaints you need to make:
- Your room is unsatisfactory (why?).
- The swimming pool is much smaller than the brochure showed, and is always crowded.
- Your children aren't happy with the Kids Club (why?).

A is the travel agency representative at the resort.
He / She looks quite young and inexperienced so you're sure you are going to have the upper hand. You just hope he / she's not one of those over-friendly people who use your first name all the time (you hate that), and pretend they're listening to your complaints and then do absolutely nothing!
- **A** will start.
- Explain your three complaints. Be more specific if asked to be.
- Be firm, but without losing your temper. Demand some kind of financial compensation. Be prepared to accept other solutions as a last resort, however.

Roleplay 2

You're a travel agency representative in a popular tourist city. You've just had the worst day of your life at work and you're about to finish an 18-hour shift. You are used to dealing with complaints, and know that the best way is to use vague expressions like 'I'll get back to you on that one' or 'I'll see what I can do' a lot.

A is a client of the travel agency and is in the city.
He / She is a difficult client and complained on the first day about the hotel. You managed, with great difficulty, to get him / her moved to another hotel. A few moments ago, **A** rang you and said he / she needed to talk to you. Your heart sinks, as you really want to go home.
- **A** will start.
- Listen to **A**, but keep looking at your watch, and try to cut short long and involved explanations.
- Make vague promises and try get rid of him / her as quickly as possible.

New English File Teacher's Book Advanced
Photocopiable © Oxford University Press 2010

1 The Hare with many friends

The hare was very popular with the other animals, and they all claimed to be her friends. One day, she heard the sound of some hunting dogs approaching and she needed to get away before they could catch her. She ran to her friends to ask them for help. First, she went to the horse, and asked him to carry her away on his back. But he said that he couldn't because he had some important work to do for his master.

She then went to ask her friend the bull for help as she hoped that he would fight off the dogs with his horns. Unfortunately, the bull couldn't help as he was meeting a cow, who was a friend of his. He suggested that perhaps the goat might be able to help her.

But the goat said he was suffering from a bad back and wouldn't be able to help. As a last resort, she went to speak to her young friend the calf to seek his assistance. However, the calf was also unwilling to help her. He claimed that he did not want to risk offending her other friends, who were older than him and had more experience.

By this time the hare could hear the dogs getting closer and closer. Desperately, she started running and luckily managed to escape.

2 The war between the Beasts and the Birds

A great battle was about to take place between the birds and the beasts. When the two armies had come together in order to fight, the bat had a serious dilemma – he didn't know which side to fight on. The birds that passed him said 'Come and fight with us,' but the bat said, 'No, I am a beast,' and stayed where he was. Later on, some beasts who were passing underneath him looked up and said 'Come and fight with us,' but he said, 'No, I am a bird,' and stayed where he was.

Luckily, at the last moment the battle didn't take place and peace was made. So, the bat went to the birds and said that he wanted to join their peace celebrations. The birds were indignant and they all turned their backs on him, and so the bat had to fly away. He then went to the beasts to see if he could celebrate with them. But they threatened to eat him alive if he tried to join the party.

So the bat was left on his own while the birds and the beasts celebrated.

3 The Fox and the Stork

At one time the fox and the stork seemed to be really good friends. So, it was not surprising when, one day, the fox invited the stork to dinner. As a joke, the fox decided to serve up some soup in a very shallow dish. The fox had absolutely no problem eating the soup as he could easily lap it up and drink it, but the stork could only wet the end of her long beak in it. At the end of the meal she was as hungry as she had been at the beginning!

'I am sorry,' said the fox, 'that you don't like the soup.'

'Please don't apologize,' said the stork. 'Come round to my place and have dinner with me next Saturday.'

So, the following Saturday, the fox went to his friend the stork's house for dinner. The stork served the dinner in a very long-necked jar with a narrow mouth. The fox, of course, couldn't even get his nose into it. In fact, all he could manage to do was to lick the outside of the jar.

'I won't apologize for the dinner,' said the stork.

4 The Lion and the Mouse

Once when a lion was asleep, a little mouse began running up and down his body. The lion woke up and was absolutely furious to have had his nap disturbed. His immediate reaction was to put a huge paw on the mouse and to open his big jaws to swallow him. The little mouse was terrified and cried 'I'm sorry, O King. Forgive me this time and I'll never forget your kind pardon. Who knows, maybe one day I'll be able to do something for you!'

The lion laughed at the idea of the mouse being able to do something for him, but as he admired the mouse's bravery, he decided to let him go.

Some time later, the lion was caught in a trap. The hunters tied him to a tree with a piece of rope while they went to fetch their cart. Just then, the little mouse happened to pass by, saw the lion's terrible situation, and bit through the rope to which the lion was tied. The lion was free once again.

New English File Teacher's Book Advanced
Photocopiable © Oxford University Press 2010

1 A Hungarian, born in Budapest, his family emigrated to Wisconsin when he was two. Inspired by a childhood visit to see a magician, he began to give performances at amusement parks and fairs. His fame grew world-wide as a man who could escape from any kind of locked container, even underwater. He died from peritonitis after inviting someone to punch him in the stomach to demonstrate the strength of his muscles.

2 A star in several of Pedro Almodóvar's early films, he surprised some of his fans by moving to Hollywood and marrying a well-known actress several years older than himself, with whom he had a daughter. Despite living in the US, he retains close links to his native country and promotes Andalusian products all over the world.

3 Brought up in Austria by very strict parents, he took up bodybuilding at the age of 15, and six years later, after winning the title 'Mr Universe', he moved to the USA. He had a very successful career as an actor, in both action and comedy films, and subsequently went into politics, after marrying a member of a famous American political family.

4 The daughter of a former wrestling champion and a 400m runner, she received her first racquet at the age of five, and when she was ten showed such promise that she moved to Florida from Moscow to train at a well-known academy. Famous as much for her blonde good looks as for her on-court ability, she never managed to win a Grand Slam singles title, and since retiring has made her home in Miami.

5 This film director left his native Taiwan to study theatre at the University of Illinois. One of the most successful directors of his generation, with several Oscars to his name, the importance of his roots is exemplified by one of his most successful films, *Crouching Tiger, Hidden Dragon*, which was filmed in Mandarin.

6 Born in Hungary, as a young man he emigrated to the USA, where he made his fortune through a very successful career in journalism, becoming one of the most powerful newspaper publishers in the United States. When he died, his will provided for the financing of a prize bearing his name, which today is the most prestigious award in US journalism.

7 The first Mexican actor to be nominated for an Academy award, she was born in Veracruz and first made her name in the Mexican soap opera *Teresa*. Although she didn't speak very fluent English at the time, she moved to Los Angeles in 1991, and is now acclaimed for her work both as an actor and a producer.

8 He was a German immigrant who sailed to the United States with his mother and two sisters at the age of 18. He first lived in New York before finally settling in San Francisco where he set up a clothing company at the time of the 'Gold Rush'. With a partner, he patented a method for strengthening men's work trousers, and later founded a company which still bears his name today.

9 Born in the UK and christened Archibald Leach, he travelled to the US as a teenager with a theatre group, and decided to settle there and make a career as an actor. He later changed his name, and went on to become one of the most popular cinema actors of his era, famous for his roles as a handsome, charismatic leading man in several of Hitchcock's thrillers.

10 He was born in Łódź, Poland, but emigrated with his family to the USA in the early 1900s. He set up his own business selling cosmetics to movie actors in Hollywood, and developed make-up and lipstick which made actors look more natural on screen. Later he began selling the same products to women, and today his name is synonymous with women's beauty products.

11 Born in Havana, Cuba, she was brought up in Miami after her father was forced to flee following the 1959 coup by Castro. After auditioning to sing in a local wedding band she went on to become one of the biggest singing stars of the 80s and 90s, with a succession of dance hits, in Spanish and English, rooted in the rhythms of her native country.

12 This Russian-born author has an asteroid and a crater on Mars named after him. One of the most prolific writers of all time, he is best known for his science fiction novels and books on popular science. One of his stories, *Nightfall*, was voted the best science fiction short story of all time. In 2004 one of his most famous novels was turned into a film starring Will Smith.

A

Perfect scrambled eggs | Ingredients per person

a Look at the recipe and make sure you understand it.

b Use the pictures to explain to **B** how to make perfect scrambled eggs. **B** should make notes.

c Listen to **B** explaining how to make perfect roast potatoes. Take notes.

B

Perfect roast potatoes | Ingredients for 4 people

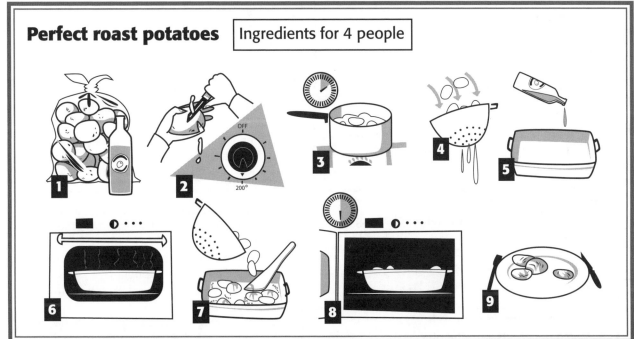

a Look at the recipe Two and make sure you understand it.

b Listen to **A** explaining how to make perfect scrambled eggs. Take notes.

c Use the pictures to explain to **A** how to make perfect roast potatoes.

New English File Teacher's Book Advanced
Photocopiable © Oxford University Press 2010

1 Look at the people above. Where are they from, and what sport were they famous for?
a Martina Hingis
b Nadia Comăneci
c Mark Spitz
d Sergey Bubka
e Hugo Sánchez

2 Name a sport where you can …
a tackle
b score a try
c volley
d serve
e dribble
f ask for a time out

3 In which sports might you talk about…?
a a header
b a drop shot
c a birdie
d the lotus position
e a somersault
f slam dunk

4 Name a sport you can do at the following places.
a a track
b a ring
c a court
d a rink
e a slope

5 Match the sports with the objects.
a a saddle   swimming
b a shuttlecock   hockey
c pads   snooker
d a cue   badminton
e goggles   horse riding

6 What's the name of the person who…?
a always wears gloves in a football match
b sits in a high chair during a tennis match
c decides which players should be substituted in a basketball match
d gives out yellow and red cards for committing fouls
e carries the equipment for a golf player and gives him / her advice

7 What do you use to hit the ball in the following sports?
a tennis   c hockey
b baseball   d golf

8 What do you think the following commonly used idioms mean? What sport do they all come from?
a Your comment about my mother's cooking was **a bit below the belt**.
b Don't try waking him – he's **out for the count**!
c Even though he was unseeded, he had the Wimbledon champion **on the ropes** in the third set.
d Don't **throw in the towel** just yet – you've still got a chance with her.
e What happened at the wedding? I want you to give me **a blow by blow account**.

Joke 1

A man with a dog goes to the cinema and buys a ticket to see *The Lord of the Rings*. He sits down in the back row and the dog sits in an empty seat next to him.

After about half an hour the manager of the cinema notices the dog and whispers to the man:

'I'm very sorry sir, but dogs are not allowed in the cinema – you will have to take him outside.' The man sadly leads the dog outside. As he passes the ticket office the girl says: 'What's the problem, sir? Why are you leaving?'

The man says:

'The manager says I can't have the dog in the cinema. It's a pity, because he was really enjoying the film.'

'How amazing,' said the girl.

'I'm surprised too,' said the man. 'He didn't like the book at all.'

Joke 2

A group of friends who are all single women decide to go on holiday together. They see a five-storey hotel with a sign that reads: 'For Women Only', and they decide to go in. The receptionist explains how the hotel works:

'There are five floors. You can go up floor by floor, and once you find what you are looking for, you can stay there. It's easy to decide as each floor has a sign telling you what's inside. But remember you can only go up - you can't go down again.'

The women start going up. On the first floor the sign reads: 'All the men on this floor are short.' The friends laugh and go straight up to the next floor. The sign on the second floor reads: 'All the men on this floor are short and handsome.' This still isn't good enough, so the friends go up to the next floor.

When they get to the third floor, the sign there says: 'All the men on this floor are tall and handsome.' But the women still want to do better, and so they continue going up. On the fourth floor, the sign says: 'All the men here are tall, handsome and rich.' Now the women get really excited, and are just about to go in when they remember there's still one floor left. They all rush up to the fifth floor.

But when they get there they find a sign which says 'There are no men here. **This floor was built to prove that women are never satisfied.'**

Joke 3

A mother and baby camel are talking one day when the baby camel asks:

'Mum, why do I have these huge feet with three toes?'

The mother replies, 'Well, son, when we walk across the desert your toes help you to stay on top of the soft sand.'

'I see,' said the son. A few minutes later he says, 'I've got another question, Mum. Why do I have these long eyelashes?'

'They're to keep the sand out of your eyes on the trips through the desert.'

After a little while the son comes back and asks:

'Mum, why do I have these enormous humps on my back?'

The mother, who is now getting a bit impatient with the boy, replies:

'They're to help us store water for our long journeys across the desert, so we can go without drinking for long periods.'

'That's great Mum, so we have these huge feet to stop us sinking, and long eyelashes to keep the sand from our eyes, and these humps to store water. But Mum – just one more question.'

'Yes, son?' says the mother.

'Why are we in London Zoo?'

Joke 4

A man is reading his paper when his wife walks up behind him and hits him hard on the back of the head with a frying pan.

'What was that for?' he asks.

She says, 'I found a piece of paper in your pocket with 'Mary Jane' written on it.'

The husband says, 'Darling, don't you remember last week I went to that horse race? 'Mary Jane' was the name of the horse that I bet on.'

His wife gives him the benefit of the doubt and believes him.

Three days later he's reading his paper when the phone rings. A minute later his wife walks up behind him and hits him even harder on the back of the head with the frying pan.

'What was that for?' he asks.

'Your horse just phoned,' his wife says.

1 Work

A A paraphrasing activity

SS rewrite sentences to practise expressing work-related concepts in different ways. Copy one sheet per SS.

> **LANGUAGE** Adjectives for describing a job, nouns that are often confused, collocations

- Give out one sheet per student. Focus on the instructions, and elicit the answer to **1**. Then set a time limit.

  Extra support Give SS a few minutes to revise Vocabulary Bank *Work* on *p.157* before they start.

- Get SS to compare their answers with a partner. Then check answers.

> **1** charge of **2** off **3** a team **4** prospects **5** be / get promoted **6** short-term **7** employees **8** staff **9** training **10** qualifications **11** self-employed **12** made redundant **13** out of work **14** voluntary / unpaid **15** challenging **16** repetitive **17** career **18** benefits / perks

1 Family

B A card game

SS define words / phrases for other SS to guess. Copy and cut up one set of cards per pair or small group.

> **LANGUAGE** 21st century families, describing families, family idioms

- Put SS in pairs or small groups. Give each group a set of cards face-down or in an envelope.

  Extra support Give SS a few minutes to revise Vocabulary Bank *Family* on *p.158* before they start.

- Demonstrate the activity by choosing another word or words (not one of the ones on the cards), e.g. *sibling*, and describe it to the class until someone says the word, e.g. *It's a formal noun. It's used for either a brother or sister.* **Highlight that SS are not allowed to use any of the words on the card in their definition.**

- SS play the game, taking turns to take a card and describe the word or phrase. The student who is describing mustn't let anyone see their card. Tell SS to wait until the person has finished their description before trying to guess.

  Extra idea Get SS to play this in groups as a competitive game. The student who correctly guesses the word first keeps the card. The player with the most cards at the end is the winner.

  Non-cut alternative Put SS in pairs. Copy one sheet per pair and cut it down the middle. SS take turns to describe the words or phrases to their partner until he / she guesses the word.

1 Language terminology

C A pairwork question and answer activity

SS ask each other questions recycling language terminology and new lexis from File 1. Copy one sheet per pair and cut into **A** and **B**.

> **LANGUAGE** Language terminology, e.g. *collocate*, *synonym*. Vocabulary from File 1

- Put SS in pairs, ideally face to face, and give out the sheets. **Make sure SS can't see each other's sheets.** Give SS time to read their questions.

- Tell **A** to ask his / her first question to **B**. Then **B** asks his / her first question to **A**, etc.

2 Abstract nouns

A A revision activity

SS revise and extend their knowledge of abstract nouns. Copy one sheet per student.

> **LANGUAGE** Abstract nouns ending in *-hood*, *-dom*, *-ship*, *-ness* and *-tion*, and ones which are new words (no suffix)

- Give out one sheet per student and focus on **a**. Tell SS they don't just have to write words from the lesson, they can write any other ones they know. Give SS four minutes to write words in the circles. **Stress that the words must be abstract nouns, not nouns that describe things, e.g. *station*.**

- Get SS to compare with a partner. Check answers, making sure SS stress the words correctly.

> **Possible answers**
> | | |
> |---|---|
> | ***-hood*** | childhood, adulthood, neighbourhood, brotherhood, knighthood |
> | ***-dom*** | boredom, freedom, wisdom, kingdom, stardom |
> | ***-ship*** | friendship, relationship, membership, partnership, censorship, fellowship |
> | ***-ness*** | happiness, kindness, illness, sadness, weakness |
> | ***-tion*** | imagination, celebration, competition, education |
> | **no suffix** | fear, shame, belief, death, hatred, loss, poverty |

- Focus on **c**. Give SS time to write their sentences and discuss in small groups or pairs. Monitor and get feedback.

2 'Time' race

B A gap-fill activity

SS complete sentences with time expressions. Copy one sheet per pair.

> **LANGUAGE** Expressions with time, e.g. *save time, by the time*, etc.

- Put SS in pairs and give out the sheets. Set a time limit, e.g. three minutes. Tell SS that they have to complete as many gaps as they can within the time limit. The pair who complete all the phrases correctly first are the winners.

  Extra support Give SS a few minutes to revise Vocabulary Bank *Time* on *p.159* before they start.

> **1** from time to time **2** save time **3** pushed for time / short of time **4** time on her hands **5** a long time ago **6** on time **7** by the time **8** time off work **9** before her time **10** the time of our lives **11** at times **12** spare / free time **13** take your time **14** ran out of time **15** giving me a hard time **16** This time last year **17** just in time **18** waste your time **19** a question / a matter of time **20** time's up

2 get phrases

C — A re-writing activity

SS replace phrases using expressions with *get*. Copy one sheet per student or pair.

LANGUAGE	Expressions with *get* e.g. *get, rid of, get a joke*, etc.

- Give out one sheet per student, or one per pair. Focus on **1** and elicit that you could substitute *get rid of* for *throw away*. Point out that they should use the correct form of *get* (gerund, past, etc.) depending on the sentence.

Extra support Give SS a few minutes to revise Vocabulary Bank *get* on *p.160* before they start.

- Set a time limit, e.g. three minutes. If SS have done it individually, get them to compare with a partner. Check answers.

> **1** get rid of **2** get it **3** getting together **4** get around **5** get away **6** got the wrong end of the stick **7** get on like a house on fire **8** gets on my nerves **9** get through to him **10** get her own way **11** gets me down **12** get her own back **13** got the chance **14** get the message **15** got a (terrible) shock **16** getting on **17** getting by **18** get out of the / my way

3 Sounds and the human voice

A — A pairwork question and answer activity

SS ask each other questions recycling lexis from the Vocabulary Bank *Sounds and the human voice*. Copy one sheet per pair and cut into **A** and **B**.

LANGUAGE	Sounds and the human voice, e.g. *bang, drip, whisper*, etc.

- Put SS in pairs, ideally face to face, and give out the sheets. Give SS time to read their questions. Tell them that they have example answers in brackets, but that they should accept any answer that they agree with.

Extra support Give SS a few minutes to revise Vocabulary Bank *Sounds and the human voice* on *p.161* before they start.

- Tell **A** to ask his / her first question to **B.** Then **B** asks his / her first question to **A**, etc.

- When SS have finished, get feedback to see if anyone came up with different answers to those on the sheet.

3 Adjectives and adverbs

B — An information gap activity

SS define words / phrases to help their partner complete a crossword. Copy one sheet per pair and cut into **A** and **B**.

LANGUAGE	Adjectives to describe books and films, and adjectives and adverbs from Lexis in context on *p.42* of the Student's Book

- Put SS in pairs, ideally face to face, and give out the sheets. **Make sure SS can't see each other's sheets.** Explain that **A** and **B** have the same crossword but with different words missing. They have to describe / define words to each other to complete their crosswords.

- Give SS a minute to read their instructions. If SS don't know what a word means, they can look it up in lesson **3B**.

- SS take turns to ask each other for their missing words (e.g. *What's 1 down?*). Their partner must define / describe the word until the other student is able to write it in his / her crossword. SS should help each other with clues if necessary.

- When SS have finished, they should compare their crosswords to make sure they have the same words and have spelt them correctly.

3 Money

C — A paraphrasing exercise

SS rewrite sentences to practise expressing money-related concepts in different ways. Copy one sheet per student.

LANGUAGE	Nouns for money or payments, money in today's society, adjectives and idioms related to money

- Give out one sheet per student. Focus on the instructions, and elicit the answer to **1**. Then set a time limit, e.g. three minutes for SS to complete the other sentences.

Extra support Give SS a few minutes to revise Vocabulary Bank *Money* on *p.162* before they start.

- Get SS to compare with a partner. Then check answers.

> **1** mortgage **2** loan **3** instalments **4** fees **5** fare **6** donation **7** interest rate **8** currency **9** exchange rate **10** in debt **11** income **12** cost of living **13** loaded **14** hard up **15** tight-fisted **16** make ends meet **17** the red **18** cost a fortune **19** beyond their means **20** grant **21** savings **22** deposit

4 History and warfare

A — An information gap activity

SS define words / phrases to help their partner complete a crossword. Copy one sheet per pair and cut into **A** and **B**.

LANGUAGE	Weapons, people and events, and verbs describing warfare

See instructions for **3B Adjectives and adverbs**. If SS aren't sure what one of their words means, they can check with Vocabulary Bank *History and warfare* on *p.163*.

4 Compound adjective race

B — A gap-fill revision race

SS complete compound adjectives. Copy one sheet per student.

LANGUAGE	Compound adjectives, e.g. *duty-free, last-minute*, etc.

- Give out the sheets. Set a time limit, e.g. three minutes. Tell SS that they have to write as many words in the **Missing Word** column as they can within the time limit. Check answers.

> **1** duty-free **2** last-minute **3** second-hand **4** home-made / home-cooked **5** worn-out **6** air-conditioned **7** badly-behaved **8** hand-made **9** blue-eyed **10** easy-going **11** left-handed **12** mass-produced **13** short-sighted **14** narrow-minded **15** well-off **16** absent-minded **17** short-term **18** self-sufficient **19** bad-tempered **20** self-employed

- Focus on **b**. Give SS time to revise and then test themselves.

4 Phone language

C — A definitions activity

SS write words for definitions to revise phone language. Copy one sheet per student.

- Give out one sheet per student. Focus on the instructions, and elicit the answer to **1**. Then set a time limit for SS to write the other words or phrases.
- Get SS to compare with a partner. Then check answers.

1 hang up **2** top up **3** put sb through **4** charge **5** landline **6** directory enquiries **7** engaged / busy **8** voicemail **9** pay phone **10** text message **11** missed call **12** speak up **13** be cut off

5 A Word formation: prefixes
A pairwork activity

SS listen to sentences with a missing word and complete them by adding prefixes to a given word. Copy one sheet per pair and cut into **A** and **B**.

| LANGUAGE | Prefixes, e.g. *over-*, *under-*, *out-*, etc. |

- Put SS in pairs, ideally face to face, and give out the sheets. **Make sure SS can't see each other's sheets.** Focus on instructions a–c, and give SS time to read through them and to read their sentences.
- Demonstrate the activity. Write *pay* on the board. Then tell SS you are going to say a sentence with the invented word BLEEP in it. They have to make a word from *pay* by adding a prefix and changing the form if necessary, so that it fits the sentence. Then say to the class *I don't think nurses earn enough money. They're really BLEEP.* Elicit that BLEEP should be *underpaid*.
- Now get SS to continue in pairs, reading their sentences alternately for their partner to make the missing word.

5 B Place and movement
A vocabulary discrimination activity

SS circle the right word, or tick if both are possible. Copy one sheet per student or per pair.

| LANGUAGE | Place and movement, e.g. *to*, *towards*, etc. |

- Give out the sheets to individual SS or to pairs and set a time limit. Focus on the instructions. Give SS time to circle the words. If they did the activity individually, get them to compare with a partner before checking answers.

Extra support Give SS a few minutes to revise Vocabulary Bank *Place and movement* on *p.164* before they start.

1 towards **2** on **3** at **4** into **5** outside **6** over, ✓ **7** ✓ **8** out of **9** onto, off **10** in **11** at **12** under **13** round **14** through **15** below **16** inside **17** along **18** on top **19** in **20** ✓ **21** ✓ **22** through, out **23** in **24** on

5 C Medical words and similes
A pairwork definitions activity

SS define words / phrases for their partner to guess. Copy one sheet per pair and cut into **A** and **B**.

| LANGUAGE | Medical words and phrases, e.g. *stitches, a virus,* and similes, e.g. *as stubborn as a mule* |

- Put SS in pairs and give out the sheets. **Make sure SS can't see each other's sheets.** Focus on a and b, and give SS time to write their definitions. Monitor and check their definitions while they are writing.

- Focus on **c**, and get SS to read their definitions alternately to each other to see if their partner knows the word.
- Get feedback to see how many words they each knew.

Extra challenge Get SS to give their definitions orally without writing them down.

See Student's Book *pp.76–79*.

6 A Travel and tourism
An error correction activity

SS correct vocabulary mistakes related to travel and holidays. Copy one sheet per pair.

| LANGUAGE | Compound adjectives e.g. *duty-free* |

- Put SS in pairs. Give out the sheets, and focus on the instructions. Focus on **1**, and elicit that it is wrong, as the phrase should be *cut the trip short*.
- SS continue in pairs. Check answers.

Extra support Give SS a few minutes to revise Vocabulary *Travel and tourism* on *p.165* before they start.

1 cut the trip short **2** a package holiday **3** trip to Hong Kong **4** take out travel insurance **5** ✓ **6** setting off / out **7** far too touristy **8** ✓ **9** off the beaten track **10** Guided tours **11** a stopover **12** ✓ **13** low-cost airline **14** put off **15** overrated **16** ✓ **17** went on a safari **18** lively **19** ✓ **20** ✓

6 B Animal idioms
A gap-fill activity

SS complete animal idioms. Copy one sheet per student or per pair.

| LANGUAGE | Animal idioms, e.g. *a dark horse* |

- Give out the sheets, either to individual SS or to pairs. Focus on the instructions. Set a time limit, e.g. 3 minutes.
- If SS did the exercise individually, get them to compare with a partner before checking answers.

Extra support Give SS a few minutes to revise the animal idioms in Vocabulary Bank *The natural world* on *p.166* before they start.

1 a dark horse **2** a real pig of yourself **3** the last straw **4** like water off a duck's back **5** kill two birds with one stone **6** count your chickens **7** smell a rat **8** let sleeping dogs lie **9** tail between his legs **10** like a fish out of water **11** the lion's share **12** do all the donkey work

6 C What's the difference?
A card game

A team game for SS to revise confusing words from this lesson and previous lessons. Make one copy and cut up into cards.

| LANGUAGE | Confusing words, phrases with *take* |

- Divide SS into two teams, or more if you have a lot of SS.
- Give team 1 a card. The team have 30 seconds to decide what the difference is between the two words. A spokesman from the team explains it to the rest of the class. If the explanation is correct, they get a point. If not, the card is passed to team 2, who also have 30 seconds to explain the difference. If neither team remembers the difference, explain it to the class. Then give team 2 a card. Continue until all the cards have been used up.

- Write up the teams' points on the board and finally add up the points to see which team has won.

Non-cut alternative Put SS in pairs. Copy one sheet per pair. SS take it in turns to explain the difference between the words.

1 like (adj) = having similar qualities to sb or sth
  alike (adj) = in a very similar way (only used at the end of a sentence or clause)

2 especially = above all, for a particular purpose (often followed by past participle)
  specially = particularly (often used before an adjective or adverb)

3 actually = in fact, to tell the truth
  currently = at the moment

4 affect = verb meaning to produce a change in sb or sth
  effect = noun meaning the consequence of an action

5 economic = related to the economy
  economical = spending money in a careful way

6 beside = next to or at the side of sb / sth
  besides = in addition to, apart from

7 ache = to feel continuous dull hurt
  pain = the feeling that you have in your body when you've been hurt

8 campsite = a place where you can put up tents, etc.
  camping = living in a tent, etc. on holiday

9 suit = a jacket with matching trousers or skirt
  suite = a set of rooms, esp. in a hotel, usually with a bedroom, a living area, and a bathroom

10 sight = the ability to see / the act of seeing / an interesting place
   site = a place where a particular building was, is, or will be / a place on the Internet with information

11 ashamed = feeling bad about sth you have done
   embarrassed = shy or awkward in a social situation

12 argument = a conversation in which two or more people disagree, often angrily
   discussion = talking about sth or sb in detail

13 view = what you can see from a particular place
   scenery = the natural features of an area

14 deny = to say sth is not true
   refuse = to say that you won't do sth sb has asked you to do

15 lay = put sth or sb in a particular position or put something down on sth (past *laid*, past participle *laid*), e.g. *He laid his hand on my arm.*
   lie = put yourself in a horizontal position (past *lay*, past participle *lain*)

16 compromise = an agreement between two parties or groups in which each side gives up some of the things they want. Also a verb, e.g. *We had to compromise.*
   commitment = a promise to do sth or to behave in a particular way

17 wages = a regular amount of money that you earn, usually every week
   salary = money that employees receive for their job, especially professionals, usually paid monthly

18 journey = travelling from one place to another, especially when they are far apart
   trip = a journey to a place and back again, especially a short one for a particular purpose or pleasure

19 career = the series of jobs that a person has in a particular area of work, usually involving more responsibility as time passes
   job = work which you do to receive regular payment

20 announce = to tell people sth officially, especially about a decision, plans, etc.
   advertise = to tell the public about a product or service so that they will buy it

7 A Preparing food

An information gap activity

SS define words / phrases to help their partner complete a crossword. Copy one sheet per pair and cut into **A** and **B**.

LANGUAGE	Preparing food and cooking: *ribs*, *whipped*, *shellfish*, *oven*, etc.

See instructions for **3B Adjectives and adverbs**. If SS aren't sure what one of their words means, they can check with Vocabulary Bank *Preparing food* on *p.167*.

7 B Word building race

A gap-fill activity

SS form words to complete gaps in sentences. Copy one sheet per pair.

LANGUAGE	Making verbs, nouns, adverbs, etc. from adjectives, e.g. *strong, strength, strengthen*, etc.

- Put SS in pairs and give out the sheets. Focus on the instructions. Tell SS that they need to think carefully about what part of speech they need in each sentence.
- When the time is up tell SS to stop and check answers.

STRONG	A strengthen B strength
LONG	A lengths B lengthen
DEEP	A depth B deeper
SHORT	A shortly B shortness
WIDE	A widely B width
HIGH	A height B highly
WEAK	A weaknesses B weakened
THICK	A thickly B thickened
FLAT	A flattened B flatness

Revision: describing game

A group card game

SS define words / phrases for other SS to guess. Copy and cut up one set of cards per pair or small group.

LANGUAGE	Revision from Files 1–7

- Put SS in pairs or small groups. Give each group a set of cards face down or in an envelope.
- Tell SS that they have to pick a card. They then have two minutes to try to describe the seven words or phrases on the card for their partner or other group member to guess. **Highlight that SS are not allowed to use any of the words on the card in their definition.** Tell SS to wait until the person has finished his / her description before trying to guess the word or phrase.
- Start the game. Get S1 to pick a card, and then say '*Go!*' After two or so minutes say '*Time's up*', and find out how many words or phrases S1 managed to communicate. Then get S2 to pick a card. Continue until all the cards have been used, or until you run out of time.

Non-cut alternative Put SS in pairs. Copy one sheet per pair and cut it down the middle. SS take turns to describe the groups of words / phrases for their partner.

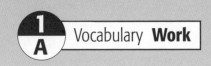

● Complete the second sentence so that it means the same as the first.

1 I'm responsible for the marketing department.

I'm in _____ _____ the marketing department.

2 I'm not working right now because I'm ill.

I'm _____ work right now because I'm ill.

3 I don't like working alone. I prefer working with others.

I'd rather not work by myself. I prefer working in _____ _____.

4 There will be lots of promotion opportunities in this job.

This job has good _____.

5 After a few months I could go from being Assistant Managing Director to Managing Director.

I could _____ _____ to Managing Director in a few months' time.

6 My contract's only from March to June.

I've only got a _____ - _____ contract.

7 How many people do you employ in this company?

How many _____ do you have in this company?

8 The nurses who work at this hospital are fantastic.

The nursing _____ are fantastic at this hospital.

9 There are some new things I need to learn for my job.

The boss is sending me on a _____ course.

10 He's got a degree, a Master's degree, and a 'B' at First Certificate.

He's got good _____.

11 I work for myself.

I'm _____ - _____.

12 I lost my job last year as the company I was working for wasn't making a profit.

I was _____ _____ last year.

13 My sister's been unemployed for well over a year.

My sister has been _____ _____ _____ for well over a year.

14 Adrian doesn't get any money for the charity work he does.

The charity work that Adrian does is _____.

15 My job is very high pressure and stressful.

I have a very _____ job.

16 He works on a car production line and does exactly the same thing every day.

His job on a car production line is very _____.

17 He worked successfully for many years both as a teacher and a teacher trainer.

He had a very successful _____ in education.

18 Apart from my salary I also get a company car and free lunches, which is brilliant.

The _____ are brilliant in this job. I get a company car and free lunches.

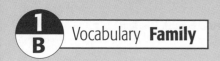

New English File Teacher's Book Advanced
Photocopiable © Oxford University Press 2010

one-parent family	extended family	be spread out	an only child
bring up **PHR V**	a get-together	a skeleton in the cupboard **IDM**	see eye to eye **IDM**
the black sheep of the family **IDM**	a father figure	self-sufficient	cautious
a gut feeling **IDM**	catch your eye **IDM**	face something head on **IDM**	take after **PHR V**
be on speaking terms **IDM**	alike	a grown-up	a relation
loyal	easy-going	get stuck	conscientious

A

a Ask your partner your questions. The answers are in brackets.

1 What word collocates with the word 'maternity' to mean 'time off work to have a baby'? (**leave**)

2 What's a more formal way of saying 'need'? (**require**)

3 How can you say 'children' in a more colloquial way? (**kids**)

4 What idiom can you use to say that the wife is more dominant than the husband in a marriage? (**She wears the trousers.**)

5 What phrasal verb is a less formal way of saying 'omit'? (**leave out**)

6 What's a synonym for 'recently'? (**lately**)

7 Can you explain the metaphor 'She has a heart of stone'? (**She has no feelings and is unsympathetic to other people's suffering.**)

8 What's a more informal way of saying 'I recall'? (**I remember**)

9 What's a formal way of saying 'to make sure'? (**to ensure**)

10 What's the phrasal verb which is a synonym for 'postpone'? (**to put off**)

b Now answer your partner's questions.

B

a Answer your partner's questions.

b Now ask your partner your questions. The answers are in brackets.

1 What phrasal verb can you use to say you have a similar personality to someone? (**take after**)

2 What word beginning with the letter *t* is a synonym for boring? (**tedious**)

3 What idiom with *mind* can you use to mean that you can't decide about something? (**I can't make up my mind or I'm in two minds.**)

4 What phrasal verb means to 'become an adult'? (**grow up**)

5 What's an American English word for 'stupid'? (**dumb**)

6 Can you tell me a more formal expression meaning 'because of'? (**due to** or **owing to**)

7 What do you think this metaphor means? 'When I asked my dad for more money he exploded.' (**He got very angry.**)

8 Can you explain the idiom 'to go with your gut feeling'? (**to use your instinct to decide what to do in a situation**)

9 What's a more informal way of saying 'to adhere to a rule'? (**to follow a rule**)

10 Do you know what the British slang word 'quid' means? (**a pound**)

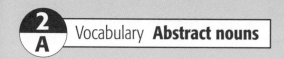

New English File Teacher's Book Advanced
Photocopiable © Oxford University Press 2010

a You have five minutes to write four abstract nouns in each circle.

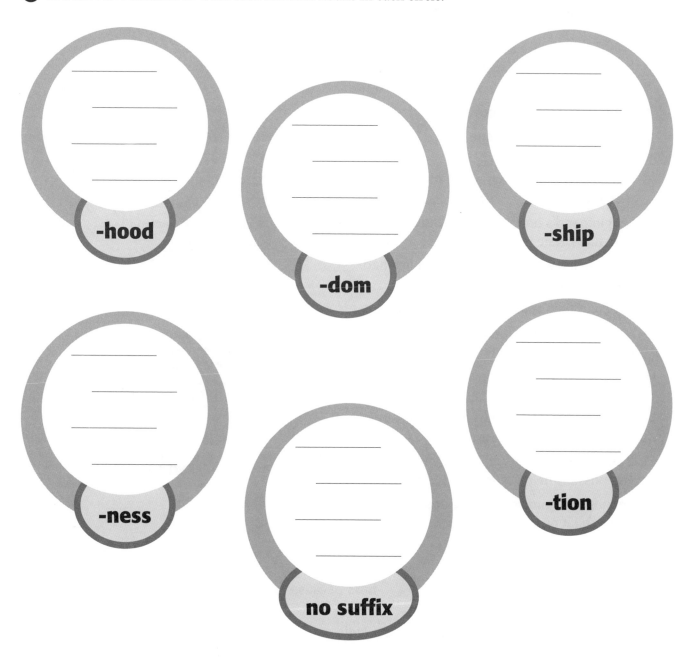

-hood

-dom

-ship

-ness

no suffix

-tion

b Compare your answers with a partner. Do you have the same words or different ones?

c Choose one word from each circle, and use it in a sentence which expresses something you agree with, e.g. *People's memories of their childhood are not always reliable.* Then compare your sentences with a partner.

● Work with a partner. You have three minutes to complete the sentences.
Don't run out of time!

1 I only see my half-brother _____ **time** _____ **time**.

2 We can cut across the park **to** _____ **time**.

3 Sorry, I can't help you now. I'm a **bit** _____ _____ **time**.

4 Now that she's retired she's got a lot of **time** _____ **her hands**.

5 I can't remember much about my school days, as it was **such a** _____ **time** _____.

6 My girlfriend's never _____ **time**. She's the least punctual person I know.

7 The actual wedding ceremony had finished _____ **the time** we got there.

8 I need to take **some time** _____ work to recover.

9 My niece was born in the nineties so The Beatles were _____ **her time**.

10 Our honeymoon was fantastic! We had **the time of our** _____.

11 Generally speaking I enjoy living on my own, but _____ **times** I miss having someone to talk to.

12 If you have any _____ **time** this afternoon, could you possibly help me to draft the report?

13 I'm not in a hurry for an answer so you can _____ **your time** and think it over for a while.

14 I couldn't answer the last question because I _____ _____ **of time**.

15 My stepfather's _____ **me a** _____ **time** because he thinks I'm going out too much.

16 _____ **time last year** we were in the middle of moving house.

17 We thought we were going to miss our connecting flight, but we made it **just** _____ **time**.

18 Don't _____ **your time** trying to convince him. He'll never change his mind.

19 They're always arguing. It's only a _____ **of time** before they split up.

20 OK, **time's** _____! Stop writing now.

2C Vocabulary *get phrases*

● Replace the **bold** words or phrases with a phrase using *get* in the correct form.

1 Please could you **throw away** all the old clothes you don't wear any more. _____

2 It's embarrassing when someone tells the punchline to a joke, everyone laughs, and you don't **understand it**! _____

3 My family love **meeting up** at Christmas. _____

4 What do you think is the best way to **move from one place to another** in this city? _____

5 Once my brother-in-law starts talking to you it's practically impossible to **escape**! _____

6 I thought we'd made it clear that we'd meet at the restaurant, but she **misunderstood** and was waiting for us to pick her up. _____

7 They've only just met, but they **already have a very good relationship**. _____

8 It really **annoys** me when you eat my chips. _____

9 I tried to explain the problem to my father, but **I just can't make him understand**. _____

10 My parents always let my little sister **do whatever she wants** – that's why she's so spoiled. _____

11 Not having enough time for myself really **depresses me**. _____

12 Martha was dumped by her ex-boyfriend and now she wants to **take revenge** on him. _____

13 If I **had the opportunity** to go and live abroad, I think I'd probably take it. _____

14 I've told him time after time that I don't want to go out with him, but he just doesn't seem to **hear what I'm saying**! _____

15 She **had a terrible surprise** when she discovered that she had been adopted as a baby. _____

16 Both of my parents are **becoming older**, but they still lead very active lives. _____

17 It's not easy **managing to live** on a student grant, especially in a big city. _____

18 I tried to walk past him but he wouldn't **move to the side to let me pass**. _____

A ● Ask your partner the questions. One point for each correct answer.

> **1** Can you name two animals that hiss?
> (*e.g. a snake, a cat*)
>
> **2** How do people often close the door when they're angry?
> (*They slam it*)
>
> **3** Can you name two things that drip?
> (*e.g. a tap, an ice cream*)
>
> **4** What noise do lions and tigers make?
> (*They roar*)
>
> **5** Give two reasons why someone might whisper.
> (*e.g. so as not to be overheard, so as not to disturb other people in a cinema, etc.*)
>
> **6** What unpleasant noise do some people make when they eat soup?
> (*They slurp*)
>
> **7** Why might you start stammering?
> (*e.g. because you are nervous or frightened*)
>
> **8** What sound would you hear if someone jumped into a swimming pool?
> (*a splash*)
>
> **9** Name two insects that buzz.
> (*e.g. a mosquito, a wasp*)
>
> **10** What sound might you make if you were feeling very disappointed or sad?
> (*a sigh*)

B ● Ask your partner the questions. One point for each correct answer.

> **1** Can you name two parts of the body we use to tap with?
> (*e.g. your fingers, your foot*)
>
> **2** What noise does a balloon make when it bursts?
> (*a bang*)
>
> **3** Give two situations when a driver might hoot.
> (*e.g. when the driver in front is slow to move at a traffic light, when another driver has done something dangerous*)
>
> **4** What noise does a time bomb make?
> (*It ticks*)
>
> **5** If someone's mumbling, what might you say to them?
> (*Please can you speak more clearly?*)
>
> **6** What noise does a door make when it needs oil?
> (*It creaks*)
>
> **7** Can you name two situations where people giggle?
> (*e.g. when they think something is funny, when they are nervous*)
>
> **8** What noise do people sometimes make when they have a cold, but they don't have a tissue?
> (*They sniff*)
>
> **9** What do people sometimes hum?
> (*A tune*)
>
> **10** What noise do you often hear if somebody who is driving brakes suddenly?
> (*A screech*)

A **a** Look at your crossword and make sure you know the meaning of all the words you have.

b Now ask **B** to define a word for you. Ask e.g. *'What's 1 down? What's 12 across?'* Write the word in.

c Now **B** will ask you to define a word.

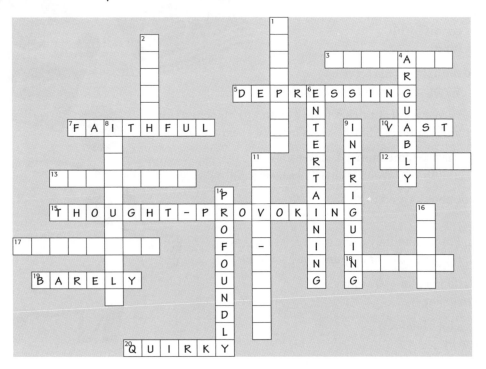

- -

B **a** Look at your crossword and make sure you know the meaning of all the words you have.

b **A** will ask you to define a word.

c Now ask **A** to define a word for you. Ask e.g. *What's 5 across? What's 14 down?* Write the word in.

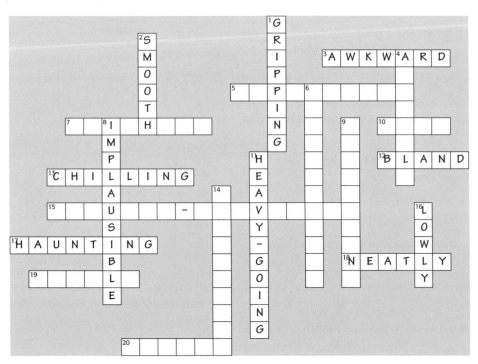

● Complete the sentence with a 'money' word or phrase so that both sentences mean the same.

1 The bank lent me some **money specifically to buy a house**.
I've got a _ _ _ _ _ _ _ _ from the bank.

2 Peter **lent** Luke €500.
Peter gave Luke a €500 _ _ _ _.

3 She's paying for the car **bit by bit**.
She's paying for the car in _ _ _ _ _ _ _ _ _ _ _.

4 My lawyer **charged me** a lot for his services.
My lawyer's _ _ _ _ for his services were very high.

5 It's incredible how expensive **a train ticket** from London to Manchester is.
The train _ _ _ _ from London to Manchester is incredibly expensive.

6 I **gave** my favourite charity **some money** last week.
I made a _ _ _ _ _ _ _ _ to my favourite charity last week.

7 My bank **charges me** about 4% on my loan.
I am paying a 4% _ _ _ _ _ _ _ _ _ _ _ _ _ on my bank loan.

8 The **money used** in France and Italy is the same – it's the Euro.
The _ _ _ _ _ _ _ _ is the same in France and Italy – it's the Euro.

9 **How many** pounds do I get for $100 today?
What's the pound to dollar _ _ _ _ _ _ _ _ _ _ _ _ _ today?

10 The company **owes** a lot of money.
The company is heavily _ _ _ _ _ _.

11 He doesn't have to work because he **gets** about $250,000 a year from the properties he rents out.
He has an _ _ _ _ _ _ of about $250,000 a year from the properties he rents out.

12 **Everything's** more expensive than it was this time last year.
The _ _ _ _ _ _ _ _ _ _ _ _ _ is higher now than it was this time last year.

13 My friend **is incredibly wealthy**.
My friend's _ _ _ _ _ _.

14 I **don't have much money** at the moment so I can't buy you a drink.
I'm a bit _ _ _ _ _ _ right now.

15 She has to be one of the **meanest** people I've ever met.
She's one of the most _ _ _ _ _-_ _ _ _ _ people I've ever met.

16 I have a lot of outgoings and sometimes I **don't have enough money to get to the end of the month**.
I sometimes find it hard to _ _ _ _ _ _ _ _ _ _ _ _.

17 Have you ever **spent more money than you had in your account**?
Have you ever been in _ _ _ _ _ _?

18 That dress is stunning. It must have been **very expensive**.
That dress is stunning. It must have _ _ _ _ _ _ _ _ _ _ _ _.

19 They seem to have a **very expensive lifestyle considering that they don't earn much money**.
They seem to be living _ _ _ _ _ _ their _ _ _ _ _.

20 The government **gave me some money** to study abroad.
I was given a _ _ _ _ _ by the government to study abroad.

21 Luckily I'd **put some money away** in the bank so I could pay to have the roof repaired after the storm.
Luckily I had some _ _ _ _ _ _ _ _ in the bank so I was able to pay to have the roof repaired after the storm.

22 When I got my new flat I had to pay one month's rent **in advance**.
I had to pay a _ _ _ _ _ _ _ of one month's rent when I got my new flat.

A ⓐ Look at your crossword and make sure you know the meaning of all the words you have.

ⓑ Now ask **B** to define a word for you. Ask e.g. *What's 2 down? What's 17 across?* Write the word in.

ⓒ Now **B** will ask you to define a word.

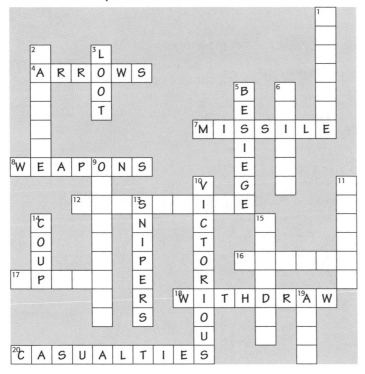

B ⓐ Look at your crossword and make sure you know the meaning of all the words you have.

ⓑ **A** will ask you to define a word.

ⓒ Now ask **A** to define a word for you. Ask e.g. *What's 3 down? What's 18 across?* Write the word in.

a In three minutes write the missing word in the **Missing Word** column
to make a compound adjective.

b Cover the column and test yourself. How many can you remember?

Missing Word

1	I always get my perfume from the duty- ▮▮▮ shop at the airport.	_____
2	On my final day in Paris I did some last- ▮▮▮ shopping before I went to the airport.	_____
3	We love going round second- ▮▮▮ shops to see if we can find any bargains.	_____
4	I'd rather have home- ▮▮▮ food than eat out.	_____
5	Those jeans are really worn- ▮▮▮ . Look at the holes in the knees!	_____
6	It would be impossible to drive in summer if my car wasn't air- ▮▮▮ .	_____
7	My godson's so badly- ▮▮▮ that you can't take him anywhere!	_____
8	The sweaters are all ▮▮▮ -made by local craftsmen.	_____
9	Most Siamese cats are blue- ▮▮▮ , unlike other breeds.	_____
10	My sister's boyfriend is really easy- ▮▮▮ . He never gets upset about anything!	_____
11	Being left- ▮▮▮ is often considered an advantage for sports players.	_____
12	Those paintings aren't originals! They're ▮▮▮ -produced in a factory just outside London.	_____
13	She's really short- ▮▮▮ . That's why she wears such thick glasses.	_____
14	The people in this town are very narrow- ▮▮▮ . They're just not open to new ideas.	_____
15	She comes from a very ▮▮▮ -off family, and had a privileged upbringing.	_____
16	My boss is incredibly absent- ▮▮▮ . He always needs reminding about everything.	_____
17	My contract is only a short- ▮▮▮ one. It runs from October to December.	_____
18	They're completely self- ▮▮▮ . They produce all their own food on their farm.	_____
19	I'm definitely not a morning person. I'm usually a bit bad- ▮▮▮ until I've woken up properly.	_____
20	Phil hated his previous job with a big company. Now he's self- ▮▮▮ he's much happier.	_____

● Read the definitions and write the word or phrase in the space provided.

1 _____ _____ `PHR V` to end a telephone conversation by putting the receiver down or switching the phone off

2 _____ _____ (your mobile phone) `PHR V` to buy more time for calls

3 _____ _____ `PHR V` to connect somebody by telephone

4 _____ (your mobile phone) *v.* to pass electricity through a phone so that it is stored there

5 _____ *n.* a phone connection that uses wires carried on poles or under the ground, in contrast to a mobile phone

6 _____ _____ *n.* a telephone service you can use to find out a person's telephone number

7 _____ *adj.* a telephone line being used

8 _____ *n.* an electronic system which can store phone messages, so that somebody can listen to them later

9 _____ _____ *n.* a telephone, usually in a public place, that is operated using coins or a card

10 _____ _____ *n.* a written message that you send using a mobile phone

11 _____ _____ *n.* a notice displayed on your mobile to tell you that somebody called

12 _____ _____ `PHR V` to tell somebody to speak more loudly

13 _____ _____ `PHR V` to be interrupted when talking on the phone by a break in the connection.

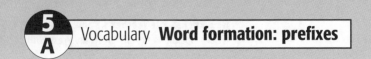

A

a B is going to read a sentence to you, including the sound BLEEP, which means that a word is missing. Guess the missing word by adding a prefix (e.g. *anti*, *re*, etc.) to the first word in your list (*cook*), and make any other necessary changes.

1 cook	2 social	3 pay	4 consider	5 line
6 national	7 pronounce	8 react	9 play	10 mature

b Read your first sentence in **c** to **B**. **B** will try to guess the missing word.

c Continue taking turns to read your sentences.

1 The film isn't as good as the reviews say. It's very BLEEP. (**overrated**)
2 You got the wrong end of the stick and completely BLEEP what I said. (**misunderstood**)
3 He might look a bit tired now but don't BLEEP him. He could still win this match. (**underestimate**)
4 My boss isn't happy with my report so he's asked me to make some changes and has asked me to BLEEP it. (**rewrite**)
5 Visitors to the hospital have to wash their hands with BLEEP soap before they enter a ward. (**antibacterial**)
6 In hot weather it's easy to become BLEEP if you don't drink enough liquids. (**dehydrated**)
7 BLEEP forces managed to put down the rebellion. (**pro-government**)
8 I proposed having the Christmas party on December the 23rd, but I was BLEEP by my colleagues. (**outvoted**)
9 I've been living in the village for years, but I still feel like an BLEEP. I don't feel part of the community. (**outsider**)
10 It was a BLEEP attack. The criminals had been watching his house for several days. (**premeditated**)

- -

B

a Read your first sentence in **c** to **A**. Explain that the sound BLEEP represents a missing word. **A** will try to guess the missing word.

b Now **A** is going to read a sentence to you, including BLEEP. Guess the missing word by adding a prefix (e.g. *anti*, *re*, etc.) to the first word in your list (*rate*), and make any other necessary changes.

1 rate	2 understand	3 estimate	4 write	5 bacteria
6 hydrate	7 government	8 vote	9 side	10 meditate

c Continue taking turns to read your sentences.

1 Sorry, but my steak is a bit BLEEP. I asked for it to be well-done. (**undercooked**)
2 The government are introducing new measures to try to control BLEEP behaviour in young people. (**antisocial**)
3 Please return this form in the BLEEP envelope provided. (**prepaid**)
4 I want you to BLEEP your decision to leave the company. (**reconsider**)
5 Could you give me a brief BLEEP of tomorrow's events? (**outline**)
6 The opposition party are pressing the government to BLEEP the health service. (**denationalize**)
7 The problem with my name is because it's foreign, people always BLEEP it. (**mispronounce**)
8 My dad totally BLEEP when I told him I'd failed my exams. In fact, he went crazy! (**overreacted**)
9 The champion completely BLEEP his rival, and the match was over very quickly. (**outplayed**)
10 He looked BLEEP old because he had such an unhealthy lifestyle. (**prematurely**)

a Look at the sentences and circle the correct preposition.

b If you think both prepositions are possible, tick (✓) them.

1   When the bull ran **to / towards** me, I leapt over the fence.

2   My house is **in / on** a really busy main road. The noise of the traffic sometimes gets on my nerves.

3   I always try to arrive **to / at** the office before the boss gets there.

4   He saw a parking space in the car park and drove right **into / in** it.

5   Birpeck is a really pretty village just **outside / out of** the city centre.

6   The burglar climbed **above / over** the wall and ran **off / away**.

7   We've been driving **round / around** for hours. Why don't we ask someone the way?

8   Tina panicked as her credit card just wouldn't come **out / out of** the cash machine.

9   The cat climbed **onto / on** the table and then jumped **off / away**.

10 Your mobile won't work unless you put **in / into** your SIM card first.

11 Go straight on and turn right **in / at** the next set of traffic lights.

12 It's considered bad luck to walk **under / below** a ladder.

13 There was a hole in the middle of the road and I had to drive **past / round** it.

14 The tunnel's about four kilometres long and lots of people feel a bit claustrophobic when they drive **through / across** it.

15 The temperature at night falls to 5° **below / under** zero.

16 It was boiling **inside / into** the cinema because the air conditioning wasn't working.

17 If you walk **along / across** this aisle, you'll see the frozen food cabinet near the end.

18 Their wedding cake had little figures of a bride and groom **on top of / on top**.

19 He's been **in / at** hospital for the last couple of days as he's had his appendix removed.

20 I wonder what's **inside / in** that box?

21 The flat's a bit small, but at least we've got a roof **over / above** our heads.

22 If you want a short cut you can walk **across / through** the department store, and then when you come **out / outside** the other side turn left into Shelton Street.

23 You'll never ever see him **in / into** the kitchen – he loathes cooking.

24 Just put the shopping on top **of / on** the table please.

A

a Look at your ten words and similes.

b Write definitions for your partner to guess. Try not to use any part of the word or phrase in your definition!

c Read your definitions to your partner. Does he / she know the word and similes?

Words	Definitions
a placebo	_____
stitches	_____
as stubborn as a mule	_____
a GP	_____
as quick as a flash	_____
a plaster	_____
hypnosis	_____
to watch your weight	_____
he drinks like a fish	_____
a rash	_____

B

a Look at your ten words and similes.

b Write definitions for your partner to guess. Try not to use any part of the word or phrase in your definition!

c Read your definitions to your partner. Does he / she know the words and similes?

Words	Definitions
a virus	_____
food poisoning	_____
as white as a sheet	_____
a scan	_____
needles	_____
a bruise	_____
as blind as a bat	_____
a bruise	_____
an osteopath	_____
it works like a dream	_____

New English File Teacher's Book Advanced
Photocopiable © Oxford University Press 2010

● Right (✓) or wrong (✗)? If you think the word or phrase in **bold** is wrong, correct it and write the new word or phrase in the space provided.

1 He was in Dubai for work, but he had to **cut** the trip **down** because his wife was taken ill. _____

2 We're going on a **parcel** holiday. _____

3 What was your **travel** to Hong Kong like? _____

4 We never bother to **take on** travel insurance when we go on holiday. _____

5 I think **backpacking** would be the cheapest way to travel round Europe. _____

6 What time are you **setting away** tomorrow morning?
_____

7 The resort was far too **touristic** for us. _____

8 In winter, only a few people come here, but in the summer it gets seriously **overcrowded**. _____

9 Our hotel is up in the hills and completely **off the bitten track**.
_____

10 **Guided trips** round the museum start at 11 a.m.
_____

11 There are two flights to New Zealand – a direct one (which is more expensive) and another one with a **stayover** in Bangkok.
_____

12 The views from the mountain are **breathtaking**.
_____

13 Have you seen there's yet another **cheap-cost airline** with flights to Paris? _____

14 We're going to have to **put out** our trip until the end of the month. _____

15 I think the cathedral is **overstated**. It's not nearly as beautiful as people say. _____

16 Is it cheaper to book a **round trip**, or to get two one-way flights?
_____

17 Last year we **went to a safari** and it was absolutely fantastic.
_____

18 The town is very **lifely** at this time of year, as it's packed with holidaymakers. _____

19 Flying **long haul** can be exhausting if you're travelling in economy. _____

20 It used to be quite a pretty town, but they've really **spoilt** it with all those high-rise buildings. _____

● Complete the animal idiom in the dialogues.

1 A What's your new boss like as a person?

  B I'm not too sure as she doesn't talk about herself much. She's a bit of a _ _ _ _ horse.

2 A You're going to be sick if you have any more chocolates. You're making a real _ _ _ of _ _ _ _ _ _ _ _.

  B OK, but hide them somewhere I can't see them.

3 A What finally made you split up with your partner?

  B Well, things were already pretty bad, but the last _ _ _ _ _ _ was when he admitted that he'd had an affair!

4 A I've told Andy a million times he has to keep his room tidy.

  B If he's anything like my son, he'll nod and do nothing about it. It's like _ _ _ _ _ _ off a _ _ _ _ ' _ back.

5 A Can you go and get some milk from the petrol station?

  B No problem. I need to get some petrol anyway so I can kill _ _ _ birds with _ _ _ _ _ _ _ _.

6 A The interview went really well. I'm absolutely sure I'm going to get the job!

  B Well, I wouldn't count your _ _ _ _ _ _ _ _ until you hear from them.

7 A Does your wife know about the surprise birthday party you're organizing for her?

  B I think she might _ _ _ _ _ _ a rat as she saw me unloading 50 bottles of champagne from the car!

8 A Do you think we should bring up the question of possible redundancies with the boss?

  B No, I would just let _ _ _ _ _ _ _ _ _ dogs _ _ _. He hasn't mentioned it for several months now.

9 A Did you tell Jack what you thought about his behaviour at the party?

  B I did, and he was so ashamed that he went off with his _ _ _ _ between his _ _ _ _.

10 A I wish I hadn't moved back to the UK.

  B Why?

  A Things have changed a lot since I last lived here and I sometimes feel like a fish _ _ _ of _ _ _ _ _.

11 A What happened with your grandfather's will?

  B Well my uncle was always his favourite child, so he got the lion's _ _ _ _ _.

12 A Why are you so fed up at work?

  B Because I always do all the _ _ _ _ _ _ work but my boss gets all the credit!

New English File Teacher's Book Advanced
Photocopiable © Oxford University Press 2010

● Explain the difference between the following pairs of words.

1 like (adj) alike (adj)	**2** especially specially	**3** actually currently	**4** affect effect
5 economic economical	**6** beside besides	**7** ache pain	**8** campsite camping
9 suit suite	**10** sight site	**11** ashamed embarrassed	**12** argument discussion
13 view scenery	**14** deny refuse	**15** lay lie	**16** compromise commitment
17 wages salary	**17** journey trip	**19** career job	**20** announce advertise

225

A **a** Look at your crossword and make sure you know the meaning of all the words you have.

b Now ask **B** to define a word for you. Ask e.g. *What's 13 across? What's 6 down?* Write the word in.

c Now **B** will ask you to define a word.

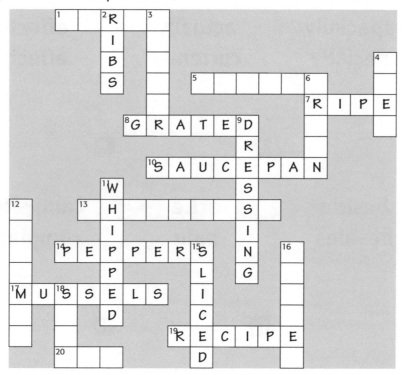

- -

B **a** Look at your crossword and make sure you know the meaning of all the words you have.

b **A** will ask you to define a word.

c Now ask **A** to define a word for you. Ask e.g. *What's 10 across? What's 2 down?* Write the word in.

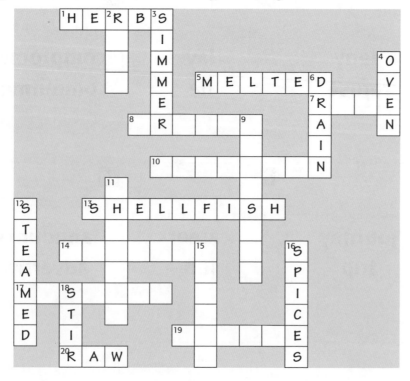

New English File Teacher's Book Advanced
Photocopiable © Oxford University Press 2010

● Work with a partner. You have ten minutes to complete the sentences
with the correct form of the word in **bold**.

STRONG

A You need to _ _ _ _ _ _ _ _ _ _ your stomach muscles by doing more sit-ups.

B He just doesn't know his own _ _ _ _ _ _ _ _! He pulled the cord so hard, the blinds broke.

LONG

A I swim at least 20 _ _ _ _ _ _ _ of the pool every morning.

B The dress is a bit short. Would it be possible to _ _ _ _ _ _ _ _ it?

DEEP

A When I did a scuba diving course, I went down to a _ _ _ _ _ of five metres.

B The water is much _ _ _ _ _ _ in the middle of the lake than round the edge.

SHORT

A She won't be long. She'll be with you _ _ _ _ _ _ _.

B I have asthma and I sometimes suffer from _ _ _ _ _ _ _ _ _ of breath, especially in the spring.

WIDE

A English is _ _ _ _ _ _ spoken around the world.

B The wardrobe is about two metres high and one and a half in _ _ _ _ _.

HIGH

A The crisis was at its _ _ _ _ _ _ in 2009.

B In literary circles, the book is _ _ _ _ _ _ thought of.

WEAK

A One of my sister's _ _ _ _ _ _ _ _ _ _ is never accepting that she's in the wrong.

B His long illness _ _ _ _ _ _ _ _ him considerably.

THICK

A My favourite breakfast is hot toast _ _ _ _ _ _ _ spread with marmalade.

B The fog _ _ _ _ _ _ _ _ _ and it became increasingly difficult to see where we were going.

FLAT

A The child jumped on the sandcastle and completely _ _ _ _ _ _ _ _ _ _ it.

B The trip was made even more boring by the _ _ _ _ _ _ _ _ of the landscape.

Work	The family	Idioms	Formal verbs
a short-term contract	a step brother	to get the wrong end of the stick	to omit
to get a rise	a distant relative	to smell a rat	to transcribe
to be made redundant	a single-parent family	to see eye to eye	to ensure
challenging	to bring up	to kill two birds with one stone	to require
perks	a close family	his bark is worse than his bite	to adhere to
staff	a get-together	to have a skeleton in the cupboard	to conduct business
to be fired	the black sheep of the family	it's like water off a duck's back	to view

Phrasal verbs	Time	Sounds	Money
to hang up	to have time on your hands	to drip	a mortgage
to run out of sth	time's up	to sniff	loaded
to take after sb	to kill time	to hoot	to be in the red
to blow sth up	to make up for lost time	to mumble	tight-fisted
to set off /out	to give somebody a hard time	to stammer	an income
to get over sth	for the time being	to hum	the stock market
to cut off	to take your time	to giggle	an instalment

History	Compound adjectives	Confusing words	Humour
to loot	high-heeled	a suite	witty
a spear	narrow-minded	besides	to make fun of
to retreat	well-behaved	to announce	a cartoonist
a ceasefire	absent-minded	a stranger	to get a joke
a coup	easy-going	ashamed	a pun
to surrender	second-hand	commitment	to burst out laughing
to overthrow	mass-produced	to deny	hilarious

The natural world	Food	Travel	get
a hive	to stir	long-haul	to get to know
endangered species	a chopping board	a round trip	to get a shock
fins	poached eggs	a package holiday	to get rid of sth
battery hens	to drain	to take out travel insurance	to get your own back
a puppy	to heat	an outing	to get on your nerves
to sting	a frying pan	off the beaten track	to get a life
an animal activist	a recipe	touristy	to get into trouble

1 The Logical Song 1.8   CD1 Track 9

B

Intensive listening (individual words) and song interpretation

| LANGUAGE | Adjectives (mainly describing personality, e.g *sensible*, *cynical*) |

- Copy one sheet per student and give them out. Focus on **a**. Tell SS to read the song once to get a rough idea of what it is about and to think briefly what some of the missing words might be.
- Focus on **b**. Tell SS that you are going to play the song once all the way through, and then with pauses. Play the song once. Then play it again pausing after every four lines (and after the chorus) to give them time to fill in the missing words.
- Get SS to compare with a partner, and then check answers. Make sure SS are clear about the meaning of all the adjectives, most of which they have already seen. You may need to highlight the meaning of *cynical* (= believing that people only do things to help themselves rather than for good or honest reasons), and *presentable* (= looking clean and suitable to be seen in public), and remind them of the meaning of *sensible* (= able to make good judgements based on reason and experience rather than emotion).

1 wonderful	2 magical	3 sensible	4 responsible
5 practical	6 dependable	7 cynical	8 simple
9 absurd	10 fanatical	11 respectable	12 presentable

- Now focus on **c**. Give SS a few minutes in pairs to discuss what they think is the message of the song.

Suggested answer
The singer compares his childhood, when life seemed wonderful and magical, to the time when he was sent away to boarding school to learn to be a model citizen (sensible, logical, responsible, clinical, etc). This kind of education (which seems to lack any idea of creativity or freedom of thought) turned him into 'a vegetable', somebody who cannot question anything for fear of being labelled a radical or liberal. It also leaves him wondering, 'Who am I?'

- Get SS to read **Song facts**.
- Finally, you may want to play the song again for SS to sing along.

2 50 Ways to Leave Your Lover 2.12   CD1 Track 32

C

Intensive listening (individual words)
Understanding idiomatic and colloquial language

| LANGUAGE | Idiomatic and colloquial language: *drop off (the key)*, *hop on the bus*, *sleep on it*, etc. |

- Copy one sheet per student and cut into two pieces. Give each student the top half of the sheet and focus on **a**. Tell SS that you are going to play the whole song and that they will hear the chorus three times. Play the song, pausing after each verse and chorus to give SS time to answer the questions. Replay as necessary. Check answers.

1 The problem is in the man's head. He will find the solution by thinking logically.
2 I don't usually interfere in other people's problems. I hope what I am saying won't be misunderstood / misinterpreted.
3 Jack, Stan, Roy, Gus, Lee.
   Slip out the back / Make a new plan / Hop on the bus / Drop off the key.
4 He feels pain.
5 Go to bed and think about the problem. She thinks that in the morning the man will understand clearly what he has to do.

- Now give out the song lyrics (the bottom half of the photocopy). Focus on **b**. Play the song again, and then give SS time, in pairs, to discuss what the highlighted phrases mean. Elicit suggestions and check answers.

slip out the back: slip = to go somewhere quickly and quietly, especially without being noticed
out the back = out of the back door.
coy = shy or pretending to be shy and innocent, especially about love or sex
Hop on the bus: hop = (informal) to jump quickly onto sth. (*Hop* also means to jump on one foot.)
drop off the key = leave the key somewhere or with sb. *Drop off* can also be used for leaving people somewhere, e.g. *Can you drop me off at the doctor's on your way to work?*
It grieves me = (formal, old fashioned) It makes me feel very sad. In other contexts *grieve* means feel sad after the death of a loved one
sleep on it = to delay making a decision about sth until the next day, so that you have time to think about it
see the light = to finally understand or accept sth, especially sth obvious

- Get SS to read **Song facts**.
- Finally, you may want to play the song again for SS to sing along.

3 A Lady of a Certain Age 3.16   CD2 Track 20

C

Intensive listening for meaning
Paraphrasing idioms and metaphors

| LANGUAGE | Idioms and metaphors: *chase the sun, the smart set*, etc. |

- Copy one sheet per student and cut into two pieces. Give each student the top half of the sheet and focus on the title of the song. Ask SS what they understand by the expression 'of a certain age' (= a polite way of saying that someone is no longer young / becoming old).
- Focus on **a** and give SS a few moments to read the questions. Tell SS that you will play the song once, pausing after each verse and chorus to give them time to answer the questions. Play the recording, replaying sections as necessary, giving SS time to discuss what they have understood and to answer the questions. Check answers.

1 She had been part of high society, having holidays with royalty and eating with celebrities. She travelled the world, wore designer clothes and expensive perfumes, and attended famous people's parties.
2 She is no longer young and she is alone.
3 'You wouldn't think that I was seventy.' The young man pretends that he is surprised at her age, and that she looks younger.
4 She married a rich man so that she could keep her extravagant lifestyle (she had lost a lot of her wealth through paying high taxes under a socialist government).
5 She employed a nanny to look after them and later they were sent away to boarding school.
6 She now says that she is seven years younger than before (sixty-three).
7 He doesn't stay very long ('leaves in a hurry').
8 Her daughter married 'a strange young man' who she didn't like.
9 He left their villa to his mistress (his lover).
10 She now claims to be fifty-three.

- Now give out the other half of the sheet with the lyrics, and focus on **b**. Play the song again for SS to listen and read. Give SS time, in pairs, to discuss what the highlighted phrases mean. Elicit suggestions and check answers. You could elicit the meaning of other useful vocabulary, e.g. *starlet* = young female celebrity, *sip* = drink taking very small amounts each time.

> *the smart set* = an exclusive group of rich, fashionable people   *smart* = well dressed (also 'the jet set')
> *Scaling the dizzy heights* = IDM climbing to the top of high society   *scale* = to climb   *dizzy* = the feeling that everything is spinning around
> *Armed only with a cheque book and a family tree* = all she needed to climb in high society was her family background (her family were presumably wealthy)
> *the light of youth became obscured* = she became old and her beauty faded   *became obscured* = became difficult to see
> *in the shade* = (literally) in a dark, cool area where the sun's light doesn't reach. Here it probably has the double meaning that she no longer sits in the sun, and also that she is no longer an important figure in high society.
> *conspiratorial wink* = adj from *conspiracy*, a secret plan made by a group of people. She winks at him to show that a secret is being shared between them, i.e. that she is not giving her real age.
> *keep your sanity* = so that she did not go mad with the stresses of bringing up children
> *Your son's in stocks and bonds* = her son made his money from investing in the stock market   *a stock* = a share that sb has bought in a company or business   *a bond* = an investment product where a government or company pay you interest on money you lend them
> *of whom you don't approve* = she didn't think her daughter's husband was suitable   *approve* = to think that sb / sth is good or acceptable
> *Your husband's hollow heart gave out* = her husband died of a heart attack   *give out* = PHR V stop working. His heart is *hollow* (= having an empty space inside), i.e. he had no feelings of love for her.

- Get SS to read **Song facts**.
- Finally, you may want to play the song again for SS to sing along.

4 C Addicted to Love 4.14   CD3 Track 4
Guessing verbs

LANGUAGE	Physical symptoms of addiction: *sweat, shake, tight throat*, etc.

- Copy one sheet per student and give them out. Focus on **a**. Give SS time to read the song lyrics and to try and guess the missing verbs. SS could do this in pairs or individually and then compare guesses with a partner. Elicit ideas as to what the missing verbs might be, but don't check answers at this stage.
- Focus on **b** and play the song for SS to check their answers. Replay particular verses or the chorus as necessary. Check answers. Elicit the meaning of *to face sth* = accept that a difficult situation exists (and deal with it), *your teeth grind* = to rub your teeth together hard.

> 1 shakes 2 sleep 3 eat 4 breathe 5 face 6 read
> 7 beats 8 crave 9 mind 10 grind

- Focus on **c**, and give SS time in pairs to discuss what the highlighted phrases mean. Check answers.

> *This lights are on, but you're not at home* = You're not paying attention to what's happening around you. This comes from the humorous idiom *the lights are on but nobody's home*, which is used to describe sb who is stupid, not thinking clearly, or not paying attention, e.g. 'He never pays attention to what's going on. The lights are on but nobody's home!'
> *You're in deep* = ambiguous: it could mean 'You are deeply in love', 'You have a serious problem', or both.
> *you're immune to the stuff* = you are not affected by this (i.e. by love)
> *a one-track mind* = only being able to think about one particular subject obsessively, usually sex-related
> *Oblivion is all you crave* = wanting to reach a state where you are not aware of what is happening
> *Your will is not your own* = you are not in control of your own decisions

- Get SS to read **Song facts**.
- Finally, you may want to play the song again for SS to sing along.

5 B Vincent 5.15   CD3 Track 24
Intensive listening (understanding phrases with linked words)

LANGUAGE	Metaphoric language: *flaming flowers, virgin snow*, etc.

- Copy one sheet per student and give them out. Focus on the painting of Van Gogh and elicit what they know about him.
- Focus on **a** and play the song, pausing after each verse for SS to write the missing words. Emphasize that each phrase has three words. Replay each verse as necessary. Check answers after each verse. Elicit the meaning of *crush* in 13 (= press or squeeze sth so hard that it is damaged or injured).

1 blue and grey	2 in my soul	3 tried to say

1 blue and grey   2 in my soul   3 tried to say
4 set them free   5 they'll listen now   6 Vincent's eyes of
7 lined in pain   8 left in sight   9 took your life
10 As beautiful as   11 in empty halls   12 watch the world
13 crushed and broken   14 think I know   15 set them free
16 they will never

- Now focus on **b** and give SS, in pairs, time to discuss what they think the phrases mean. Check answers.

snowy linen land = the white canvas which Van Gogh
    painted on
flaming flowers = flowers which are the colour of flames
    (red, orange, and yellow)
swirling clouds = clouds which are moving around in a
    circle
morning fields of amber grain = fields of grain which look
    amber coloured (a yellowish brown) in the morning
    light
weathered faces = faces which have been wrinkled and
    darkened from the sun, wind, and cold
ragged clothes = clothes which are falling to pieces
the virgin snow = snow that is perfectly white and
    untouched, i.e. nobody has walked on it

- Get SS to read **Song facts**.
- Finally, you may want to play the song again for SS to sing along.

6 A I Wish I Could Go Travelling Again 6.1 CD4 Track 3

Intensive listening for meaning
Idiomatic language

LANGUAGE   Travel lexis: *jet-lagged, overpriced hotel, tropical rain,* etc.

- Copy one sheet per student and cut into two pieces. Give out the top half of the sheet and focus on the title of the song.
- Focus on **a** and give SS time to read the list of problems. Tell SS you are going to play the song once all the way through and then again, pausing after each verse. Don't check answers at this point.
- Now give out the song lyrics (the bottom half of the photocopy). Focus on **b**. Play the song again for SS as they read, and check answers to **a**. Then elicit from the class which problems should be ticked and what words / phrases in the song gave them the answer.

Problems which should be ticked are:
Feeling tired after a long-haul flight ('jet-lagged')
Losing a suitcase ('our luggage gone astray' = got lost or stolen)
Rude waiters ('give us a reprimand'= a negative comment about your behaviour)
Almost missing a flight ('sit in traffic anxious about our plane')
Being irritated by a travelling companion ('your blasé comments drive me half insane'. *blasé comments* = comments which show he is not worried about the situation because he has experienced it many times before)
Bad weather ('the tropical rain')
Unsatisfactory accommodation ('an overpriced hotel devoid of charm')

- Focus on **c**, which consolidates some of the phrases which came up in **b** and focuses on some other interesting lexis in the song.

1 shades   2 sip   3 awning   4 go astray   5 blasé
6 dash   7 faulty   8 overpriced   9 devoid

- Focus on **d** and do this as a whole class activity. Elicit ideas.

Possible answer
The singer regrets the break-up of a relationship with a person with whom she travelled a lot in the past. She wishes she was still with this person and could go travelling again. She says she would even enjoy all the travel problems they had previously experienced and which had then irritated her. Finally she realizes she doesn't want go travelling again, as it would just keep reminding her of her loss.

- Get SS to read **Song Facts**.
- Finally, you may want to play the song again for SS to sing along.

7 B Eye of the Tiger 7.8 CD4 Track 30

Intensive listening (to complete phrases)
Understanding idiomatic language

LANGUAGE   Idioms: *face to face, go the distance, lose your grip*

- Copy one sheet per student and cut into two pieces. Give out the top half of the sheet and focus on **a**. Give SS time to read the list of words and phrases **a–l**. Tell SS not to worry about the meaning of individual words at this stage. Play the song, pausing after each verse for SS to complete the phrases. Replay as necessary. Check answers.

a street   b chances   c distant   d feet   e glory   f grip
g fight   h challenge   i face   j odds   k top   l guts

- Now give out the song lyrics (the bottom half of the photocopy). Focus on **b**. Play the song again for SS to listen and read. Then give them time to complete the task and to compare their answers with a partner. Check answers. Highlight the literal meaning of *grip* = hold tightly. Explain that *stack* = pile up, and *the odds* = the probabilities of success or failure. This is a reference to the idiom *the odds are stacked against us* = it is more likely that we will fail than succeed. Focus on the photo and elicit / explain that it comes from the film *Rocky III* (which starred Sylvester Stallone and is about a boxer who is the world heavyweight champion.)

1 lose your grip   2 go the distance   3 rise to the challenge
4 stack the odds   5 have the guts

- Focus on **c** and do this as a whole-class activity.

Possible answer
The song has a positive message which encourages people to continue, even if the situation looks bad. 'The eye of the tiger' means to be confident, focused, determined to win, strong, etc.

- Get SS to read **Song facts**.
- Finally, you may want to play the song again for SS to sing along.

New English File Teacher's Book Advanced
Photocopiable © Oxford University Press 2010

a Read the song lyrics and think about what the missing words might be (they are all adjectives).

b Listen to the song and fill in the missing words.

The Logical Song

When I was young, it seemed that life was so **w**_____,[1]
A miracle, oh it was beautiful, **m**_____,[2]
And all the birds in the trees, well they'd be singing so happily,
Oh joyfully, oh playfully, watching me
But then they sent me away to teach me how to be **s**_____,[3]
Logical, oh **r**_____,[4] **pr**_____.[5]
And then they showed me a world where I could be so **d**_____,[6]
Clinical, oh intellectual, **c**_____.[7]

There are times when all the world's asleep,
The questions run too deep
For such a **s**_____[8] man.
Won't you please, please tell me what we've learned
I know it sounds **a**_____,[9]
(But) please tell me who I am.

I say now watch what you say or they'll be calling you a radical,
A liberal, oh **f**_____,[10] criminal
Won't you sign up your name, we'd like to feel you're
Acceptable, **r**_____,[11] oh **pr**_____[12] a vegetable?

Oh take it, take it, take it, yeah

But at night, when all the world's asleep,
The questions run so deep, etc.

c Read the lyrics again. With a partner, discuss what you think the message of the song is.

Song facts

The Logical Song was an international hit single for the group Supertramp from their best-selling album *Breakfast in America*. The song was inspired by the experience of Roger Hodgson, the lead vocalist in this song, who was sent to boarding school as a boy.

a In this song the singer's new lover gives examples of how a man can leave his lover.
Listen to the song, and answer the questions.

1   Where is the problem, according to the woman?
    How does she think the man will find the solution?   _____

2   What do you think these phrases in the second verse mean?
    It's really not my habit to intrude.   _____
    I hope my meaning won't be lost or misconstrued.   _____

3   Write down two of the men's names you can hear in the
    chorus, and one of the ways that they leave their lover.   _____

4   How does the man seem to feel about breaking up
    with his partner?   _____

5   In the final verse, what does she suggest they both do?
    What does she think will happen in the morning?   _____

- -

b Now listen again with the lyrics and check your answers.

50 Ways to Leave Your Lover

'The problem is all inside your head,' she said to me
'The answer is easy if you take it logically
I'd like to help you in your struggle to be free
There must be fifty ways to leave your lover.'

She said 'it's really not my habit to intrude
Furthermore, I hope my meaning won't be lost or
   misconstrued
So I'll repeat myself, at the risk of being crude
There must be fifty ways to leave your lover
Fifty ways to leave your lover.'

Chorus
You just slip out the back, Jack
Make a new plan, Stan
You don't need to be coy, Roy
Just listen to me / Just get yourself free
Hop on the bus, Gus
You don't need to discuss much
Just drop off the key, Lee
And get yourself free.

Ooo slip out the back, Jack
Make a new plan, Stan
You don't need to be coy, Roy
Just listen to me
Hop on the bus, Gus
You don't need to discuss much
Just drop off the key, Lee
And get yourself free.

She said 'It grieves me so to see you in such pain
I wish there was something I could do to make you
   smile again.'
I said 'I appreciate that and would you please explain
About the fifty ways?'

She said 'Why don't we both just sleep on it tonight
And I believe in the morning you'll begin to see the
   light?'
And then she kissed me and I realized she probably
   was right
There must be fifty ways to leave your lover
Fifty ways to leave your lover.

Chorus

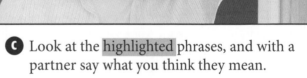

c Look at the highlighted phrases, and with a
partner say what you think they mean.

Song facts

This song, from the album *Still Crazy After All These Years*, was a big hit
for the singer Paul Simon. In a 1975 interview, Simon told the story of
this song: 'I woke up one morning in my apartment on Central Park and
the opening words just popped into my mind: "The problem is all inside
your head, she said to me..." That was the first thing I thought of. So I
just started building on that line.' According to Simon's younger brother
Eddie (from the same interview), Paul made this song up while teaching
his son how to rhyme.

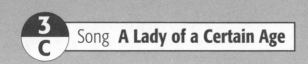

a Listen to the song once, pausing after each verse and chorus, and answering the questions with a partner.

Verse 1
1 What kind of lifestyle did the woman use to have?

Chorus 1
2 What impression do you get of the woman now?
3 How old does she say she is to the young man? What does he reply?

Verse 2
4 Why kind of man did she marry? Why?
5 How did she bring up her children?

Chorus 2
6 What has changed in what she says to the young man?

Verse 3
7 What happens now when her son visits her?
8 What happened to her daughter?
9 What unpleasant surprise did she get when her husband died?

Chorus 3
10 What has changed in what she says to the young man?

---

b Read the glossary, and listen to the song again with the lyrics. With a partner look at the highlighted phrases, and decide what you think they mean.

A Lady of a Certain Age

Verse 1
Back in the day you had been part of the smart set
You'd holidayed with kings, dined out with starlets
From London to New York, Cap Ferrat to Capri
In perfume by Chanel and clothes by Givenchy
You sipped Camparis with David and Peter
At Noel's parties by Lake Geneva
Scaling the dizzy heights of high society
Armed only with a cheque book and a family tree

Chorus 1
You chased the sun around the Côte d'Azur
Until the light of youth became obscured
And left you on your own and in the shade
An English lady of a certain age
And if a nice young man would buy you a drink
You'd say with a conspiratorial wink
'You wouldn't think that I was seventy'
And he'd say, 'no, you couldn't be!'

Verse 2
You had to marry someone very very rich
So that you might be kept in the style to which
You had all of your life been accustomed to
But that the socialists had taxed away from you
You gave him children, a girl and a boy
To keep your sanity a nanny was employed
And when the time came they were sent away
Oh that was simply what you did in those days

Chorus 2
You chased the sun around the Côte d'Azur
Until the light of youth became obscured
And left you on your own and in the shade
An English lady of a certain age
And if a nice young man would buy you a drink
You'd say with a conspiratorial wink
'You wouldn't think that I was sixty-three'
And he'd say, 'no, you couldn't be!'

Verse 3
Your son's in stocks and bonds and lives back in Surrey
Flies down once in a while and leaves in a hurry
Your daughter never finished her finishing school
Married a strange young man of whom you don't approve
Your husband's hollow heart gave out one Christmas Day
He left the villa to his mistress in Marseilles
And so you come here to escape your little flat
Hoping someone will fill your glass and let you chat about how

Chorus 3
You chased the sun around the Côte d'Azur
Until the light of youth became obscured
And left you all alone and in the shade
An English lady of a certain age
And if a nice young man would buy you a drink
You'd say with a conspiratorial wink
'You wouldn't think that I was fifty-three'
And he'd say, 'no, you couldn't be!'

Song facts
A Lady of a Certain Age was written by Neil Hammond, the lead singer and founding member of the band The Divine Comedy, and was released in 2006 on the album *Victory for the Comic Muse*.

Glossary
Côte d'Azur = an area on the south coast of France, popular with tourists and famous for being glamorous
Campari = a drink
Finishing school = a private school where young women from rich families are taught how to behave in fashionable society

a Read the song lyrics. Try to guess the missing verbs.

b Listen to the song and check.

Addicted to Love

The lights are on, but you're not home
Your mind is not your own
Your heart sweats, your body **sh**_____ [1]
Another kiss is what it takes
You can't **sl**_____, [2] no, you can't **e**_____ [3]
There's no doubt, you're in deep
Your throat is tight, you can't **br**_____ [4]
Another kiss is all you need

Chorus

Whoa, you like to think that you're immune to the stuff, oh yeah
It's closer to the truth to say you can't get enough
You know you're gonna have to **f**_____ [5] it
You're addicted to love

You see the signs, but you can't **r**_____ [6]
You're running at a different speed
Your heart **b**_____ [7] in double time
Another kiss and you'll be mine, a one-track mind
You can't be saved
Oblivion is all you **cr**_____ [8]
If there's some left for you
You don't **m**_____ [9] if you do

Chorus

Might as well face it you're addicted to love (x5)
The lights are on, but you're not home
Your will is not your own
Your heart sweats, your teeth **gr**_____ [10]
Another kiss and you'll be mine

Chorus

Might as well face it you're addicted to love (x5)

c Look at the highlighted phrases, and with a partner say what they mean.

Song facts

This 1985 song was number one in the US and number five in the UK charts for the British singer
Robert Palmer. The video became an icon of the 1980s, and is constantly parodied, including in a
Pepsi commercial with Britney Spears. Palmer died of a heart attack in 2003, aged 54.

a Listen to the song verse by verse. Complete each gap with a three-word phrase. Be careful, because the words are often linked together.

Vincent

Starry starry night
Paint your palette _____ [1]
Look out on a summer's day
With eyes that know the darkness _____ [2]
Shadows on the hills
Sketch the trees and the daffodils
Catch the breeze and the winter chills
In colours on the snowy linen land

Chorus
Now I understand
What you _____ [3] to me
And how you suffered for your sanity
And how you tried to _____ [4]
They would not listen,
They did not know how
Perhaps _____ [5]

Starry starry night
Flaming flowers that brightly blaze
Swirling clouds in violet haze
Reflecting _____ [6] china blue
Colours changing hue
Morning fields of amber grain
Weathered faces _____ [7]
Are soothed beneath the artist's loving hand

Chorus
For they could not love you
But still your love was true
And when no hope was _____ [8]
on that starry starry night,
You _____ [9] as lovers often do,
But I could have told you, Vincent
This world was never meant for one
_____ [10] you

Starry starry night
Portraits hung _____ [11]
Frameless heads on nameless walls
With eyes that _____ [12] and can't forget
Like the strangers that you've met
The ragged men in ragged clothes
The silver thorn of bloody rose
Lie _____ [13] on the virgin snow

Now I _____ [14]
What you tried to say to me
And how you suffered for your sanity
And how you tried to _____ [15]
They would not listen
They're not listening still
Perhaps _____ [16]

b Look at the highlighted phrases which help to convey Van Gogh's style of painting. With a partner say what you think they mean.

Glossary
daffodil = tall yellow spring flower shaped like a trumpet
china blue = the blue colour in Chinese porcelain
hue = a particular shade of a colour

Song facts
This song, a tribute to Vincent Van Gogh, was written by Don McLean and first recorded by on his album *American Pie*. He wrote the song after reading a book about Van Gogh and it reflects his admiration not only for his paintings, but also for the man himself.

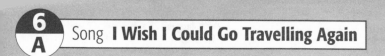

a Listen to the song once. Tick (✓) the travel-related problems that the singer mentions.

Feeling tired after a long-haul flight   **Losing a suitcase**   **Being robbed**

Rude waiters   **Flight overbooking**   **Almost missing a flight**

Being irritated by a travelling companion   **Disappointing food**

Bad weather   **Unsatisfactory accommodation**   **Crowded beaches**

---

b Now listen again with the lyrics and check your answers.

I Wish I Could Go Travelling Again

I wish I could go travelling again
It feels like this summer will never end
And I've had such good offers from several of my friends
I wish I could go travelling again

I want to sit in my shades, sipping my latte
Beneath the awning of a famous café
Jet-lagged and with our luggage gone astray
I wish I could go travelling again

I want a waiter to give us a reprimand
In a language neither of us understand
While we argue about the customs of the land
I wish I could go travelling again ·

I want to sit in traffic anxious about our plane
While your blasé comments drive me half insane
I want to dash for shelter with you through the tropical rain
I wish I could go travelling again

I want to be awakened by a faulty fire alarm
In an overpriced hotel devoid of charm
Then fall asleep again back in your arms
I wish I could go travelling again

But how can I ever go travelling again
When I know I'll just keep remembering again
When I know I'll just be gathering again
Reminders to break my heart?

I wish could go travelling again, etc.

c Find words in the song which mean:

1 _____ *noun (informal)* sunglasses

2 _____ *verb* drink, taking very small amounts each time

3 _____ *noun* a sheet of strong cloth that stretches out from above a door or window to keep off the sun or rain

4 _____ **IDM** to become lost / stolen

5 _____ *adj* not impressed, excited or worried about sth, because you have seen or experienced it many times before

6 _____ *verb* go somewhere suddenly and quickly

7 _____ *adj* not perfect; not working correctly

8 _____ *adj* too expensive; costing more than it is worth

9 _____ ~ of sth, completely lacking in sth

d Read and listen to the song again. What do you think the main message of the song is?

Song facts

This song was sung by Stacey Kent, an American jazz singer. The lyrics were written by Kazuo Ishiguro, the Japanese / British writer, most famous for the novel *The Remains of the Day*.

New English File Teacher's Book Advanced
Photocopiable © Oxford University Press 2010

a Listen to the song and complete the phrases with a word from the list.

challenge	chances	distance	face	feet	fight
glory	grip	guts	odds	street	top

a back on the _____

b took my _____

c went the _____

d back on my _____

e passion for _____

f lose your _____

g the thrill of the _____

h rising up to the _____

i face to _____

j stack the _____

k straight to the _____

l have the _____

----

b Listen again and read the lyrics. Check your answers. Which phrase in **a** means?

1 to become unable to understand or control a situation ☐

2 to continue playing in a competition or sports contest until the end ☐

3 to show that you are able to deal with an unexpected problem ☐

4 to increase the possibilities of sb losing ☐

5 be brave enough (to do sth) ☐

Eye of the Tiger

Rising up, back on the street
Did my time, took my chances
Went the distance, now I'm back on my feet
Just a man and his will to survive

So many times, it happens too fast
You change your passion for glory
Don't lose your grip on the dreams of the past
You must fight just to keep them alive

Chorus
It's the eye of the tiger, it's the thrill of the fight
Rising up to the challenge of our rival
And the last known survivor stalks his prey in the night
And he's watching us all with the eye of the tiger

Face to face, out in the heat
Hanging tough, staying angry
They stack the odds 'til we take to the street
For the kill with the skill to survive

Chorus

Rising up, straight to the top
Have the guts, got the glory
Went the distance, now I'm not gonna stop
Just a man and his will to survive

Chorus

c Why do you think this has become a motivational song for sportspeople all over the world? What do you think 'the eye of the tiger' means?

Song facts

The actor Sylvester Stallone asked the American rock group Survivor to write the theme song for the film Rocky III (1982) in which he starred. *Eye of the Tiger* became a motivational song for anyone facing a challenge, and this aspect of the song was parodied when *Eye of the Tiger* was used in an advert for the Starbucks chain of coffee shops in the United States in 2005.

● Cover the PREPOSITION column on the right, and test yourself.

Adjective + preposition

		PREPOSITION
1	We weren't **aware** ____ the problem with our ticket until we got to the airport.	of
2	The film, which is set in Sweden, is **based** ____ a best-selling novel.	on
3	I can't eat prawns because I'm **allergic** ____ seafood.	to
4	Are you **familiar** ____ the computer software we use?	with
5	As marketing manager I am **responsible** ____ all our publicity campaigns.	for
6	Her dress was **identical** ____ mine. It was so embarrassing!	to
7	I'm **fed up** ____ waiting for the electrician to come. I'm going out.	with
8	My grandmother is especially **fond** ____ her eldest grandchild.	of
9	My wife is not very **keen** ____ me buying a sports car.	on
10	My cousin is a great linguist – she's **fluent** ____ four languages.	in
11	We're very **dissatisfied** ____ the service we received at your establishment.	with
12	She may be old, but she's quite **capable** ____ looking after herself.	of
13	The flight was delayed for two hours **due** ____ a technical fault.	to
14	My younger brother is absolutely **mad** ____ motor racing.	about
15	My family are **hooked** ____ that new series – we never miss it.	on
16	I'm **sick** ____ listening to her complain about how many hours she has to work.	of
17	Jack is very **upset** ____ the way the company treated him when he was ill.	about
18	My wife's name is Fran, which is **short** ____ Francesca.	for

Preposition + noun

1	____ **theory** it only takes two days to renew the visa, but ____ **practice** it takes a week.	In/in
2	The travel agent has asked us to pay 50% of the cost of the holiday ____ **advance**.	in
3	I'm quite sure that he did that ____ **purpose**, because he knew it would annoy her.	on
4	The teacher makes us learn lots of phrases ____ **heart** and then tests us on them.	by
5	I need a definite answer from you by the end of next week ____ **the latest**.	at
6	We didn't arrange to meet. I just saw her on the bus ____ **chance**.	by
7	I saw the interview with the President ____ **the news** last night.	on
8	Climate change is always ____ **the news** these days – on TV, radio, and in the newspapers.	in
9	Be careful with Nora today. She's ____ a very **bad mood**.	in
10	It was very difficult at first but everything worked out well ____ **the end**.	in
11	I sent a very romantic email to my boss instead of my girlfriend ____ **mistake**.	by
12	I did all that work ____ **nothing**. The teacher forgot to collect in our essays.	for
13	My sister and her husband broke up last year, but they are still ____ **good terms**.	on
14	I don't eat in that restaurant ____ **principle**. I've heard they treat their staff very badly.	on
15	____ **principle**, they have agreed to rent the house to us, but we need to work out the details.	In
16	The company are heavily ____ **debt** and may have to close down.	in
17	In California smoking on beaches is ____ **the law**.	against
18	____ **a rule** I'm usually in bed by 11.00 during the week. At weekends I stay up later.	As

● Keep a record of other examples of dependent prepositions. These can also be found in dictionaries, such as the *Oxford Advanced Learner's Dictionary*.

● Cover the PREPOSITION column on the right, and test yourself.

Verb + preposition

	PREPOSITION
1 Simon **insisted** _____ paying for everything when we went out.	on
2 The exam **consists** _____ speaking, writing, listening, reading, and English in use papers.	of
3 I can't **concentrate** _____ what I'm doing with all that noise outside.	on
4 His ex-wife **took revenge** _____ him by cutting up all his suits.	on
5 The government was heavily **criticized** _____ not acting faster.	for
6 I need to **translate** this document _____ German. Can you help me?	into
7 My brother is a lawyer who **specializes** _____ criminal law.	in
8 We're still waiting for Laura to **apologize** _____ her awful behaviour last night.	for
9 Everyone **blamed** me _____ the mistake, even though it wasn't my fault.	for
10 The police have **accused** her _____ stealing from her employer.	of
11 I'm so hard up I'm going to have to **borrow** some money _____ my sister.	from
12 It's often not a good idea to **lend** money _____ a friend.	to
13 We have **succeeded** _____ reducing unemployment to less than 5% of the workforce.	in
14 I think the film is definitely **aimed** _____ people under 25. I didn't enjoy it at all.	at
15 I was **named** _____ my grandmother, who died before I was born.	after
16 I know I can **rely** _____ you to keep a secret.	on
17 We need to **divide** this _____ four equal parts	into
18 I'm going to **complain to** the manager _____ this.	about

Noun + preposition

1 There doesn't seem to be an easy **solution** _____ the problem.	to
2 The **reason** _____ the delay was the late arrival of the incoming flight.	for
3 I have quite a lot of **difficulty** _____ remembering names and faces.	in
4 There is an urgent **need** _____ qualified teachers to work in developing nations.	for
5 The police have reported a sharp **increase** _____ crimes involving identity theft.	in
6 I have absolutely no **intention** _____ resigning.	of
7 There is going to be a full **investigation** _____ the causes of the accident.	into
8 I'm sure there is going to be a lot of **protest** _____ the new law.	against
9 Jack has a lot of **respect** _____ his grandfather's achievements.	for
10 There's no **point** _____ getting angry about it. It's too late now.	in
11 The rescue services say that there is no **hope** _____ finding any more survivors.	of
12 My boss has asked me to write a **report** _____ the new computer system.	on / about
13 The **lack** _____ water is becoming a very serious problem in some countries.	of
14 The new managing director has a **reputation** _____ being very ruthless.	for
15 I think the government's **attitude** _____ single-parent families is changing.	to / towards

● Keep a record of other examples of dependent prepositions. These can also be found in dictionaries, such as the *Oxford Advanced Learner's Dictionary*.